MASTERING
FILM PHOTOGRAPHY

THE DEFINITIVE GUIDE FOR PHOTOGRAPHERS

CHRIS GATCUM

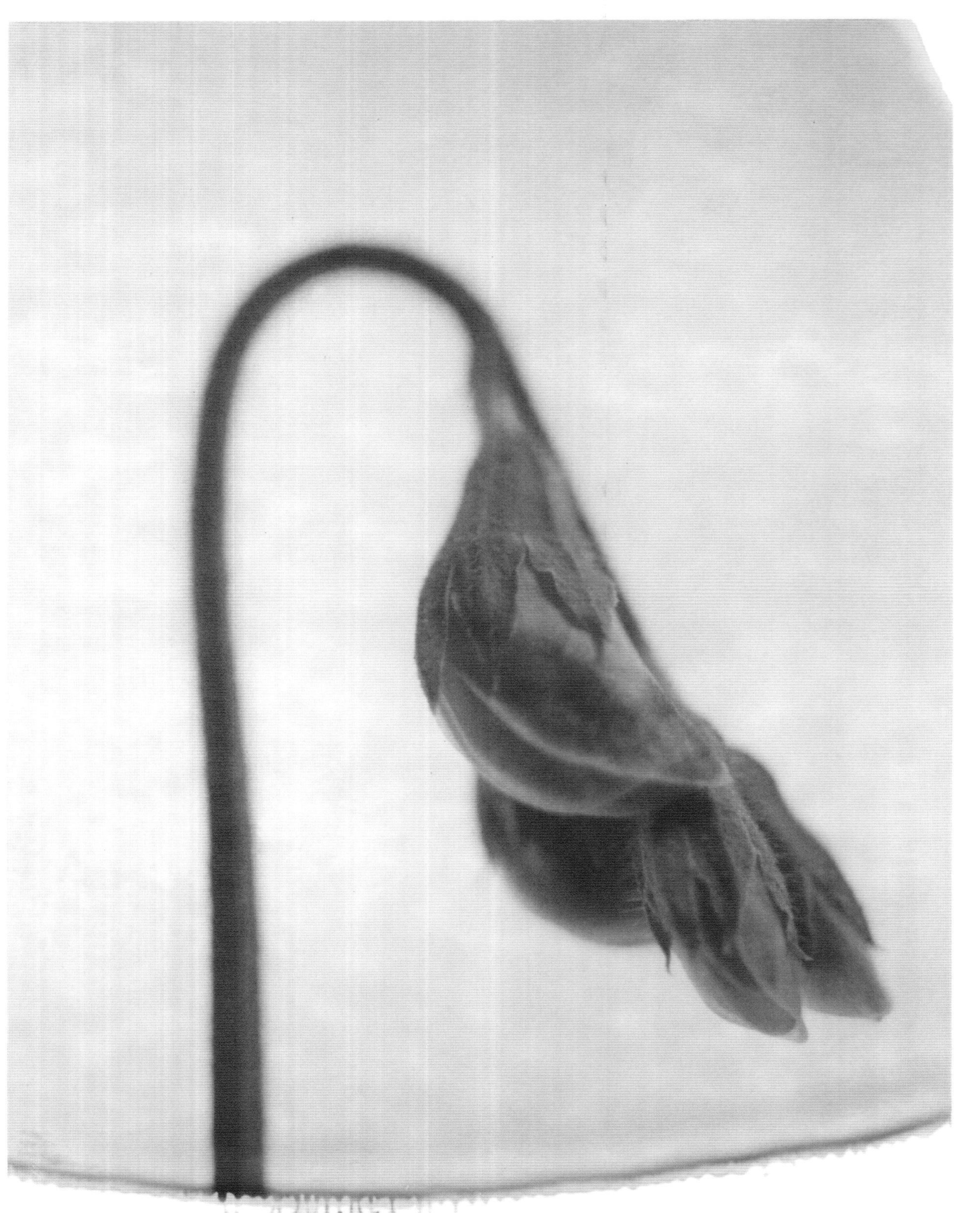

MASTERING
FILM PHOTOGRAPHY

THE DEFINITIVE GUIDE FOR PHOTOGRAPHERS

CHRIS GATCUM

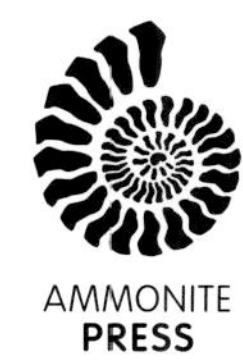

AMMONITE
PRESS

First published 2019 by
Ammonite Press
an imprint of Guild of Master Craftsman Publications Ltd.
Castle Place, 166 High Street, Lewes, East Sussex, BN7 1XU, United Kingdom

ISBN 978-1-78145-351-3

British Library Cataloging in Publication Data: A catalog record of this book is available from the British Library.

Publisher: Jason Hook
Design Manager: Robin Shields
Designer: Luke Herriott
Editor: Tracy Calder

Typeface: Helvetica Neue
Color reproduction by GMC Reprographics
Printed in China

Contents

Introduction

I love film. I love the look of it, the feel of it, and I even love the smell of it. I guess this isn't too surprising, because when I started out in photography almost 30 years ago film was the only option. As I learnt about exposure, color, focus, and composition, film was not only my companion and mentor, but also my greatest critic: it's a huge slap in the face to pay for a roll of film and processing only to discover that the camera wasn't loaded properly and you've made 36 exposures on air, not emulsion…

A few years after I graduated from art school I found myself reviewing digital cameras for a photography magazine, but even though I was at the "bleeding edge" of technology (and the world was going crazy for affordable digital SLRs) I would still try and encourage the editor to include a few pages of pinhole photography, a review of a Chinese TLR or large-format camera, or a couple of paragraphs on the plastic curiosities from a still relatively unknown company called Lomography. You see, despite the general excitement surrounding digital developments in those early days, film—to me—was still important, and on a personal level I didn't want to see the friend that had taught me everything I knew about photography get tossed aside like week-old pizza.

Don't get me wrong, I am not one of those old-school film fundamentalists screaming "shoot film or die" through rose-tinted glasses, as I deny the digital age, and nor am I the hipster eagerly embracing an old technology in the name of fashion. No, for me, it is simply the case that digital came, but film never went away: they both became options for photography.

In embracing both technologies I have come to appreciate them for what they are, and to see where they diverge. This understanding is crucial, regardless of whether you are using film as an antithesis to digital capture, or as your first foray into photography. It is easy to assume that as film and digital cameras both ostensibly do the same job—take pictures—they are essentially interchangeable, but this is not the whole truth.

Before we look at where the two mediums converge and diverge, perhaps the first thing you have to accept is that today's digital sensors have obliterated (almost) every argument for shooting film on a technical level. This might be a strange claim in a book promoting the virtues of film, but virtually all of the historic arguments for film being superior in terms of its image quality have now been answered: digital capture is cheaper, cleaner, and quicker, and when it comes to dynamic range and low-light shooting, film isn't in the race any more. About the only time film now comes close to matching or exceeding the quality of film is if you shoot medium- or large-format through a high-quality lens.

So, if that's the case, why bother with film? Why shoot on a technically "inferior" medium?

Everyone who continues to shoot film will have his or her own answer here, but mine is based on my own photographic journey, which has allowed me to experience hundreds of different cameras. These have ranged from miniature format to large format, modern to vintage, automatic to manual, but the ones I have enjoyed the most—and the ones I return to still—invariably shoot film. These are not necessarily the same cameras that have given me my favourite photographs, or the best images. They have done more than that: in some small way they have stirred my soul.

This may sound slightly melodramatic, but when you look at it objectively it's easy to see why. At a fundamental level, digital photography is a world of zeros and ones; on and off; yes and no; right and wrong. Because of this, it removes all doubt in a shot and excludes the possibility of a happy accident. For many people, this is reason enough to abandon film and embrace digital capture in totality, and who can blame them—it is impossible to deny that today's digital cameras are anything other than phenomenally functional tools. But therein lies their profound "soullessness."

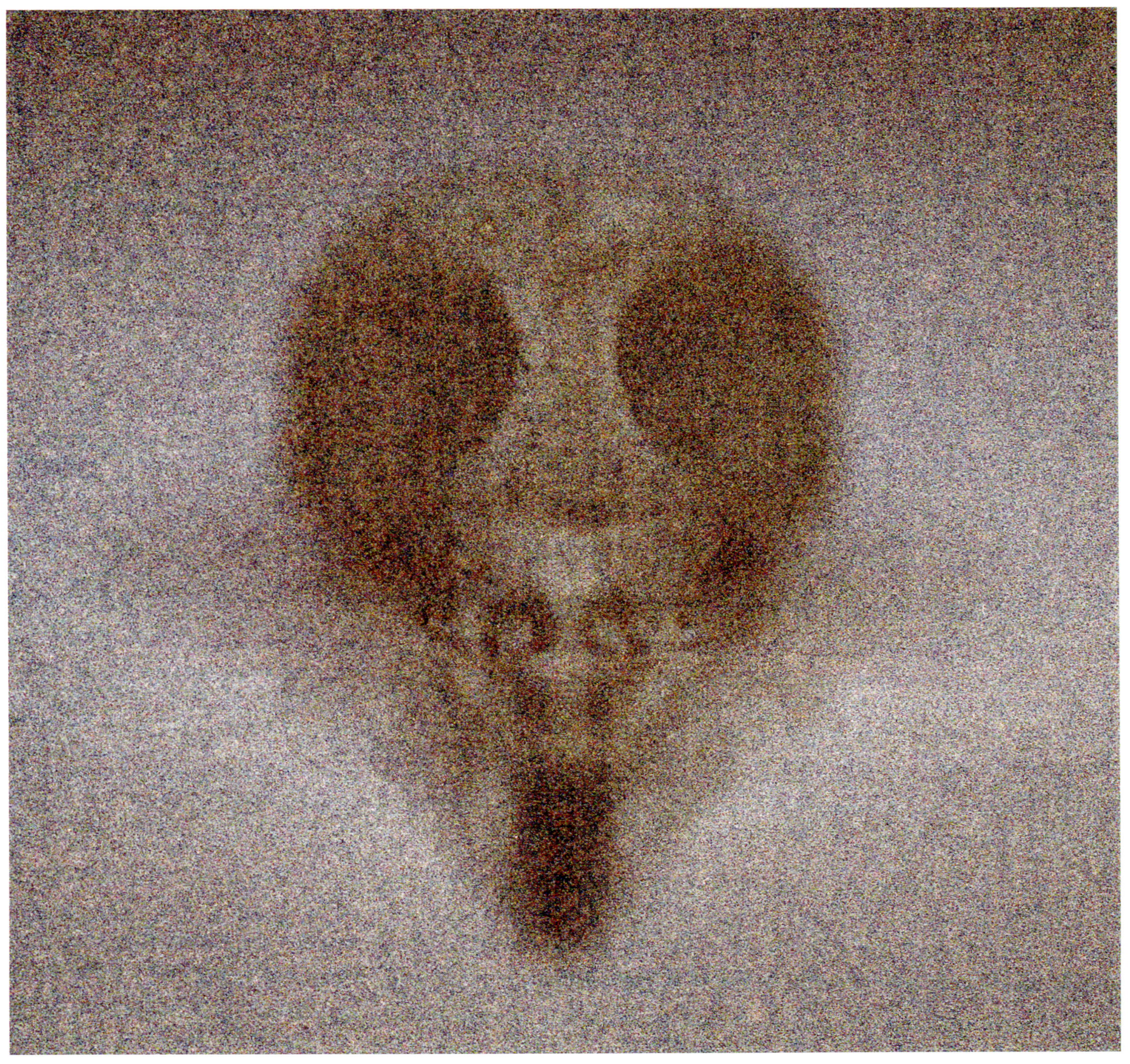

A digital camera is a cold, robotic eye capable of pixel-perfect precision with every click of the shutter, and barring a corrupt memory card or hard drive the images it produces are virtually indestructible; like a virus they can be transmitted from one device to another, creating an unlimited army of perfect replicas.

By comparison, shooting film is a much more intense and emotive journey. The cameras themselves often have more quirks, demanding greater concentration, while the film itself is far more delicate: light can leak and fog your frames; chemical processes can go awry; airport X-ray machines can irreparably damage it; it will attract dust and scratches; and so the list goes on. We also have to pay greater attention to what we are photographing, as every time we open the shutter there is an immediate financial cost. However, it is this fragility, effort, and intrinsic value that makes each frame all the more special. To get to the end result often requires us to weather a greater storm, battling multiple elements to realize our vision. It is, in short, a much greater achievement.

Film is also a wonderfully tangible medium, and this—I believe—brings us much closer to the images we shoot. We load our film by hand, physically touching the material that will hold our pictures, and we hold it again when we unload our camera, now handling the sheet or roll that contains our still-invisible images. We make a deliberate and concerted effort to take the film (or mail it) to a lab or process it ourselves, in either case handing it over to the chemical gods and praying for success, waiting with a unique combination of fear and excitement to see if that once-in-a-lifetime shot is good, bad, or indifferent. Then, after a pregnant pause, our pictures are born and we get to hold in our hands the images we have made; we get to hold our negatives and pass round our prints.

So, yes, you could say that a digital camera and a film camera both produce photographs, but I would argue it is much more than that. With film we *create* pictures, we don't just record them, and with this book you will learn how.

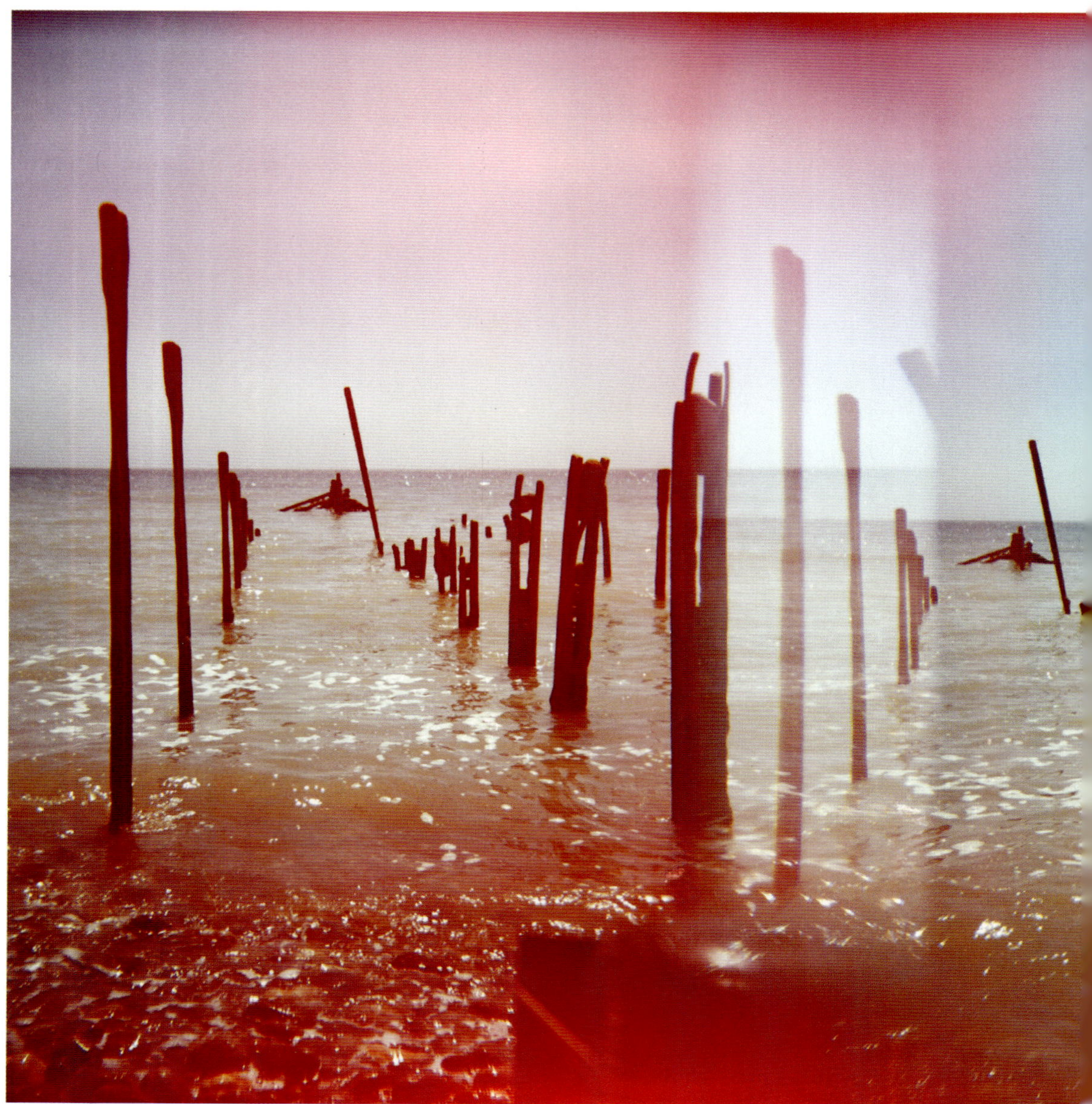

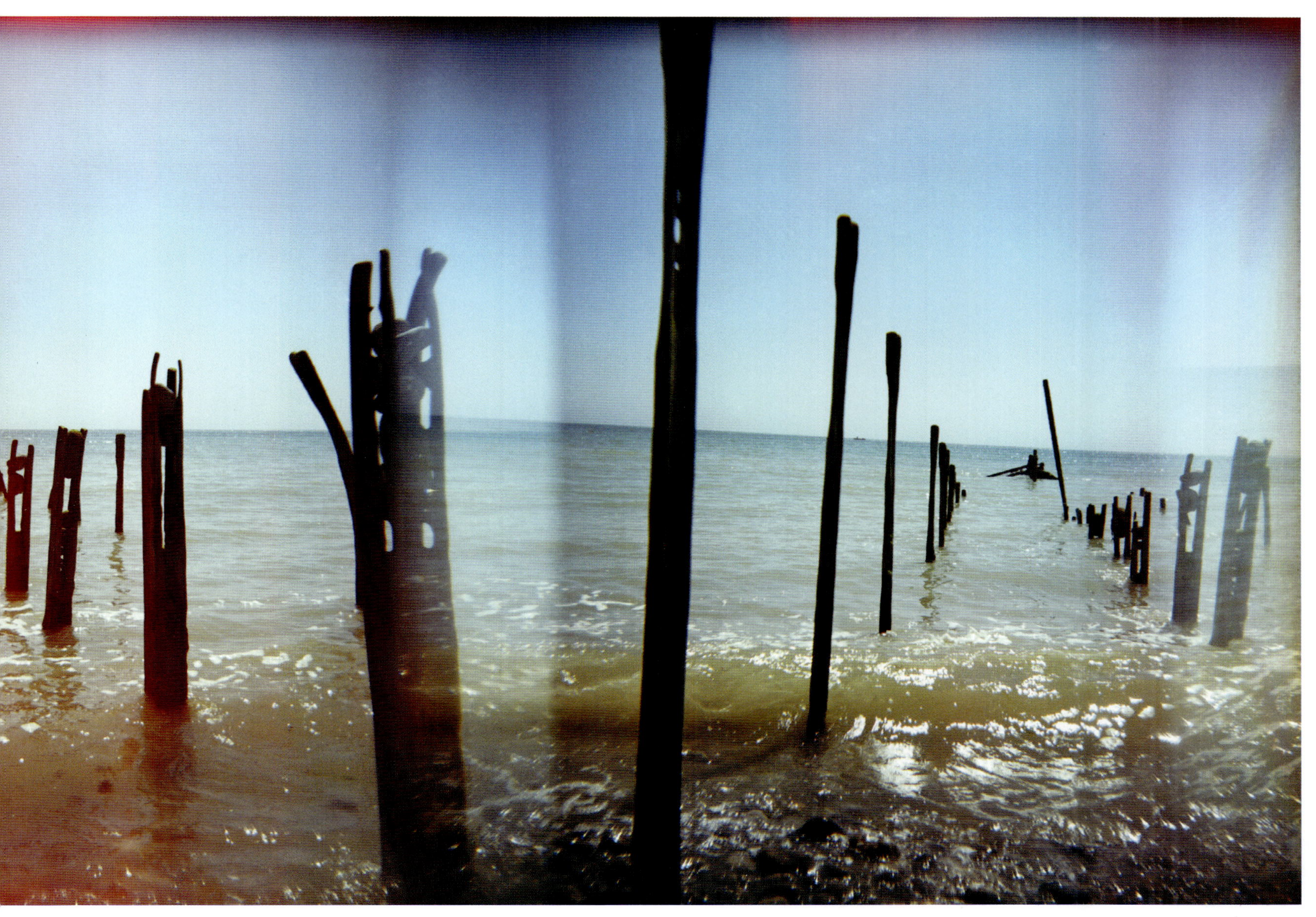

Above: This shot was taken with a medium-format Holga camera, which shoots either 6x4.5cm or 6x6cm format images. In this instance I shot 6x6cm shots, but wound the film on as if it were 6x4.5cm, creating a series of overlapping frames. I couldn't be entirely sure what (if anything) I would get, and the light leak was serendipitous. This type of wonderful uncertainty can never be delivered by a digital camera.

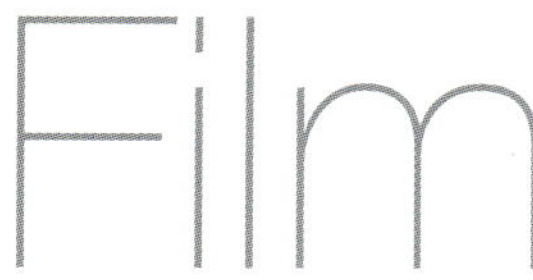

Chapter 1
Film

The film you choose to take your photographs on is one of the most fundamental decisions you have to make. Unlike a digital image, which can be easily edited, manipulated, and distorted until it becomes something very different to the object or scene that was originally in front of the lens, a film image is far less mutable. Sure, you can change the processing to alter the contrast of a black-and-white film, tweak the colors when you print from a color negative, or even scan your shots and open them in your choice of image-editing program, but broadly speaking your ability to make global or local changes to a film image is far less sweeping. Therefore, it is not only important to get as much of the image "right" in camera as you can—exposure, focus, and so on— but it is imperative that you choose the right film to start with.

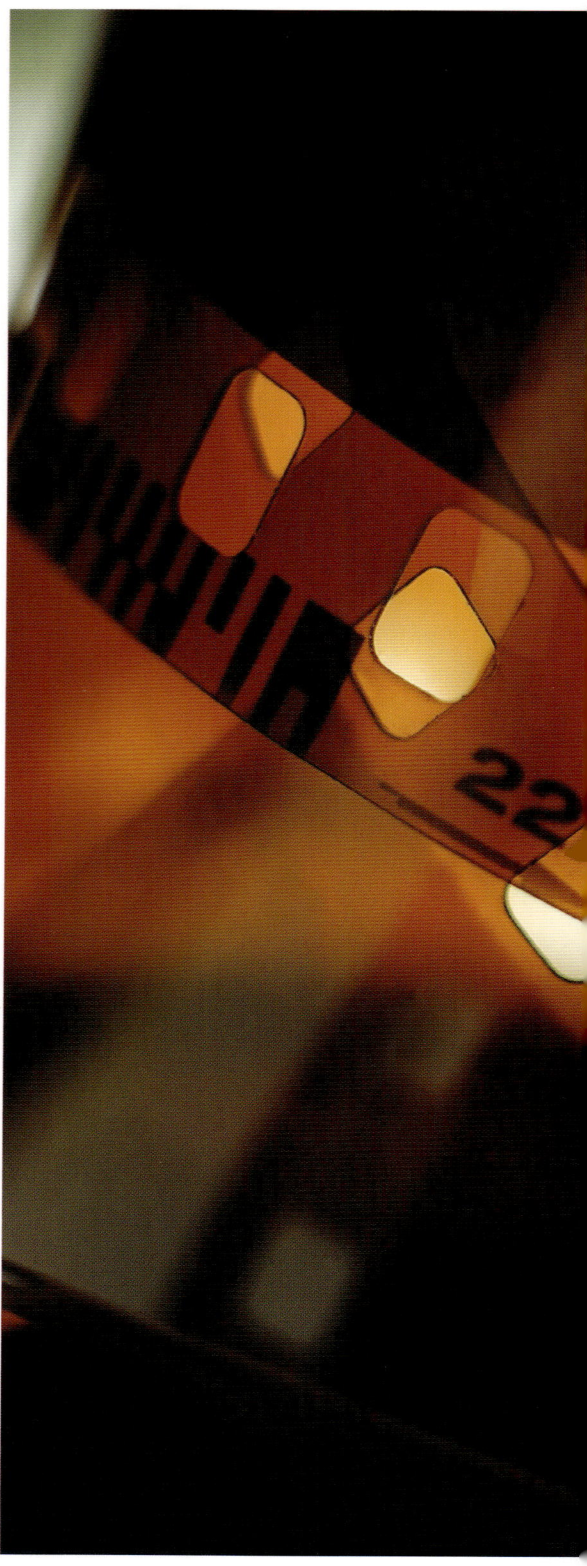

Right: Unlike a digital image, a photograph made on film is tangible: you can hold it in your hands. However, this also makes it susceptible to attracting dust and scratches, so always handle it with care and only when it's absolutely necessary.

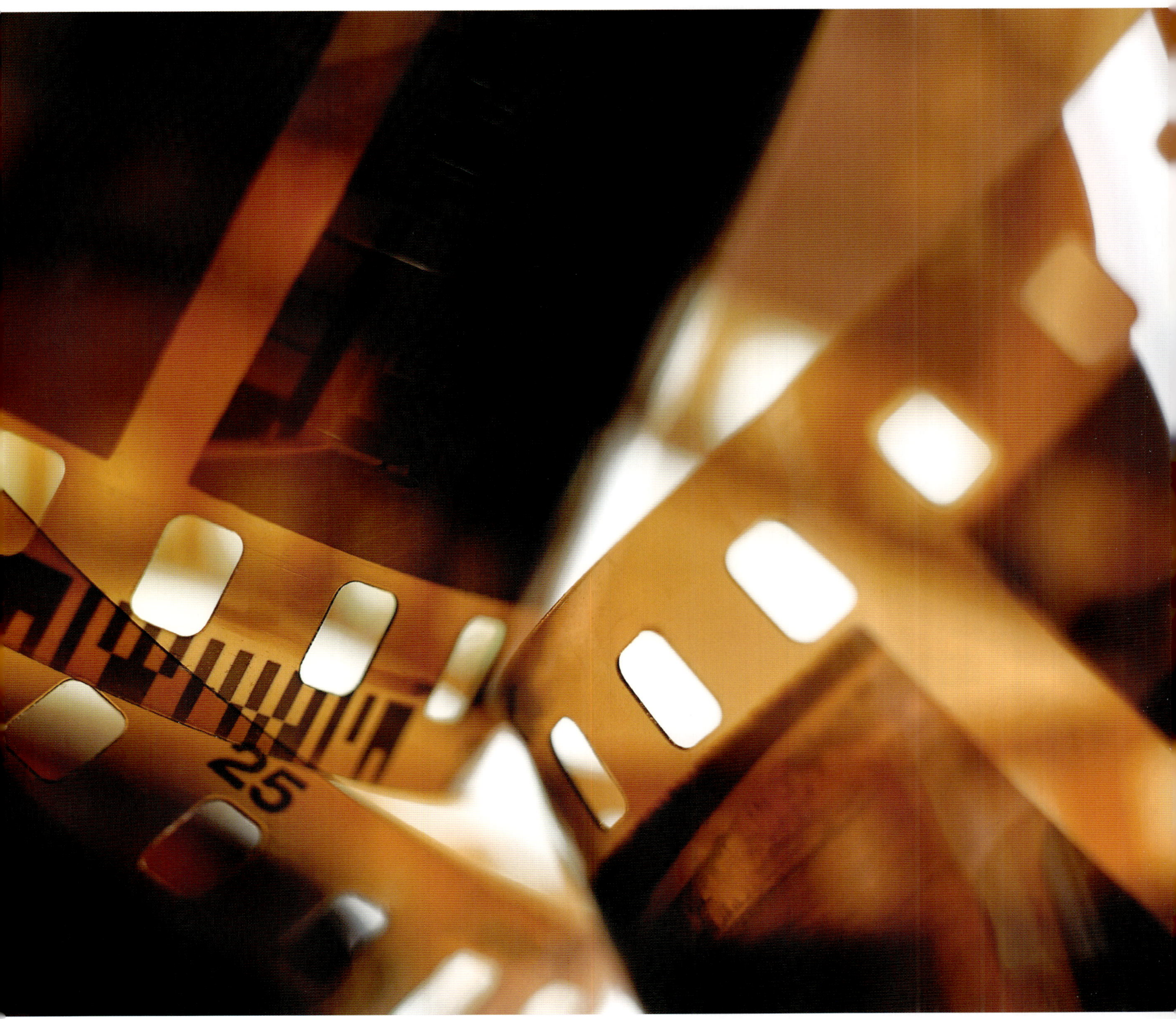

The Mechanics Of Emulsion

In its simplest sense, all film consists of two key ingredients: a light-sensitive emulsion and a base to support it. In the early years of photography the emulsion was coated onto glass plates, but in the late 1800s George Eastman coated a flexible paper base, creating the forerunner to film as we know it today. A few years later, the paper base was replaced with a nitrocellulose base (creating highly flammable nitrate film), which was in turn replaced by a variety of much safer cellulose acetates (safety film); film today typically has either a cellulose triacetate or polyester base.

However, while the base gives film a flexible substrate, it is the light-sensitive emulsion that creates photographs. This gelatin emulsion contains microscopic silver-halide crystals that are sensitive to light; these crystals react to the light striking them to form a latent image that is subsequently revealed through chemical processing (as outlined in chapter 7).

In essence, that is all you need to make film, but not all photographic emulsions are the same. The silver-halide crystals can be combined with various sensitizers to control their sensitivity to different wavelengths of light, for example, creating different responses or film types, such as panchromatic black-and-white film, or color negative film. Additional non-image-forming layers can also be added to filter the light, affect the way in which the layers are chemically processed, or simply to protect the film, while a film's sensitivity to light can be controlled by changing the size of the silver-halide crystals: the larger the crystals used in an emulsion, the more sensitive it is to light and the "faster" the film is. So, while only two ingredients are needed to make film—a base and an emulsion—there are countless permutations, which we will explore on the following pages.

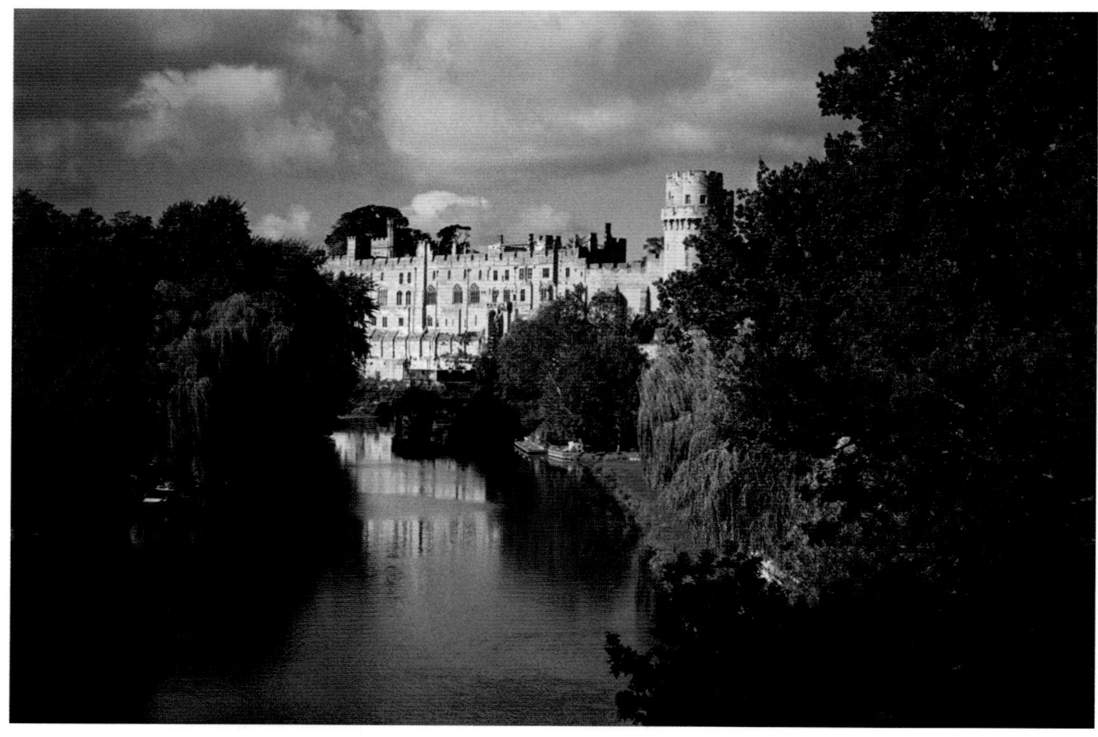

Above: This is one of my earliest photographs, taken almost 30 years ago. Not only is the film it was taken on (Ilford HP5 Plus) essentially the same today as it was then, but apart from a bit of dust, the negative is still in perfect condition. By comparison, I have Raw digital images from as little as 10–15 years ago that I simply cannot access because technology has rendered them obsolete. Pixels may be widely accepted as the face of modern photography, but emulsion can offer far greater longevity.

X-RAYS

X-rays can ruin film of all types, and security points at airports and other venues around the world have been responsible for countless lost or ruined vacation photographs over the years. This remains a problem today, so always keep your film—exposed and unexposed—in your carry-on luggage when you are traveling and ask for a hand search to avoid your film being X-rayed. This is particularly important if you have multiple flights and security checkpoints to pass through.

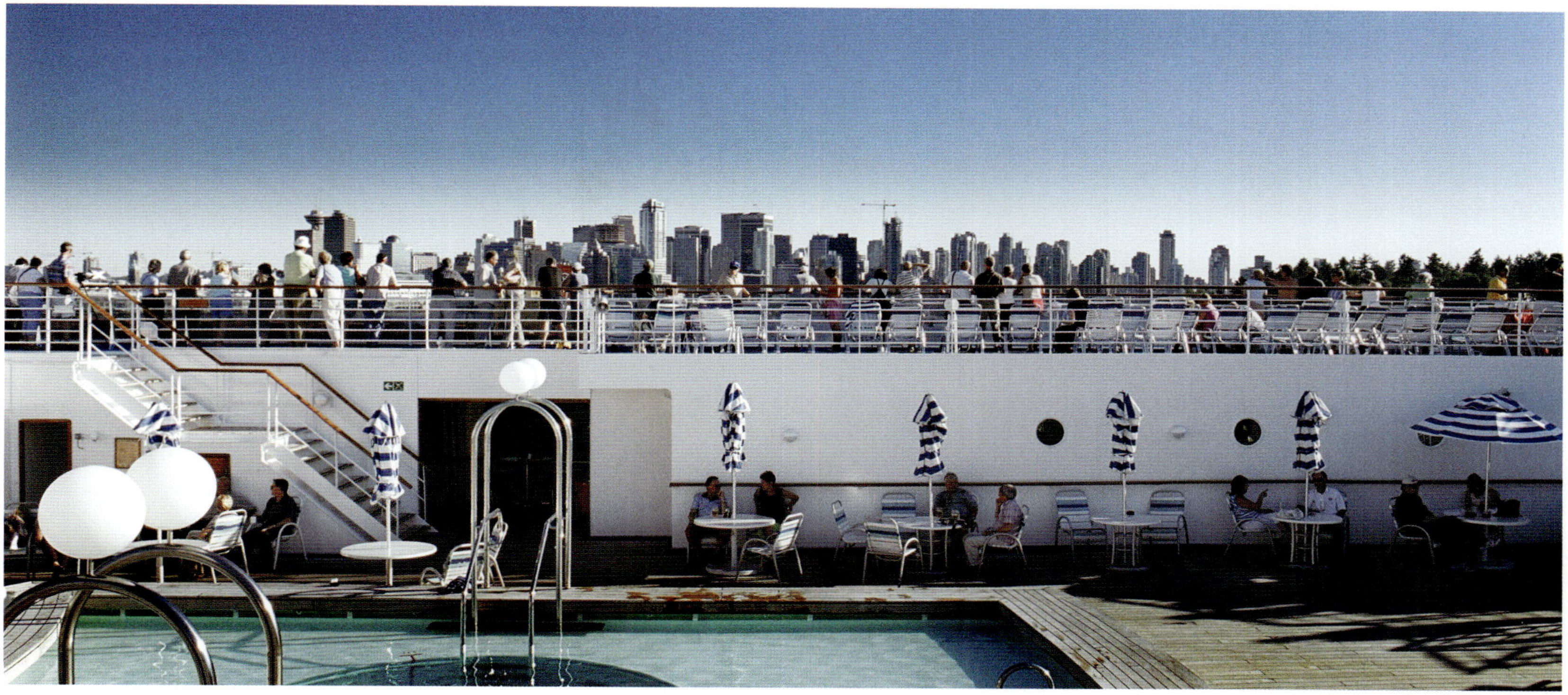

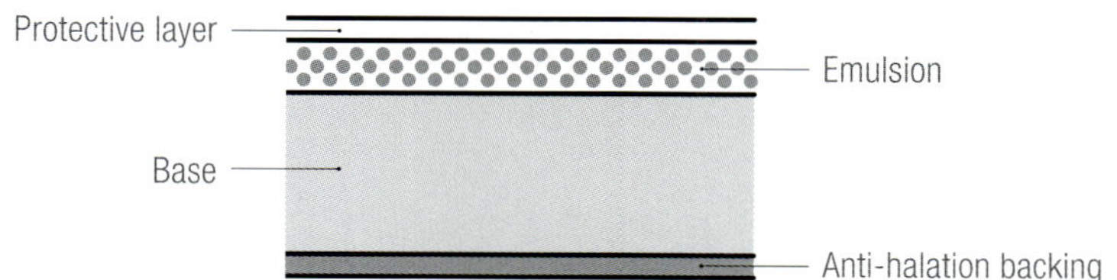

Cross Section of Black & White Film

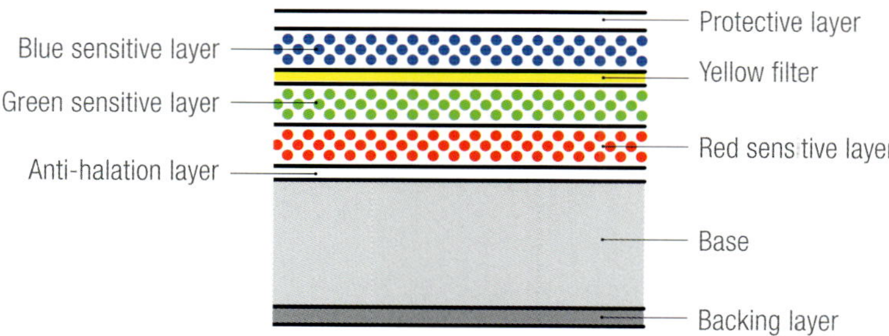

Cross Section of Color Film

Above: I took this on board a cruise ship leaving Vancouver, having traveled there from the UK via North America. Including return flights my film was checked four or five times in total, and at each point I requested a hand search to avoid any X-ray damage. An alternative approach to taking film overseas is to buy it at your final destination, although this depends on its availability.

Left: Black-and-white film and color film have quite different structures, but they essentially share two fundamental elements: light-sensitive emulsion and a base to support it. The difference between films generally comes down to how many layers are used—both image forming and non-image-forming—and their composition.

Film Characteristics

Whether it's black and white, color negative, or color positive, there is a wide range of different films available from different manufacturers and each has its own unique set of characteristics. It is these individual traits that combine to give a film its personality. It's what makes Ilford HP5 Plus different to Kodak Tri-X in the world of black and white, or Fujifilm's Velvia 100 color slide film distinct from Provia 100F. The following are the fundamental properties that go into giving each film its own look.

Speed

As noted previously, silver-halide crystals make a film sensitive to light and the larger the crystals, the more sensitive the film. This sensitivity is given as an ISO rating, which indicates a film's sensitivity to light or its "speed": the higher the ISO, the greater the sensitivity to light, or "faster" the film is said to be.

However, the ISO rating given on the box of a film (known as its box speed) is not absolute. You might find that you can actually get better results in terms of the look you want to achieve by rating a film at a slightly higher or lower ISO speed (see Testing, page 24), and you can also experiment with push and pull processing (see page 159).

Tips

- Fast films generally exhibit lower contrast than slow films, but this is not always the case; the emulsion and the way it is processed are more important factors.

- ISO stands for International Organization for Standardization, which is the body that defines the standard. Prior to this a range of systems were used to indicate sensitivity, including ASA, DIN, and GOST.

Grain

As well as determining the speed of a film, the silver-halide crystals also determine the amount of "grain" in an image, which we see as an underlying texture. This is a result of the silver particles in black-and-white film, or the dye clouds in color film, appearing to clump together; the larger the particles or dye clouds appear, the "grainier" the image.

To give an indication of the graininess of a film, most manufacturers give emulsions an RMS (Root Mean Square) value, with a lower value indicating lower potential levels of grain. But exposure, development (particularly of black-and-white film), and even the subject being photographed can all affect the appearance of grain.

Tips

- The RMS figures for negative and positive films cannot be directly compared; they only work in a like-for-like comparison.

- Grain and sharpness are often seen as closely related, with finer-grained films being sharper, but this is really only part of the story. High-contrast films generally appear sharper than low-contrast ones, and the way in which edge contrast is handled also plays a part.

- Film manufacturers generally work toward having the finest possible grain at any given ISO, but sometimes this might not be what you want: in fact, grain can sometimes be an intrinsic part of a photograph.

Below: The appearance of grain is usually related to film speed: the faster the film, the grainier it is. However, grain can also be increased and decreased through development. Here the grain of an ISO 160 slide film was exaggerated massively by cross processing it (see page 160).

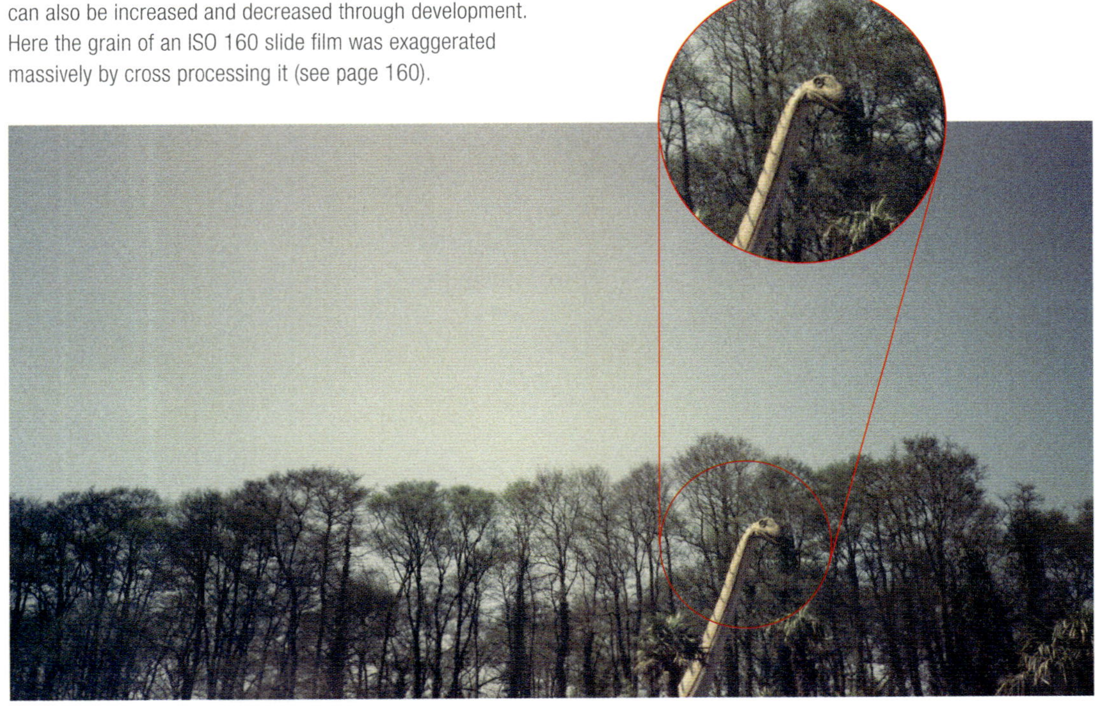

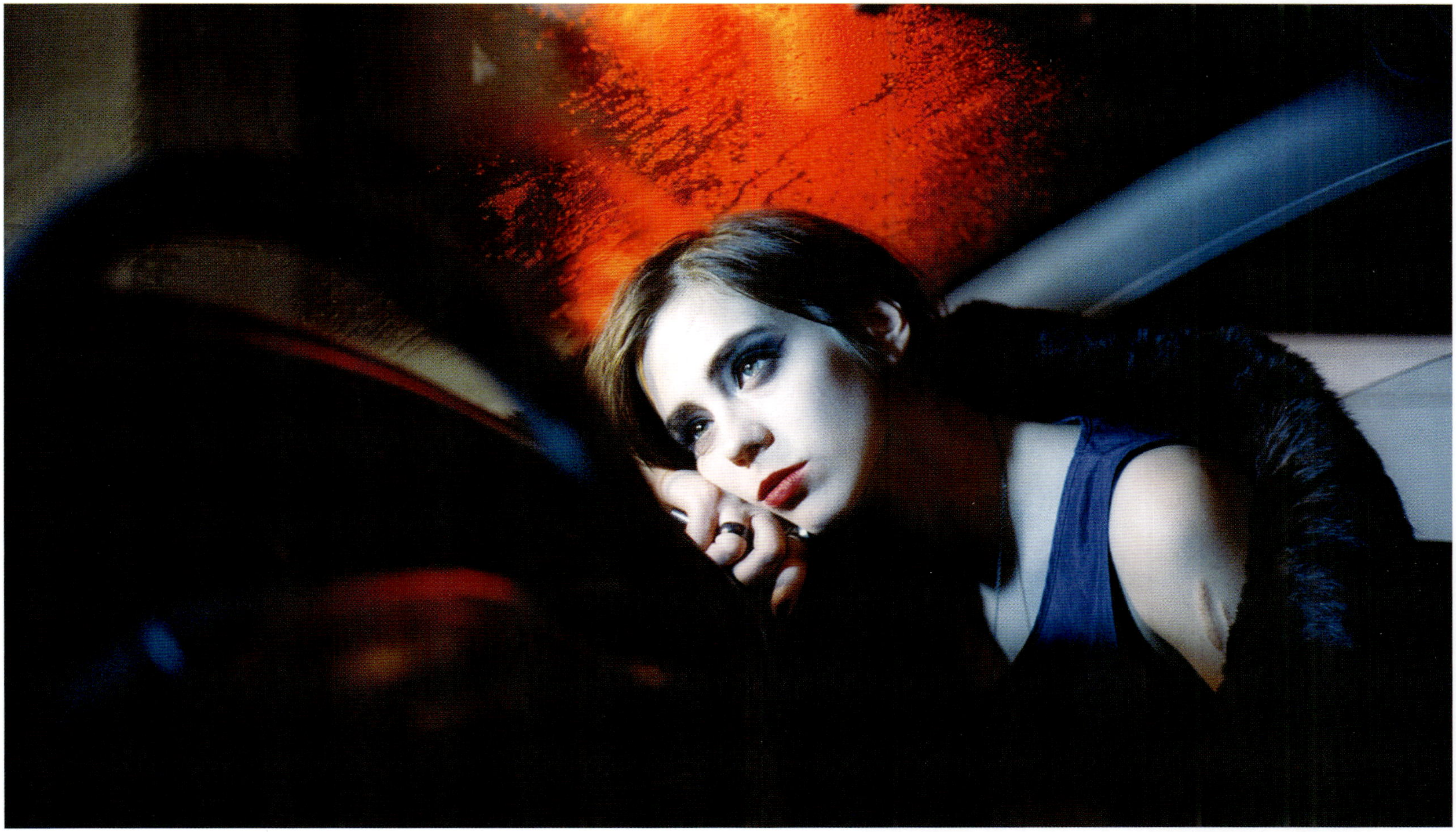

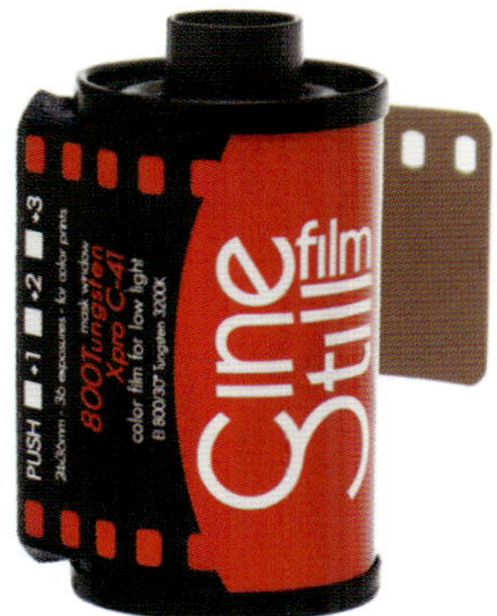

Daylight Vs. Tungsten

The vast majority of color film available today is daylight balanced, which means it will give color-accurate results under sunny daylight conditions or with flash. Any light source with a different color temperature will appear warmer or cooler, and to correct this you will need to use filters, as outlined in chapter 5. However, if you are shooting under tungsten lighting (quite a rarity nowadays) you could always use one of the few remaining tungsten-balanced films instead; a letter "T" in the name typically identifies these films.

Above: This picture was taken using CineStill 800T tungsten-balanced film, at a parking lot on a rainy night. The main light source was a tungsten bulb rigged up to a battery pack, just out of frame, with a neon light in the background and other colored lights nearby.

Above: There are very few tungsten-balanced emulsions available for still photography, but they are fairly common in the motion picture industry. For its 800T tungsten film, CineStill uses a process that makes motion picture film suitable for regular color negative (C41) processing.

Tips

- Shooting tungsten film under daylight conditions will result in images with a strong blue color cast. This can work surprisingly well with some subjects.

- Try combining daylight-shot tungsten film with cross processing (see page 160) for a dramatic boost to contrast and saturation.

Characteristic Curves

Every film has what is known as a "characteristic curve," which plots the film's density against exposure. This is an unnecessary complication for most people, with seemingly little real-word relevance, but a rudimentary understanding can help you recognize the key characteristics of a film without running a roll through your camera.

The main thing to appreciate here is how film responds to light in a different way to a digital sensor. With a digital camera, the response to light is linear, so the "curve" is actually a straight line, as you see when you open up the Curves window in your image-editing software. In essence this is showing 256 distinct steps from pure black ("0") right through to pure white ("255"). From this base you can push and pull the curve to control the tones in the image—applying an S-shaped curve to boost contrast, for example.

In contrast, film does not have a linear response; highlights and shadows react differently from emulsion to emulsion, and the contrast also varies. However, as with a digital image the curve can be manipulated through processing (albeit chemical processing), which is why it can be important to test your film (see page 24).

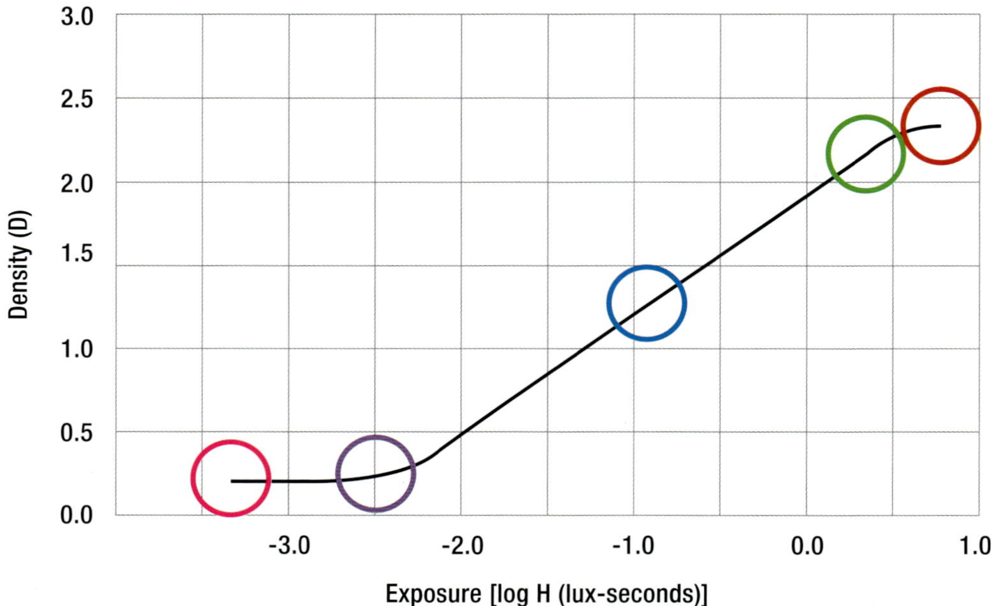

The highest and lowest points of the curve on the graph show the film's minimum and maximum density (DMin and DMax). When it comes to scanning, you need to ensure that the DMax of your scanner exceeds that of the film, otherwise the scanner will not be able to see detail in the darkest areas of the film.

The bottom of the curve, or "toe," shows how the darkest areas transition to pure black.

The "shoulder" is the highest part of the curve, and this shows where and how highlights transition from very bright to pure white. The way that light areas "roll off" into pure white with film is arguably more attractive than the sudden cut-off experienced with digital cameras.

The relatively straight line between the shoulder and toe gives an indication of contrast; the steeper the line, the greater the contrast.

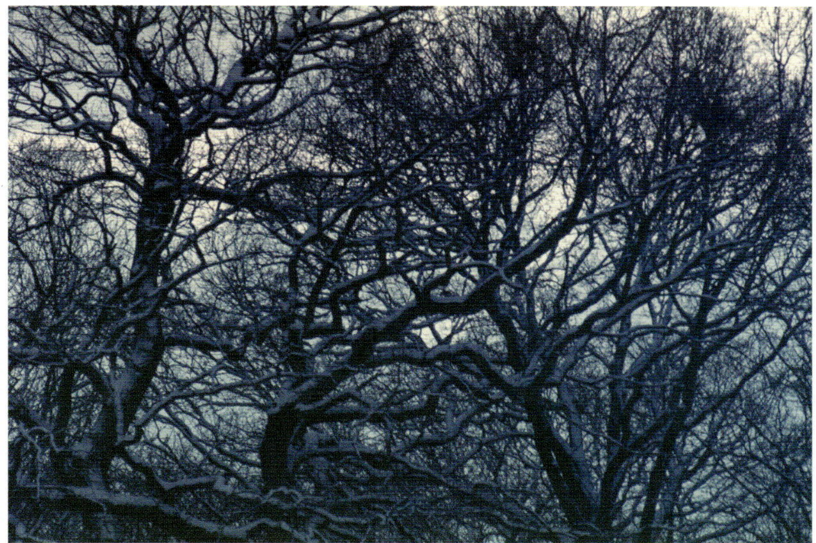

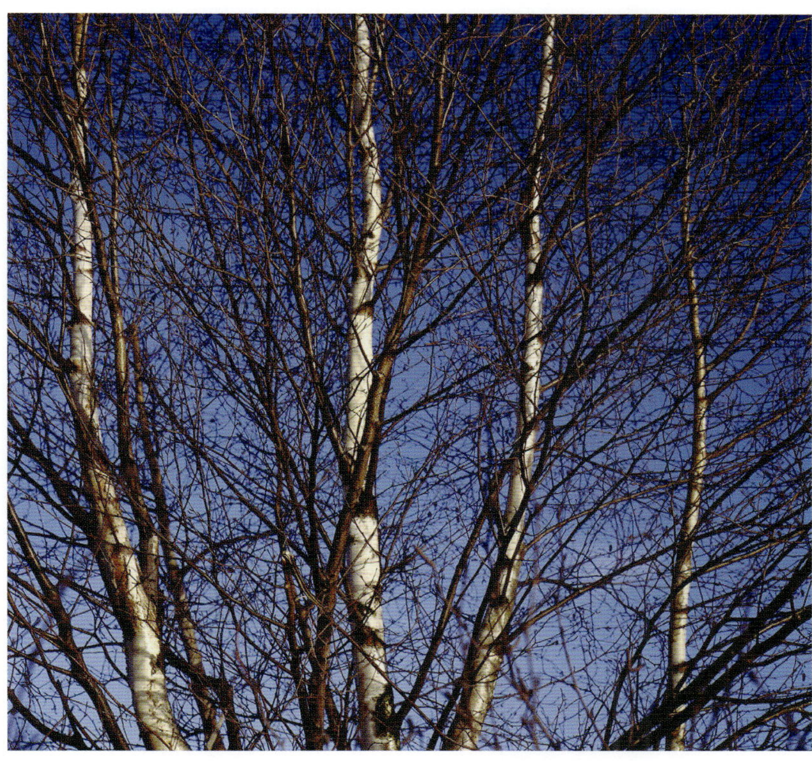

Above: This shot was taken on a roll of 35mm color negative film found among the possessions of my late grandmother. It was definitely outside its "best before" date, and there was no way of knowing what results—if any—it would deliver. The answer was "thin" (heavily underexposed) negatives with a decidedly strong color shift.

Above: Strong, direct lighting can create a high dynamic range scene as it creates bright highlights and deep shadows. You may have to sacrifice detail in one of the tonal extremities or else be ultra precise with your exposure. In any case, the greater the dynamic range of a scene, the less exposure latitude you will have.

Dynamic Range

Dynamic range is the difference—usually given in stops—between the brightest and darkest areas that detail can be recorded in, so a film with a 6-stop dynamic range would be able to record detail in both the shadows and the highlights of a scene, as long as those areas are no more than 6-stops apart. In general, slide film has the most limited dynamic range (up to 7 stops at best), which is why precise exposure readings and filters are often essential; color negative film has a greater dynamic range, of maybe 10 stops or so, depending on the emulsion; and the dynamic range of a black-and-white film can be controlled through development (from as few as 3 stops with a high-contrast developer to as many as 15 or more stops with a low-contrast developer, depending on the film stock).

Exposure Latitude

Exposure latitude and dynamic range are often—and wrongly—used interchangeably. Specifically, exposure latitude refers to the amount that an individual image can be under- or overexposed by and still fall within the dynamic range. For example, if your film had an 8-stop dynamic range and the scene you were photographing had a 6-stop dynamic range, you've got 2-stops of exposure latitude. This means you could underexpose the scene by 1 stop to make it slightly darker and moodier, or overexpose it by 1 stop to make it brighter and fresher, but in each case the film would still record the full tonal range.

BEST BEFORE

Film has a "best before" date that gives you an idea of how long you've got to shoot it and get it processed before it's passed its best; once this happens film tends to become increasingly less sensitive and, with color film, the colors can shift. But this date is just a guide, and storing your film in a fridge or freezer slows the ageing process. The film must be unopened and in its original foil packaging or film pot, and then brought up to the ambient temperature before you use it. For casual photography expired film can produce unique and quirky results.

Film Types: Black & White

Some people prefer to shoot in color, but there are a lot of good reasons to try black-and-white film, including the option to process it yourself at home (see page 150). Black-and-white film is the simplest of all film types, and typically consists of a single layer of light-sensitive emulsion. Even this simplicity allows a plethora of options.

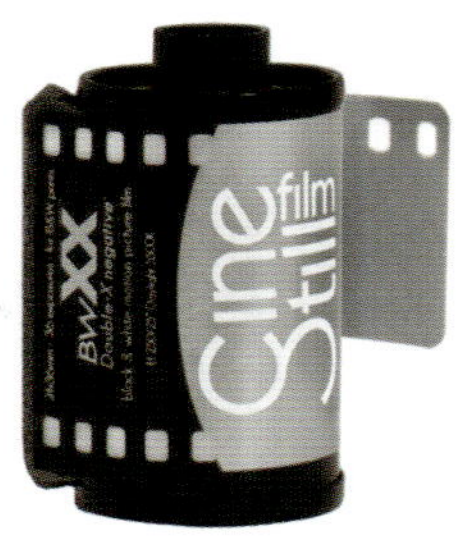

Above: CineStill's BwXX negative film uses the same black-and-white motion picture stock (Eastman Double-X) that was used to shoot movies such as *Raging Bull* and *Schindler's List*. Double-X is relatively unchanged since its introduction in 1959.

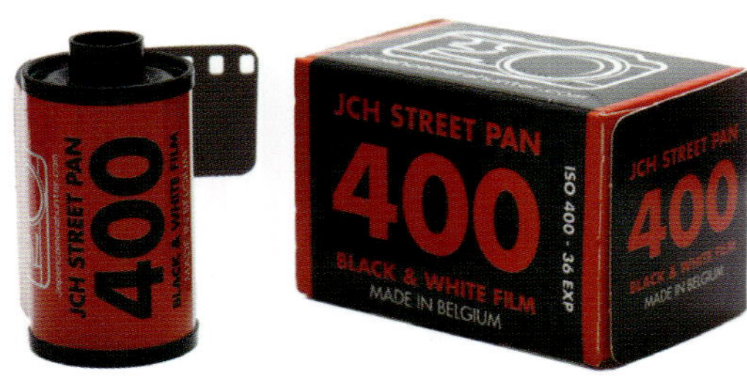

Above: Japan Camera Hunter's StreetPan 400 is based on fast, black-and-white surveillance film. The results are subtly different to more established emulsions of the same speed, thanks in part to its near-infrared sensitivity.

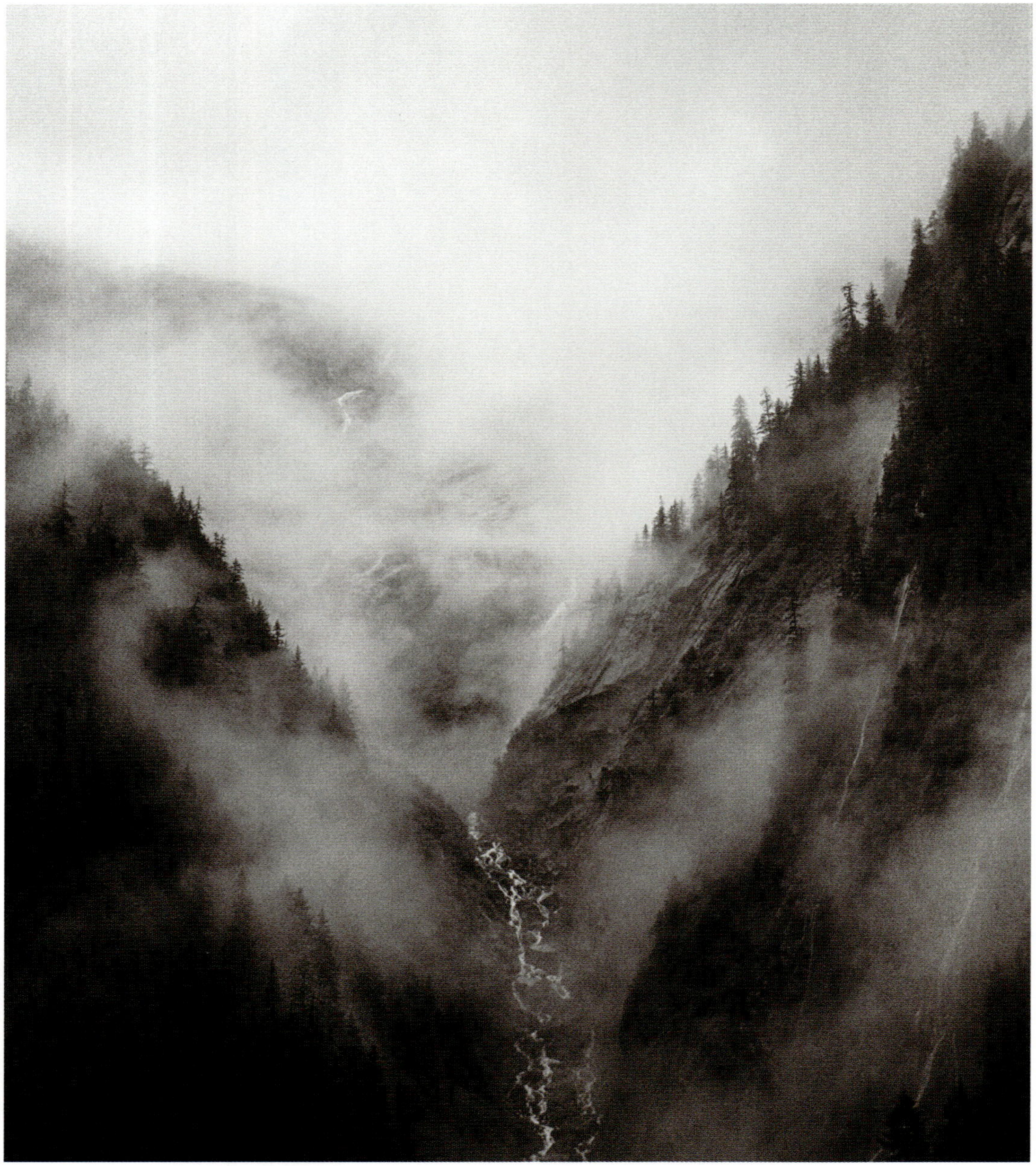

Above: For me, one of the biggest appeals of using black-and-white film is the way it can reduce and simplify a scene. Free from the "distraction" of color, shape and tone become everything, and mood is more readily revealed.

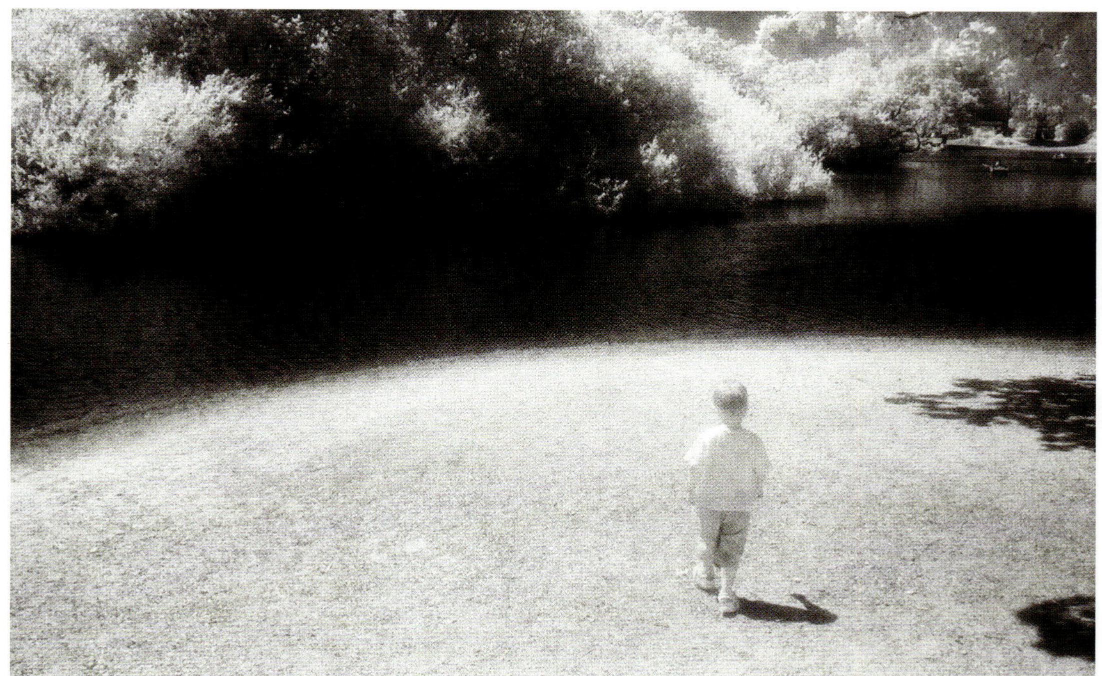

Orthochromatic & Panchromatic

In the early days of photography, black-and-white emulsions were orthochromatic, which meant that they were far more sensitive to blue wavelengths of light (and UV light) than they were to red and green wavelengths. As a result, a black-and-white image wouldn't necessarily reflect the world as it appeared to the human eye: blues would appear brighter than expected, while reds would look far darker. This changed when panchromatic films—which are sensitive to all wavelengths of light—were introduced at the turn of the 20th century, allowing the colors in a scene to translate into natural-looking tones. Today, the vast majority of black-and-white film is panchromatic, although there are a few orthochromatic films still available if you want to experiment.

Old & New Technology

In the mid 1980s, a new kid appeared on the black-and-white film block: tabular-grain film. The technology used flatter and broader silver-halide crystals resulting in less grain and higher resolution than traditional emulsions. A number of these films remain in production today, notably the Ilford Delta and Kodak T-Max families.

Chromogenic Film

Most black-and-white film requires specialist black-and-white chemistry, but a number of films are produced that use the C41 (color negative) process. The advantage of films such as Ilford XP2 and Fuji Neopan 400CN is that shooting and printing black and white becomes quick, cheap, and accessible. However, because the films use dyes in their construction, the grain and contrast tend to be softer than traditional black-and-white emulsions, while machine-made prints on color paper often have a sepia or blue color cast.

Black & White Reversal

Technically, any black-and-white film can be processed to produce slides instead of negatives, but the processing is more complex and few films have a clear enough base for it to be successful. One exception is ADOX Scala 160.

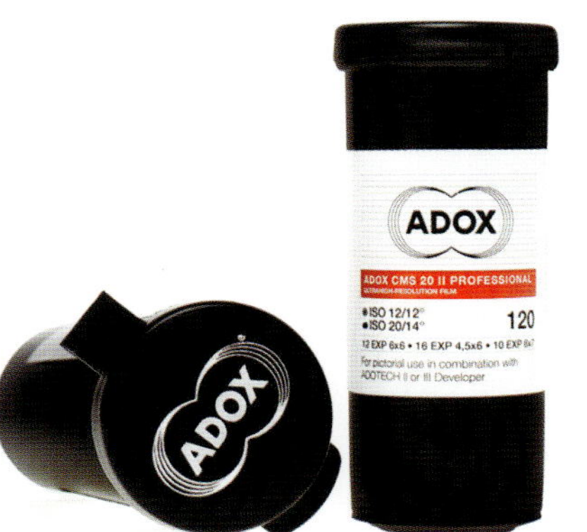
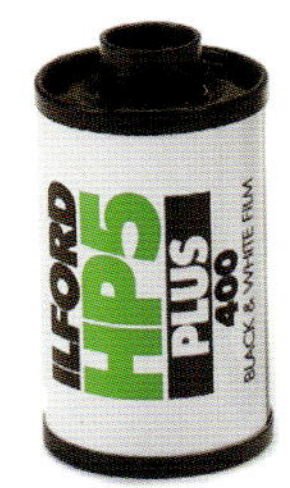
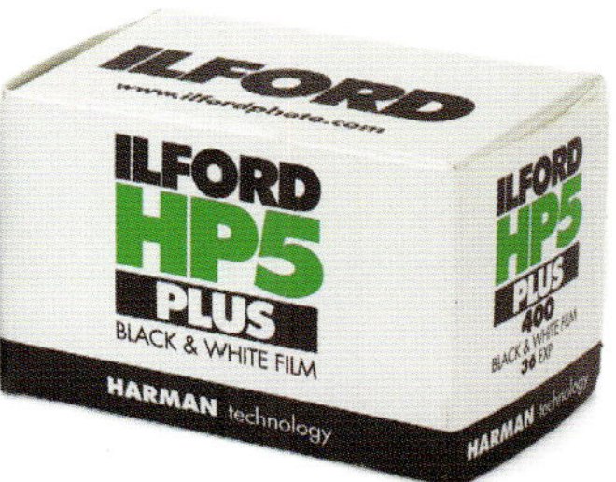

Above: Infrared (IR) film has increased sensitivity to the infrared wavelengths of the electromagnetic spectrum. Using a filter to block the visible light often leads to glowing white foliage and deep black skies

Far left: ADOX CMS 20 has an ISO of 12 in sunlight, which makes it "slow," but capable of almost grain-free images.

Left: Ilford's HP5 Plus can be traced back to the company's Hypersensitive Panchromatic plates, dating back to 1931.

Film Types: Color Negative

Color negative film is designed to be printed, rather than viewed directly, which is why it's also known as print film. Compared to the sheer simplicity of black-and-white film, color film requires far more layers of emulsion, filters, and so on, with different layers designed to catch different wavelengths of light: a red layer records red wavelengths, a green layer records green wavelengths, and a blue layer records blue (the same RGB trio used by most digital cameras). Some films use additional layers, such as Fujicolor Reala, which was the first film to add a fourth, cyan layer to help photographers cope with mixed lighting conditions.

We will look at color negative (C41) processing in greater detail in chapter 7, but in each of the image-forming layers there is a chemical known as a "coupler." During development, these couplers form colored dyes, which ultimately create a color image. However, because a negative image is being created, these layers are not red, green, and blue, but their opposites: cyan, magenta, and yellow respectively. It is only during printing (or when scanning) that a color positive image is created.

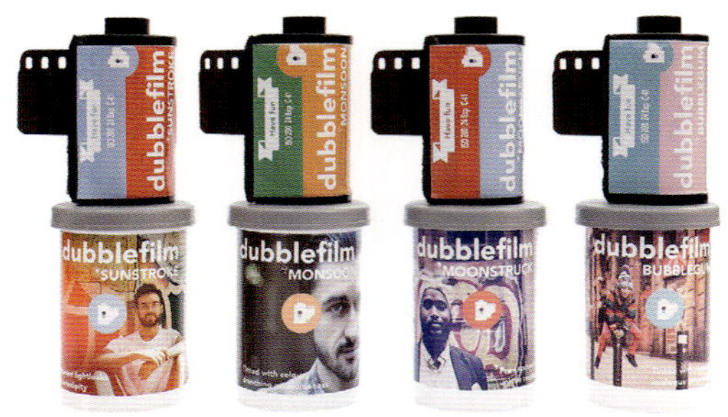

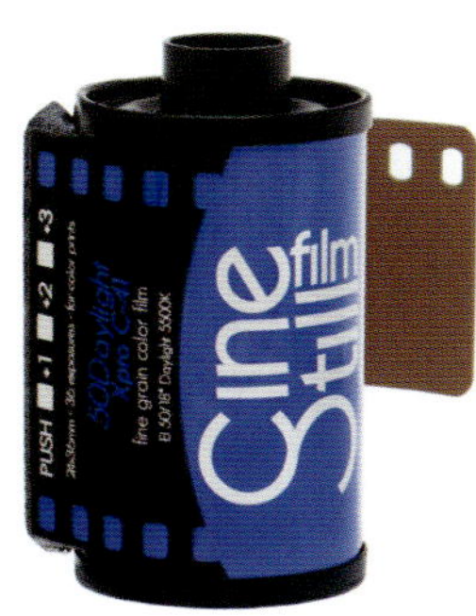

Above: 50Daylight is another film from CineStill that uses its proprietary "premoval" process, which allows motion picture film to be developed using the standard C41 photographic process (see page 158). In this instance the result is an ISO 50 daylight-balanced color negative film that claims to deliver the world's smallest grain for a film of its type.

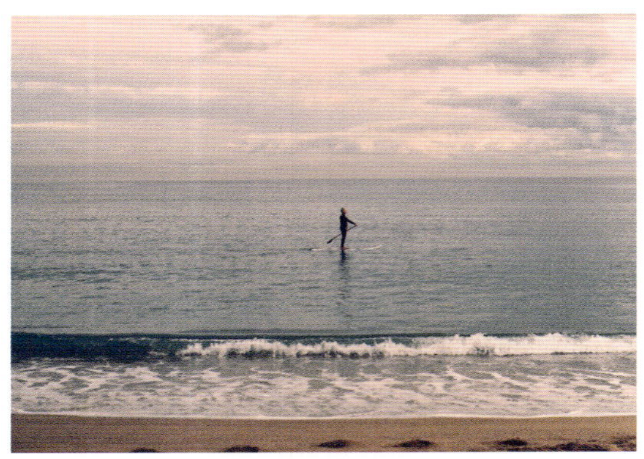

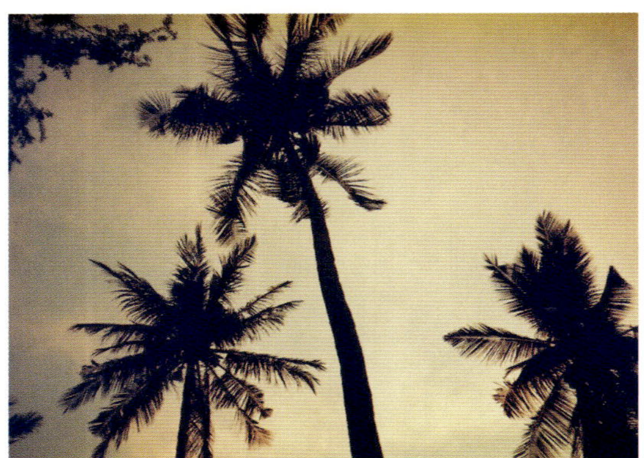

Above: Dubblefilm's range of "alternative" color negative films includes the emotively named Bubblegum, which adds "sweet" pinkish color to your shots (center) and Moonstruck, which leans toward cooler colors (bottom). Other films in the range include the color-shifting Monsoon and Sunstroke, which has been pre-exposed with light leaks.

Right: Redscale film, such as KONO! Rotwild 400, is color negative film that has been loaded "back to front." This means that the layers in the emulsion are exposed in the opposite order, resulting in an image that often exhibits a strong yellow-red color shift.

Redscale

One of the great things about color negative film is its versatility, and a wide range of "creative" films are currently available that use negative film as their start point. One of these—redscale film—is simply film that is deliberately loaded back to front so the base layer is facing the lens, rather than the emulsion. This means that the emulsion's layers are reversed, with the red-sensitive layer exposed first and the film's base acting like a colored filter. The result is images with a strong red-yellow color bias, which can work well with an appropriate subject. If you're shooting large-format sheet film, you load your film back to front to get the look (which some say is how redscale was "discovered" in the first place), but with 35mm and 120 it can be much easier to buy redscale film off the shelf from manufacturers such as KONO! and Lomography.

Tip

Negative film is more forgiving of exposure errors than positive film, but that doesn't mean you can be sloppy with your technique: A quick film test (see page 24) will help you to judge how best to expose your negatives.

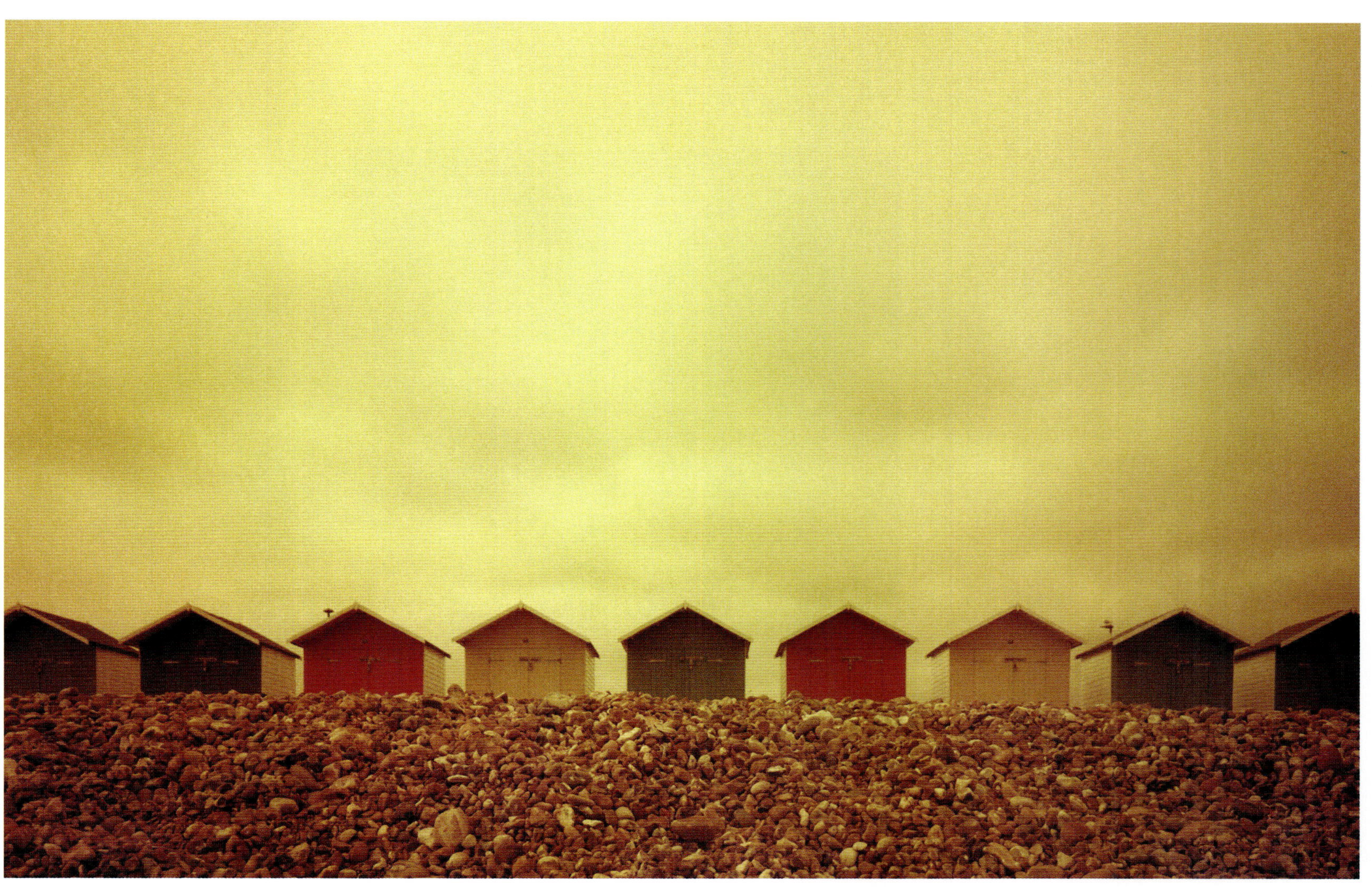

COLOR NEGATIVE FILM PROS AND CONS	
PROS	**CONS**
Greater dynamic range than positive film, so a greater level of shadow and highlight detail can be held in a single exposure; also more forgiving of exposure errors.	*Lab printing will attempt to "normalize" any color shifts, so you need to make staff aware if you have used filters to change the color, or if you have used a "creative" film, such as redscale.*
Slight color shifts can be removed at the printing stage.	*Harder to get accurate colors when scanning, due to the orange film base.*
Low DMax compared to positive film; easier to scan the film's full dynamic range.	*Doesn't cross process as well as color positive film (see page 160).*
Low cost: the cheapest color film to buy and process.	*Much harder to push/pull film (see page 159) as all films—regardless of speed— use the same basic timings during development.*
Some very "creative" film options available.	*Can look softer than positive film in terms of color and contrast, and lack punch.*

Film Types: Color Positive

Color positive film—also known as transparency or slide film—produces a positive image, so the colors and tones of the film essentially appear as we see them in reality (assuming a regular exposure and color balance). Although originally designed to be projected for viewing, slides also became the mainstay of professional photographers shooting for publication, as the positive images were far easier to translate to the printed page; color transparency film still offers a relatively pain-free scanning experience when compared to color negative film.

However, slide film is a far more demanding medium than negative film. A narrower dynamic range limits exposure latitude, which means that you have to be far more precise with your exposures to avoid highlights bleaching out or shadows blocking up. This in turn leads to a greater reliance on filters. Not only are they more often needed to control exposure—graduated neutral density filters to balance the sky and ground in landscape photography, for example—but also to control color, as there isn't necessarily a traditional printing stage (scanning your film and working on it digitally overcomes this to a certain degree).

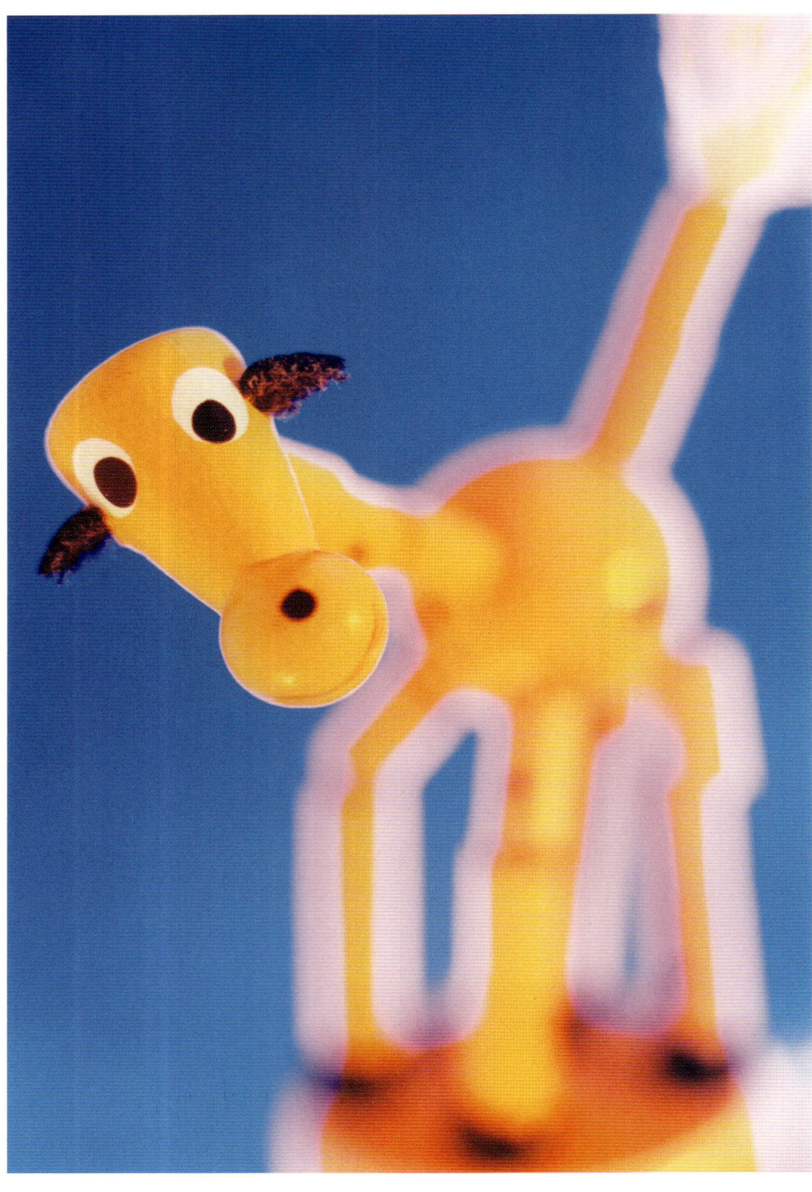

Above: To enhance the color in this shot I deliberately chose a transparency film that was designed to be slightly more saturated than others and then underexposed it by a small amount. This slight underexposure increased the saturation, but without making the overall exposure look completely "wrong."

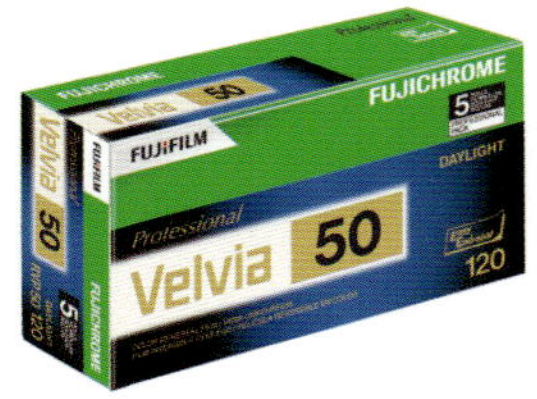

Above: Fujifilm's Velvia 50 is a "slow" transparency film known for its high saturation. Coupled with its fine grain it is a very popular choice for landscape photography.

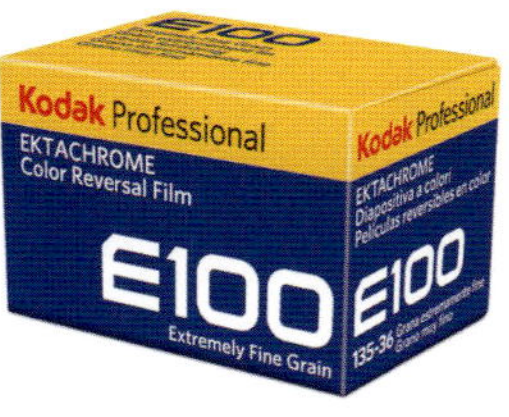

Above: Kodak relaunched Ektachrome E100 color reversal (positive) film in 35mm format in 2018, having discontinued it six years earlier. In the intervening period some materials used in the original manufacturing process became unavailable, and it had to be reformulated.

Tips

- The general rule for exposing transparency film is to ensure that you retain highlight detail where you want it and let the shadows take care of themselves; we are generally more accepting of "blocked up" shadows than we are of "blown" highlights.

- Age and temperature can affect the color of transparency film more than negative film, so for the best results you should always keep slide film in a fridge, especially if it's close to its best before date.

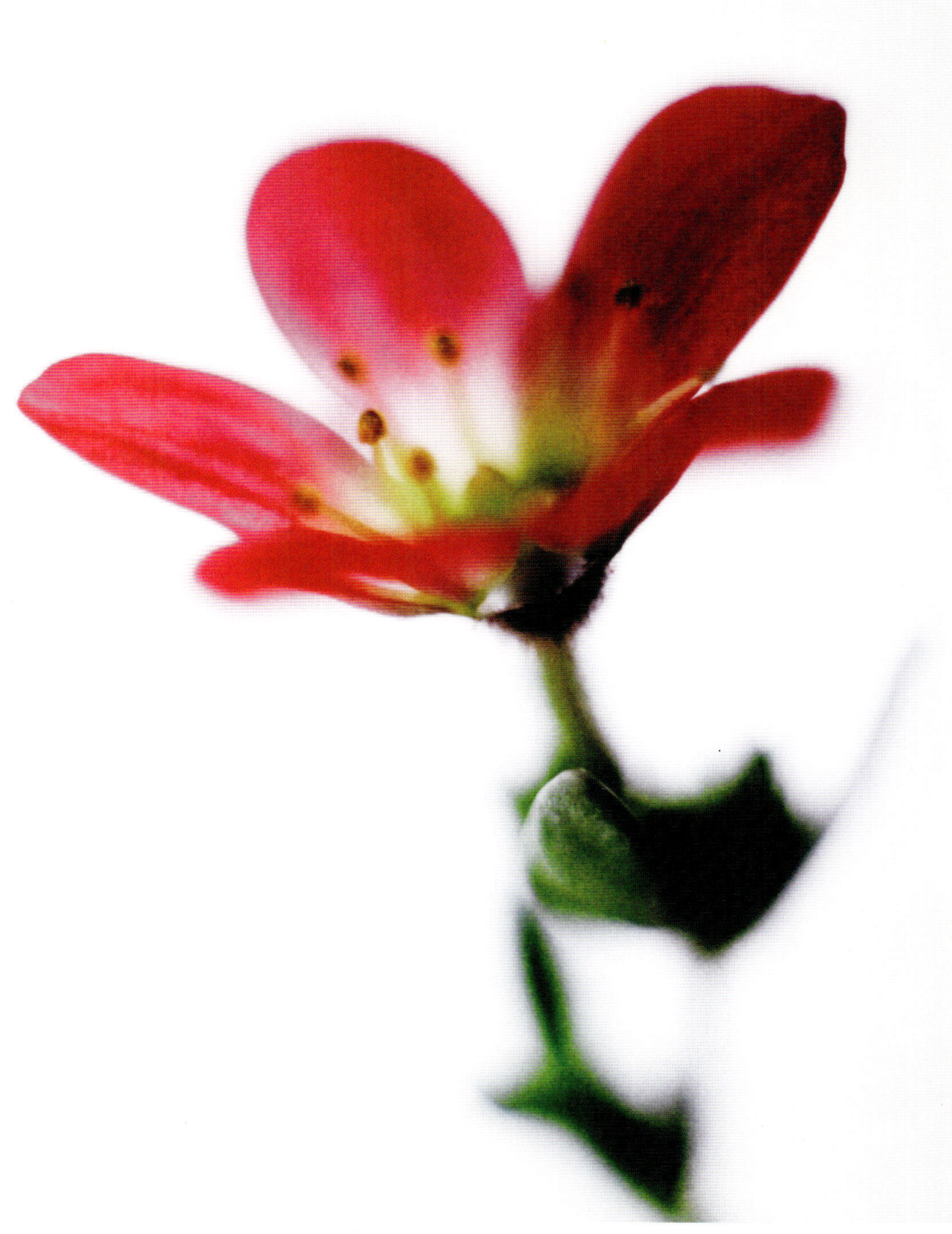

Above: If you can get it, color Polaroid or Fujifilm instant films can create images with a different "look." In this instance shooting now-obsolete 5x4in color Polaroid introduced a subtle texture to the image, which is quite different to grain.

INSTANT FILM

Instant film is perhaps the closest you can get to the instant gratification of digital photography, which is part of the reason why Fujifilm's Instax cameras go from strength to strength and Polaroid has been reborn. The ability to shoot and have a print in your hand within a couple of minutes is great fun, but you can also take it a step further and enter the realms of fine art by emulating the joiner images popularized by David Hockney in the 1980s. Most instant cameras may be simple point-and-shoot devices, but they are capable of creating some highly sophisticated images!

Testing

It's a good idea to test any film that you want to use on a regular basis, so you know how it performs under any and all conditions. This simply means that you will have a really good idea of how it responds to daylight, flash, artificial lighting, low light, and so on, and whether you need to adjust your technique.

Testing a film is pretty simple. Start by rating it at its "box speed" ISO and shoot a series of images, bracketing ±3 stops either side of the metered reading (see page 69 for details on bracketing) in ½- or ⅓-stop increments. It's important that your base exposure is as accurate as it can be, so consider using a handheld lightmeter (see page 78) or taking a light reading from a gray card (see page 80). Keep some notes so you know what the exposure is for each shot.

Take your film to a lab for processing and have prints and/or scans made from each frame. Tell the lab it's a test roll and you don't want any adjustments: you want a "normal" process and don't want them to try and compensate for the exposure (or color) when they print or scan the film. This is absolutely vital, because the sole aim of this exercise is to see how your film reacts to different exposures.

When you get them back, compare the prints or scans against your notes to see which frames look best. It might be that slight overexposure gives a better look with some negative films, for example, while a tiny amount of underexposure makes the colors in slide film pop. However, it will all depend on the individual film and the look you are after.

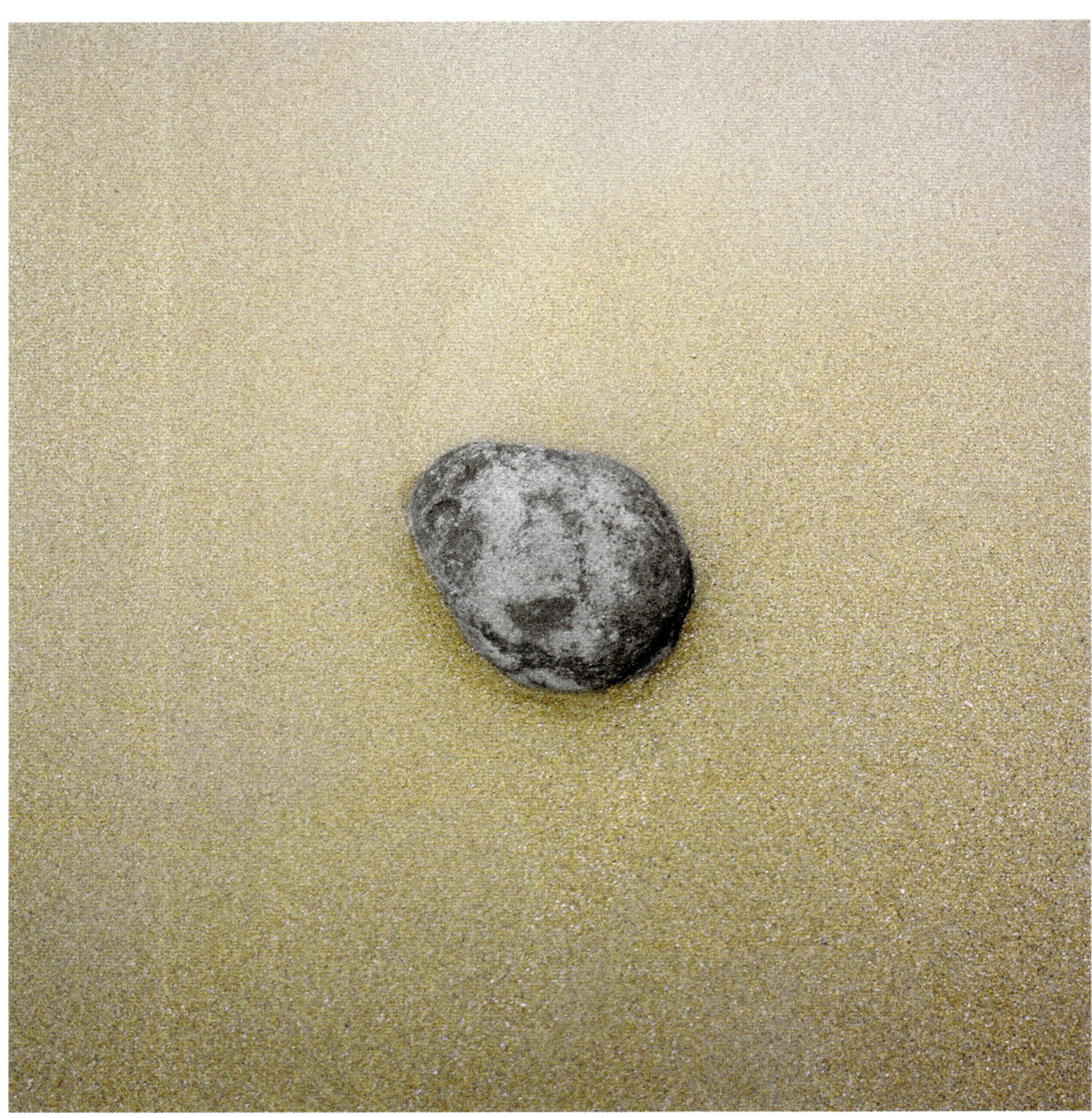

Above: For this simple square shot I used one of the more "neutral" transparency films available, knowing that the subject wouldn't be subjected to any radical saturation or contrast boosts. The film was exposed at its box speed (ISO 100), and processed normally.

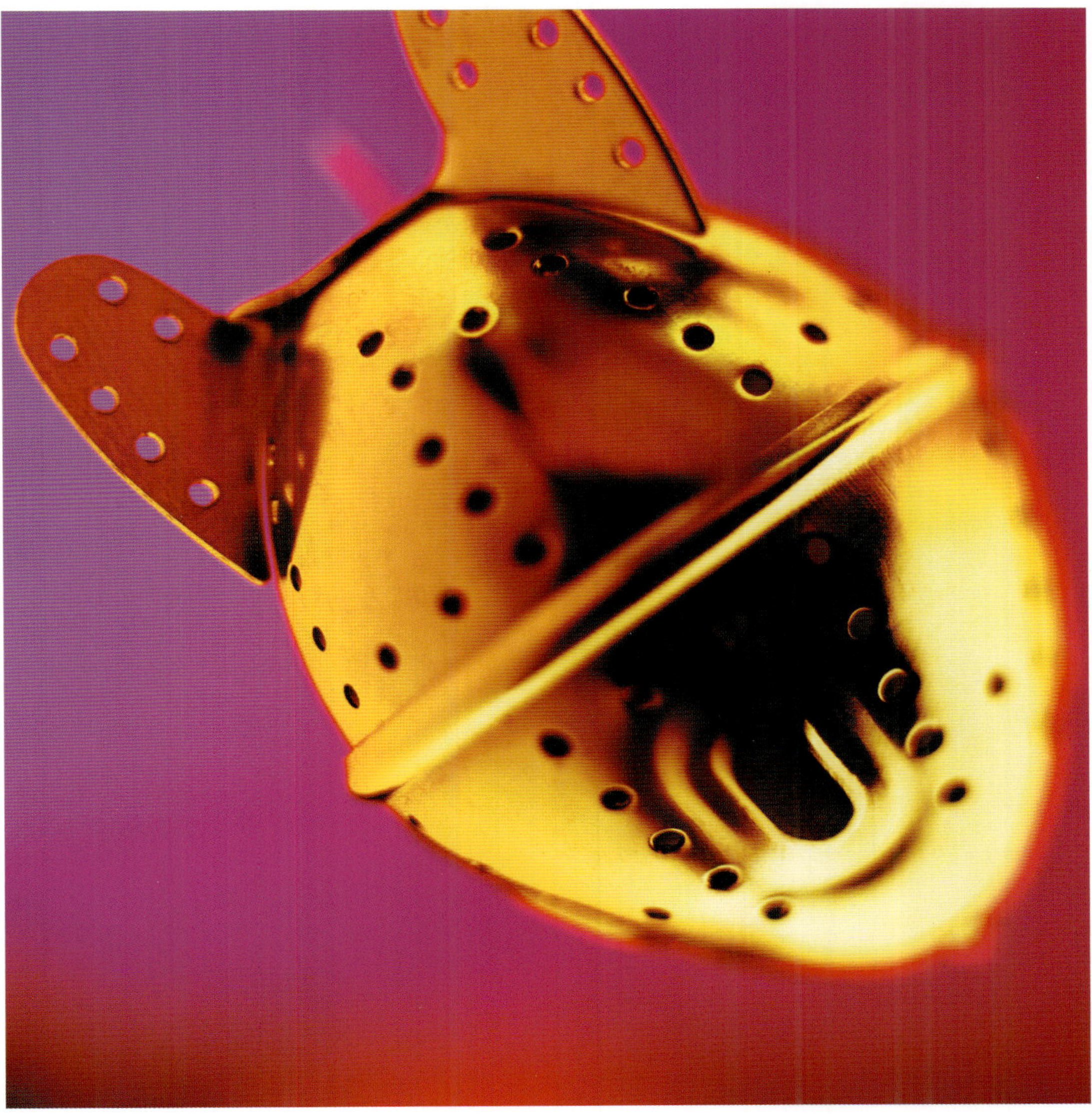

Above: I wanted to bump up the saturation in this still-life shot of a rocket-shaped tea infuser, which I photographed against a lightbox covered with colored gels. From testing I knew that slightly underexposing the film I was using (Fujichrome Provia 100) would help to make the colors pop, so I rated it at ISO 125 and processed it normally.

Film Formats

There are three broad camera formats (and, by extension, film formats): small, medium, and large. This simply refers to the type of film a particular camera can take, whether it's 35mm cassettes, rollfilm, sheet film, or one of the other formats outlined in the grid below right. The general rule when it comes to film formats is quite simple: the bigger the format, the bigger the prints, scans, or projections you can make from it. However, what and how you shoot also needs to be taken into account; you probably wouldn't want to shoot fast action on a large-format camera any more than you would want to shoot a billboard on 110 film. The format you choose will largely be driven by the type of photography you do; the end result you're looking to achieve; and the features you need from your camera.

Tips

- If you want to minimize the appearance of grain, larger formats, slow-speed films, and minimal enlargement is the ideal combination. Alternatively, choose small formats, fast film, and big enlargements if you want to produce grainier images.

- As well as increasing the appearance of grain, enlarging an image will also magnify any other "defects," such as dust and scratches on the film's surface, chromatic aberration, or any softness caused by the optical properties of the lens, focusing issues, or camera shake.

Film Format & Grain

There's a common misconception that film grain and film format are related, and that larger film formats are less grainy than smaller film formats, but this simply isn't true. If you had a 35mm film of a certain emulsion and a 10x8in sheet of film of the same emulsion, the grain on each would be the same because the emulsion used to coat them is identical. For example, Fujifilm Velvia 50 is the same emulsion, with the same structure, regardless of whether it's on small, medium, or even large-format film.

The reason larger formats are often thought to be less grainy (and smaller formats thought to be more grainy) comes purely from the enlargement of the image. Let's say that you want to create a 10x8in (25x20cm) print. If you were shooting on 35mm film (with a frame size of roughly 1½x1in or 36x24mm) you would need to enlarge the image approximately eight times to make your print. However, if you were shooting 10x8in film it would require no enlargement at all, so the grain isn't enlarged either. The result is that when you look at the prints side by side, the print from 35mm film appears grainier. The same thing happens when you scan film, and the rule is simple: the greater the enlargement, the more apparent the grain.

FORMAT	DIMENSIONS
10x8 sheet film	10x8in (25.4x20.32cm)
5x7 sheet film	5x7in (12.7x17.8cm)
5x4 sheet film	5x4in (12.7x10.16cm)
6x9	6x9cm (2¼x3½in)
6x7	6x7cm (2¼x2¾in)
6x6	6x6cm (2¼x2¼in)
6x4.5	6x4.5cm (2¼x1¾in)
35mm	24x36mm (1x1½in)
110	13x17mm (½x⅔in)

Right: Film comes in a wide range of formats, from small to large. This illustration overlays frames of all the commonly available and used formats at their actual size, from the miniature 110 format up to 10x8in sheet film (the image itself was shot on 35mm film).

Note: the dimensions given in the grid (left) are given first in their accepted unit of measurement: sheet film is typically measured in inches; medium format in centimeters; and small formats in millimeters. This is followed by an approximate metric/imperial conversion.

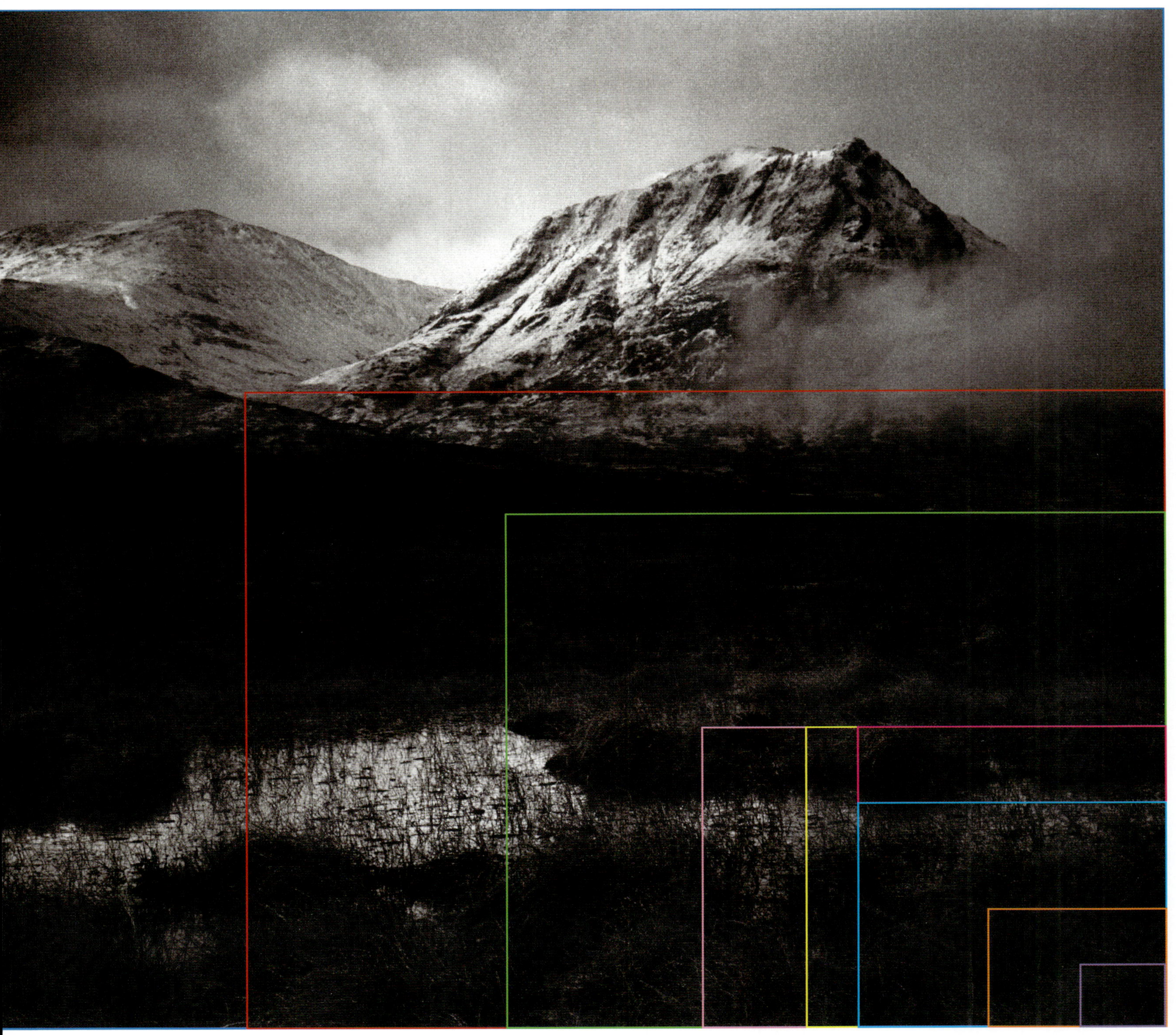

Profile: Andrea & Francesco Padovani

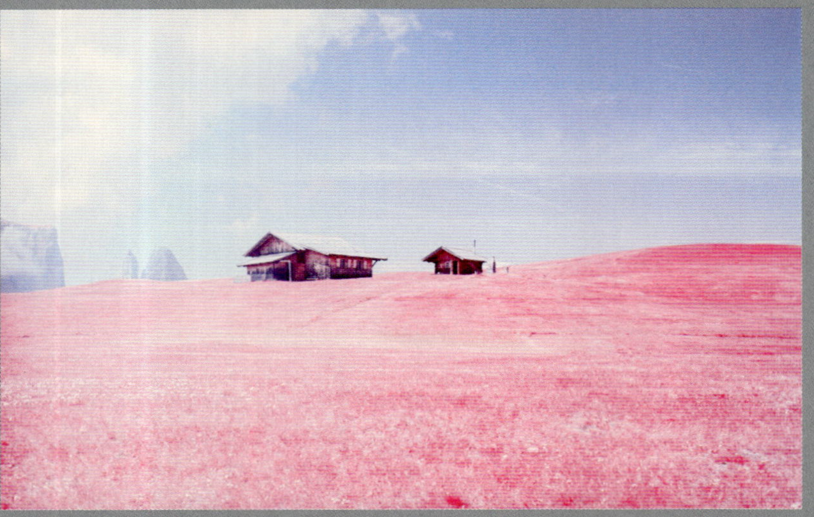

Left:
The view from Alpe di Siusi, with Sciliar in the background. This came from an early experimental roll and was heavily overexposed. It took quite a lot of work to recover it digitally.

Q) What film do you use to create the colors in your #DolomitesinInfrared landscapes?

A) We use 35mm FPP (Film Photography Project) InfraChrome. This is a color positive infrared film that is virtually identical to Kodak Aerochrome. We discovered the existence of infrared film not long ago, and having seen a lot of fantastic results from some great photographers, it was an obvious choice for an unusual look. We also discovered that this kind of film was rare, so we wanted to give it a try before it was too late!

Q) How easy is it to get the film?

A) When we first decided to experiment with this particular film, there was only one place to buy it new: the Film Photography Project's online store. That was in 2016, but now it seems that this stock has been discontinued, so if somebody wanted to experiment with color infrared film now it would probably mean buying some expired film from eBay or somewhere similar. Luckily we still have a few rolls left in the fridge.

Q) What cameras do you use?

A) It's important to avoid cameras that have automatic film advance systems, because they use tiny IR LEDs that can cause light leaks and ruin your pictures. We use a Canon AE-1 and an Olympus OM2n, each with a 50mm lens for consistency across the images.

Q) Do you use filters?

A) With IR film you're forced to use filters. We experimented with yellow and orange filters to start with, and preferred the chromatic rendition of the orange filter, so we pretty much always use that now.

Q) How do you determine your exposures?

A) This is quite tricky, because you have to consider how much infrared light is coming through the lens, rather than visible light. To start with we kept notes about every shot we took and played around with different settings so that we could learn what worked and what didn't. We wouldn't say we're experts on the subject, but it's definitely getting easier.

Q) Where and how is your film processed? Is the processing modified in any way?

A) The film goes through a standard E6 process, but as recommended by FPP, we ship our rolls to the guys at The Darkroom in California, who know exactly how to handle infrared film. Once we get the scanned images back we do a bit of editing in Photoshop to make the pictures sit together.

Q) What would be your top tip for anyone looking to shoot IR images?

A) Take notes about your shots: the shutter speed, aperture, if you metered for the highlights or shadows, the weather, and even the time of day. Shooting IR allows you to capture something that you cannot actually see, which forces you to think more about your subject choice and make guesses at times. This creates a bit of uncertainty, but for us that's a huge part of the fun of shooting film!

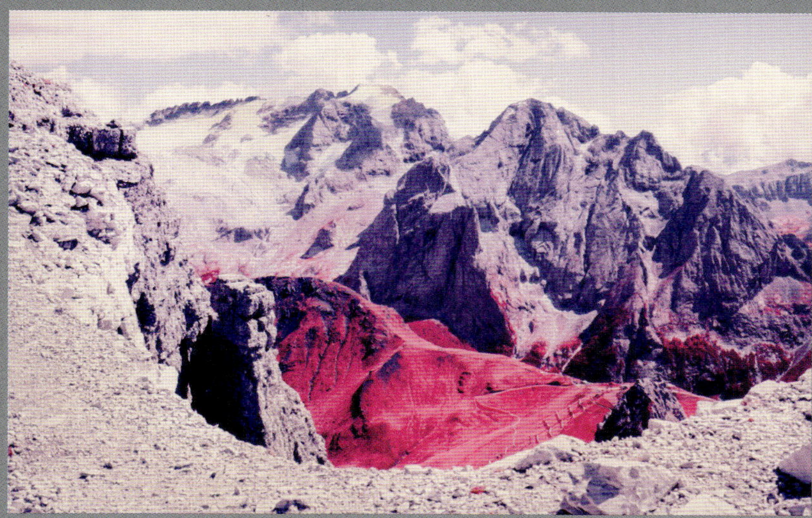

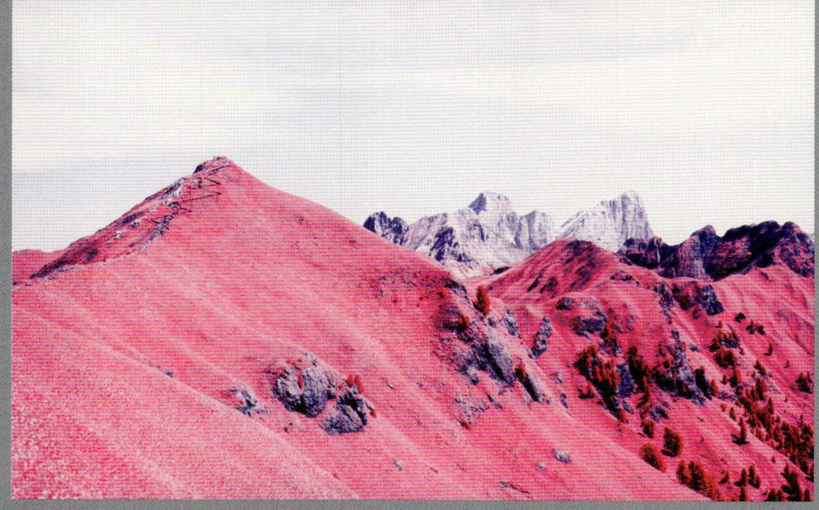

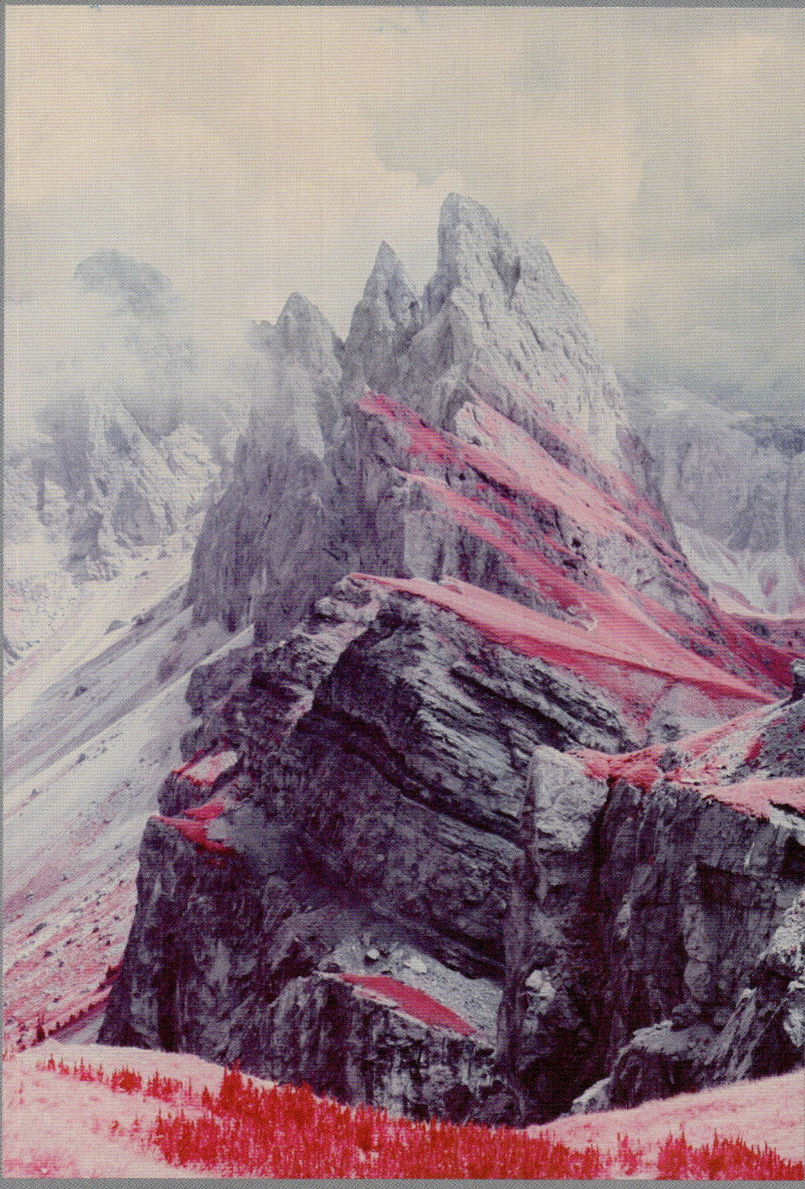

Top:
View from the top of Sass Pordoi, with Marmolada (the highest peak in the Dolomites) in front.

Above:
Sass de Dama with the peaks of Marmolada visible behind.

Right:
Seceda with the Odle mountains in the background.

Chapter 2
Cameras & Lenses

Over the last 200 years there have been countless variations on the basic premise of a light-tight box. Although some of these are now obsolete thanks to the discontinuation of certain film formats, many more remain usable, and this is one of the joys of shooting film: there is so much more on offer than there is in the digital realm. So, whether you opt for a large-format wood and brass field camera, a fully manual Leica or Hasselblad, a high-end 35mm SLR, or something in between, there is plenty to choose from. In this chapter we cast an eye over the various usable camera types you are likely to encounter today.

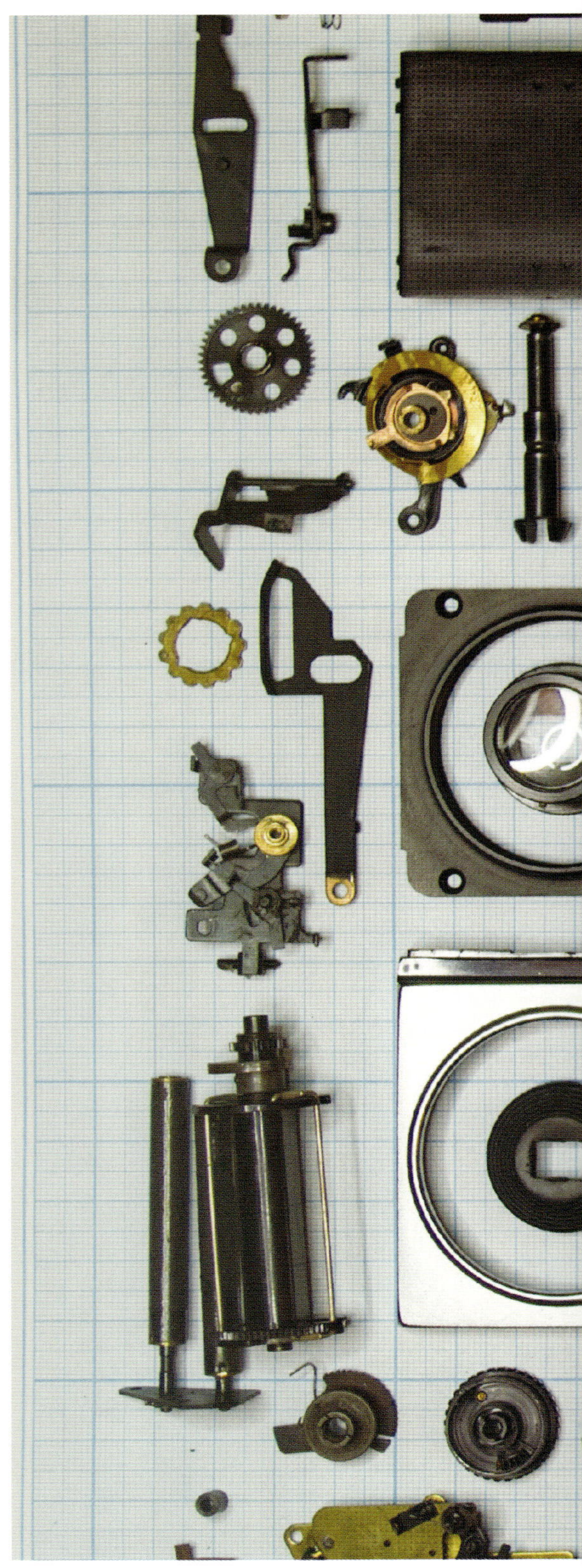

Right: A mechanical film camera relies primarily on screws and gears to make it function, meaning it is possible to strip down and repair a lot of vintage kit. This is not always the case with electronic cameras, and electrical failure can leave you with a camera-shaped paperweight…

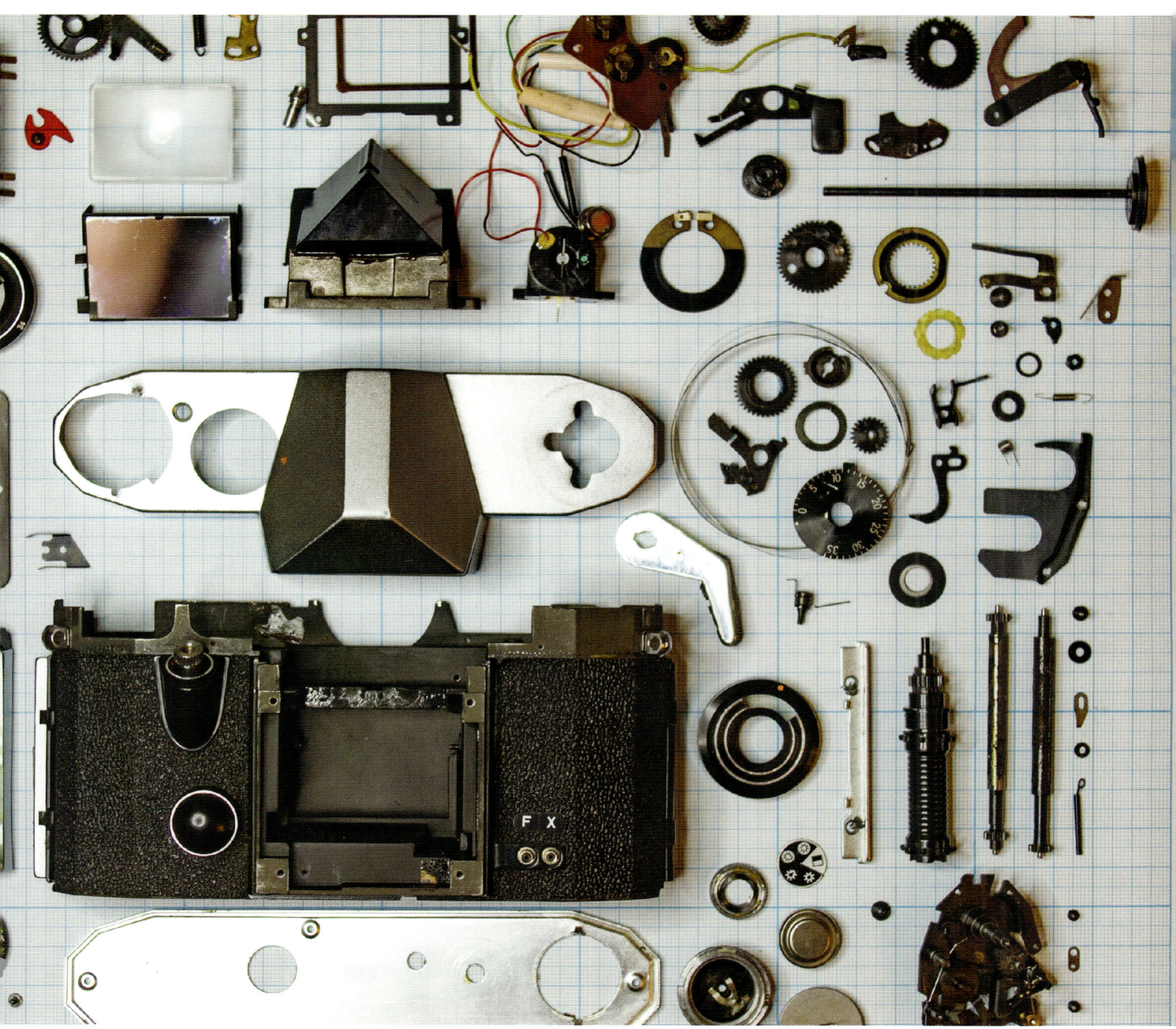

F X

Camera Types

Compact Cameras

In the loosest sense, a compact camera is simply a small and pocketable camera with a fixed lens. This covers a wide range of camera designs and styles from the past 50 years or so, from cameras offering point-and-shoot simplicity through fixed lenses and limited shutter speeds, to high-end models with bitingly sharp lenses and manual and semi-automatic shooting options.

Between these extremes lies a smorgasbord of plastic-shelled automated cameras, some with fixed focal length lenses and some with zoom lenses covering a useful range of focal lengths from modest wide-angle to mild telephoto. A few of these cameras were good (surprisingly so in some instances), some were bad, and the majority were decidedly average. However, they did what the non-photographer of any age needed them to do and they did it without any fuss, making them the mass-market "go anywhere" memory taker in the pre-digital, pre-smartphone age.

Tips

- Mass market compacts are best suited to negative film, as its wide exposure latitude can often accommodate wayward exposures.

- Premium compacts, such as the Contax T2 and T3, Minolta TC-1, Nikon 28Ti and 35Ti, and Ricoh GR models (film, not digital) offer greater exposure control, making transparency film a more viable option.

- Beware of compact cameras that use obsolete batteries, especially mercury cells. Although silver oxide batteries of the same dimensions are available, these can give spurious light readings: using a specialist battery adapter is a better option.

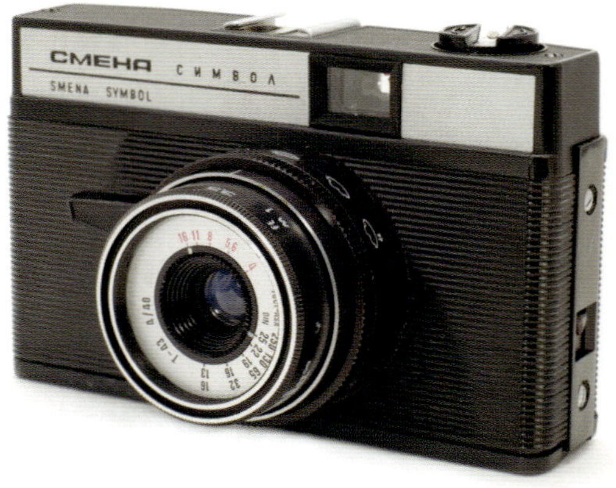

Left: The Smena Symbol is a product of the former Soviet Union and is popular among people looking to explore "lo-fi" photography with a plastic or "toy" camera without investing heavily: a used Symbol can cost as little as $10.

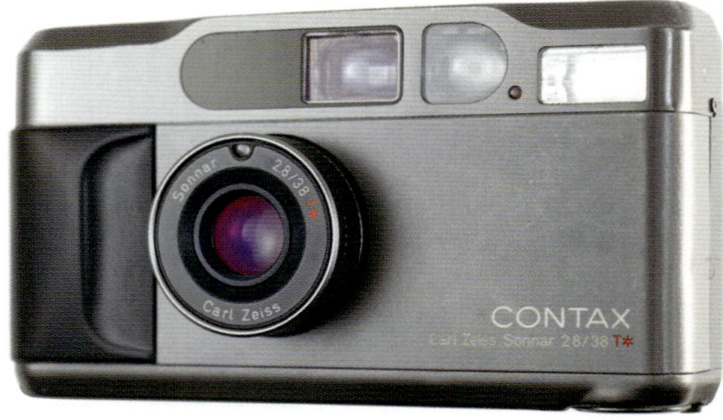

Left: With a bitingly sharp Carl Zeiss lens housed in a titanium body, the Contax T2 is one of a handful of premium compact cameras that can command an eye-watering price.

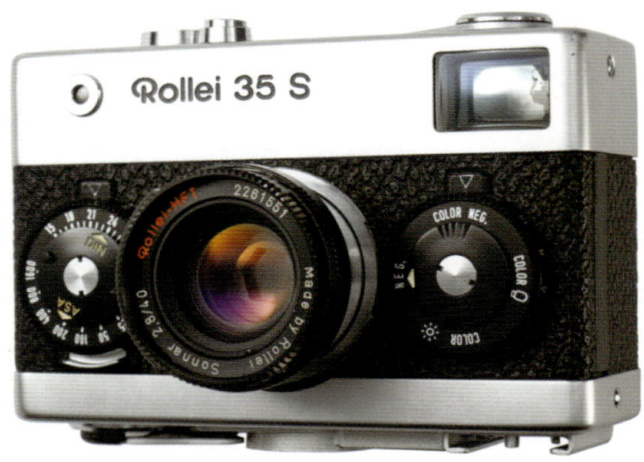

Left: When it was launched in 1966 the Rollei 35 was the smallest 35mm film camera you could buy, placing it firmly in the "compact" category. Its elegant looks and high quality Carl Zeiss lens make it as desirable now as it was then, and with full manual exposure control and focus, it's not simply a case of point and shoot.

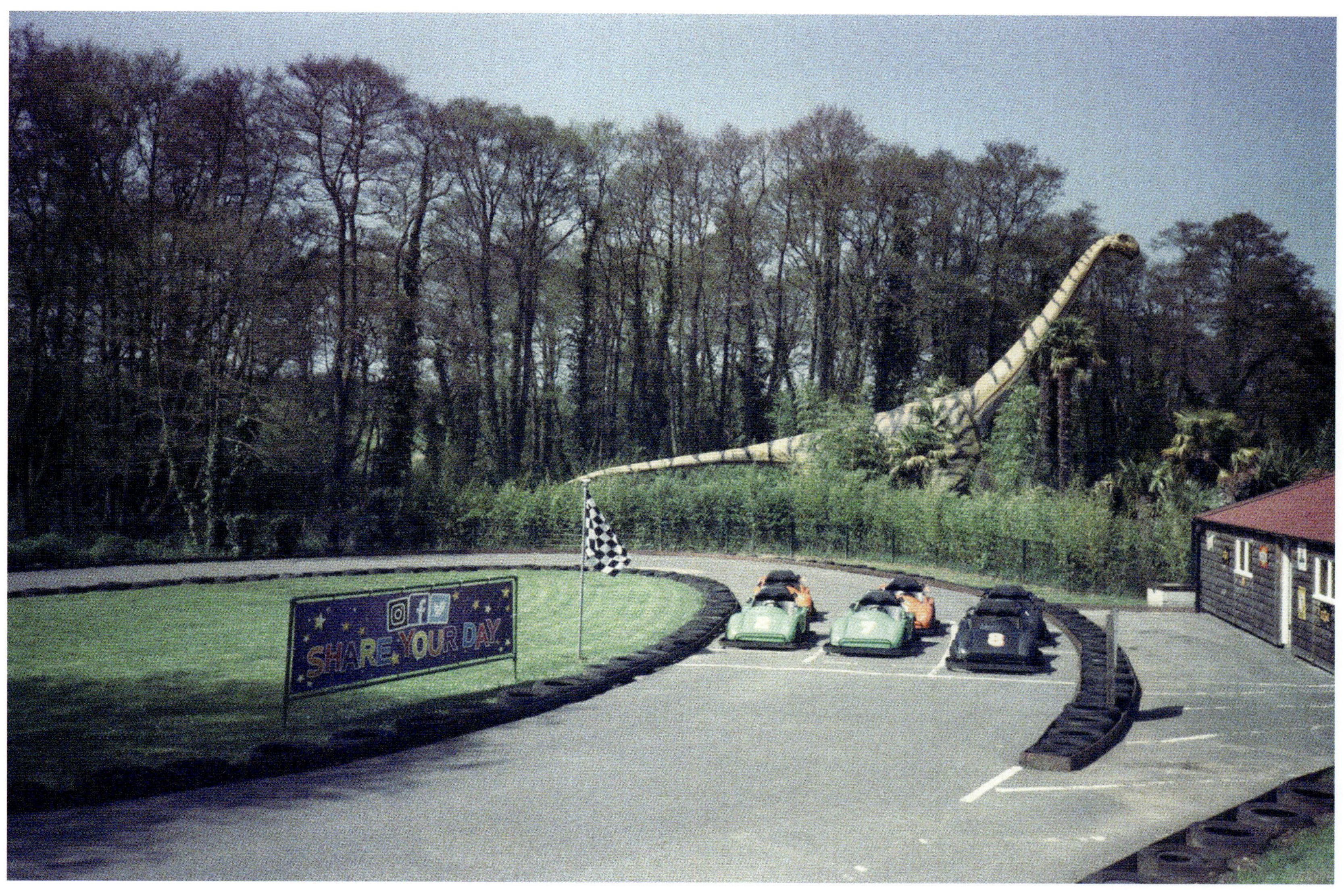

Above: A compact camera makes a great carry anywhere option. This shot was taken on an Olympus XA1 loaded with tungsten-balanced transparency film that was subsequently cross processed. That particular XA model uses a selenium light meter and doesn't require any batteries, which means it's always ready to go.

COMPACT CAMERA PROS AND CONS	
PROS	**CONS**
A great "carry anywhere" option.	*Low-end compacts can give poor-quality results.*
Thrift-store finds can give you a bit of film-based fun for next to no cost.	*The most desirable compacts command very high prices.*
The vignetting and soft edges that plague a lot of zoom compacts are now considered "characterful."	*Increasingly difficult to get compact cameras repaired, including premium models.*

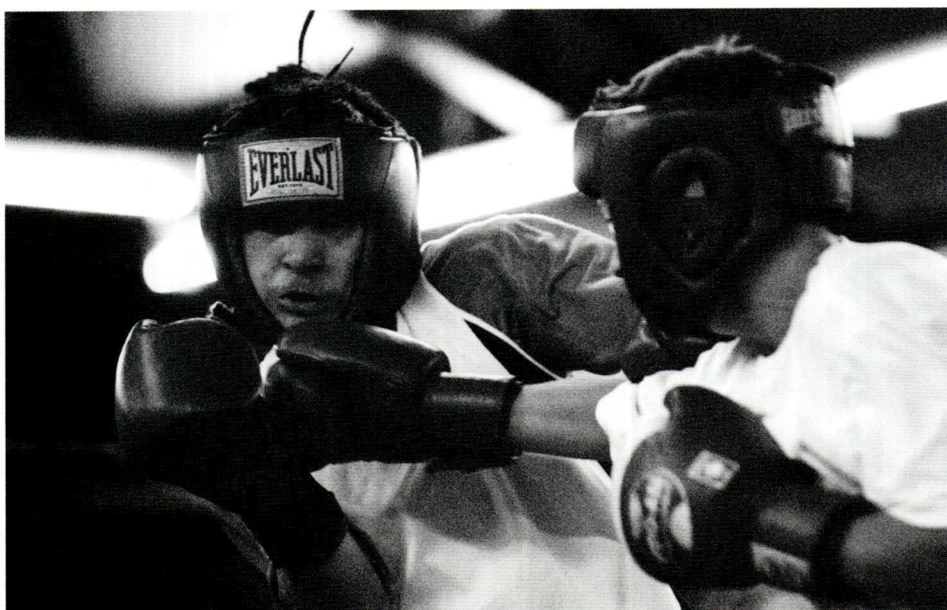

Left: To shoot sports you need a fast camera with a high drive rate and quick AF. For this indoor shoot at a boxing club I loaded a Nikon F6 with ISO 400 black-and-white film rated at ISO 3200. This allowed me to capture all the action.

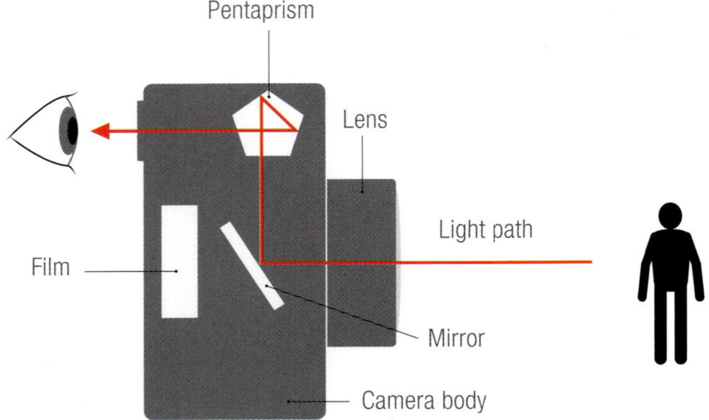

Above: The SLR design is based around a mirror and (with the exception of some medium format models) a prism, so when you look through the viewfinder you see through the lens. This gives you a fairly accurate framing mechanism, and enables you to preview the depth of field.

SLR Cameras

The Single Lens Reflex camera, or SLR, needs little introduction: this is the direct antecedent of today's digital SLRs and was, for decades, the number one choice for enthusiast photographers the world over. In addition to a through-the-lens (TTL) viewfinder, a large part of an SLR's appeal comes from the versatility afforded by interchangeable lenses and the array of accessories available. Whether it's adding a fast telephoto lens and motor drive to shoot fast-moving sports or wildlife subjects, buying a wide-aperture mid-telephoto lens for portraiture, attaching bellows and extension tubes for close-up work, or any other possible use, an SLR camera will allow you to tailor your kit to suit your particular shooting needs.

It's hardly surprising that this popularity led to a huge number of cameras being produced across most film formats, from 110 to medium format. In between these extremes were hundreds of 35mm SLRs from a multitude of manufacturers. Some, such as Canon, Nikon, Olympus, and Pentax, are still with us, while others, such as Contax, Praktica, and Topcon are now just names in the history books (at least in terms of their photographic relevance).

35mm SLRs

If you want the most "bang for your buck" then 35mm is the way to go. Look at eBay or any used camera dealer and you will find a bewildering array of 35mm SLR cameras on offer; opt for one of the more popular systems and you will find there are plenty of exotic lenses and accessories that you can attach to it.

The interesting thing here is that prices can often reflect how desirable or rare a camera is, and not necessarily how sophisticated it is. As a result, an all-manual SLR can often command a much higher price than a mid-range SLR with automatic focusing and exposure options from the same manufacturer; so a Nikon FM2 will cost you considerably more than a Nikon N90 (also known as the F90), for example. However, the key thing to remember is that they will both shoot in manual mode and if you put the same film in each camera and attached the same lens you would essentially produce images with the exact same qualities: the only difference would be the controls and general user experience. If you're on a budget this means you can often save money by buying a less desirable camera body, and then put the cash you save toward a decent lens.

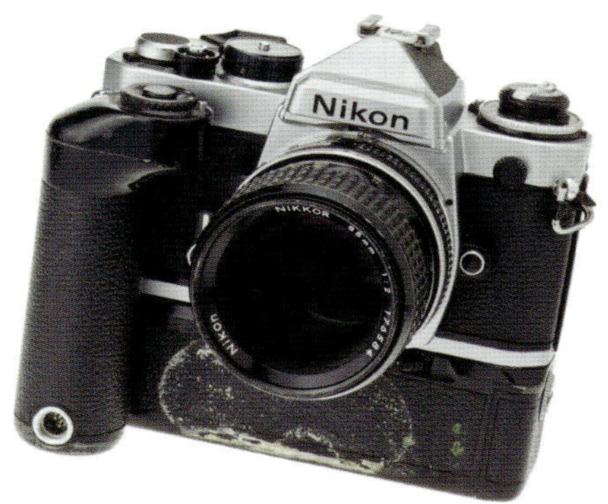

Left: One of the biggest draws of a 35mm SLR is its versatility. Accessories can be used to take your work in different directions, such as automatic film winders to increase shooting speed.

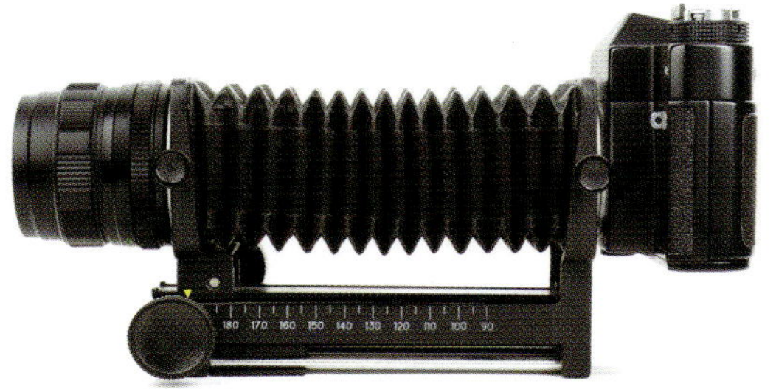

Left: Not only can you get focal lengths from 8mm right up to 1000mm (or more) with some systems, but you can also use specialist lenses and accessories such as macro bellows to open up a whole new world of subject matter.

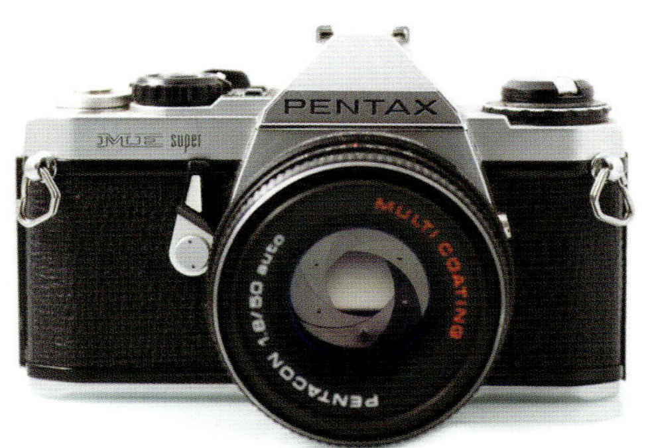

Left: The Pentax ME Super is typical of the type of SLR that was popular in the late 1970s and 1980s. Its combination of manual focus and aperture priority or manual shooting modes makes it great for anyone wanting to learn the essentials of photography.

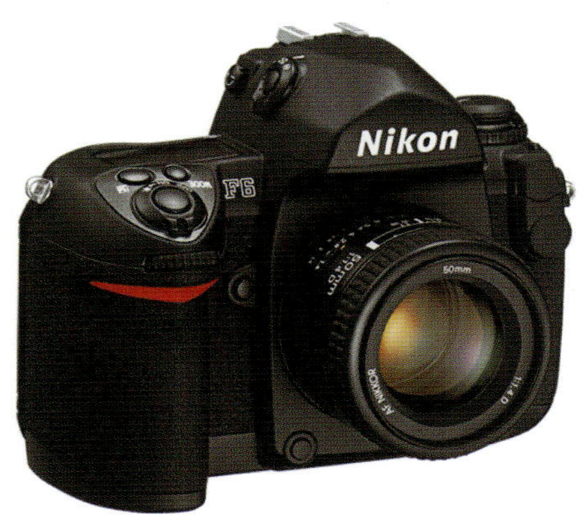

Left: Nikon's F6 was the last pro-spec 35mm SLR. It combines advanced autofocus, a range of exposure modes and metering options, and a continuous shooting mode that can shoot a 36-exposure roll of film in under seven seconds.

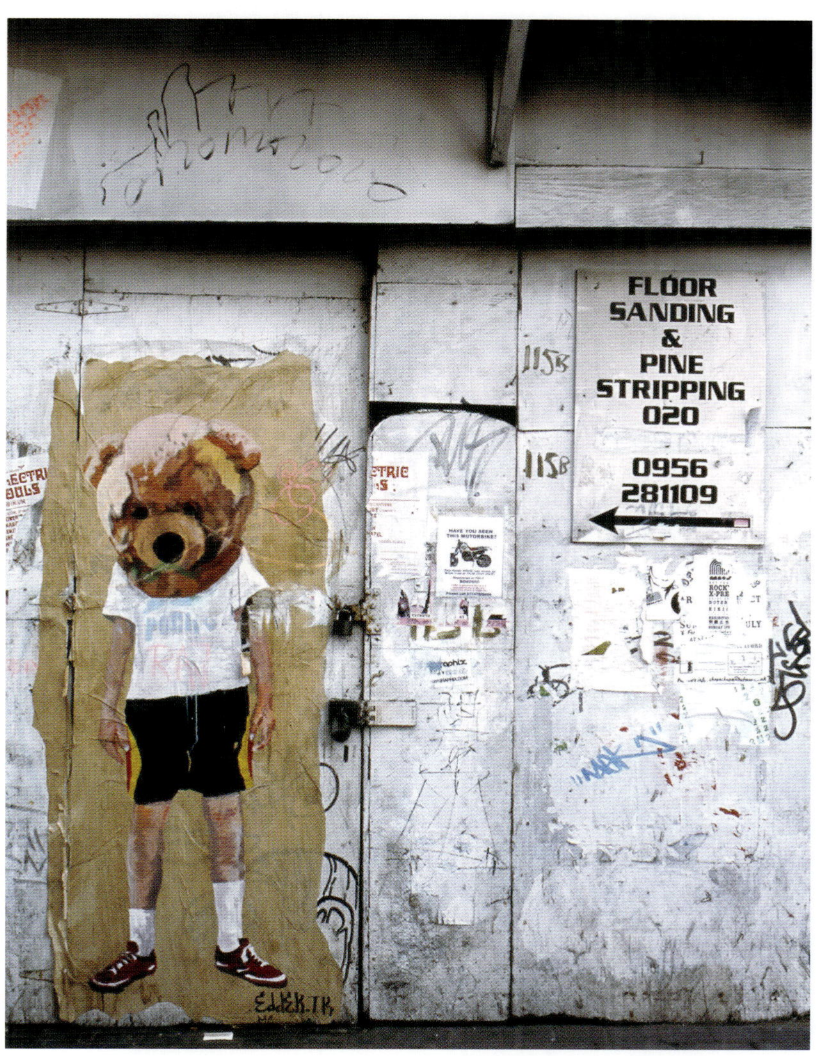

Above: A 35mm SLR with a 50mm lens is a great way to get started with film and will teach you essential skills. Just head out into your local environment and shoot what you see: I spotted this piece of wall art on a closed building and shot on transparency film using an old Olympus OM2SP.

Medium-Format SLRs

If money is no object and/or you want the highest
quality images, then medium format is a step in the
right direction. Unlike 35mm SLRs there is a huge
variety of camera body shapes and styles, from
those that look and handle like an oversized 35mm
SLR to more "boxy" designs that use a waist-level
viewfinder to display a reversed image and have
interchangeable film backs so you can switch
mid-roll between different emulsions. In addition,
some of these cameras offer automatic exposure
options while others are fully manual and will
require an external lightmeter of some sort
(although many have metered viewfinders that
are available as an optional extra). With so much
choice, determining which camera is right for you
will depend a lot on what you want to do with it, so
it really pays to do your homework before placing
a bid or getting out your money in a camera store.

Tips

- Some medium-format cameras were popular
  with professional photographers and, as such,
  may have had a hard life. While not all heavily
  used cameras and lenses will be worn out,
  some will be close to the end of their life.

- Watch out for cameras and lenses that have
  gone unused for a long period of time, as
  lubricants can dry out and mechanisms can
  jam as a result.

- Medium-format SLRs tend to have a more
  limited range of lenses in terms of focal
  lengths and maximum apertures than their
  35mm counterparts.

- Some medium-format SLRs use lenses with
  a leaf shutter (see page 52), rather than the
  camera possessing a focal-plane shutter.
  This makes the camera body simpler, but the
  lenses more complex (and more expensive).

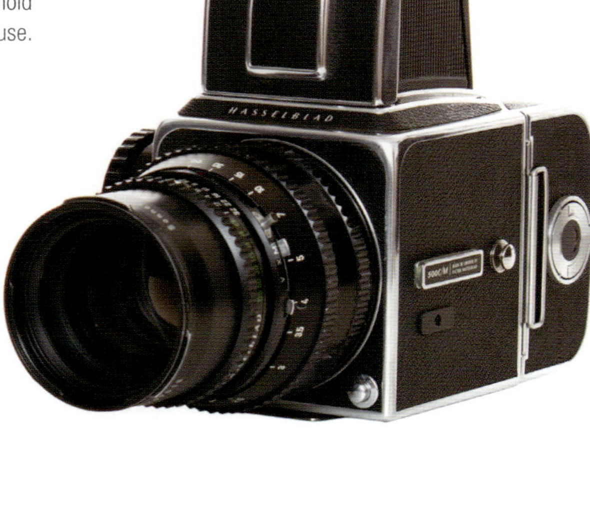

Right: You can easily argue that at the top of the
medium-format tree is Hasselblad, whose 500-series
cameras are legendary. Its Carl Zeiss lenses are super
sharp, the cameras are light enough to handhold
comfortably, and they are beautiful to use.

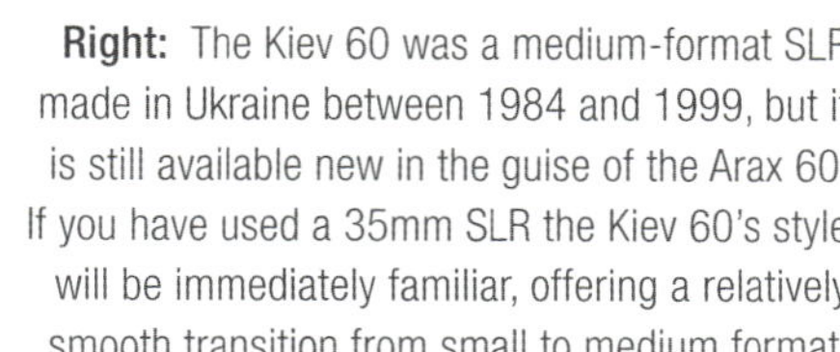

Left: Initially launched in 1970, the Mamiya
RB67 (and later RZ67) was the heavyweight
workhorse of many pro photographers.
Highlights include built-in bellows for close
focusing, interchangeable film backs, and a
comprehensive range of lenses covering focal
lengths from 37mm right up to 500mm.

Right: The Kiev 60 was a medium-format SLR
made in Ukraine between 1984 and 1999, but it
is still available new in the guise of the Arax 60.
If you have used a 35mm SLR the Kiev 60's style
will be immediately familiar, offering a relatively
smooth transition from small to medium format.

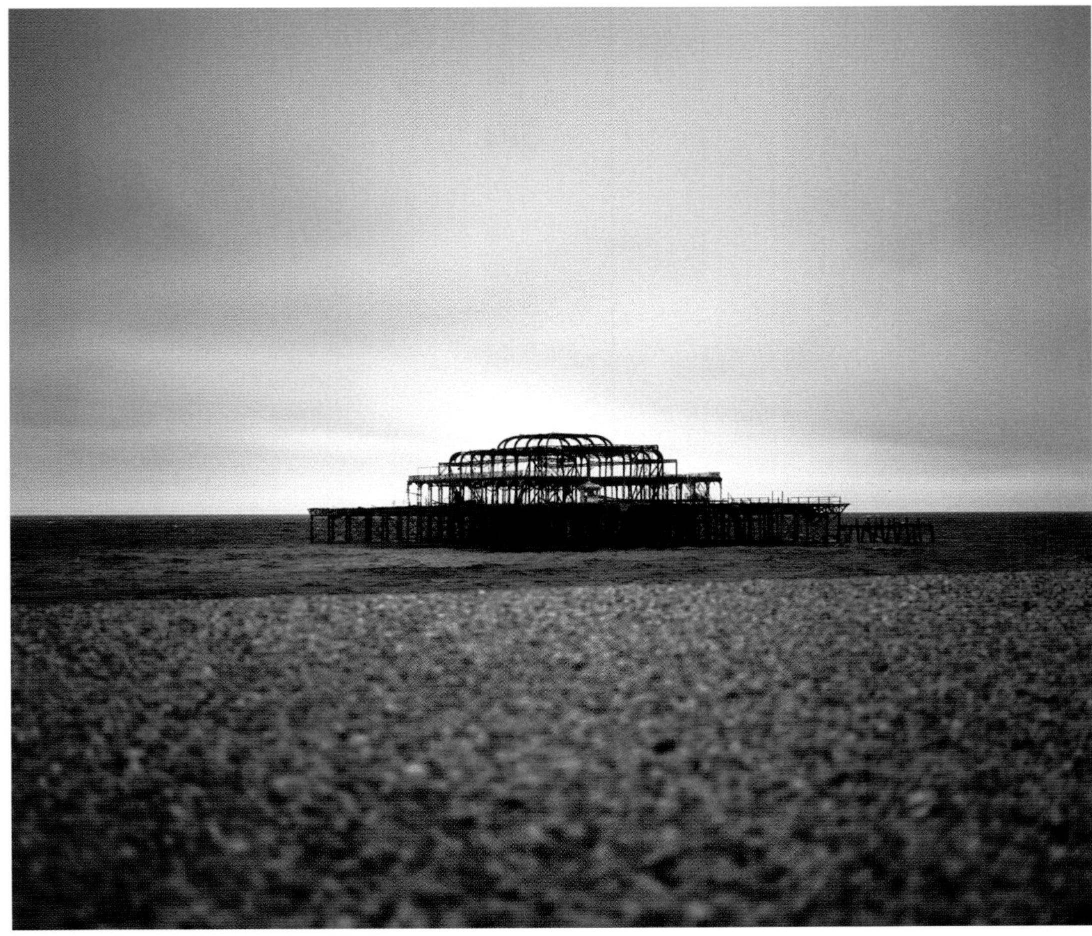

Left: This shot was taken using a Bronica SQ-A. It shoots a square image (nominally 2¼x2¼in/6x6cm) and features interchangeable film backs, lenses, and viewfinders. In this instance the standard 80mm f/2.8 lens was used at its widest aperture to throw the foreground out of focus.

SLR (SINGLE LENS REFLEX) CAMERA PROS AND CONS	
PROS	**CONS**
Established SLR systems have a huge range of lenses and accessories to tap into (especially 35mm SLRs).	"Mirror slap" can lead to slightly soft images.
Incredibly versatile: an SLR can be used to shoot everything from extreme macro to the most distant wildlife (and everything in between).	Viewfinder blacks out when the mirror flips up to make an exposure, making it harder to track moving subjects.
Through-the-lens viewing enables you to preview the depth of field and frame shots precisely.	Electronic models can suffer from "sudden death syndrome," whereby the circuitry fails and a repair is either impossible or uneconomical.
Fully mechanical SLRs have very little to go wrong (and repairs are usually possible).	A large SLR kit can be physically tiring to carry.
Choice of fully manual cameras or more automated models.	

Rangefinder Cameras

Fixed-lens 35mm rangefinder cameras, such as the Yashica Electro 35 and Minolta Hi-Matic models (among countless others), were hugely popular in the 1960s and 70s, but by the mid-80s their popularity had waned as compact cameras and autofocus became more prevalent.

However, the rangefinder design remained popular among photographers who were looking for a small, quiet, high-quality alternative to a bulky SLR. Although Leica is the brand that typifies the rangefinder genre, there were plenty of other offerings, including Voigtländer's Bessa models, with Leica-compatible lens mounts; the autofocus Contax G1 and G2 (which purists deny are "true" rangefinders); the Hasselblad XPan, which enables both 24x65mm panoramic shots and regular 24x26mm frames to be captured on 35mm film; the medium format Mamiya 6 and 7, with interchangeable lenses; and many other 35mm and medium format offerings.

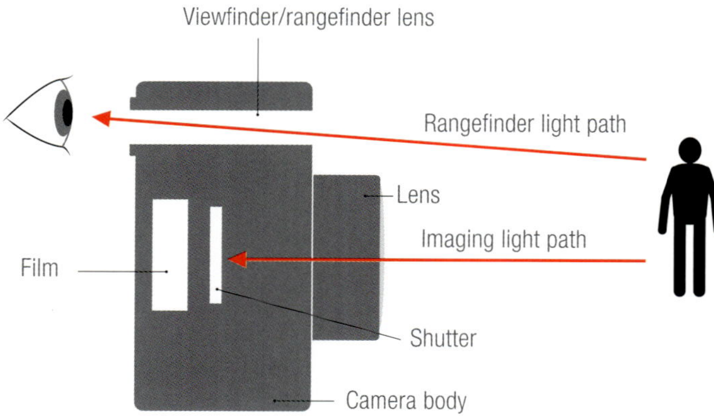

Above: Rangefinder cameras can be identified by the way in which they focus. Unlike an SLR, which lets the photographer see through the lens (see page 34), a rangefinder uses a "dual image" focusing system. The photographer looks through a direct viewfinder window and sees two superimposed images of what the camera is aimed at. Focus is adjusted until the two images are aligned, at which point the subject is in focus.

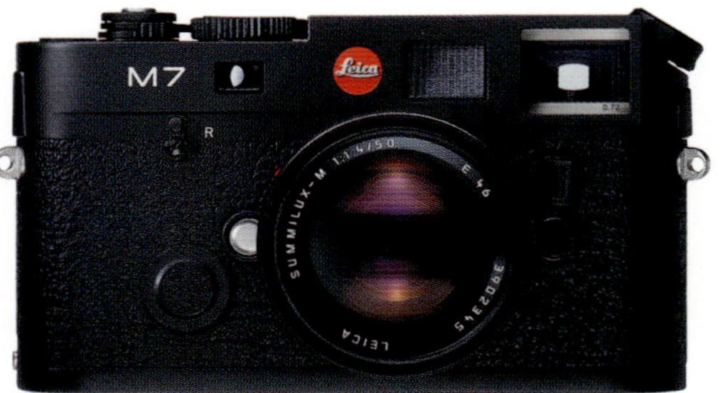

Left: Leica introduced its first 35mm rangefinder, the Leica II, in 1932. However, as well as its screw-fit camera bodies the German marque also launched the iconic M-series, which is regarded as being one of the finest camera ranges ever made.

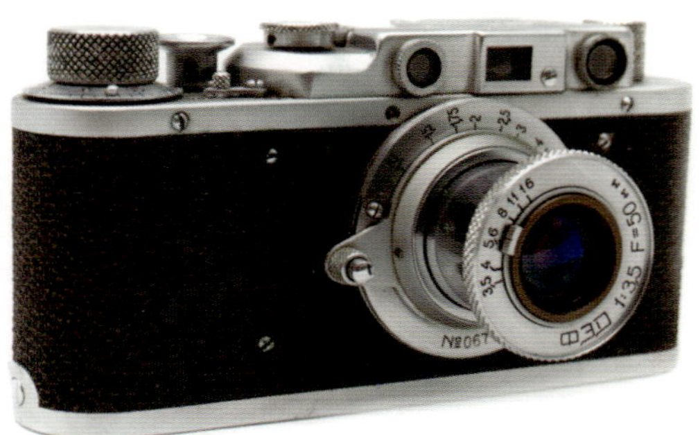

Left: Produced in the former Soviet Union shortly after World War II, early Fed cameras were shameless copies of the iconic screw-fit Leicas of the time. Some cameras and lenses were even engraved with the Leica name and sold as genuine German cameras: these counterfeit Leicas still appear for sale today.

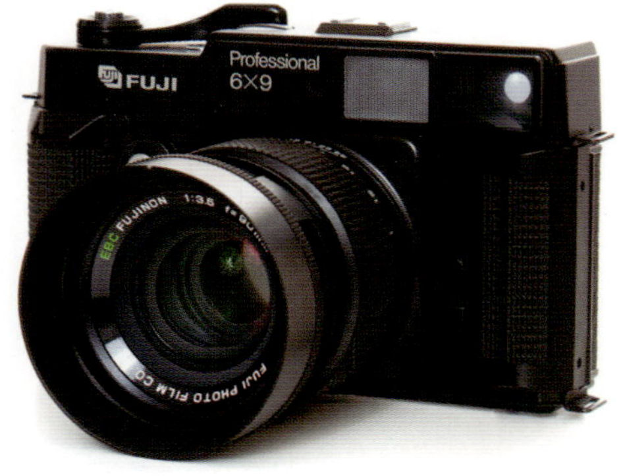

Left: If 35mm film is too small for you, Fujifilm has a history of producing medium-format rangefinder cameras. The Fuji GW690II Professional, launched in 1985, shoots 6x9cm format images and features a 90mm "standard" fixed focal length lens. Its size has led to the nickname "Texas Leica."

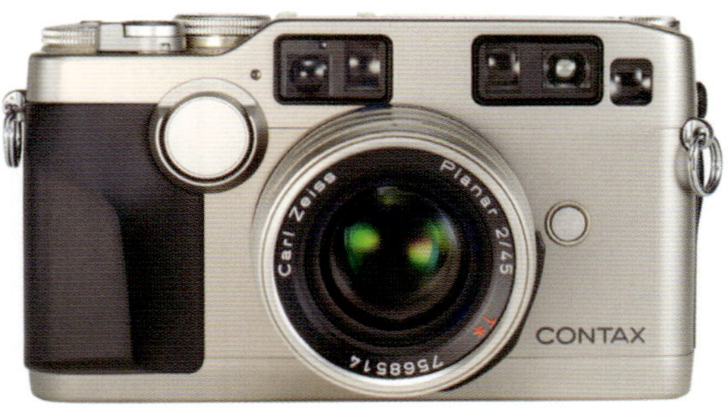

Left: The Contax G2 is unique among rangefinder cameras as it uses autofocus instead of manual focus, although some rangefinder purists argue this means it is not a "true" rangefinder.

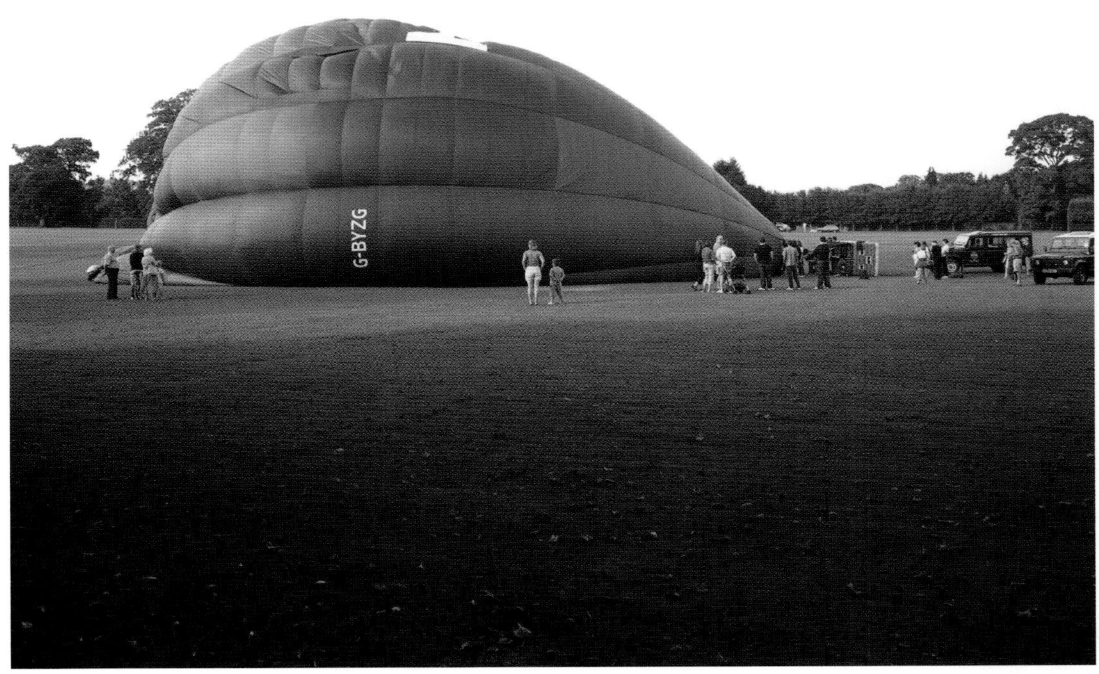

Left: There are numerous medium-format rangefinders, but my personal favorite is the Mamiya 7: it's light, shoots 6x7cm images (or 24x65mm panoramas with a 35mm film adapter), and has a useful range of interchangeable lenses, including an ultra-wide 43mm (although this shot was taken using the standard 80mm lens).

Below: I shot this when I was testing a Rollei 35 RF for a camera magazine. This 35mm rangefinder camera is essentially a rebadged Voigtländer Bessa R2 (with an inflated price tag), but it performs beautifully; for this black-and-white shot I applied a digital split tone.

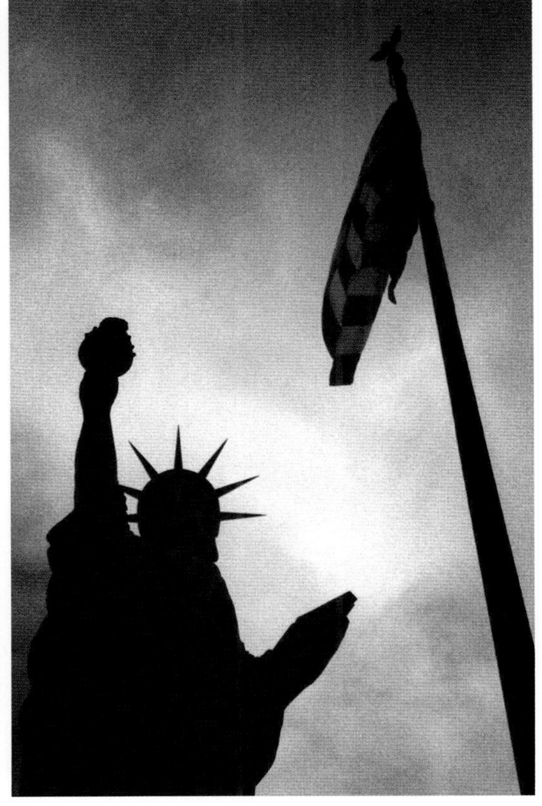

RANGEFINDER CAMERA PROS AND CONS	
PROS	**CONS**
As there is no need for a separate mirror and prism viewing system, rangefinder cameras are smaller and lighter than 35mm SLRs.	*Limited lens choice: there are very few zoom lenses or telephoto options for a rangefinder, so they are not ideal for sports and wildlife.*
No mirror means there is no chance of "mirror slap" blurring your images. This also makes it easier to handhold at slower shutter speeds.	*The distance between the lens and rangefinder creates parallax issues when you focus close up, so what the lens sees is very different to what is seen through the viewfinder. This makes them quite difficult to use for macro photography, although some complex macro accessories exist.*
The viewfinder window typically shows more than the film will record. This enables you to better predict when something might enter the frame.	*You can forget about autofocus! Although the Contax G1 and G2 use a similar "triangulating" system to focus automatically, most people agree that a true rangefinder only offers manual focus.*
A rangefinder camera is a lot quieter in use than an SLR, which is why the design is quite popular with street photographers.	*As you're not looking through the lens it's quite easy to forget to remove the lens cap, have something dangling in front of the lens, or even cover it partially with your finger when you take a shot.*
Lenses can often be made smaller (and sharper) than their SLR counterparts.	*As you're not looking through the lens you can't preview the depth of field.*

TLR Cameras

TLR or Twin Lens Reflex cameras are immediately identifiable thanks to the paired lenses that give them their name and a simple boxy shape that can be traced back to the earliest models. Although some TLRs were designed around the 127 and 35mm film formats, and a small number offer interchangeable lenses, the majority of these cameras have a remarkably similar specification: they shoot square 6x6cm frames on medium format film through a fixed focal length lens that's typically in the region of 75–80mm (the "standard" focal length for the format).

The reason they have two lenses is because each has its own role: one is used for viewing (and focusing) and the other is used for actually taking the photograph. Because both of the lenses are mounted on the same panel (or are connected using a geared mechanism) they focus at the same distance, and as they have the same focal length, the "taking" lens records pretty much what you see through the viewing lens on the waist-level finder. The beauty of this design is that each lens can be optimized for its specific role, so the viewing lens can project a bright image onto the ground glass, while the taking lens can be tuned to deliver astounding image quality. Consequently, even a mediocre TLR can deliver great results, making it as compelling today as it was in its heyday during the mid 20th century.

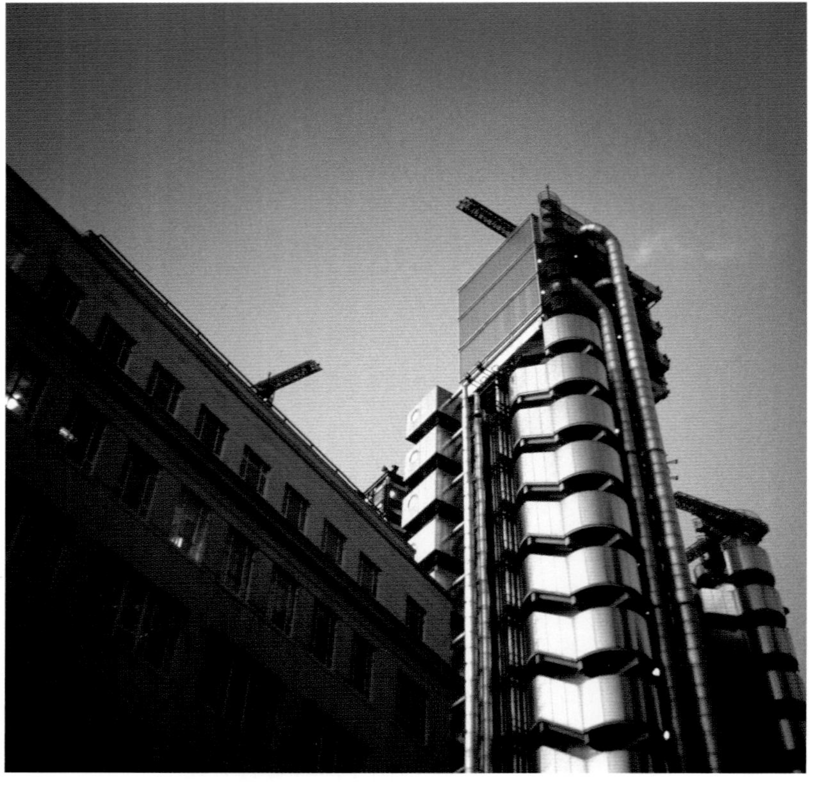

 Seagull cameras first appeared in the 1960s, and production of these TLRs continued through to the 2000s. They didn't have a great reputation for build quality and performance, but they offered a low-cost route into medium format for those on a budget. This photograph was taken on a Seagull 4A-109.

TLR CAMERA PROS AND CONS	
PROS	**CONS**
The simple mechanical design often means there's little to go wrong.	*The vast majority of TLRs have a fixed focal length lens (the notable exception being Mamiya's C series).*
Leaf shutter lenses allow flash synchronization at all shutter speeds (see page 98).	*As with a rangefinder camera (see page 38), the distance between the viewing and taking lenses can create parallax issues, making it difficult to shoot close-up images accurately.*
Using a waist-level finder means that your camera isn't in front of your face; this can make it easier to engage with portrait subjects.	*The image through the waist-level finder is reversed laterally, so the left side of the scene you are viewing appears at the right of the viewfinder. This can make it tricky to photograph moving subjects.*
As it's relatively easy to optimize a single focal length lens, TLRs can be optically superb.	*Because you're not looking through the "taking" lens you can't preview the depth of field.*
It's easy to use dense ND filters because the filter doesn't need to cover the lens you frame and focus your shots through.	*It can be difficult to position graduated filters or use a polarizer (see page 124) as you aren't seeing through the "taking" lens, so can't see the effect of the filter.*

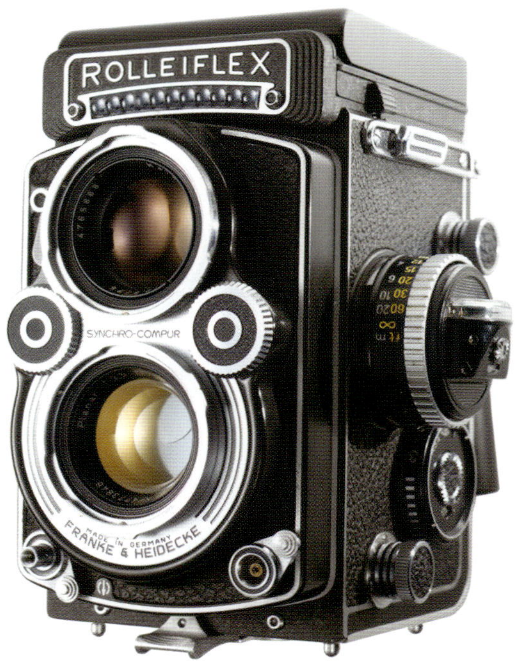

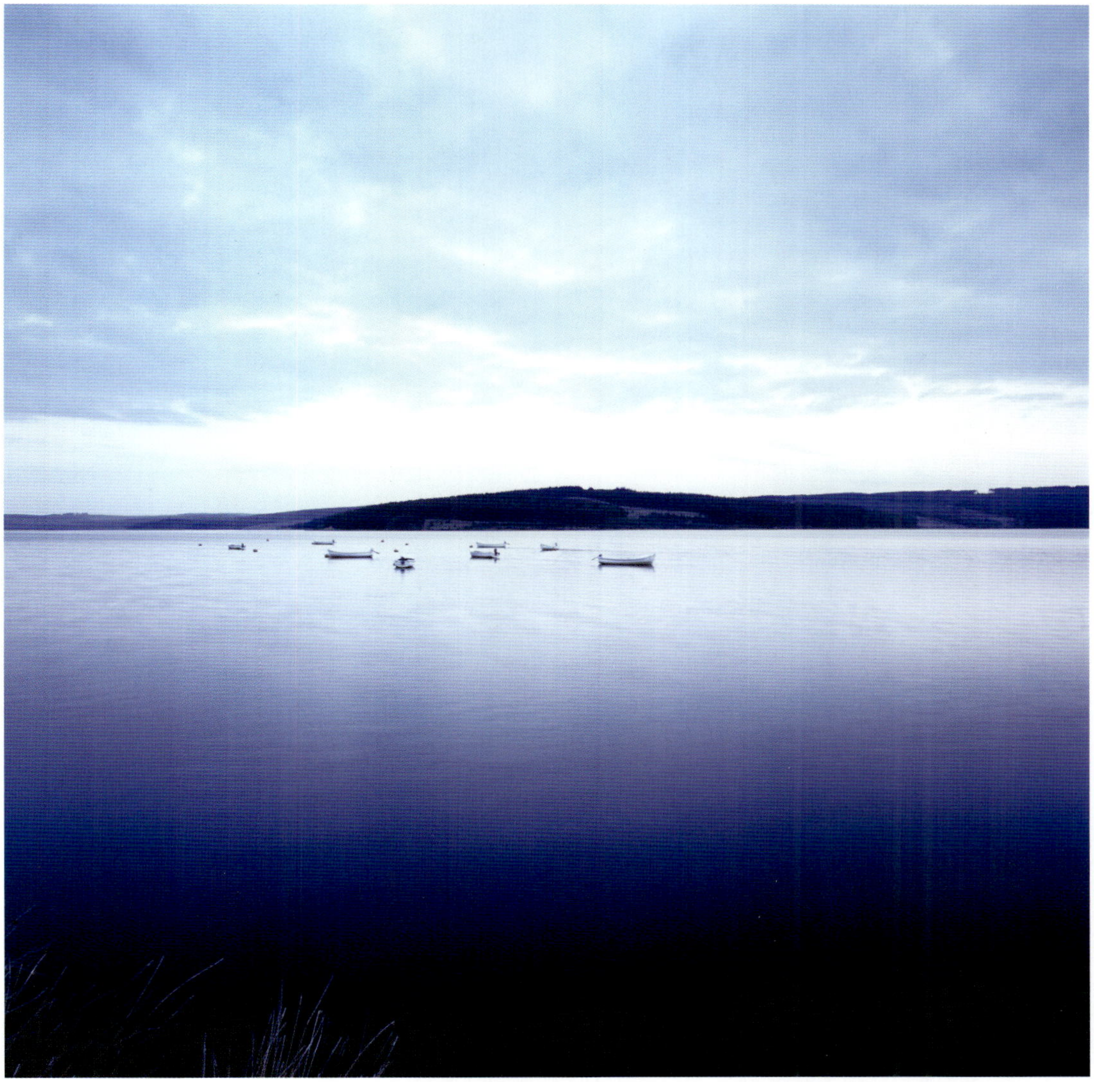

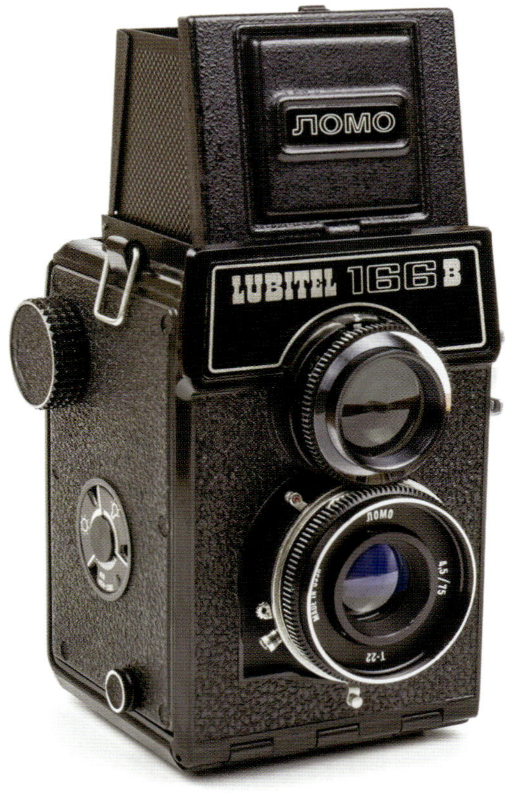

Above left: The undisputed king of the TLRs is the widely imitated (but never equaled) Rolleiflex, which is reflected in the price of even a well-used model. However, set your sights a bit lower and you will find plenty of budget-friendly Rolleicords (the Rollei TLR aimed at amateurs), Yashicamats, and Mamiyaflexes, plus a whole host of lesser-known brands on the market.

Left: The plastic-bodied Lubitel 166 is a cult classic and hipster favorite in the TLR arena, either in its original Soviet-era guise (as shown here) or brand new in the form of Lomography's Lubitel 166+ recreation, which can shoot both medium format and 35mm film.

Above: My current TLR is a Yashica A, which was manufactured from the mid-to-late 1950s until the late '60s. It's a basic camera (even by TLR standards), but it cost me less than $30, so I'm not complaining—the image quality isn't that bad, as this shot demonstrates.

Large-Format Cameras

With their bellows, ground-glass screens, and use of single sheets of film instead of rolls, large-format cameras are a natural evolution of the plate cameras that existed at the dawn of photography. Like those early cameras there is no one "large format," although the options are becoming increasingly limited: 5x4 is the most accessible format today, followed by 10x8, and then a few 5x7 options (the names refer to the size of the film, in inches, that the cameras are designed for).

Challenges

Everything about large-format photography is big, slow, and cumbersome, making a tripod almost mandatory, and that's just the start of the inconveniences: images are viewed upside down and back to front on the ground-glass screen; film-holders can be tricky to load; and there's a certain order that needs to be learnt when it comes to cocking and closing your lenses to prevent you from exposing your film accidentally. Add the high "cost per click" attached to each sheet of film and you might wonder why anyone would bother.

However, the flip side of all this is that large format makes you think harder and work harder than any other film format. Because the effort and cost invested in each shot is quite significant, every photograph naturally has greater importance. This in turn makes you pay more attention to what you are photographing and why. Large-format photography may not be an immediately accessible snapshot medium, but it will almost certainly force you to become a better photographer (or you'll bankrupt yourself trying!).

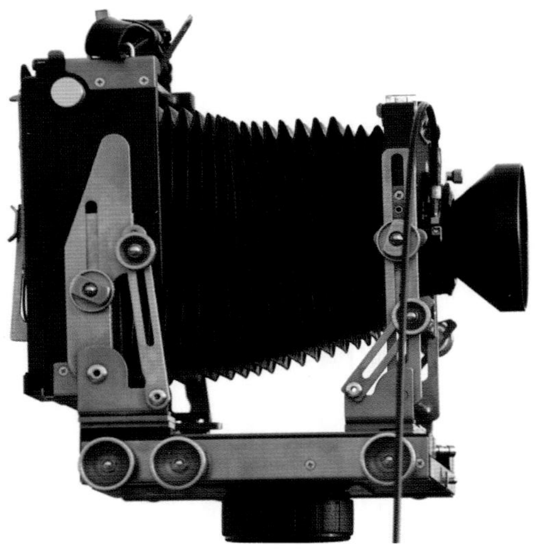

Left & below: Large-format cameras are generally based on one of two designs: "field cameras" (left) and "monorail cameras" (below). Field cameras are generally lighter and more compact, and usually fold up to make them transportable for location work, whereas monorail cameras are bigger and bulkier, but often have more comprehensive movements, precise geared controls, and longer bellows that allow better close-up shooting.

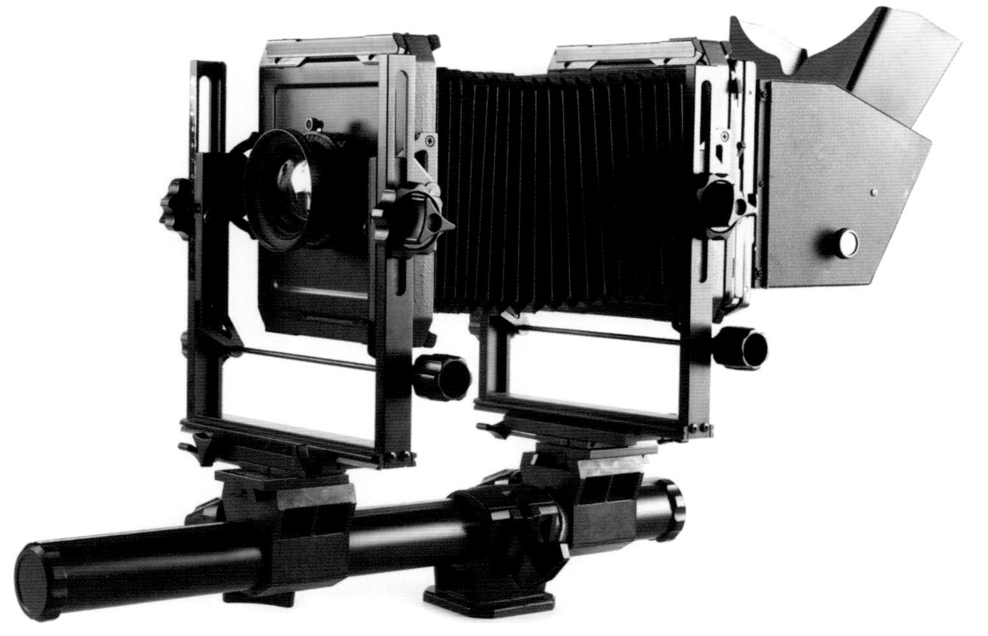

Tips

- If you're looking to buy a large-format camera think about how easy (or not) it is to get accessories or spares for it. Some makes and models might be cheap, but they can be so obscure that it's virtually impossible to buy any spare parts.

- The same sentiment as the above applies to lens panels: some cameras use unique panel shapes or sizes that can be hard to source.

CAMERA MOVEMENTS

Most large-format cameras allow you to move the lens in relation to the film plane to change the plane of focus, which opens up a host of technical and creative options. It's simply not possible to explore all of the movement permutations here—not only can they be combined, but some cameras will allow you to adjust the back of the camera (the film plane) as well as the lens—but this guide will get you started.

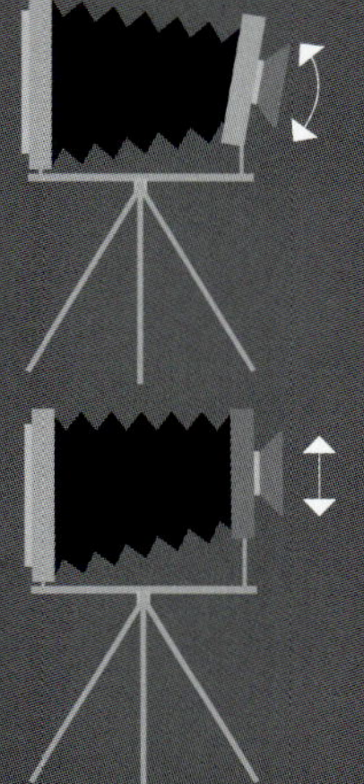

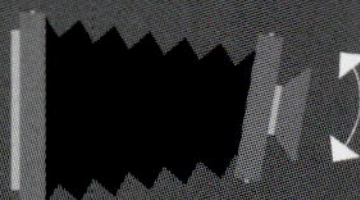

Tilt: Tilting the lens down can maximize the depth of field at any aperture (depending on the subject plane), which is particularly useful for landscape photography. Tilting the lens up can have the opposite effect, delivering a reduced depth of field (again, depending on the subject plane).

Rise/fall: A "rising front" is when the lens moves upward, but remains parallel to the back of the camera. This effectively allows the camera to see "higher up" without you having to tilt the camera upward, which means you won't suffer from any converging verticals (the perspective effect where the tops of trees or tall buildings appear to converge as they get further away). This is the classic solution to avoiding converging verticals in architectural photography. A "falling front" allows you to see lower, but is used far less often.

Swing: Swinging the lens means turning it to the left or right (as seen from above). This changes the direction of the plane of focus, so rather than running parallel to the film, it starts to run at an angle through the frame. This can be used to create a vertical "slice" of focus in the middle of the frame, which falls off at either side.

Shift: A lateral shift movement to the left or right (as seen from above) essentially allows the camera to "see" a little more to its left or right, without you turning the camera. A common use for this is in interiors photography, where you might be photographing a wall with a mirror on it. By using a shift movement you would be able to set up the camera to the side of the mirror so your reflection didn't appear in the photograph, but then "shift" the lens so that the mirror appears straight on in your shot.

LOADING A DDS (DOUBLE DARK SLIDE)

One of the immediate challenges facing a first-time large-format user is loading film. On the face of it, this is relatively simple: you have to slide a sheet of film into a holder designed to contain a single sheet. However, not only do you need to do this in complete darkness to avoid fogging the film, but you also need to ensure that the film is the right way round and has been loaded correctly under the retaining guides. Here's how it's done:

1 Pull the darkslide up in your film holder. You don't need to remove it fully (if you do, you will need to re-insert it in the dark).

2 Open the door at the bottom of the film holder and, if you're right handed, position the holder with the door facing up and to the right, as shown.

3 Take a sheet of film in your right hand, ensuring the notches in one of the shorter edges are at the upper right corner. This is incredibly important as it ensures the film will be loaded with the emulsion facing the lens.

4 Use your left hand to locate the two guide rails in the film holder and direct the end of the film under them. Make sure the film goes under both rails and slide it gently into the film holder.

5 When the film has been pushed as far as it will go, close the bottom door and slide the darkslide all the way back down. Some film holders have small locking tabs at the top, which can be used to "lock" the darkslide in place.

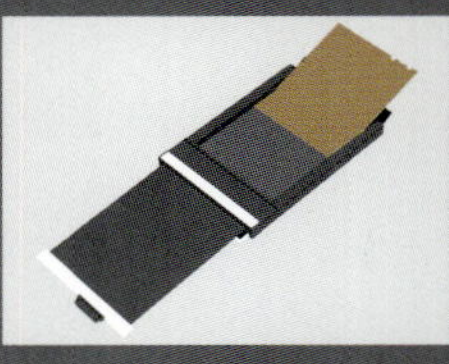

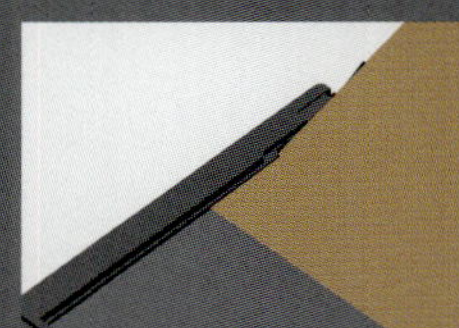

The main things to remember when you come to load a darkslide are:
- If you're right handed (and holding the darkslide in your left hand), the notches in the film need to be at the top right.
- The film needs to go under the guide rails at either side. If it doesn't, it will either pop out of the holder when you slide the darkslide back in, or it will get creased. In either case, you are likely to end up wasting a sheet of film.

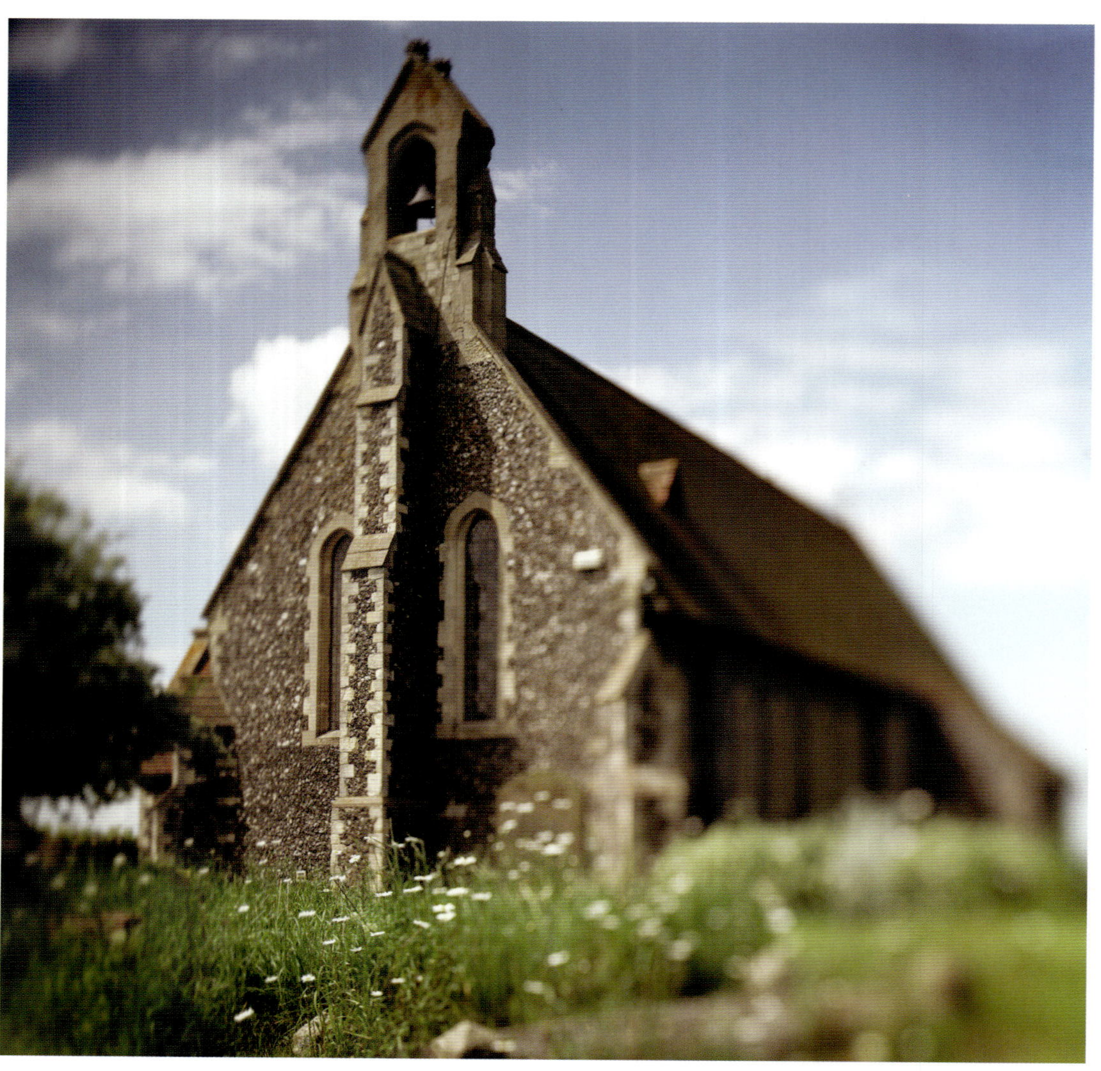

Above: An extreme example of swinging the lens to create a very narrow band of focus. However, your movements will always be limited by the coverage of the lens. In this picture, the image had to be cropped because it was "cut off" at the top left corner, where the lens' image circle wasn't big enough to cover the radical swing.

LARGE FORMAT CAMERA PROS AND CONS	
PROS	**CONS**
Camera movements provide a range of technical and creative opportunities.	*Costs can be prohibitive; a single sheet of 5x4 film can set you back almost as much as a roll of medium format to process, while a sheet of 10x8 film will cost more.*
Large film formats enable huge print sizes to be made, while keeping grain to a minimum.	*Limited film choice, especially for 5x7 and 10x8.*
You can shoot medium-format roll film using a dedicated film back.	*It's harder to process sheet film yourself.*
The slow pace (and high cost) of shooting large-format film makes you think more about what you're doing and how you go about it.	*Polaroid no longer available for checking exposure and focus.*
	Steep learning curve.

Tip

The top of the darkslide on a large-format film holder is usually reversible, with one side white and the other side black. This can be used to show whether the film inside is exposed or not: the convention is to have the white side showing when the holder contains unexposed film, and then turn it around to show the black side when the film has been exposed.

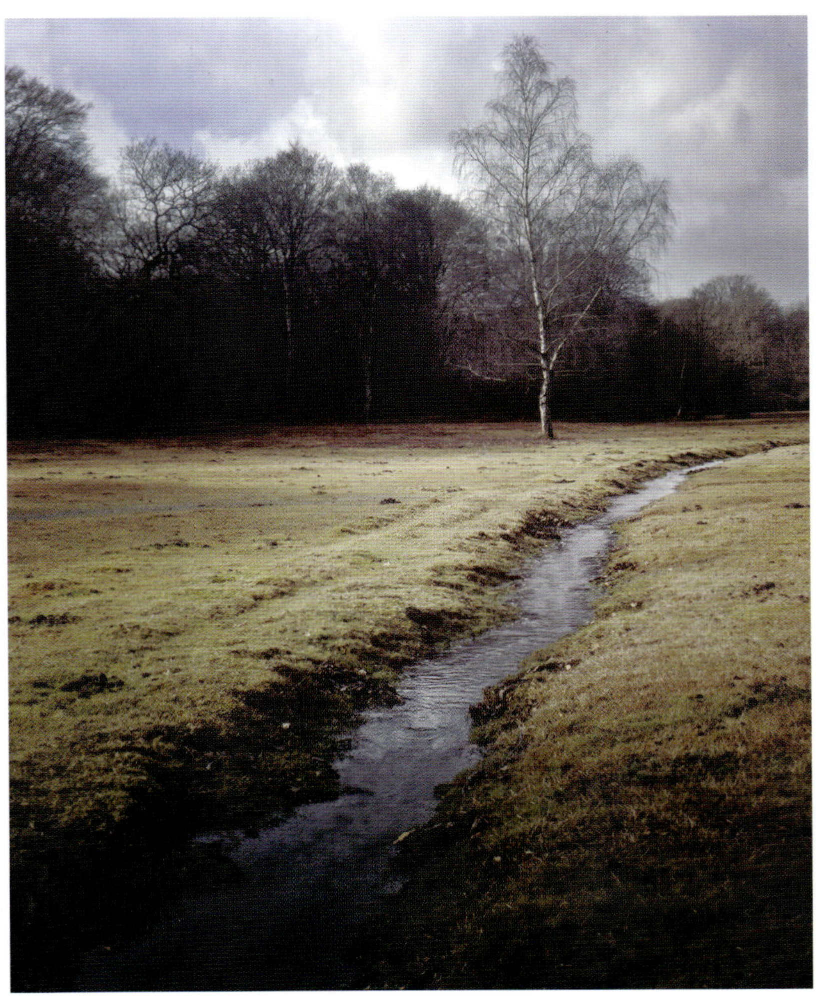

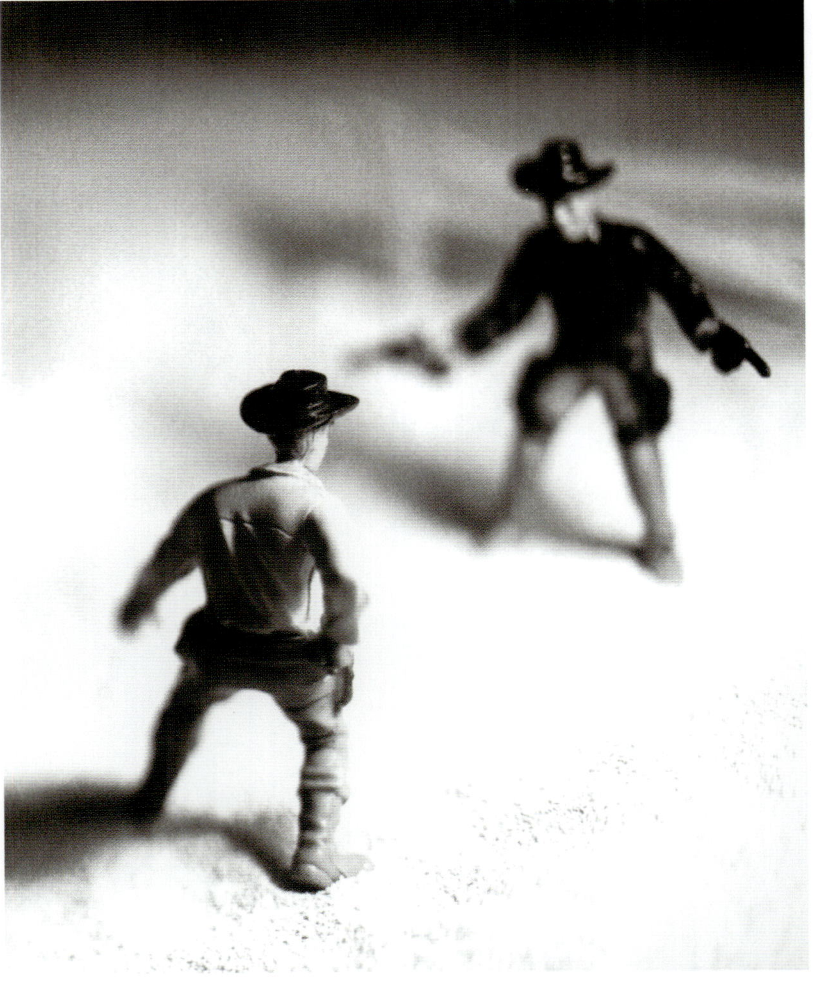

Above: Large-format photography is closely associated with two genres: landscape and still life. When it comes to landscapes, tilting the lens forward can effectively increase the depth of field at any given aperture, enabling you to keep everything in focus and/or use the "sweet spot" aperture on the lens. In this particular instance I was using a large-format field camera.

Above: Shooting close-up images with a large-format camera is made easier thanks to the camera's bellows design: for extreme macro work you can add additional bellows. Here, I didn't need anything so radical, just the standard bellows on a monorail camera and some lens swing to control the focus.

Other Camera Types

Shooting film gives you access to a whole host of different camera designs. Some of the less mainstream options can be used to take your photography in a whole new direction. These cameras may not be the epitome of cutting-edge technology, or indeed deliver tack-sharp focus, but they can give your pictures something that digital capture struggles to provide: personality.

Plastic Cameras

Also known as "toy cameras," plastic cameras celebrate all things lo-fi, with vignetting, light leaks, and dubious lens sharpness delivering quirky and fun results. There is a plethora of single-lens and multi-lens 35mm models around, ranging from cheap unbranded cameras like the Robot 3 (below), which can be picked up for next to nothing, through to Lomography's premium-priced products. The Holga and Diana are popular for those looking to shoot medium-format film.

Instant Cameras

Instant photography may have been invented by Polaroid, but the company's up-and-down history left Fujifilm and The Impossible Project flying the instant flag for a number of years, before Polaroid rose Phoenix-like from the ashes. The appeal of instant prints is undeniable, and they have a distinct look that other films cannot match. However, it can be an expensive game to play and there's no chance of enlarging your prints unless you scan them, at which point they lose a lot of their "one off" appeal.

Pinhole Cameras

Replacing the lens on your camera with a tiny hole, or even building your own pinhole camera, will enable you to see the world in a whole new light. We'll stroll down this exciting (and sedate) photographic avenue in chapter 6.

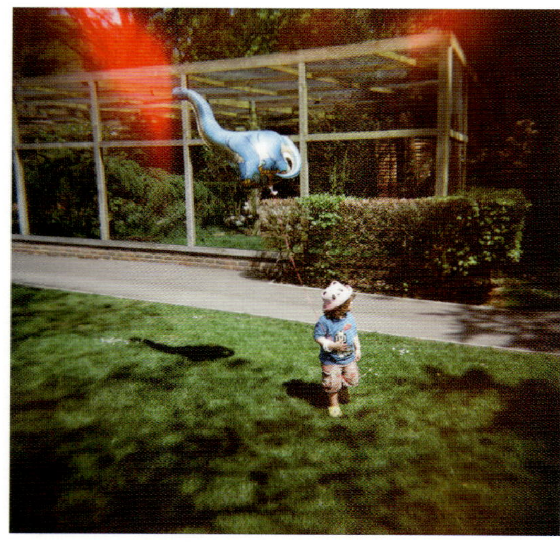

Above: Light leaks, corner shading, and a distinct fall off in focus typify plastic cameras, which is part of their esthetic. This photograph was taken using a Holga 120: one of the all-time classic plastic cameras.

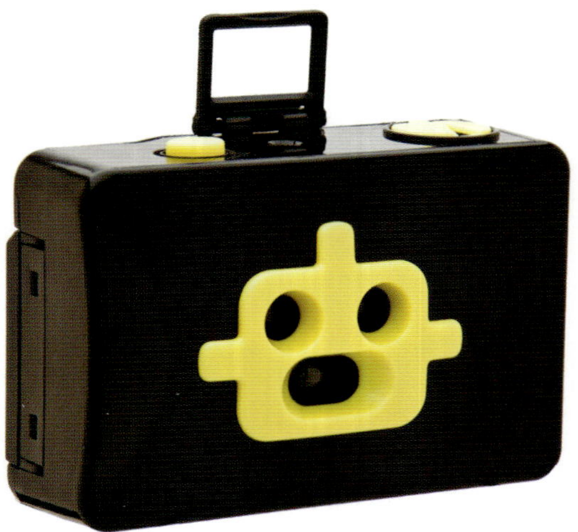

Above: Dubbed the "Robot 3" because of its triple-lens design, these plastic cameras are super cheap online.

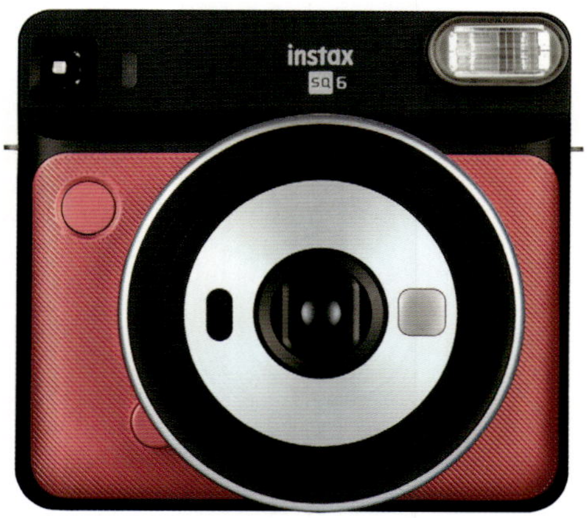

Above: Fujifilm's Instax cameras are incredibly popular thanks to their funky looks and instant pictures.

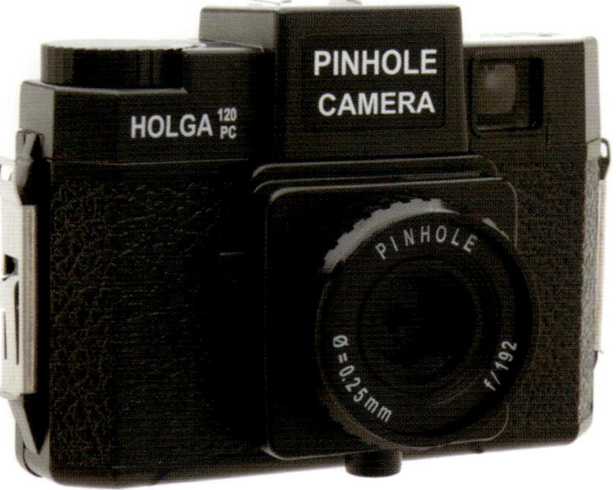

Above: Holga has made numerous iterations of its plastic medium-format camera, including this pinhole version.

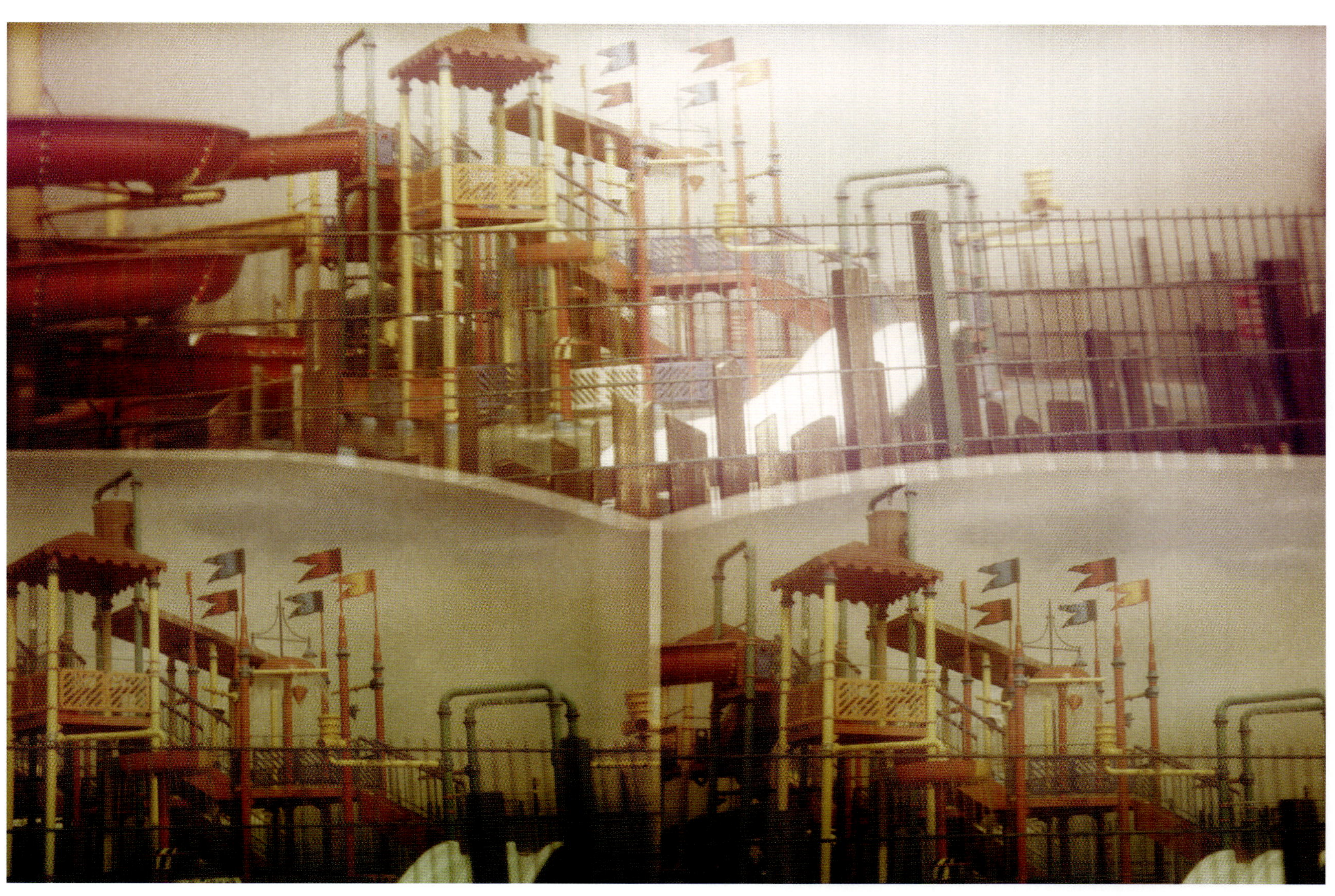

Above: The results from the Robot 3 are quite unlike any conventional camera, but they're great fun, especially when you combine them with an "experimental" film like redscale.

Panoramic Cameras

Panoramic cameras come in a range of shapes and sizes, from plastic compact cameras that simply crop a regular 35mm film frame down to a third of its height, to medium-format models that will let you squeeze four 6x17cm images onto a roll of 120 film. In addition are the "rotating" panoramic cameras, which expose the film by pulling it past a slit as either the camera or the lens turns during the exposure. What they have in common is their ability to produce an elongated image that is well suited to sweeping views of the landscape.

Box Cameras

Photography for the masses began when the Eastman Kodak Company launched its first Box Brownie in 1900. Countless variations and imitations of this simple light-tight box followed, using a variety of film formats. Although some of these film formats are now obsolete, some box cameras use 120 roll film (which was first seen in 1901) so there's nothing stopping you from loading them with modern medium-format film.

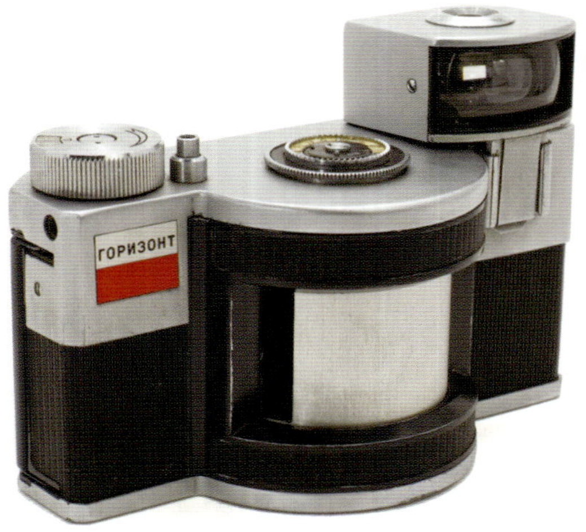

Above: "Swing lens" panoramic cameras like this Russian model hold the film in place while the lens turns from one side to the other, effectively "scanning" the scene and exposing it onto the film through a narrow vertical slit.

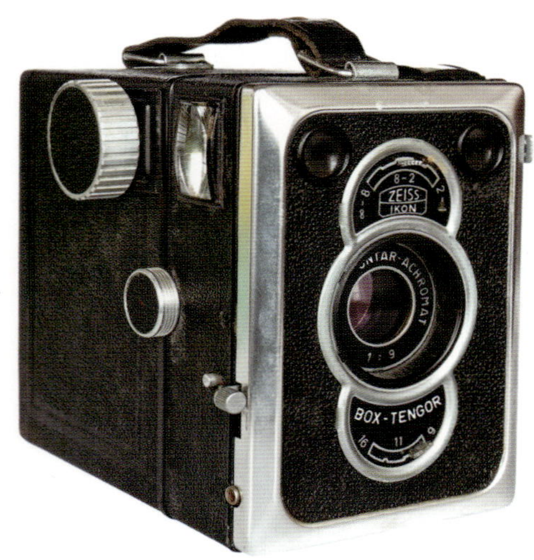

Below: Hasselblad's XPan is a high-end 35mm rangefinder camera that can switch between regular 35mm frames (24x36mm) and panoramas measuring 24x65mm; it's the panoramic format that makes it special.

Right: This Zeiss Ikon box camera might look great on your shelf, but if you want to use an old camera like this you need to check what kind of film it takes: a lot of box cameras use film formats that are now obsolete.

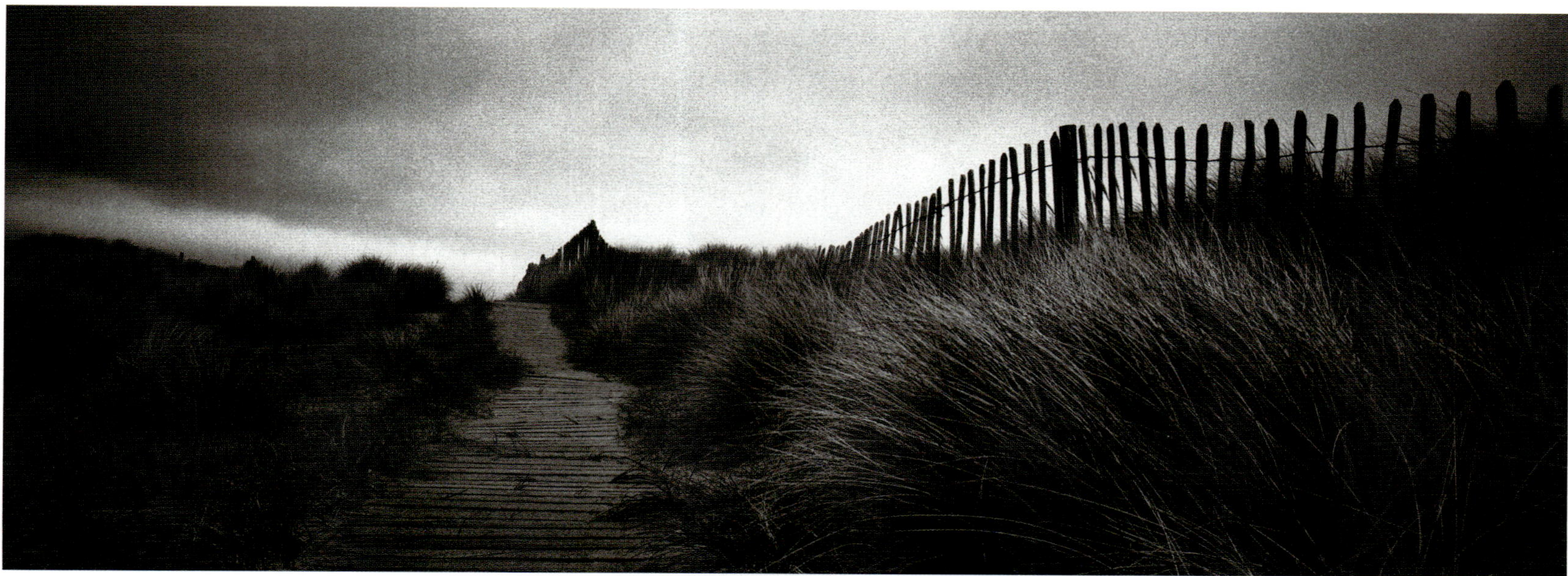

Stereo Cameras

Stereo photography is all about enhancing the 3D sense of a photograph, and was particularly popular among Victorian photographers. The basic technique is to take a pair of images from two slightly different horizontal positions and view them with a special viewer. This emulates our binocular vision and provides a much greater sense of three-dimensions. Although never really a mainstream product, stereo cameras have continued to appear on the fringes of photography throughout much of its history, and both vintage and relatively modern camera models—35mm and medium format—are still available to anyone who wants to explore photography's "third dimension."

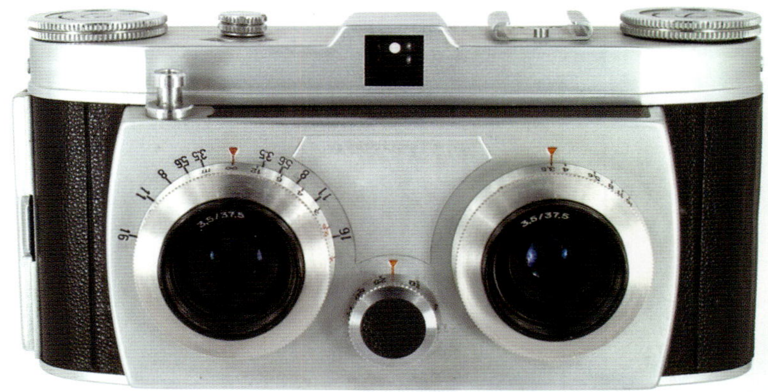

Above: Stereo cameras mimic human vision by taking photographs through a pair of lenses a short distance apart horizontally. When viewed, the images—or "stereo pair"—create the illusion of 3D.

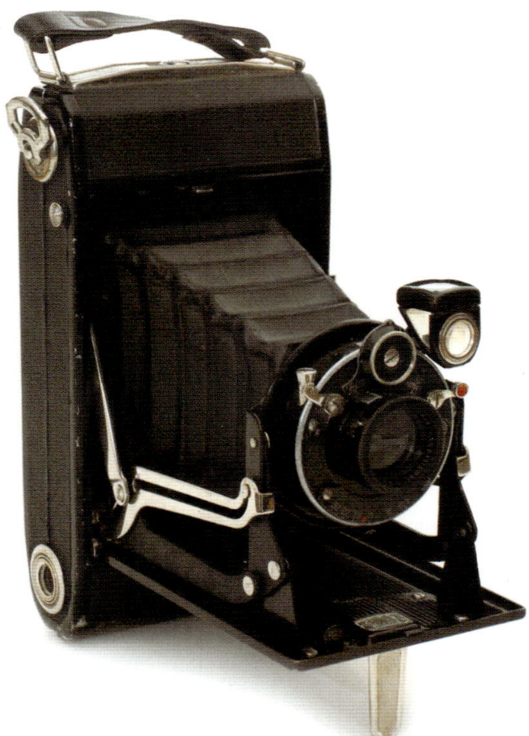

Above: Folding cameras quickly replaced box cameras as the most popular camera type, purely because they could fold down, making them smaller and much easier to carry than their boxy brethren.

Folding Cameras

If a box camera is too bulky, why not try a folder instead? By placing bellows between the film and the lens, these cameras can be folded down to make them both practical and pocketable. As with their boxy brethren, look for cameras that use 120 roll film to avoid any film format issues. Interestingly, Cosina and Fujifilm tried to resurrect the folding camera as recently as 2008, with a co-developed medium-format rangefinder camera (marketed as the Fujifilm GF670 in Japan and the Voigtländer Bessa III elsewhere). Launched in 2009 the cameras were discontinued in 2014, making them one of the last "new" film cameras.

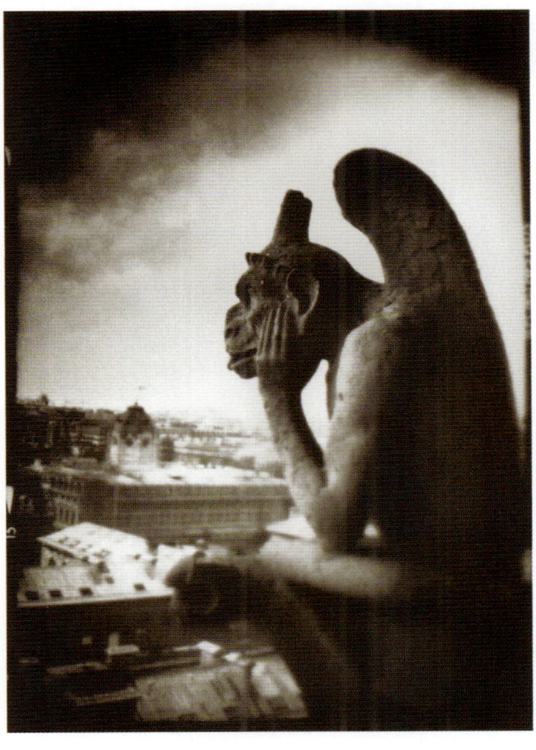

Above: Over 20 years ago I inherited a 6x9cm format folding camera (a Falcon, from the Utility Manufacturing Company in Chicago). Although the camera dates back to the 1930s it takes regular 120 roll film, so is still usable today: I love the irregular edges to the images and the way they incorporate the frame numbers and film names. This shot was created by turning a film negative into a printed paper negative.

Lenses

The lens on your camera is one of the most important parts in the imaging chain, as it dictates how accurately the scene you are photographing reaches your film, by determining sharpness and controlling distortions and aberrations. The good news is that film arguably places fewer demands on a lens than a digital sensor, because unlike a digital sensor—which has a physical depth to it and microlenses in front of its light-gathering photosites—film is a perfectly flat surface. This means that light can strike it at any angle and still expose it perfectly, ensuring more consistent exposures. Similarly, while the latest high resolution DSLRs require the highest resolution lenses to get the best out of them, film is less pernickety: a good lens will deliver good results, period.

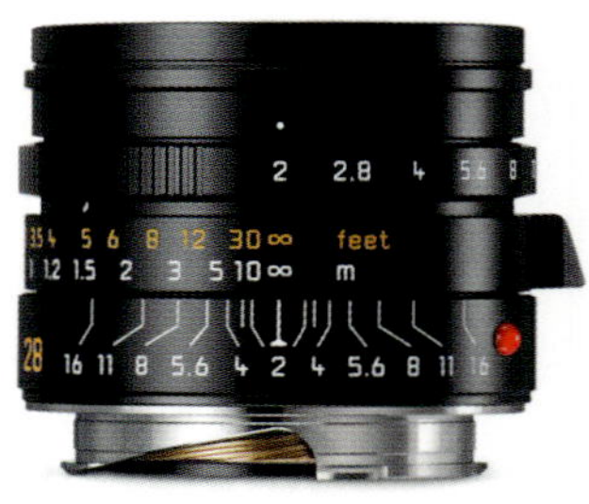
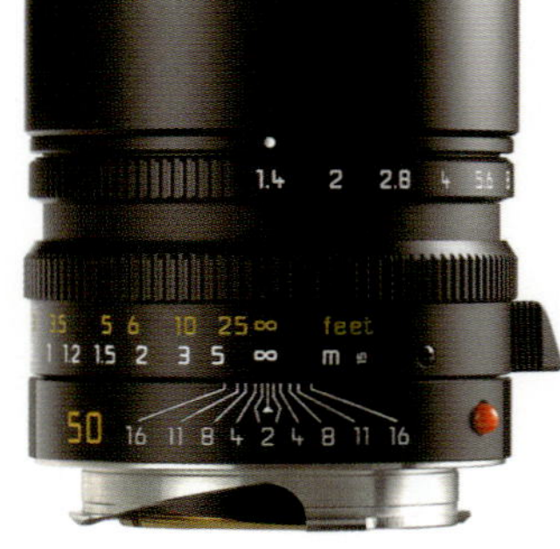
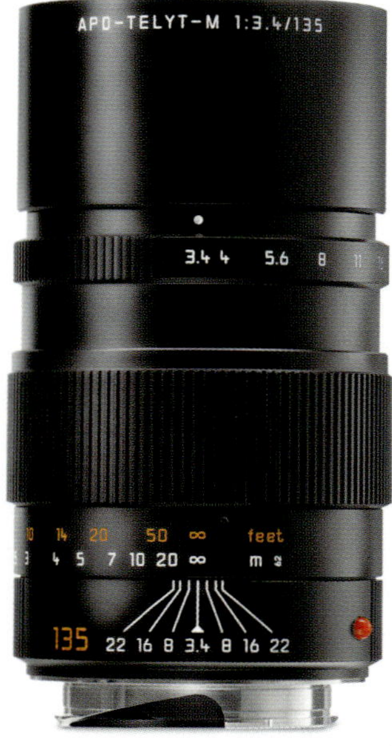

Below: Leica is renowned for producing some stunning lenses, not only in terms of their performance, but also in terms of their build quality. This trio covers three classic focal lengths—wideangle (28mm), standard (50mm), and telephoto (135mm)—which together cover most shooting situations.

STANDARD FOCAL LENGTHS	
FORMAT	**"STANDARD" FOCAL LENGTH**
110 (17x13mm)	24mm
Half frame 35mm (24x18mm)	30mm
Full frame 35mm (36x24mm)	50mm
6x4.5cm	75mm
6x6cm	80mm
6x7cm	90mm
6x8cm	100mm
6x9cm	105mm
6x12cm	120mm
6x17cm	180mm
5x4in	150mm
5x7in	210mm
10x8in	300mm

Format & Focal Length

If you've used a digital SLR or mirrorless camera before you'll no doubt be familiar with "full frame" focal lengths. These are exactly the same as 35mm film focal lengths, so a 50mm focal length on 35mm film (and full-frame digital) is considered the "standard" focal length; shorter focal lengths (28mm and 35mm for example) are wideangle; and longer focal lengths (from 60mm upward) are considered telephoto.

However, things change if you're venturing into the world of medium or large format, as the standard focal length is based on the diagonal measurement of the frame size; the "standard" is therefore different for each and every frame size, not just the film format. The grid (left) shows the accepted standards for each of the common formats. Once you know the standard you can then determine whether any other lens is wide or long (and the further the focal length is from standard, the more extreme its wideangle or telephoto effect will be).

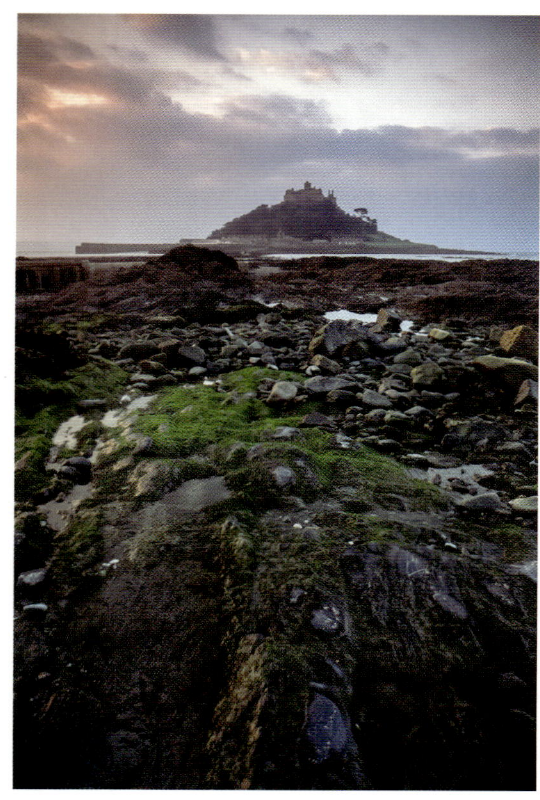

Right: Photographing in
the confines of a gun store
didn't give me much room
to maneuver, but using
a wideangle lens at least
meant I could include the
gunsmith surrounded
by his wares.

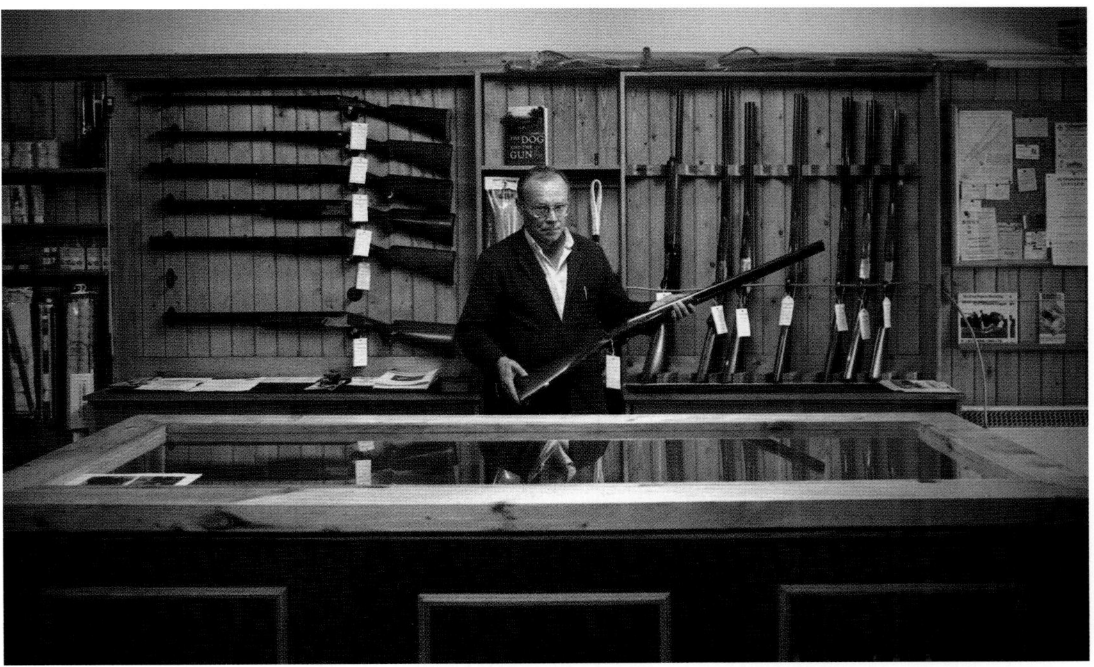

Right: I was shooting this
mountainside from quite
a distance, but a 200mm
telephoto focal length on a
35mm SLR enabled me to
pick out a small area.

Left: For this coastal
landscape I wanted to
make the most of the rocky
foreground, but didn't want
to lose the distant island.
A wideangle lens would
have been too much here,
so I opted for a 50mm
standard on my 35mm
SLR instead.

Leaf Shutter Lenses

When you use a medium- or large-format camera, there can be a change in terms of where the shutter is. The majority of 35mm SLRs use a focal-plane shutter, which consists of a pair of curtains or blinds inside the camera, in front of the film, which open and close to make an exposure.

However, while a focal-plane shutter is relatively easy to implement in a small-format camera, it is harder to employ in a medium- and large-format camera due to the physical size it would need to be. Therefore, a lot of these cameras use a leaf shutter in the lens (or just behind it) instead. In its simplest iteration a leaf shutter is a single blade that opens and closes to make an exposure, but more complex, multi-bladed shutters that are similar in appearance to the aperture are found in more sophisticated cameras.

Whether or not the type of shutter makes any difference to your photography will largely depend on what you photograph and how. If you head out in the middle of the day and shoot in sunlight then—all other things being equal—you should achieve exactly the same result from both shutter types. However, in other situations there are a couple of key differences between leaf shutters and focal-plane shutters that can have a far more profound effect on your photography:

- Leaf shutters have a limited minimum shutter speed, and usually run to 1/500 sec. at most, whereas a focal-plane shutter can shoot at 1/4000 sec. or faster. This makes a camera with a focal-plane shutter better suited to freezing fast-moving subjects.

- A leaf shutter can synchronize with flash at any shutter speed, but a camera with a focal-plane shutter will have a maximum sync speed (usually in the region of 1/125–1/200 sec.) beyond which the full film frame will not be exposed in its entirety. This makes a leaf shutter particularly useful if you're into flash; it's great for weddings and portraits, for example.

- Leaf shutters are more complex, so the lenses tend to be more expensive, both to buy and repair. Conversely, the cameras they are attached to are often simpler, so can be comparatively less expensive than a focal-plane shutter equipped alternative (although this isn't always the case).

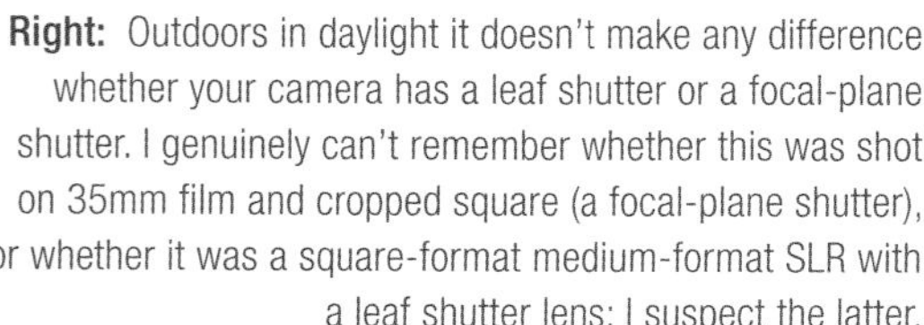

Above: Most large-format cameras use leaf shutter lenses (although press cameras can also use lenses without a shutter) and this has one main benefit for studio photography: you don't have to worry about the shutter speed when you're using flash.

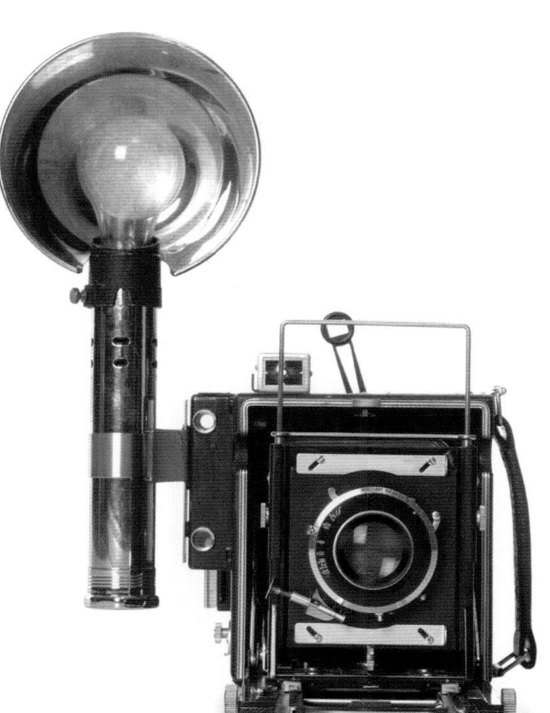

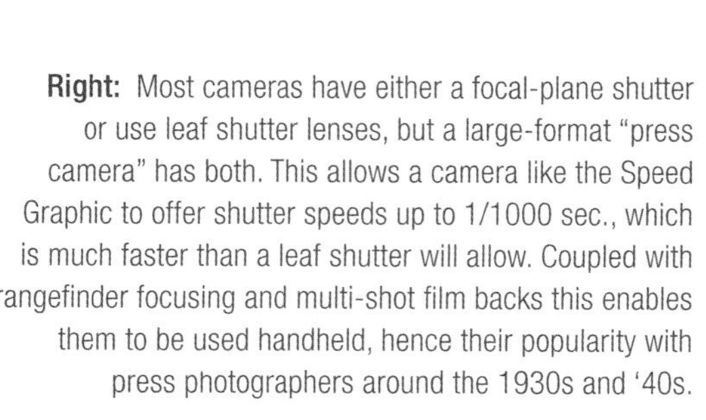

Right: Most cameras have either a focal-plane shutter or use leaf shutter lenses, but a large-format "press camera" has both. This allows a camera like the Speed Graphic to offer shutter speeds up to 1/1000 sec., which is much faster than a leaf shutter will allow. Coupled with rangefinder focusing and multi-shot film backs this enables them to be used handheld, hence their popularity with press photographers around the 1930s and '40s.

Right: Outdoors in daylight it doesn't make any difference whether your camera has a leaf shutter or a focal-plane shutter. I genuinely can't remember whether this was shot on 35mm film and cropped square (a focal-plane shutter), or whether it was a square-format medium-format SLR with a leaf shutter lens: I suspect the latter.

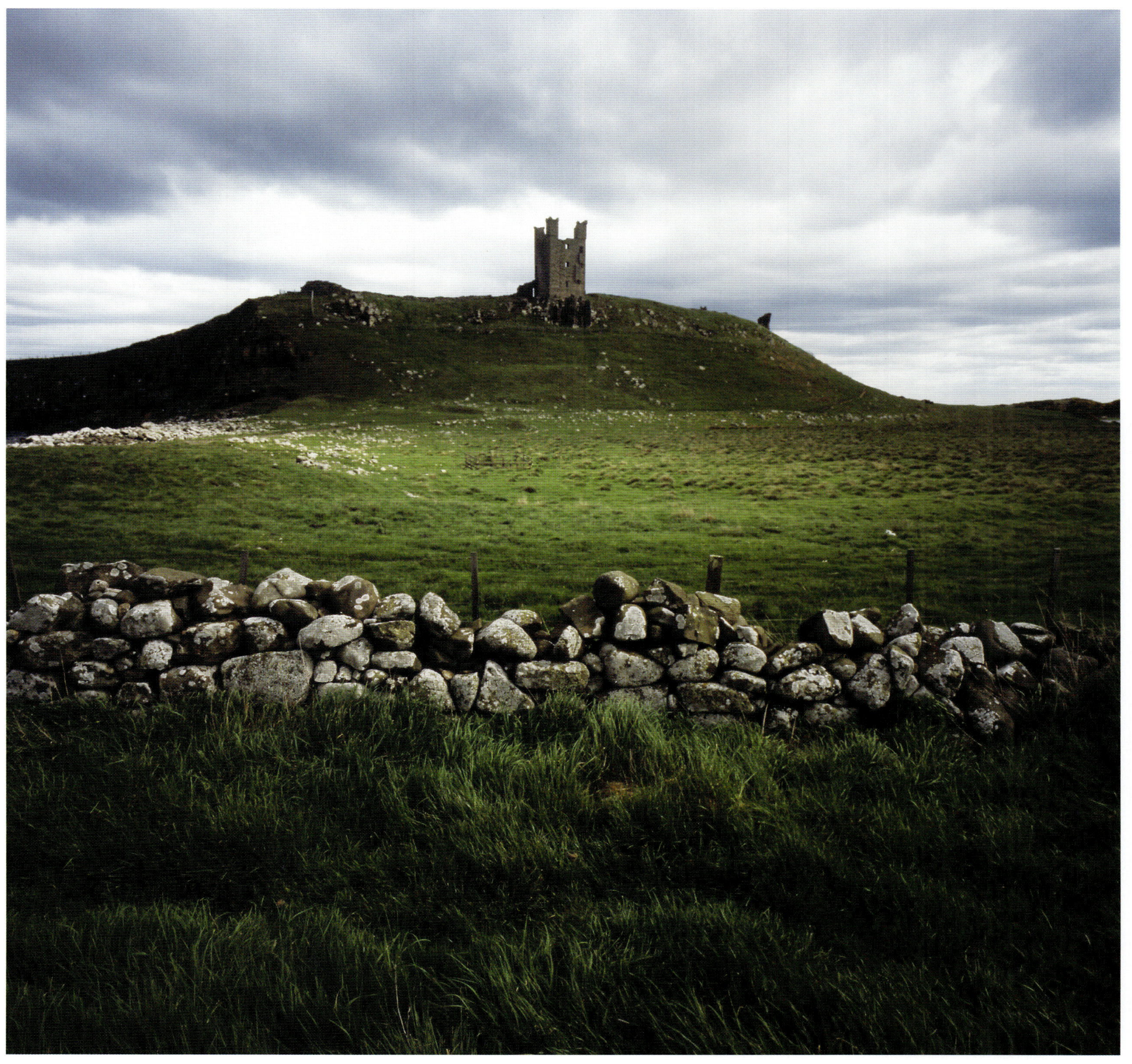

If you want to get the best results in terms of sharp, distortion-free images, then choosing quality lenses plays a significant part in the process. If you're buying used equipment, which is often the case with older film cameras, this can be a potential minefield, as a cosmetically pretty lens might have underlying issues, while a heavily battered optic might perform faultlessly. Here are a few key things to look out for (obviously, it helps if you can get "hands-on" with the lens):

With the right combination of humidity and dust, fungus can start to grow on the inside of the lens elements. This is a major problem with older lenses and can even affect lenses that are just a few years old. Lenses can be stripped down and cleaned, but the cost of having this done can easily exceed the value of a lot of older mainstream lenses (relatively specialist or expensive lenses may be worth the repair bill though).

Over time, dust will work its way inside a lens, so don't be surprised to see specks trapped between the glass elements. This may not affect your images, but you'd need to test the lens at every aperture setting to be completely sure.

Coating lenses to help reduce flare became commonplace in the 1950s-60s. If your lens is from this period (or later) look closely at the front element from different angles to see if years of cleaning have started to rub the coatings away. If they have, the lens will likely give lower contrast images and be more prone to flare (although some people find this effect attractive).

Is the front of the lens perfectly round? A slight dent in the filter mount might not look like much, but it could mean the lens has been dropped. If that's the case, can you guarantee that the elements inside haven't been knocked out of alignment?

Turn the focus ring and slowly zoom in and out (if it's a zoom lens) to check the smoothness of these actions. Both should offer slight resistance: if they are tight or slip intermittently this could be due to a lack of lubrication or degraded lubricant; too loose and they could be worn. In both cases the lens could benefit from a service.

The condition of the focusing ring (and zoom ring where applicable) is often a good indicator of how hard a life a lens has had, with heavily-worn rubber or paint suggesting heavy use. A shiny new focusing ring on a vintage lens can indicate the same thing—did the old one wear out through decades of use?

On a lens with a manual aperture, hold the lens up to a light source and check the aperture stops down as you turn the aperture ring. Note that there may be an "arm" on the back of the lens that you need to slide to stop the aperture down (something the camera will do automatically). If the aperture is controlled electronically you will need to attach the lens to a camera to check it, usually by firing the camera in Manual mode and looking through the back.

Check the exposed front and back glass elements for scratches or chips. Depending on their position and severity, these may not affect your images at all or they may render it unusable: the only way to know for sure is to shoot some film.

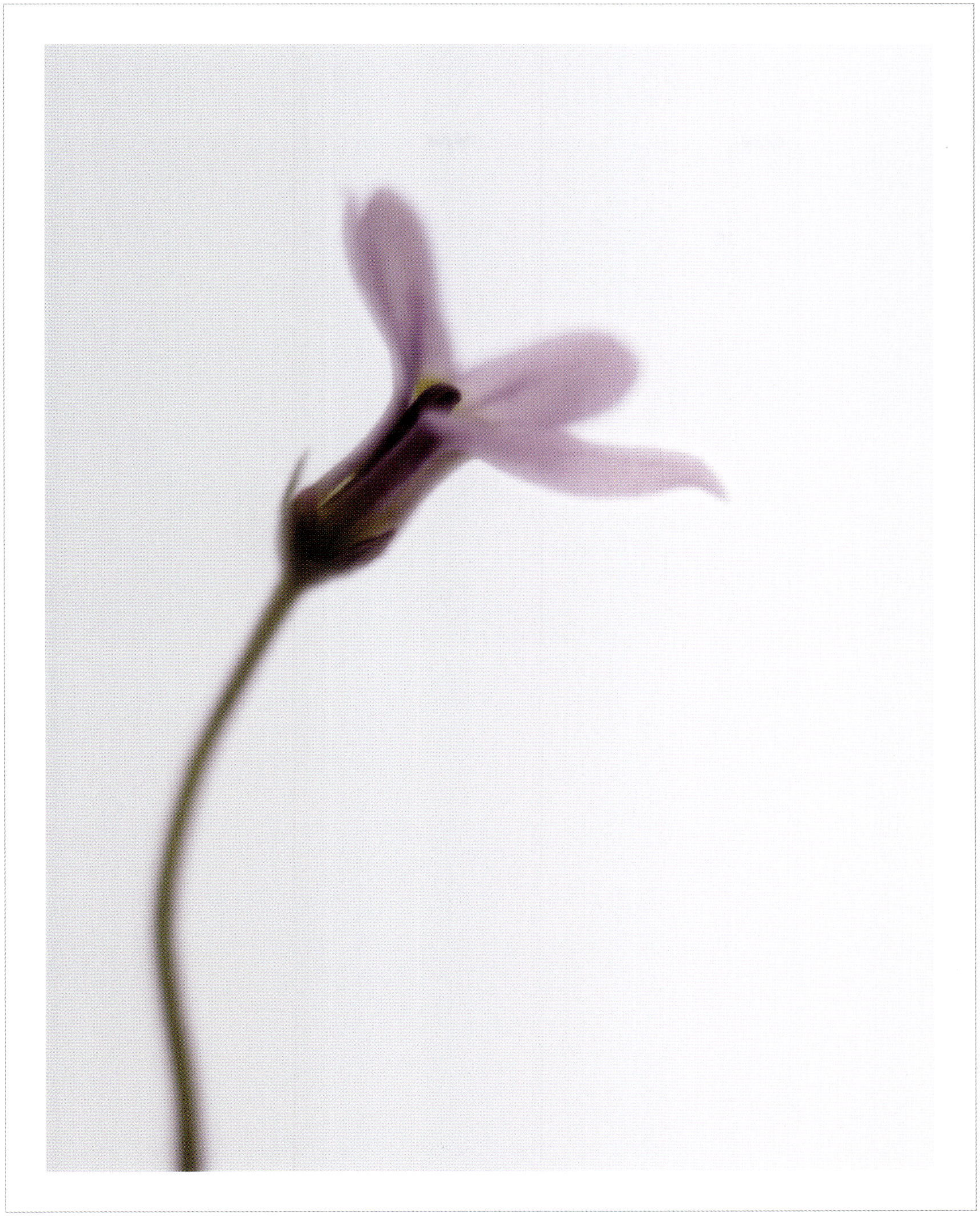

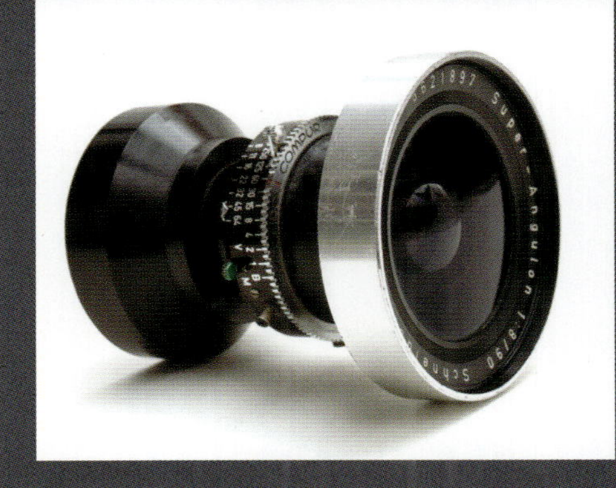

Above: A macro lens is a great way to shoot close-up images, but it is not the only way. Supplementary lenses that screw onto a regular lens like a filter can help you focus more closely, as can using extensions tubes between the camera and lens. For this shot I used a large-format view camera and simply extended its bellows.

Profile: William Jones

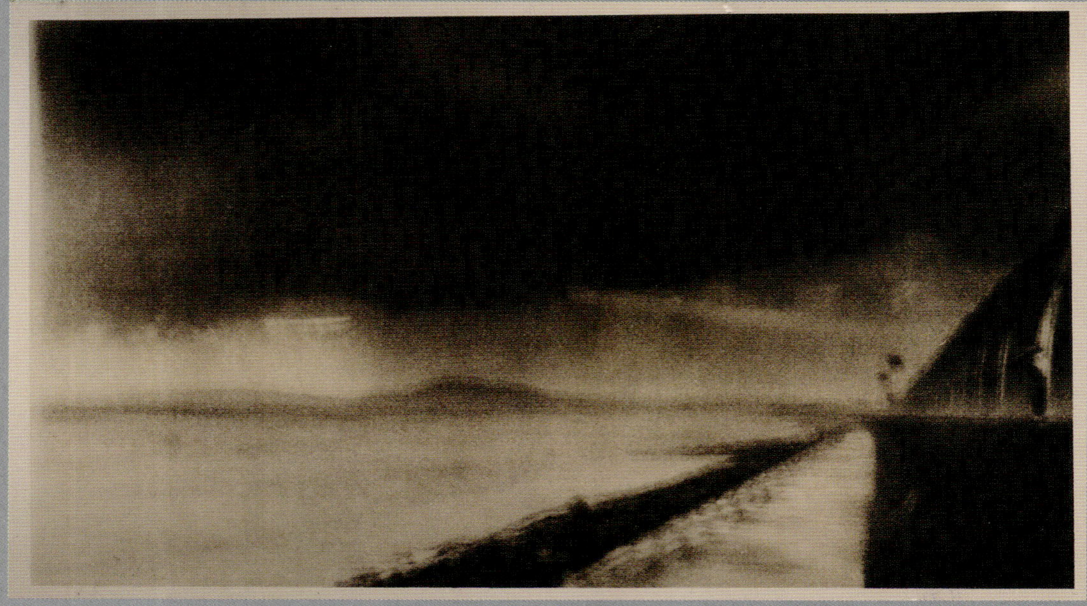

Above:
Showers and shafts
Ilford Pan F film rated at ISO 25 and developed in Rodinal (1:50). Printed on Sterling F paper, developed in Fotospeed LD20.

Below:
Altered reality
Bergger Pancro 400 film developed in Rodinal (1:50) and printed on Sterling F paper developed in Fotospeed LD 20 lith developer.

Q) How would you describe your work?
A) I'm a member of Neath Camera Club in Wales, UK, and the competitions held there have encouraged me to shoot a broad spectrum of subjects, which has helped me to develop my photographic vocabulary. I've got a wonderful variety of subjects nearby, including the coast, mountains, landscapes, heavy industry, and lots of Welsh weather! I enjoy all of these things and also shoot botanical subjects, which I find rewarding.

Q) What cameras do you use?
A) I use a Nikon F5, Bronica ETRS, Mamiya C330, and a Linhof 5x4, but the images here were taken with an Agfa Click or Agfa Clack. Wim Wenders said that the simpler your equipment, the more innovative you need to be, and I think it's true. The Agfa Clack is basically a 6x9cm box camera with a fixed shutter speed of around 1/30sec., bulb mode, and two aperture settings (f/11 and f/2.5), but even that can be creative.

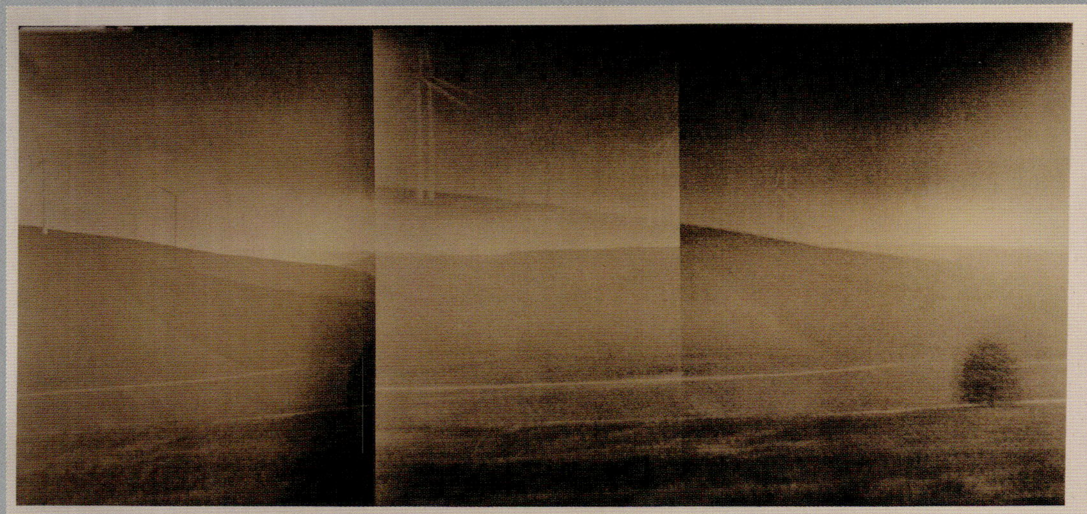

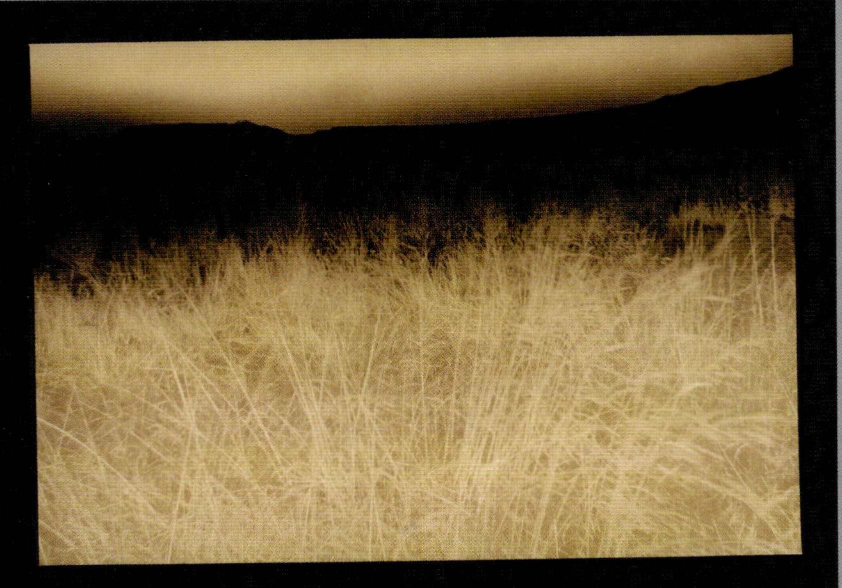

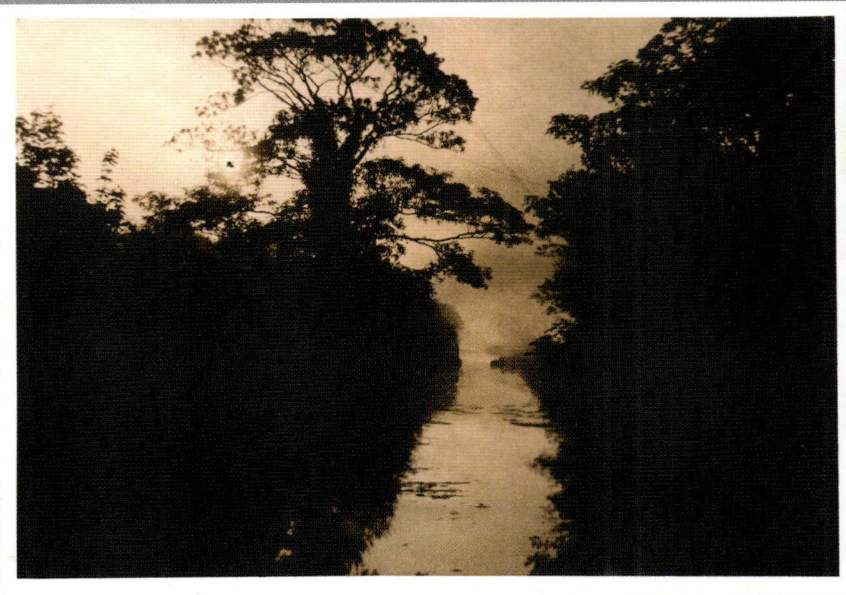

Above left:
Brwynog
Printed on Agfa Record
Rapid paper, developed
in Fotospeed LD20
lith developer, and
selenium toned.

Above right:
May morning
Ilford Pan F film rated at
ISO 25 and developed in
Rodinal (1:50). Printed on
Agfa Record Rapid paper
developed in Fotospeed LD
20 lith developer, and then
selenium toned.

Q) Why shoot on film?

A) Film allows me more avenues of expression than digital capture does, and in the darkroom I can do anything from straight printing through to lith, mordencage [a process that alters silver gelatin prints to give them a degraded effect], sun printing, chromoskedasic Sabatier [an experimental silver gelatin technique developed in the 1990s], and a host of other techniques. In each case, film allows me to put my own stamp on my images with these techniques, so they become mine, faults and all, not the result of some digital whiz kid's app.

Q) What film(s) do you use?

A) I use a wide range of films including Ilford FP4, Delta 100, and Pan F, Kodak 400 T-Max, and Adox CMS—they all have their uses. I enjoy shooting infrared as well.

Q) Where and how is your film processed? Is the processing modified in any way?

A) When I retired, I bought a Jobo processor for £120 (around $150), which is incredibly cheap compared to today's prices, and I process all my films myself. With large format (and eight 6x9 frames on 120 roll film) I find I can apply some Zone System ideas and adjust my processing to control the contrast, but 35mm film can spend weeks in my camera, so specific ideas or processing is rarely practical.

Q) Who prints your work? Are any special techniques used?

A) As with my processing, I do all of my own printing. Printing is the other skill of film photography, and the most daunting for a lot of people. It requires dedicated application, care, and plenty of attention—a colleague of mine cynically says that the best learning tool in the darkroom is the trash can!

I have been very fortunate as a darkroom worker in that I have received gifts of paper from various sources, as well as equipment, all victims of the digital revolution. Lith printing with old paper can be very surprising, but I wonder what it would have been like to use those papers in their prime—many of the papers I use are no longer available. There are still techniques to be tried. Recently I found a suitable negative that allowed me to print part in orthodox developer and part in lith developer. It wasn't easy in the twilight gloom of the darkroom, using tray development, but it's great to try something new.

Chapter 3
Exposure

Exposure is fundamental to photography, whether you're shooting film or recording to a memory card. On the face of it, exposure is the same straightforward concept for both: it's about getting the right amount of light to strike the recording medium for an appropriate amount of time to create an image. However, this is one of the areas where there is a surprising divergence between the two technologies. When it comes to determining how much light is needed and for how long—and the ways in which this can be adjusted—shooting film requires a slightly different approach to digital capture. Even if you are fully proficient shooting digitally there can be numerous pitfalls and challenges to circumvent.

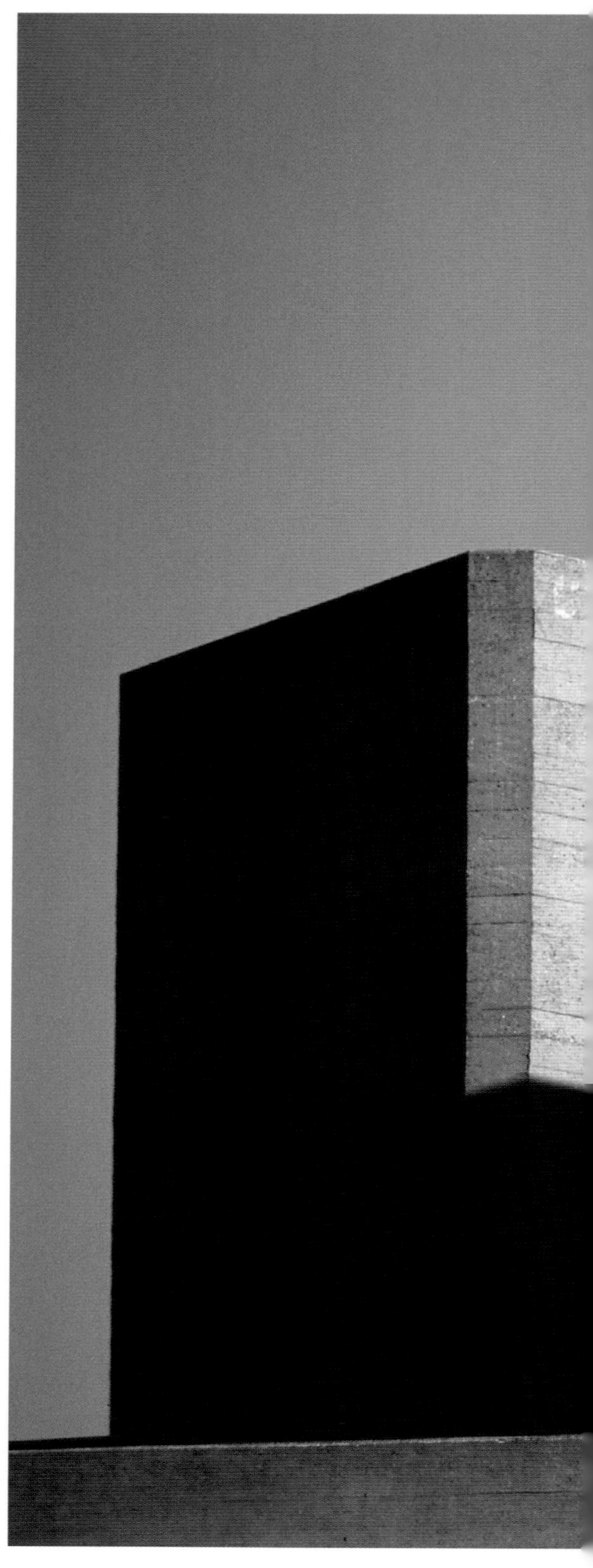

Right: Exposure on film is no different to exposure with a digital camera: you simply don't have as many ways of checking if you've got it right, so have to rely a little more on your own skills and experience.

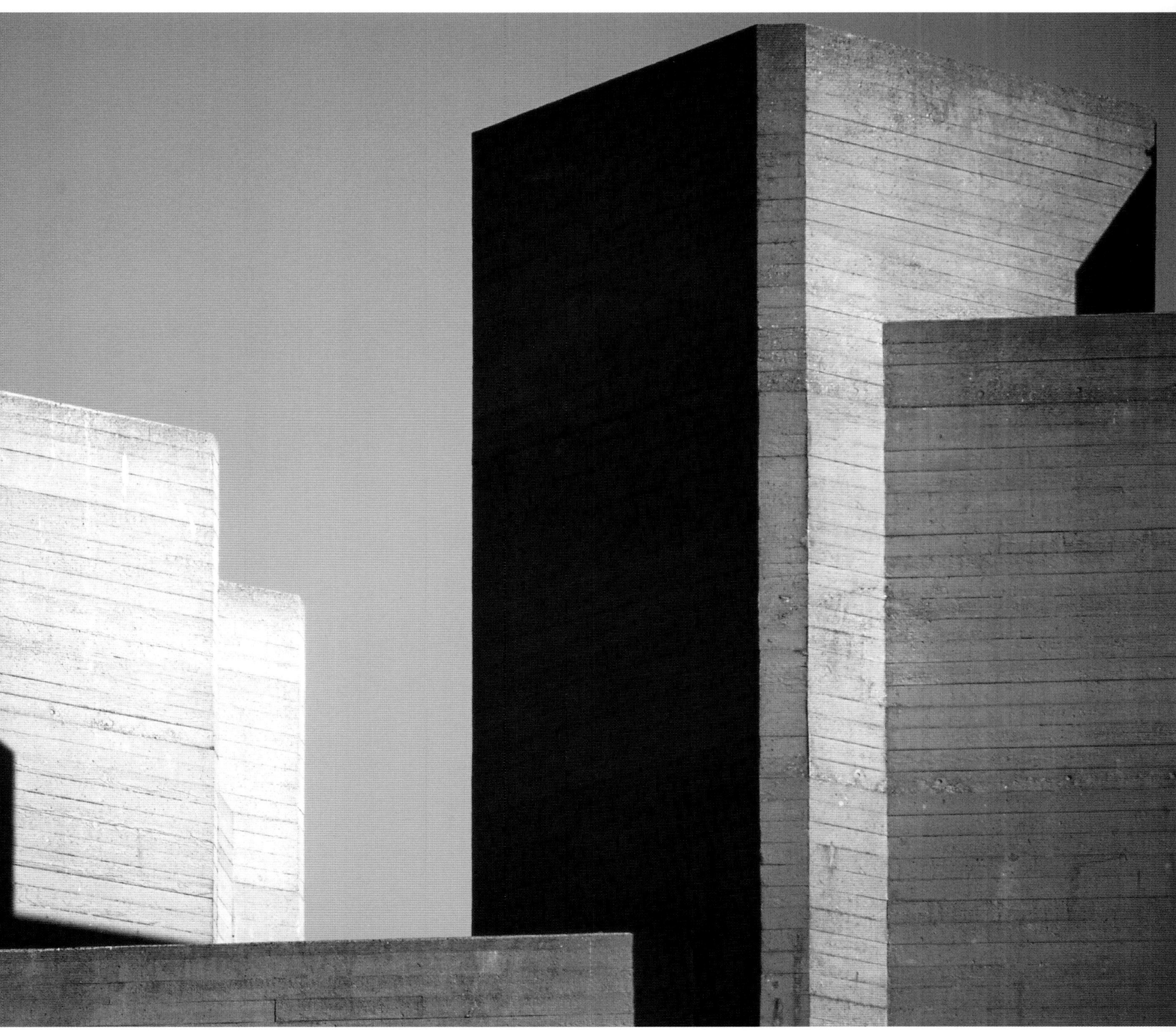

Life Without A Histogram

One of the biggest differences between shooting with a digital camera and using film is time—not in the sense that you need more or less of it, but in terms of technological development. Today, even the simplest digital SLR or mirrorless camera has exposure systems that eclipse those found on many film cameras. Such is their proficiency that modern digital cameras can increasingly be relied on to make critical decisions for you and—more often than not—deliver pixel-perfect results. Even when the camera gets a little confused it still provides a histogram to help you get things back on track; "blinkies" to warn of clipped highlights; and, as a last resort, an image played back within seconds on the rear LCD screen to confirm you have actually nailed the shot.

Below: For this pre-dawn shot I used a Leica C3 compact, which is a fully automatic point-and-shoot camera. I had no way of gauging whether the camera was doing a good job with the exposure or not and I wasn't confident that it would get this shot right, especially as I was shooting on transparency film. But it pretty much nailed it.

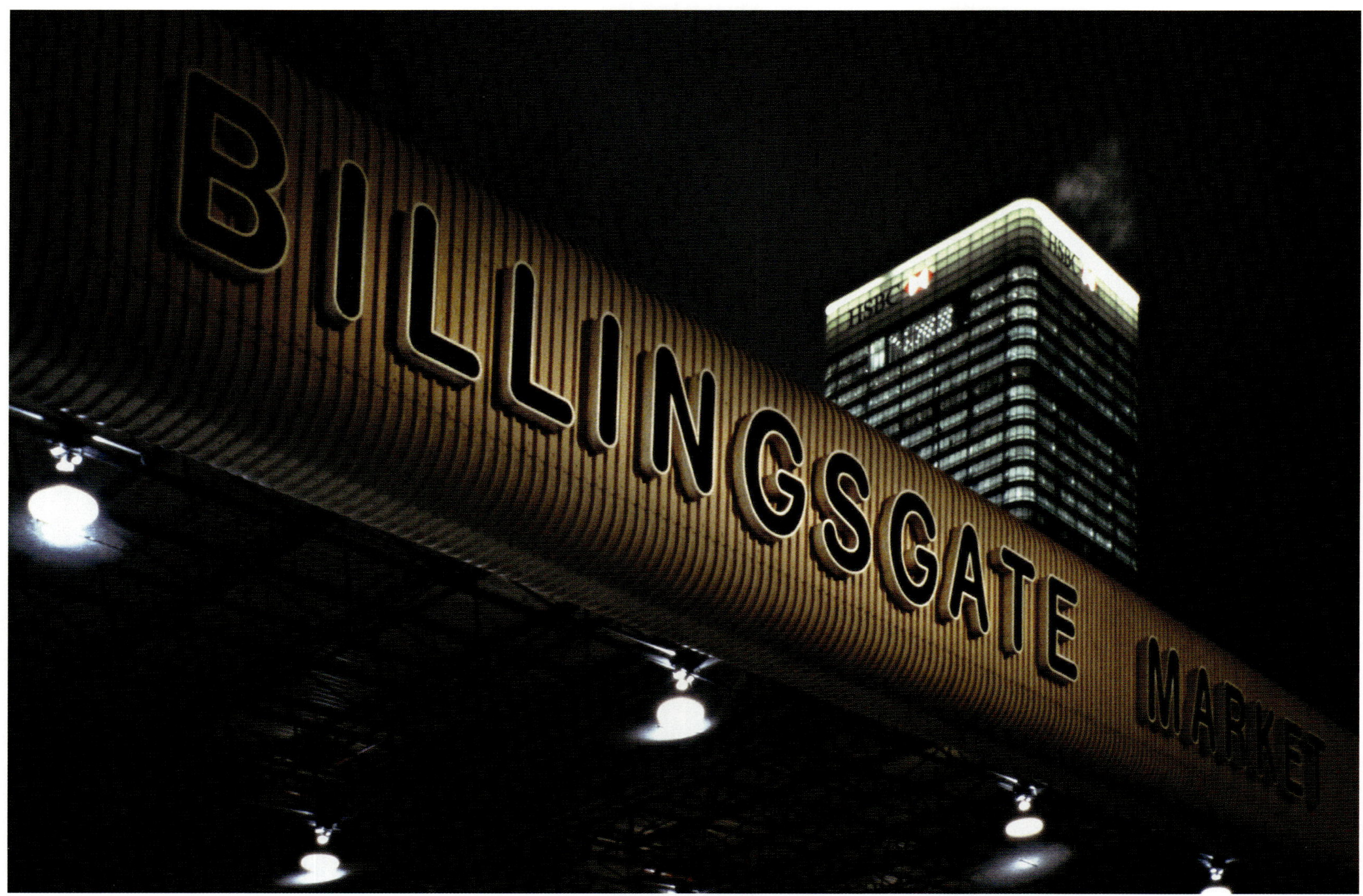

Even the most sophisticated film camera
lacks these tools, so the first thing you need to
appreciate when it comes to exposing film is that
you are effectively "shooting blind." It's not just
the digital crutches that you lose, either: with the
ISO determined by the film that you load, your
exposure options are limited to aperture and
shutter speed. This can often mean that you find
yourself using much slower shutter speeds or
wider apertures in low light conditions (especially
with low ISO film), or shooting with very small
apertures in bright sunlight because you loaded
your camera with medium-speed film.

A side effect of this is that other aspects
of photography also become more important:
if you're forced to use a wide aperture, the depth
of field in your image will decrease, placing
greater importance on focusing accurately, while
handholding your camera at slower shutter speeds
increases the risk of camera shake. Although
image-stabilized lenses will help if you're using
a compatible SLR system (Canon IS and Nikon
VR lenses first appeared for their respective film
cameras), a tripod and a cable release are arguably
much more important for film photography than
they are for digital capture.

Put simply, exposing film is not as easy as
shooting digitally. This is a major part of the
challenge (and fun) that comes with shooting film,
but it can also be a source of great frustration.
However, in this chapter we are going to work
through exposure in a way that guarantees you
will be able to nail your shots, or at least start
to understand when and why they might not
be coming out as you planned.

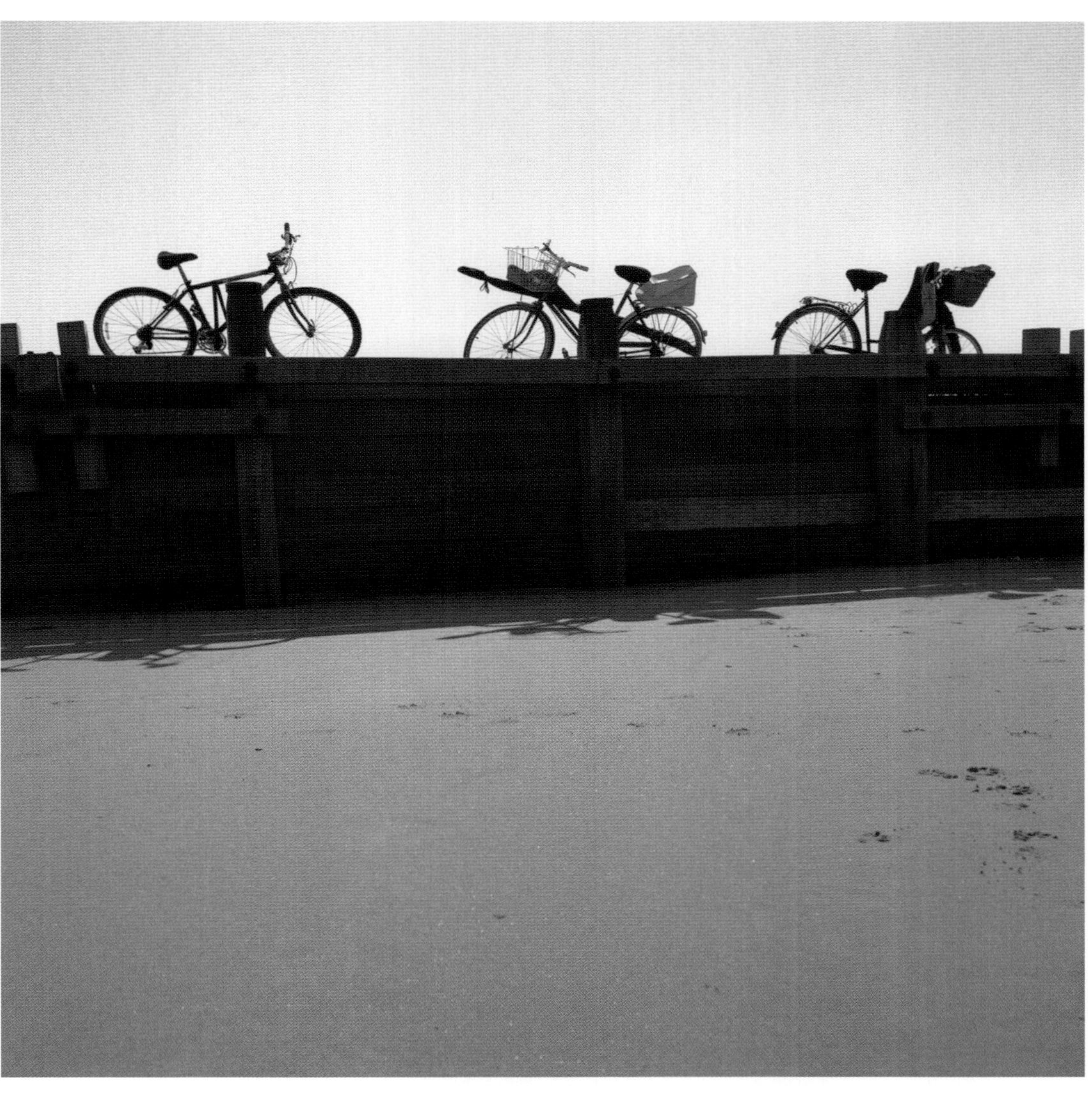

Above: If you shoot black-and-white film you will never
miss not having a histogram. Unless your exposures are
four or five stops off (and it's quite hard to get things that
wrong!) the negative will typically retain some detail.

Reading Light

Even if your camera is fully automated, or you've set it to work in a point-and-shoot fashion, it needs to know how much light the film should receive and for how long. The key to this is a lightmeter, which is simply a light-measuring device—either in the camera or a separate item—that measures the brightness of the scene you're aiming it at, or the intensity of the light falling on it.

There are several ways in which lightmeters can be used, but the principle that underpins them all is "18% gray." Essentially, lightmeters are calibrated to a mid-gray tone that has 18% reflectance (hence 18% gray) and work on the basic assumption that all of the tones in the area you are taking your meter reading from would average out to this mid-gray if they were mixed together. Depending on the meter or metering pattern (see page 67) this could be the entire scene, or just a small part of it, but in every case the lightmeter assumes the same thing: if you mixed all of the tones in that area together they would be 18% gray. Based on this assumption, the meter can then suggest an exposure for that area that would also average out at mid-gray: so it's a case of "mid-gray in, mid-gray out."

Of course, for this to work, the 18% gray assumption actually needs to hold true. Although a surprisingly large number of scenes and subjects meet the mid-gray ideal, it is not always the case: a bright beach scene with near-white sand and a bright sky; a polar bear in a snowscape; or—at the other extreme—a frame-filling shot of a black panther, are all scenes or subjects that would average out to be much lighter or darker than mid-gray. It is at this point that the exposure reading you get from your lightmeter might prove inadequate. That bright beach or snow scene will appear too dark, as your camera drags the bright tones down to mid-gray, and that panther will be too bright as its jet-black coat is lifted to the same midtone average. In both of these cases, the meter is giving you "mid-gray out," but it is not getting "mid-gray in" to start with.

If you were shooting digitally you could review the image, assess the histogram, and reshoot, but with film it's not an option. This is why you need to be more aware of how your lightmeter works, how it is measuring light, and the possible pitfalls, so that you know when problems are likely to occur, and what you can do to prevent or overcome them. And you need to be aware of all of this without the benefit of instant feedback or confirmation of success, which just adds to the tension, excitement, and overall challenge of shooting film—three things that are arguably heightened when you start to "shoot blind" and make pictures on emulsion.

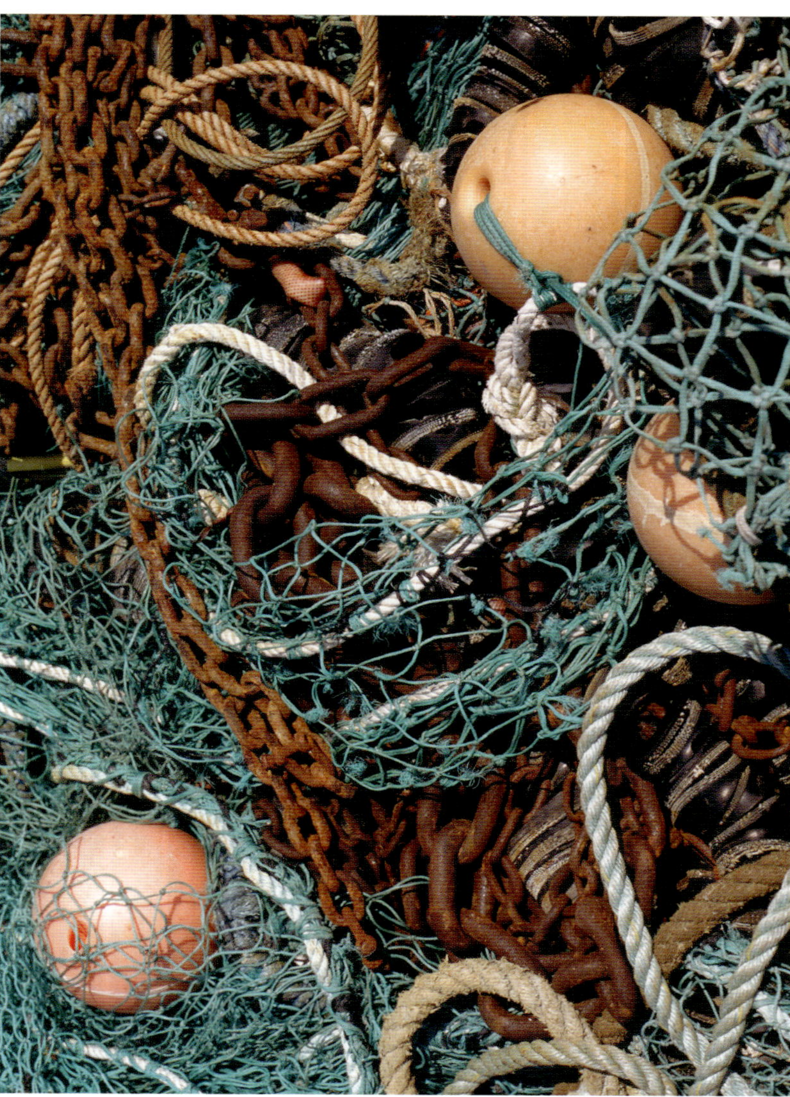

Left: With some images it's fairly easy to see that they won't cause any metering problems. Most of the objects in this collection of fishing nets and other equipment are roughly a midtone, so as a whole there wouldn't be any exposure issues.

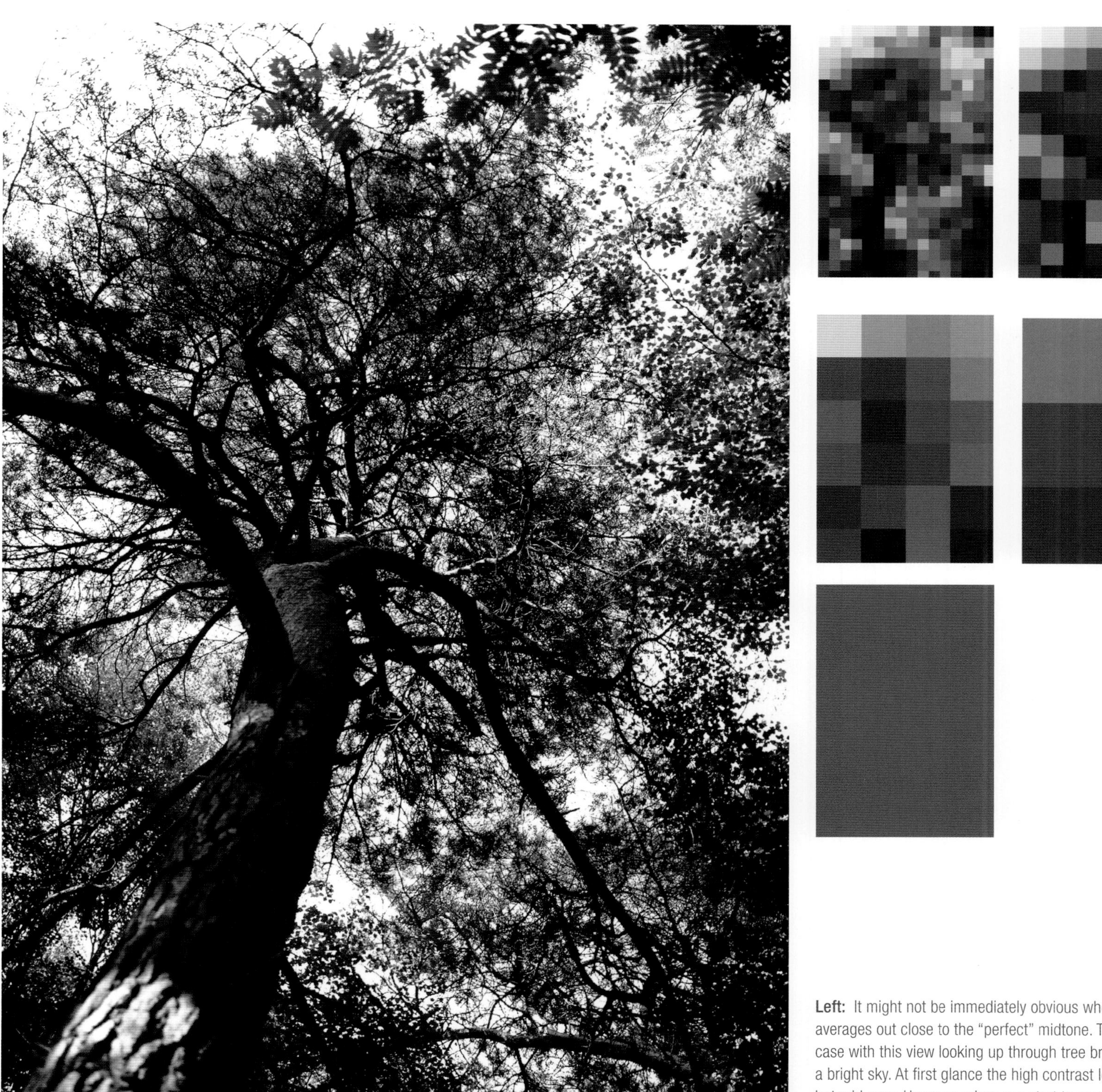

Left: It might not be immediately obvious when a scene averages out close to the "perfect" midtone. That was the case with this view looking up through tree branches at a bright sky. At first glance the high contrast looks anything but mid-gray. However, when you start to average the image out it is clear that middle gray is (roughly) the overall tone that we are left with.

In-Camera Metering

Since the dawn of photography, a number of methods have been used to determine photographic exposures, but the birth of lightmeters as we know them today came in the early 1930s. These handheld photoelectric meters could objectively read the light reaching their selenium cell and would typically provide an arbitrary number that could be cross-referenced to find an appropriate shutter speed and aperture. Over the following years these lightmeters increased in their general sophistication and sensitivity (as CdS meters replaced selenium in some instances), and by the 1950s it was not uncommon for cameras to have a built-in selenium meter that enabled automatic exposure control.

In 1960, the first camera with TTL (Through The Lens) metering arrived, and it's fair to say this revolutionized photography. It was now possible to measure the light passing through the lens to the film, rather than the light falling on an arbitrary panel on the camera, and this made exposure readings more accurate. Further developments ensued, and a variety of metering "patterns" evolved that enabled the photographer to more precisely control the area being measured and in doing so make their exposures more accurate.

Since then, metering has continued to develop, with advanced multi-area metering patterns, OTF (Off The Film) metering that measures the light in "real time" as an exposure is being made, and highlight and shadow spot metering (see page 74) with automatic averaging just some of the options that have appeared over the years. What all of these metering options have in common is the type of light they are measuring.

Below: In-camera metering can be great in a lot of situations, such as this image of a shark in an aquarium. I was using an old 35mm SLR with center-weighted and spot metering options and chose to set the exposure by spot metering (as best I could) off the moving shark's skin.

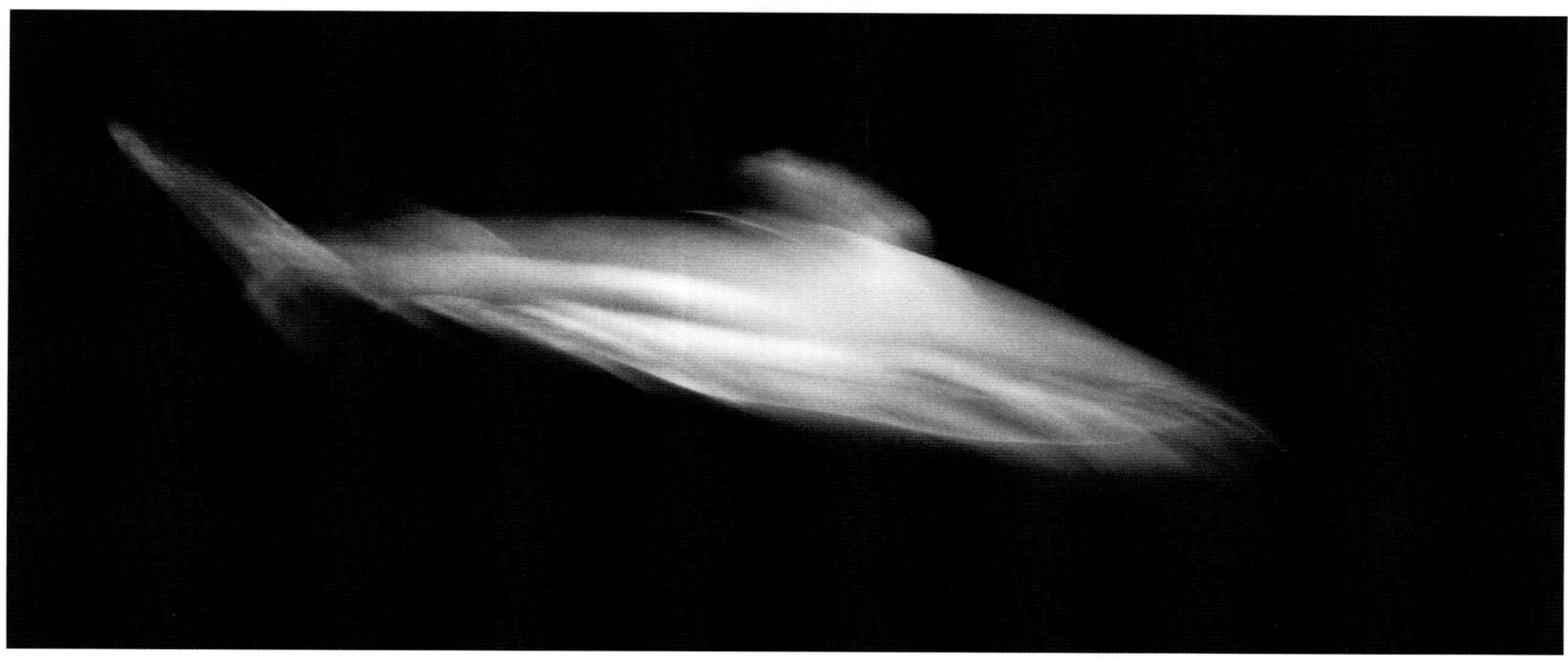

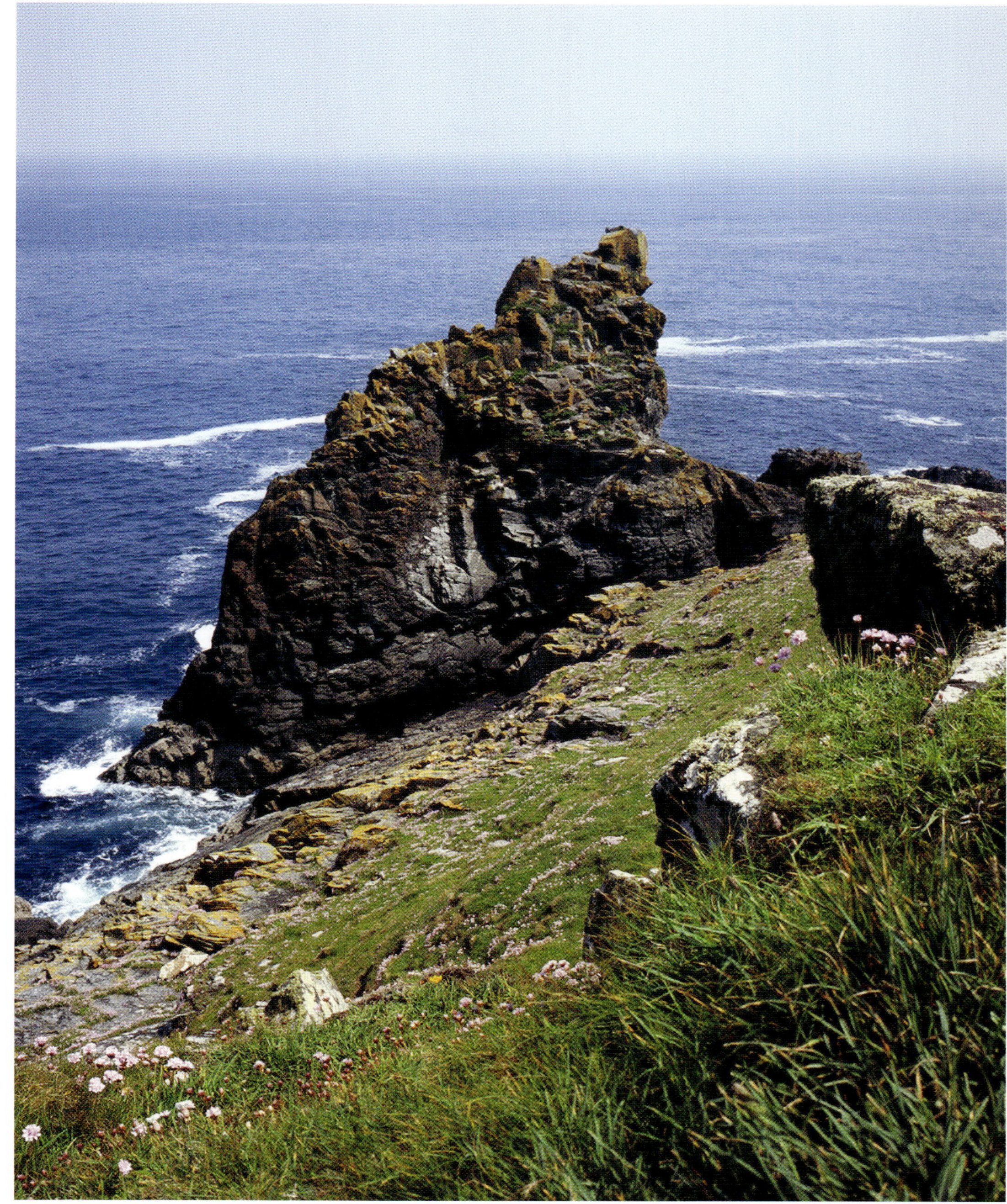

SUNNY 16

In the early days of photography, people created their own exposure tables that gave aperture settings and exposure times for a range of lighting conditions (sunny, light cloud, heavy cloud, and so on) depending on the emulsion they were using. Although crude, they were surprisingly effective, and a similar approach can be used today in the form of the "sunny 16" rule. This is especially useful if you're using a fully manual camera, as it will enable you to get a ballpark exposure without a lightmeter.

The rule is based on the simple understanding that on a sunny day you will get a "good" exposure if you set the aperture to f/16 and the shutter speed to the reciprocal of your ISO (so set a shutter speed of 1/100 sec. if you're using ISO 100 film, 1/200 sec. with ISO 200 film, and so on). It might not be a perfect exposure, but it will be close enough if you're shooting on negative film (with transparency film you will need a more accurate metering method).

From that single combination you can start to get creative. You might set a wider aperture and increase the shutter speed to compensate, or use a smaller aperture and longer exposure time. You can even start to tweak the exposure to compensate for days when it isn't sunny, although this is slightly more hit-and-miss.

Above: The "sunny 16" rule is pretty straightforward: On a sunny day and with an aperture of f/16, the bottom part of the shutter speed fraction (the "denominator") should match your ISO. So, for this shot on ISO 100 film the shutter speed was 1/100 sec.

Reflected Light

Regardless of the sophistication of your camera, all TTL lightmeters take "reflected" light readings. What this means is that they are measuring the light being reflected by your subject or scene, rather than the light falling on it (see Handheld Meters on page 78). This might seem like splitting hairs, but it's usually the Number One reason for a "bad" exposure. The problem is, because the camera's meter is reading reflected light (and assuming 18% gray, as explained on page 62) it can be influenced by the subject's apparent brightness. As a result, very bright subjects can come out darker than expected, while dark subjects appear overly bright. It's not a failing of the camera or its metering system, simply a case that the subject doesn't meet that mid-gray ideal. You can improve your chances of getting things right in a number of ways, and we will explore a range of these on the following pages. Before that, though, let's take a quick look at the first thing you need to get right to pave the way to a perfectly exposed picture: the metering pattern.

Below: Not all subjects conform to the "midtone ideal" that an in-camera lightmeter is looking for, as with this backlit flower on a lightbox. In this type of situation an in-camera meter would be liable to underexpose the image, so it pays to know a little bit about how your meter works and what you can do when it struggles.

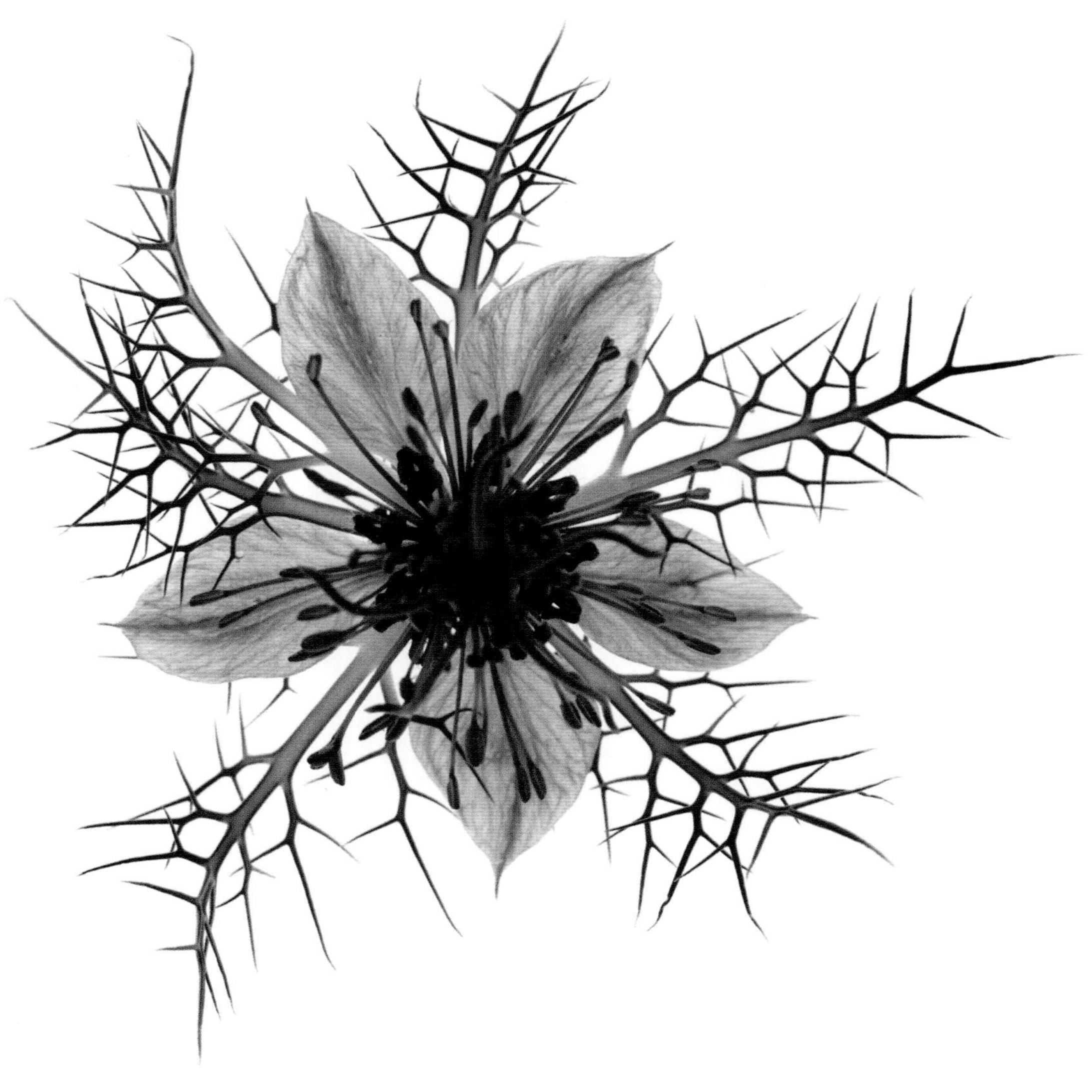

Metering Patterns

A metering pattern refers to the area of the scene that a lightmeter looks at to measure light. On some cameras there may not be a choice—there might just be a single option—while on others you may have a wider range to choose from.

Center weighted: Center-weighted metering is the staple of many manual focus 35mm SLRs, and is the only metering option on some cameras. As the name suggests, this pattern bases most of its exposure recommendation on a reading from a central part of the frame (the size of this central area varies from camera to camera). The thinking here is that this is where your main subject is most likely to be, so the brightness at the edges of the frame can be ignored.

Spot: A spot-metering pattern concentrates the light reading on a small part of the frame so you can take measurements from an ultra-precise area. As you will see later in this chapter, this can be a godsend for film photography—especially if you're shooting transparency film—as it will enable you to pick out the tiniest midtone area in a wider scene and measure the highlights and/or shadows, among other useful options.

Multi-area: Multi-area metering was first seen in the Nikon FA in 1983 (where it was known as Automatic Multi-Pattern metering) and is frequently found in relatively late 35mm SLRs, especially electronic models. The principle here is that the camera breaks the scene down into a number of different areas (sometimes called zones or segments) and takes a light reading from each of them. The individual measurements are then averaged out—sometimes with a bias toward the center of the frame—to provide an accurate exposure reading for the entire frame.

Average: A true "average" metering pattern takes a single light reading across the entire frame, with no bias toward any part of the scene. This makes it the simplest metering pattern of all, but it is readily fooled by overly light and overly dark subjects. It doesn't feature on a lot of cameras, but if this is your only option it might well be worth investing in a gray card (see page 80).

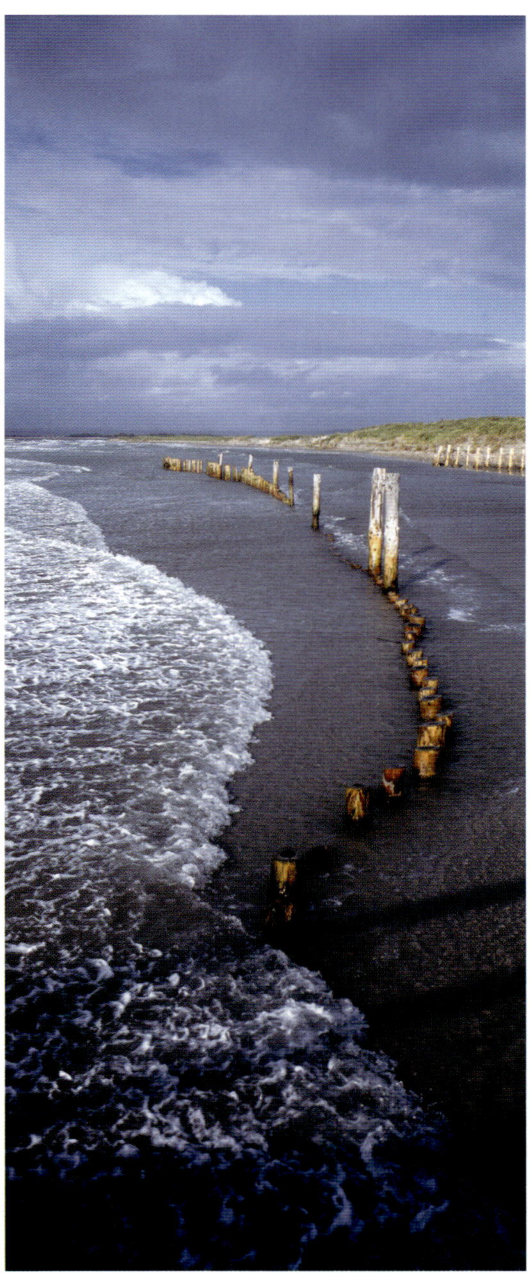

Above: For this shot I took a spot meter reading from the sunlit sand toward the center of the frame and used a 1-stop ND grad filter (see page 120) to balance the sky.

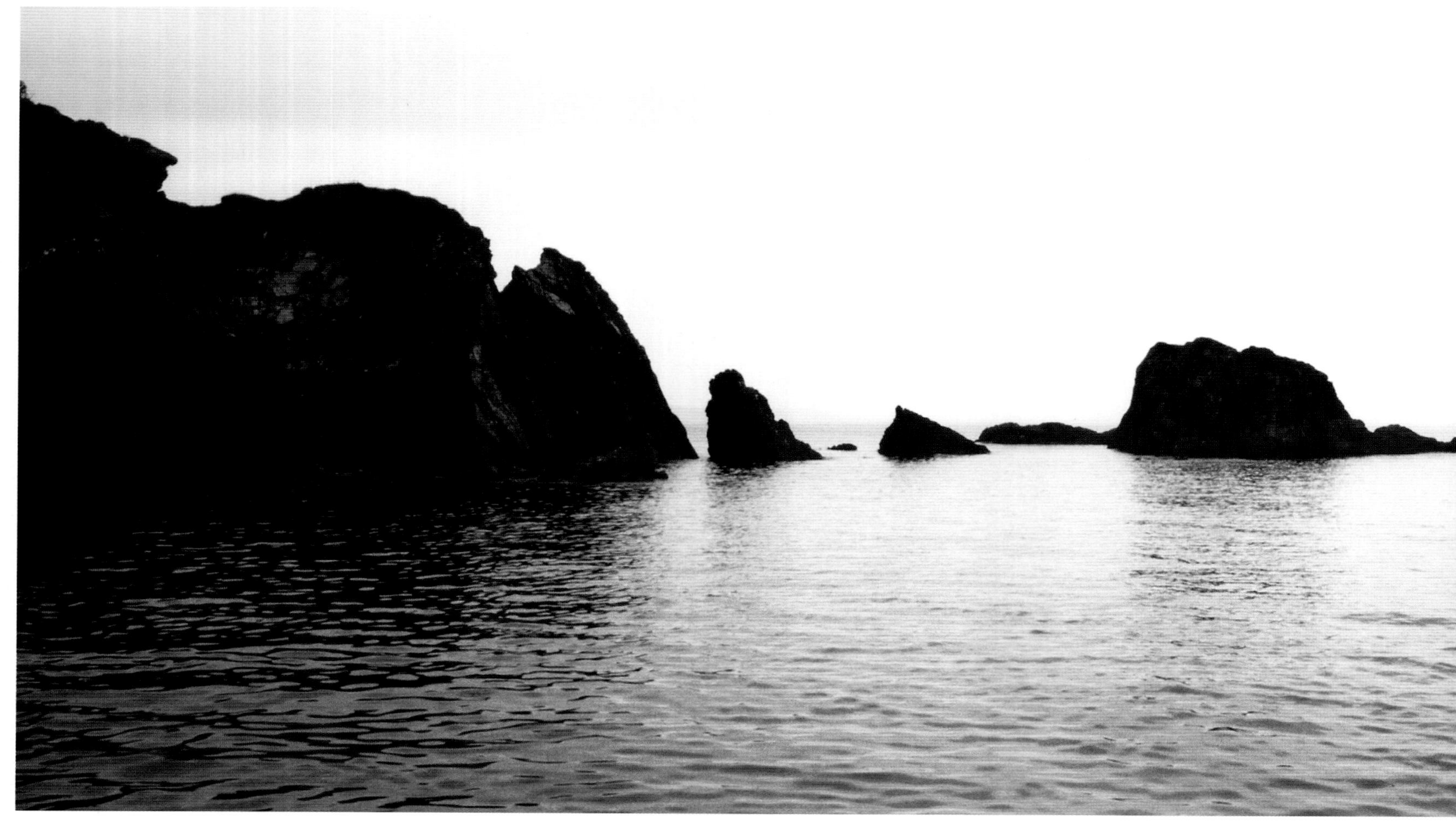

Mobile Metering

No matter which metering pattern you use, a key thing to remember is that it is a light measuring tool that can be used independently of taking a shot. It might sound obvious, but you can point your camera in any direction to take a light reading: you don't need to aim it at your subject and you certainly don't have to take a picture.

For example, let's say you're photographing a snow-covered landscape and your only option is center-weighted metering. Rather than aim your camera at the landscape—which is going to lead to an underexposed image—fill the frame with something closer to a midtone, such as tree bark or a rock, and take your light reading from that. Then, set the exposure manually so it is "locked in" and reframe your wider snowy landscape. This will give you a much greater chance of avoiding any significant exposure problems, especially when used in conjunction with bracketing.

- Although bracketing can be useful on negative film it is usually less critical given the film's wider dynamic range and exposure latitude. If you feel bracketing might be necessary, do it in 1-stop (or 2-stop) increments.

- A lot of automated cameras offer automatic exposure bracketing (AEB), which lets you set the number of frames, the exposure increment, and often the order of exposure as well. The camera will then work through the "bracket" as you shoot. If you decide to use this feature be sure to reset the camera after shooting, as you may not want to apply the same parameters to subsequent images.

Bracketing

No camera meter—or photographer—is infallible, which is where exposure bracketing comes in. Many photographers routinely bracket shots taken on transparency film, usually adjusting the exposure ½-stop either side of what they think is the "correct" exposure. This gives them a sequence of three shots, with one at the "right" setting, one that's slightly brighter, and one that's slightly darker: of these, one should be ideal.

Of course, if you're really not sure about your initial exposure (or you just want to be certain you get the shot) you can bracket more widely to cover a broader exposure range; you might also choose to bias your bracketed sequence in one direction (to make all of the shots slightly darker, for example). Alternatively, if you're fairly confident that you've nailed your initial exposure you can decrease the increment to ⅓-stop (if your camera allows it) for greater finesse. Given the limited latitude of transparency film, I find that bracketing is almost always beneficial.

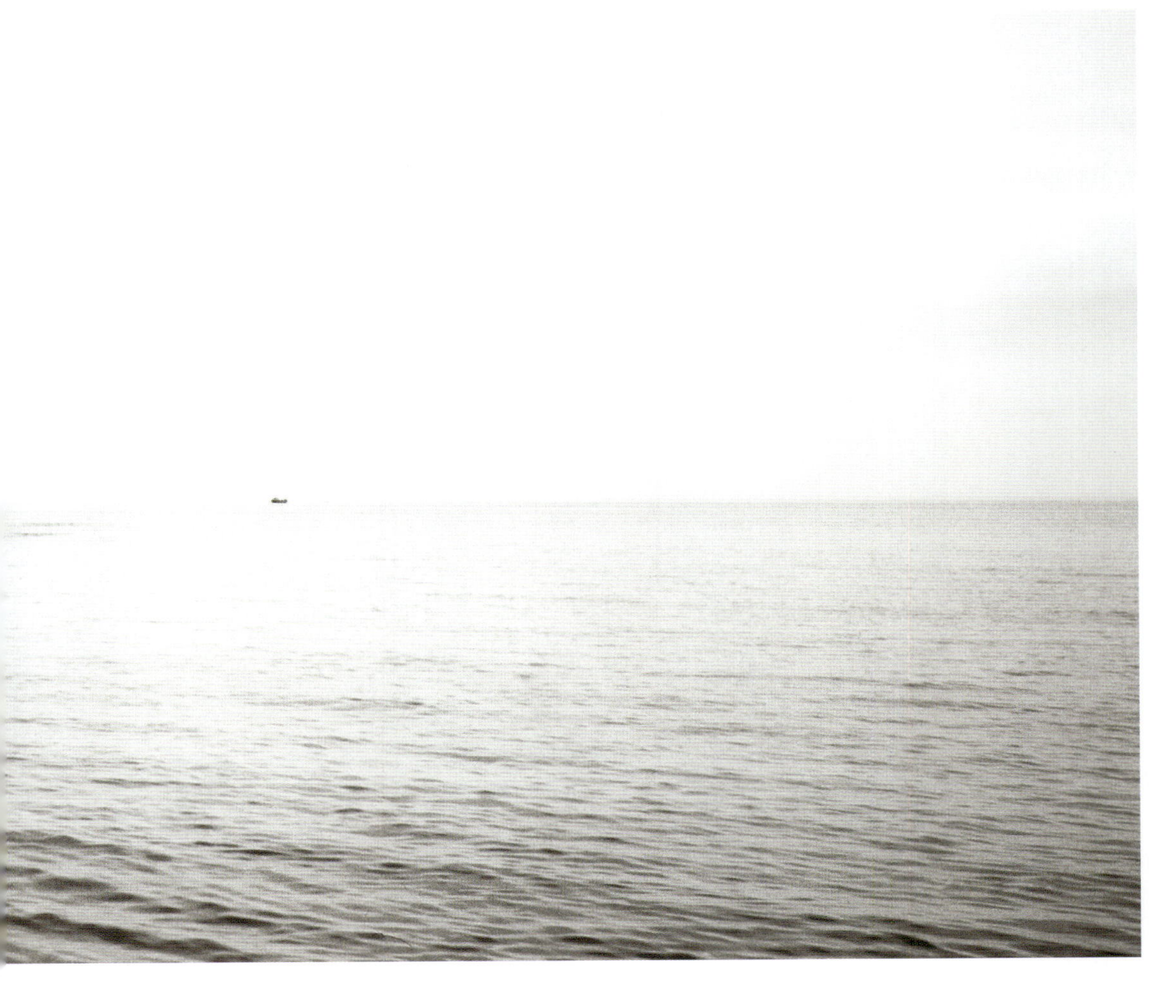

Above: With a bright, near-white sky and light-toned sea I was anticipating the camera underexposing this scene, so took a spot meter reading from a light-colored rock at my feet, set the exposure manually, and then reframed the more distant view.

Below: This trio of shots was taken on transparency film, bracketing ±½ stop either side of the "correct" exposure to ensure I got the result I was after. From left to right the sequence runs -½, 0, +½.

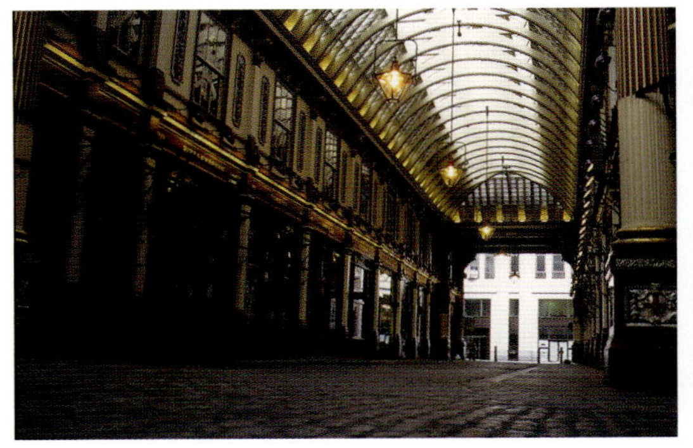
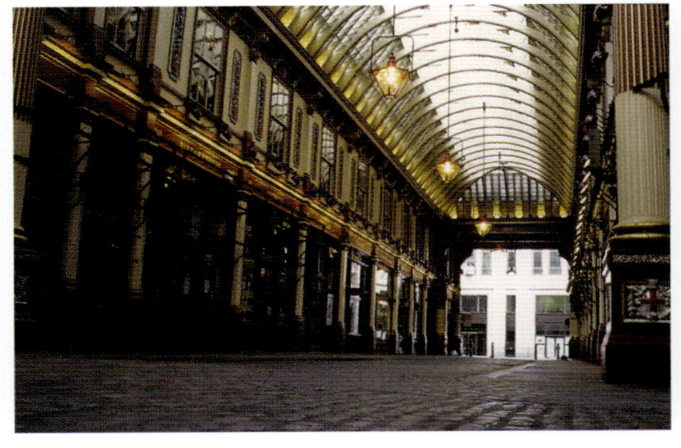
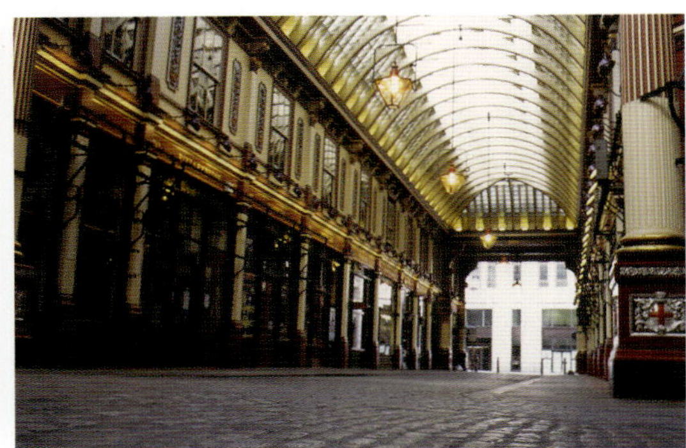

Zone System

The Zone System was developed by landscape photographer Ansel Adams, and photography instructor Fred Archer, in the late 1930s/early 40s, as a means of producing—from a technical standpoint—the best negative for printing. Some film photographers still zealously employ the Zone System in their work, while others choose to ignore it, but the most important thing to remember is that great photographs have come from both schools of thought: the Zone System is not compulsory, but nor is it redundant.

However, before we look at it in more detail, there's a caveat. Whole books have been written on the Zone System—not least by Adams and Archer—so to cover it in its entirety here is impossible. What we can do, though, is introduce its core principles and explore how they can be successfully applied today.

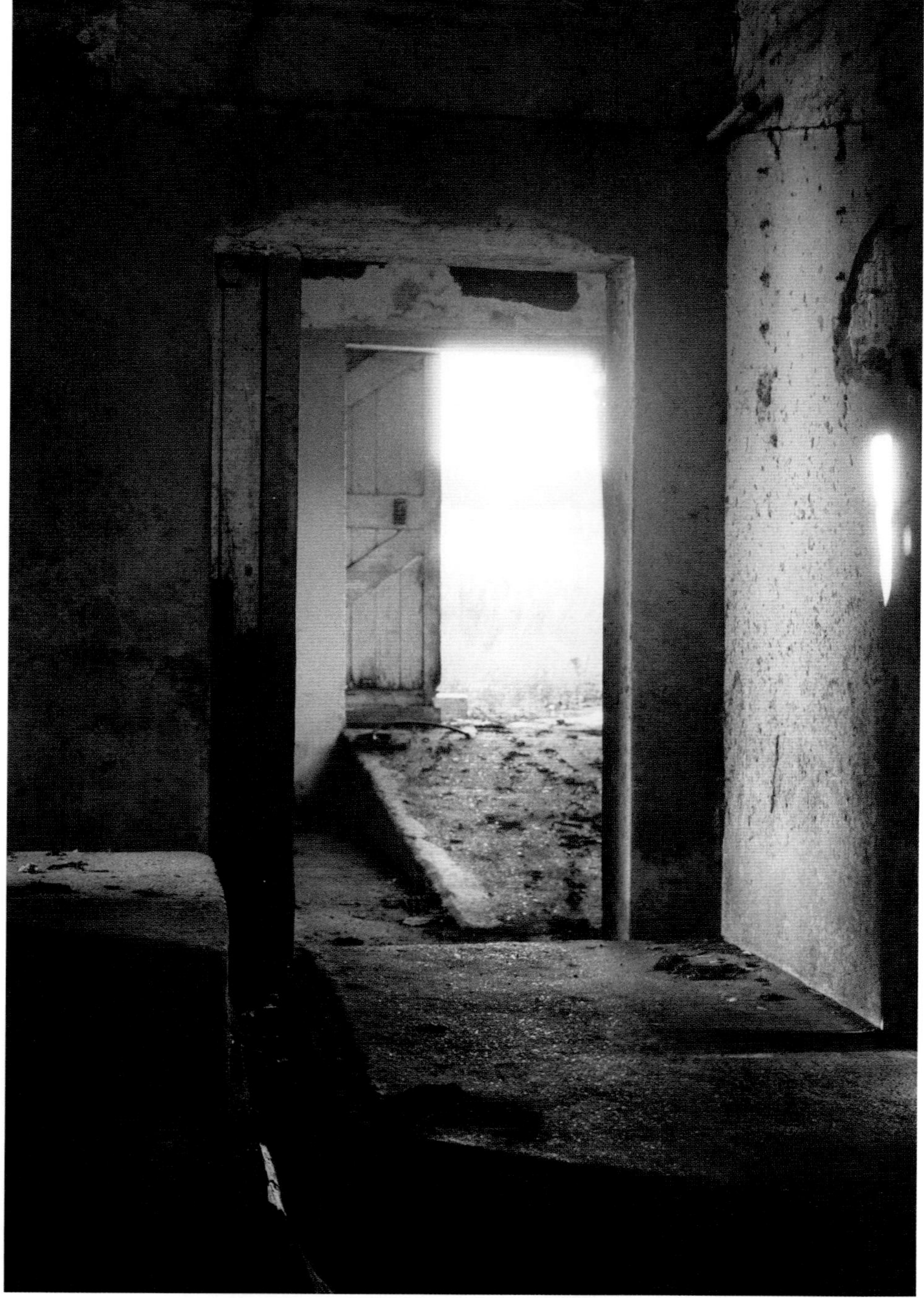

Right: I knew it was going to be a challenge to get this shot, but because I was shooting on black-and-white negative film I could follow the basic Zone System premise of exposing for the shadows at the bottom left of the frame. Were I shooting sheet film (or even roll film) I could have then decreased the development time to compensate for the high contrast, but I was shooting 35mm film, and this rarely makes sense, as there are far more frames that need to be considered. So instead, I simply let the highlights fall where they were.

In The Beginning

The Zone System was created at a time when photographers commonly shot single sheets of black-and-white negative film, and prints were made traditionally on a fixed contrast (or fixed grade) paper. So the first thing to appreciate is that it started out as a very specific system designed to deal with the challenges of the day.

The underlying principle of the Zone System is the idea that different brightness values in a scene can be placed in distinct "zones" in a photograph. Although there are variations on the system that use 9, 10, and 11 zones, the 11-zone system is arguably most widely used today. In this version the zones—which use roman numerals—run from 0 (pure black) to X (pure white), with steps from dark to light in between. Zone V (5) is the midtone.

The idea is that before doing anything else you first find the optimum Exposure Index (EI) for your film, which effectively determines the speed it is shot at, and then you determine its ideal development time. The practicalities of this are beyond the scope of this book, but it essentially involves thorough testing to find the "sweet spot."

In the field, the exposure is then based around the darkest shadow area that detail is desirable in, with the overall exposure set so that the shadows are placed in zone II or zone III. Then, a reading from the highlights is taken to see where they fall in terms of their zone. Based on the relative brightness of the shadows and highlights, the development time can be adjusted to control contrast: developing the film for longer than the "ideal" time increases contrast, while a shorter development time reduces contrast. The aim of all this precision is to produce a negative that is as close to perfect for printing on grade two photographic paper as possible.

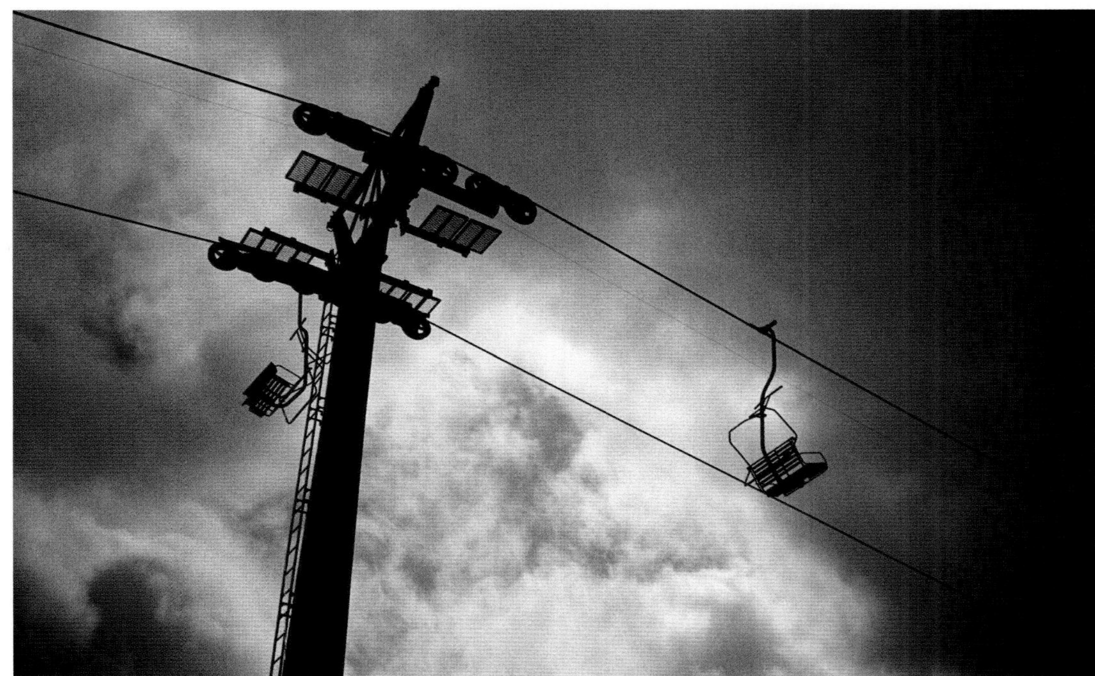

Above: To ensure this cable car tower and car were in silhouette I took a spot meter reading from the upright column and then reduced the exposure by four stops. In doing so, the exposure for that area shifted from zone V (the metered reading) to zone I, making the tower near black—just what I was looking for.

Below: The Zone System consists of 11 zones. Generally, zones 0 and X can be ignored as they refer to pure black and pure white respectively; Adams considered zones I and IX the ends of the useful range of tones, while zones II to VIII are the darkest and lightest tones to contain texture/detail.

ZONE	DESCRIPTION
0	Pure black
I	Near black (no texture; slight tone)
II	Textured black (darkest area with detail)
III	Dark materials (texture shown)
IV	Dark stone and dark foliage
V	Mid gray
VI	Light stone; average Caucasian skin
VII	Very light skin
VIII	Textured white (lightest area with texture)
IX	Near white (no texture; slight tone)
X	Pure white

The Zone System Today

The Zone System hasn't changed, and it's still a great way to pre-visualize an image and create an optimized negative. But it's important to realize its limitations. Today, we more often shoot rolls of 35mm or 120 film, so cannot develop our exposures individually, and we also shoot in color and get it lab processed, which largely removes the option to adjust development times with any real consistency (while you can get your film push- and pull-processed this can result in unwanted color shifts; see page 159). Even if you stay true to the original system and you choose to shoot large-format black-and-white negatives, traditional printing now tends to be done using variable contrast (multigrade) printing papers, or digitally after the film is scanned: both of these printing methods overcome some of the problems the Zone System set out to resolve.

However, the theories underpinning the Zone System are still useful, and on the following pages we will look at a couple of ways that the exposure element of the system can be borrowed for your own work. First, though, you need to appreciate two fundamental things:

- Zone V matches the midtone that your exposure meter is calibrated to; it is the 18% gray that we looked at on page 62.

- Each zone is 1-stop different (in terms of exposure) to its neighbor. Zone IV is 1-stop darker than zone V, zone VI is 1-stop brighter than zone V, and so on.

Armed with this knowledge—and a spot meter—you are in the unrivalled position of being able to place the tones in your images at will.

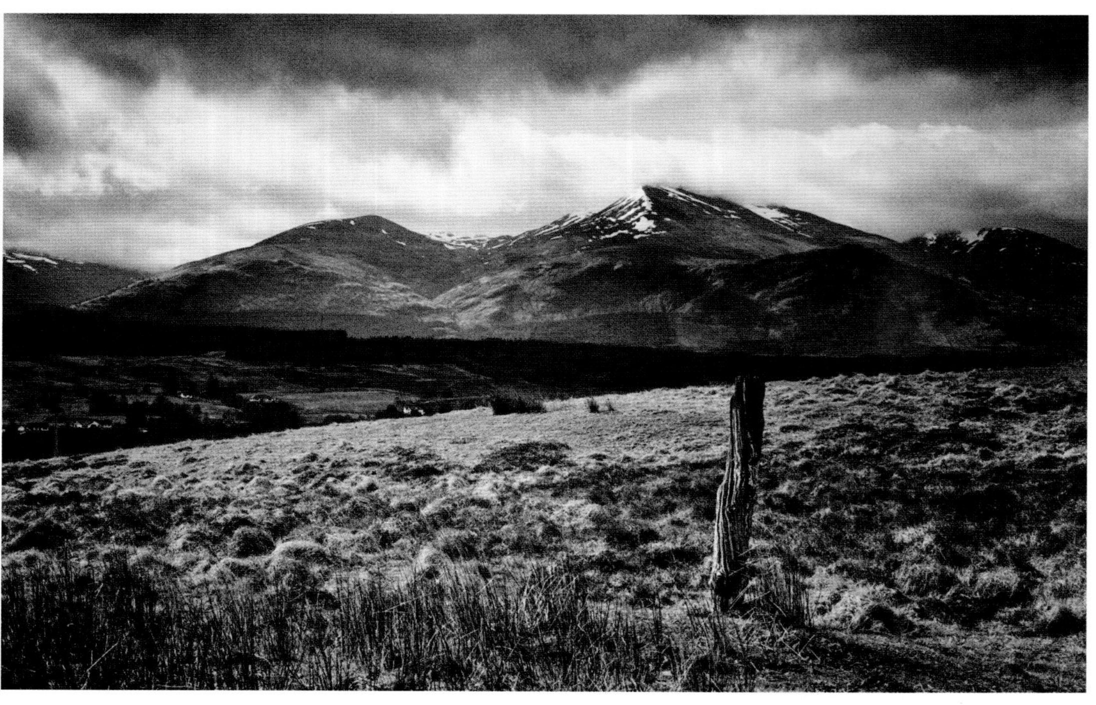

Above: It's fair to argue that the Zone System is less relevant today than it was when it was created, regardless of how you choose to work. In the darkroom, multigrade papers provide greater control over contrast when you make wet prints, while image-editing software allows you to adjust the tones in an image at will if you digitize your shots.

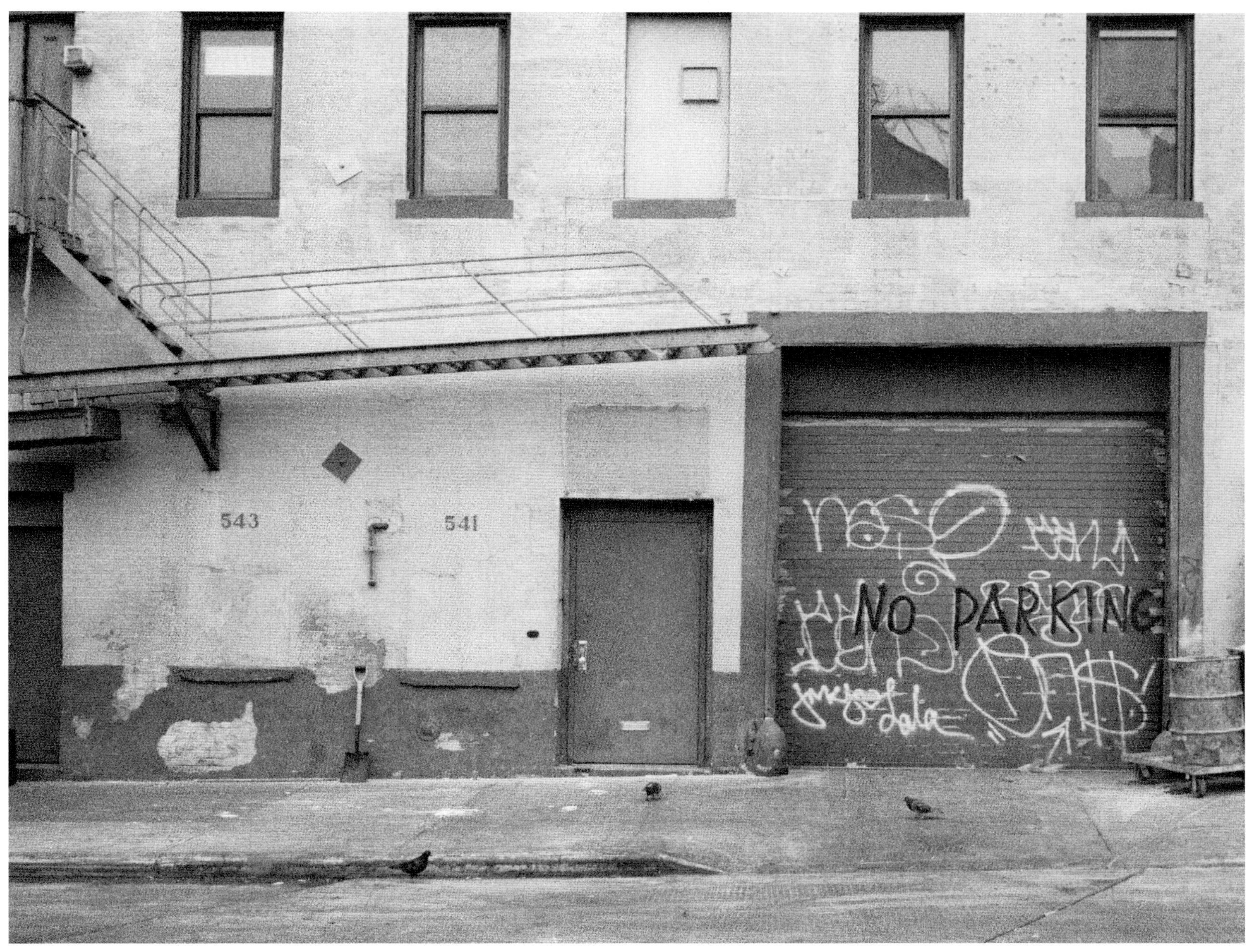

Above: Metering for this urban shot was pretty simple:
I just needed to take a light reading from the light-colored
wall with my camera's spotmeter and increase the exposure
by 1 stop, shifting the metered area from Zone V to Zone VI.

Highlight Metering

The Zone System was designed for negative film, so one of its main concerns is to prevent the shadows from blocking up (hence basing your exposure on the shadows). With transparency film the opposite is true, and setting your exposure can be summed up by the mantra "expose for the highlights and let the shadows take care of themselves." This is because, in a visual sense, we are more accepting of featureless black shadows than we are of stark areas of nothing. To put this into practice you can take the underlying principle of the Zone System and turn it on its head:

Highlight Metering In Practice

1 Take a spot meter reading from the brightest part of the scene you want detail to appear in.

2 Set this as your exposure in Manual mode, or use your camera's automatic exposure lock (AE-L) function if you're using a different mode and have this feature.

3 Increase the exposure by 2 stops, either by opening the aperture, increasing the exposure time, or using a combination of both controls. You can also use auto exposure bracketing.

4 Shoot three frames, bracketing them at ±½ stop (see page 69). This will give you three exposures that are 1½-, 2-, and 2½-stops brighter than your original spot reading, each of which lifts the highlights to a certain degree. With practice you will soon be able to identify which of these exposures you prefer in different situations.

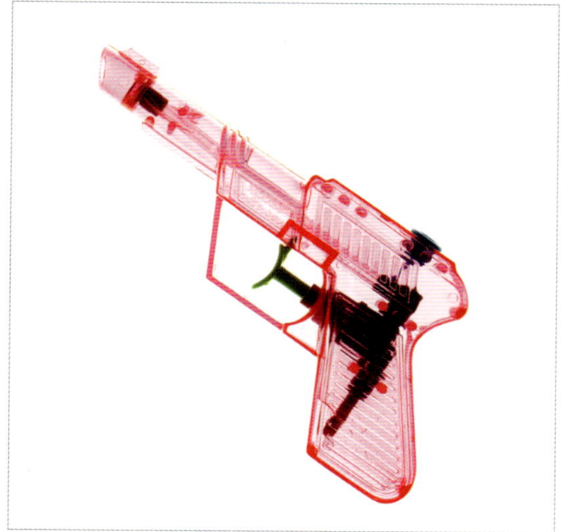

Above: This toy water gun was photographed on a lightbox, so all of the light was coming through the object. The simplest way of determining the exposure was to take a spot meter reading from the background (the lightbox), which I knew I wanted to be white, and increase the exposure by 2 stops. In this instance I also bracketed widely as I planned on cross processing the film (see page 160).

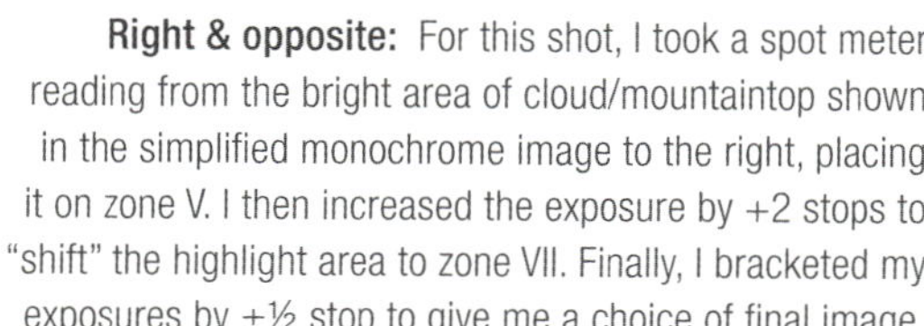

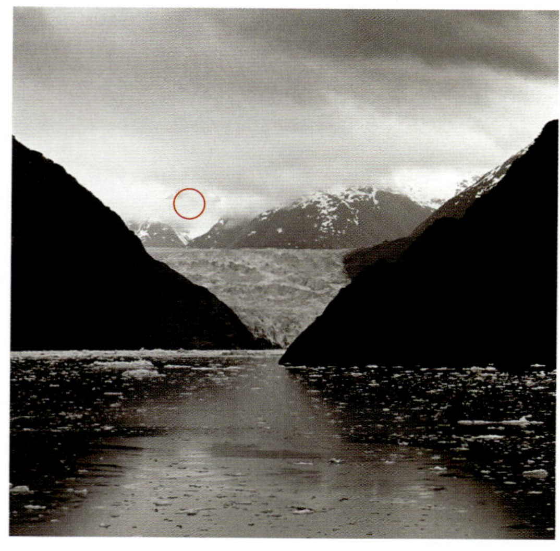

Right & opposite: For this shot, I took a spot meter reading from the bright area of cloud/mountaintop shown in the simplified monochrome image to the right, placing it on zone V. I then increased the exposure by +2 stops to "shift" the highlight area to zone VII. Finally, I bracketed my exposures by ±½ stop to give me a choice of final image.

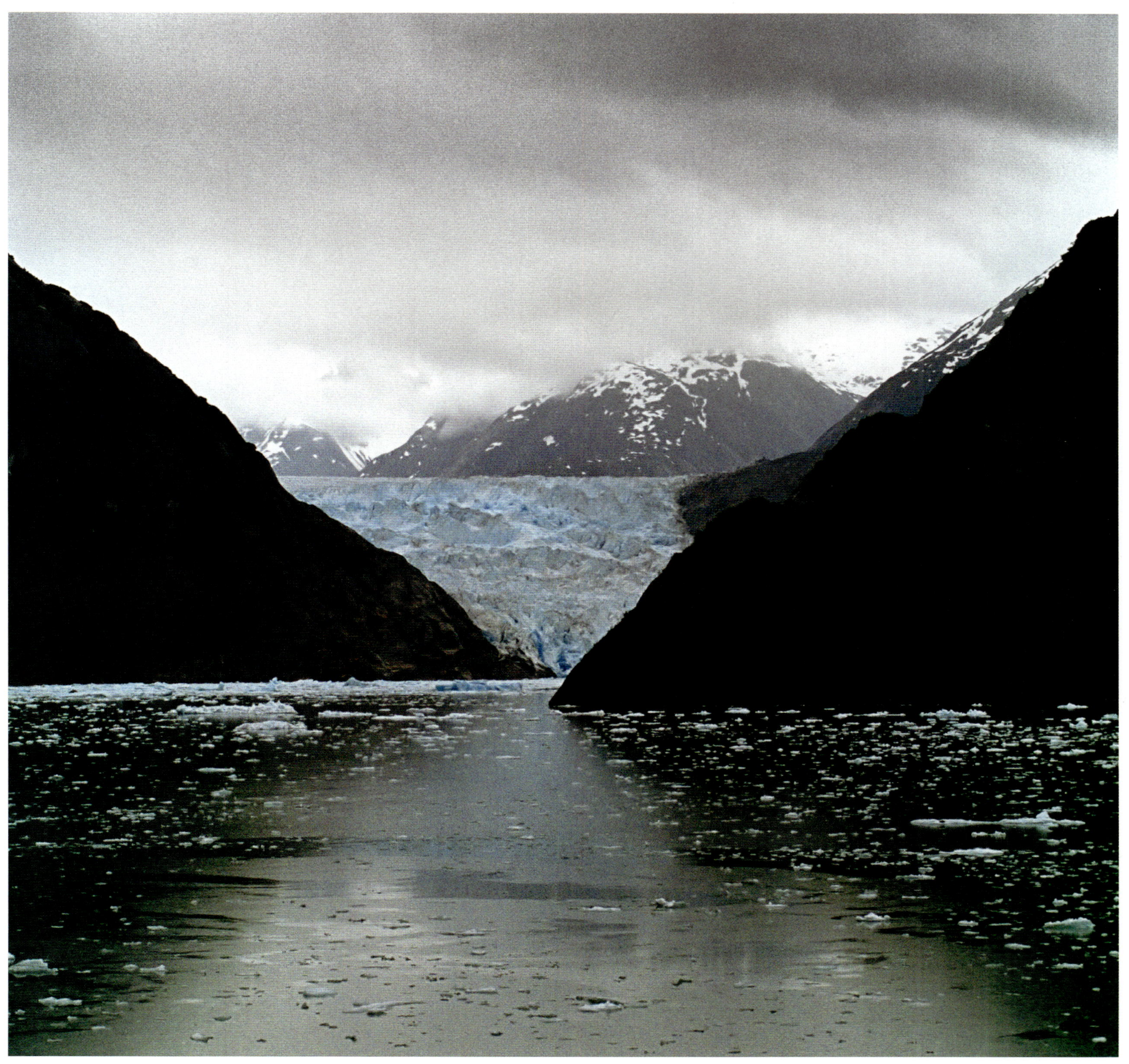

Multi-Spot Metering

In the heat of the moment we typically measure the light and take shots in such rapid succession that we treat the two things as a single action. However, if your scene allows it, there's nothing preventing you from using your spot meter to take light readings from multiple points to build up an overall brightness picture.

With some cameras, such as Canon's T90 and Olympus' OM3 and OM4, and certain handheld lightmeters, multiple spot readings can not only be taken, but also averaged out automatically. In this way you can take spot meter readings from the brightest and darkest parts of the scene—and from the tones in between—and the camera will use all of this information to set the best single exposure for your scene.

Tip

You don't need a camera with automatic multi-spot metering to employ this technique: any camera with a spot meter can be used to take multiple readings. However, it is often quicker and easier to take a midtone reading from a gray card (see page 80), rather than try to average out half-a-dozen spot readings!

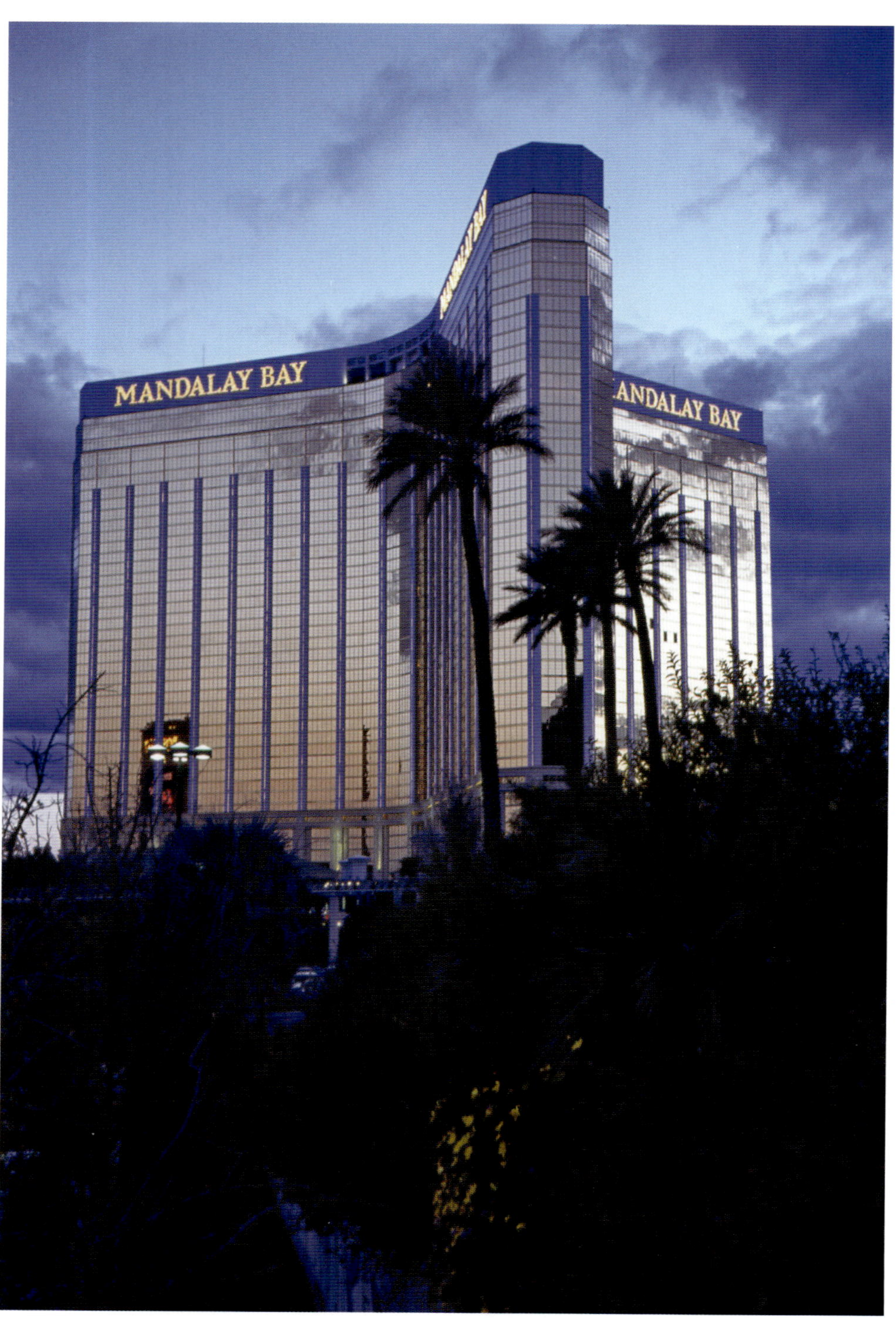

Right: When you shoot on transparency film it helps to have a good idea of the dynamic range of the scene. In most instances you will want to preserve the highlights, and so you need to meter accordingly. With this shot I didn't want the light-reflecting windows at the right of the hotel to blow out, nor did I want the lower portion of the image to block up. Taking readings from the highlight and shadow areas assured me my exposure would "fit" the film's dynamic range, leading to a pleasing result.

Dynamic Range

Although multi-spot metering sounds ideal in terms of getting your exposures spot on, it doesn't take into account the film you are using. As you saw in Chapter 2, different types of film have a different dynamic range, with transparency film being particularly limited. So, while you may arrive at the "perfect" exposure for your scene through careful multi-spot metering, the scene's dynamic range might not fit the film you are using, leading to lost shadows and lost highlights.

Unless you are lighting the scene yourself, there's not much you can do about this, but you can at least make sure you are aware of the problem. If you know what the dynamic range of your film is (or at least have a ballpark idea) you can quickly use your spot meter to see if there will be any problems, and if necessary adjust the exposure to favor the highlights or shadows, depending on your film and desired look.

1 Take a spot meter reading from the brightest area you hope to see detail in. Make a note of it.

2 Take a second spot meter reading from the darkest area you hope to see detail in. Make a note of this reading as well.

3 Work out how many stops there are between your highlight and shadow readings to determine the scene's dynamic range, and then refer to the grid (above right).

Right: Any scene where the sun appears in the frame is going to have a massively high dynamic range, so you don't need to measure it. To try and control things in this shot I "hid" the sun behind one of the turrets of Tower Bridge in London and took a spot meter reading from a light area of sky, knowing that the camera would darken it to a midtone. In doing so it would lower the overall exposure and intensify the color of the sunrise.

DYNAMIC RANGE AND FILM TYPES	
SCENE DYNAMIC RANGE (STOPS)	**COMMENT**
0–2	*Exceptionally low contrast: are you sure you metered the highlights and shadows? In any case, the dynamic range won't be a problem on any film.*
3–4	*Scene's dynamic range fits within all film types. If you're shooting black and white and want more contrast, consider a high-contrast developer and/or increased development time (see page 156).*
5–6	*If you're shooting using Fujifilm Velvia 50 or a similar transparency film you may be at the limit of its dynamic range; there's no problem if you're shooting negative film.*
7–8	*You'll be OK if you're shooting negatives (color or black and white), but you will be exceeding the dynamic range of some transparency films and at the limit of most other films of this type.*
9–11	*Beyond the range of transparency film and about the limit for negative film according to Ansel Adams and Fred Archer (there's a reason why the Zone System had 9–11 zones!). However, the Zone System was created around 80 years ago and the dynamic range of negative film had improved since then.*
12+	*You will be OK with most negative films, but you will need to be ultra-precise with your exposures: there won't be much exposure latitude at all. If you're shooting black and white you may want to use a low-contrast developer to eke out as much detail as possible.*

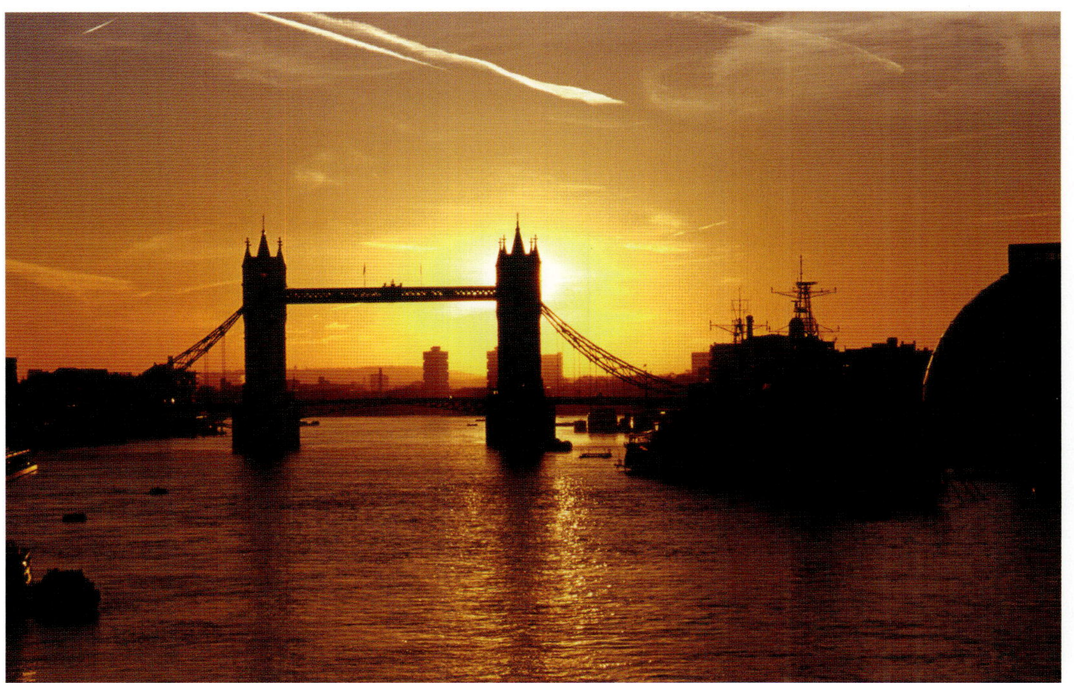

Handheld Meters

Unless you're going to rely on exposure tables, the "sunny 16" rule, or blind luck, you need some way of measuring light so that you can determine your exposures. If your camera doesn't have a lightmeter built-in, a handheld lightmeter is one option and there are plenty of models available (particularly from Sekonic).

Different lightmeters offer different metering options, which might include reflected readings, spot readings, flash metering, and cine modes, but one of the most compelling reasons to choose a handheld meter is to measure the light that's falling onto your subject (known as an incident light reading), rather than the light being reflected off it. This is a subtle difference, but it means your exposure reading won't be affected by the subject's apparent brightness: it doesn't matter if your subject is light or dark, as it's the intensity of the light falling on it that's being measured.

INCIDENT LIGHT READINGS

1 Make sure the lightmeter is set to the ISO you are using and that the lumisphere (white dome) is in place.

2 Hold the lightmeter in front of your subject, and aim it back toward the camera.

3 Activate the meter so that you can take your light reading.

4 Digital lightmeters will generally display a single shutter speed and aperture combination, but you can alter the pairing for different exposure options. Analog meters often line up a number of shutter speeds and apertures, allowing you to pick a pair.

5 Finally, set the exposure on your camera (using Manual mode).

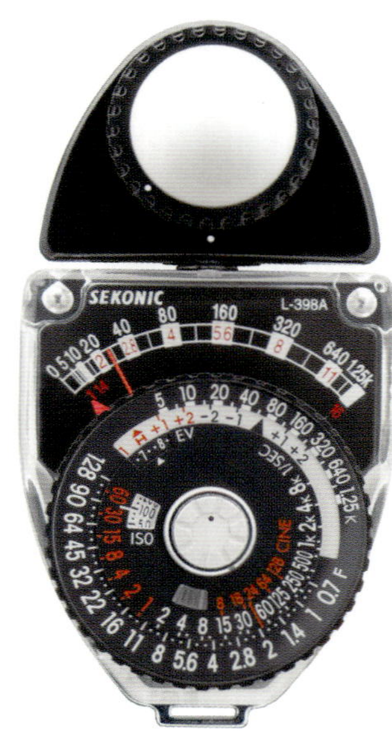

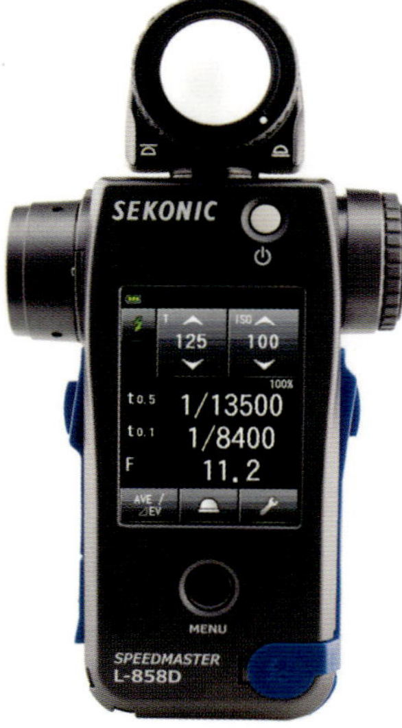

Above: Sekonic is the leading manufacturer of photographic lightmeters, with an expansive range to choose from depending on your needs and budget. Models range from the self-powered analog L-398A (top), which can take incident light readings without a battery, to the flagship L-858D (above), which includes a 1° spot meter, flash metering, and flash duration analysis, among its extensive feature list.

Smartphone Meters

A viable alternative to a dedicated photographic lightmeter is your smartphone. There are countless apps available at varying costs for iOS and Android devices, which use the phone's camera to take reflected exposure readings or—with the addition of an add-on lumisphere—incident readings, just like a "proper" handheld lightmeter.

The biggest limitation here is the smartphone itself. A lot of phones' cameras struggle in low-light conditions, and this means that your lightmeter app will also struggle; it cannot do anything that your phone camera isn't capable of. Similarly, the accuracy of your "smartphone meter" will depend heavily on the accuracy of the phone's exposure system, so if your phone's exposures are often hit-and-miss, the exposure readings you get when you convert them to a lightmeter will be equally erratic. However, if you've got a great camera in your phone it's worth a try, and it can be significantly less expensive than buying a dedicated lightmeter.

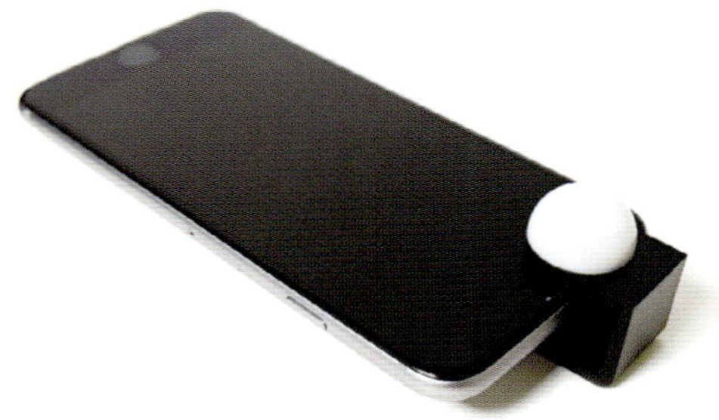

Above: The Luxi for All is a simple clip-on lumisphere that works with a wide number of free and premium apps to convert your smartphone into a lightmeter.

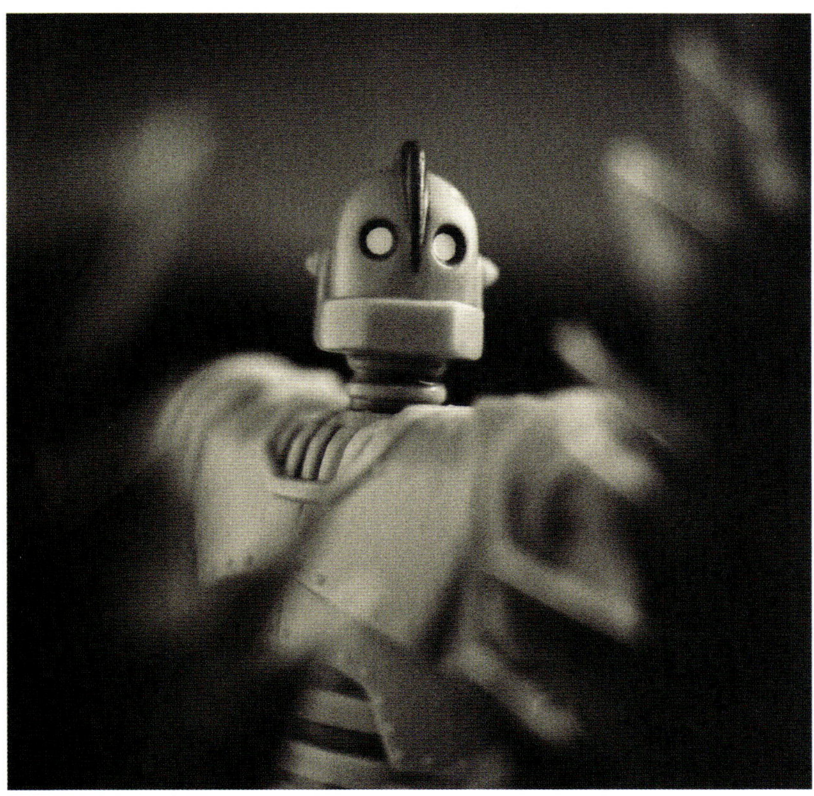

Above: A handheld lightmeter that can read flash as well as continuous lighting can come in useful in a lot of situations, including the studio.

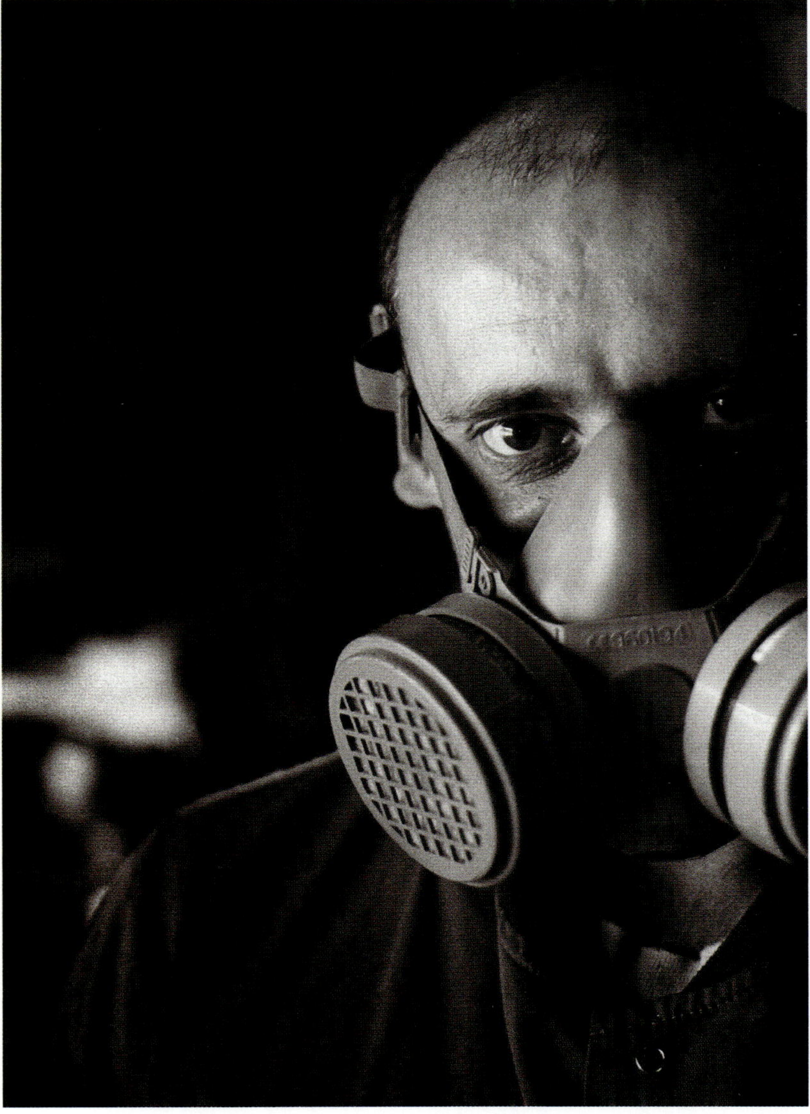

Above: Taking a light reading with a handheld lightmeter automatically balanced out the varying amounts of light falling on my subject's face.

Tips

- You might have a camera with a sophisticated TTL metering system, but the ability to take incident light readings can still be useful.

- Vintage lightmeters look great and can cost little, but they can be limited: many of them will only take reflected light readings; they may no longer be accurate (or able to be recalibrated); and they may rely on a convoluted cross-referencing system to "translate" the light readings they give.

- If you can't hold the lightmeter immediately in front of your subject (if you're shooting a landscape, for example), just hold it in the same light to take your reading.

Gray Card Metering

Perhaps one of the simplest and most underrated exposure tools is the humble gray card, which allows photographers to take accurate exposure readings in most situations. Traditionally, this is a card that reflects 18% gray, which is the same midtone that your camera or handheld lightmeter is looking for (see page 62).

All you need to do is place or hold the card so that it's under the same lighting conditions as your subject and then take a reflected light reading from it using either your camera's built-in lightmeter or a handheld meter in reflective mode. The exposure reading can then be set manually and you can be confident that you have locked in a midtone exposure that isn't affected by the broader scene; no matter how bright or dark the scene you are photographing is, the gray card will deliver the "ideal" midtone value.

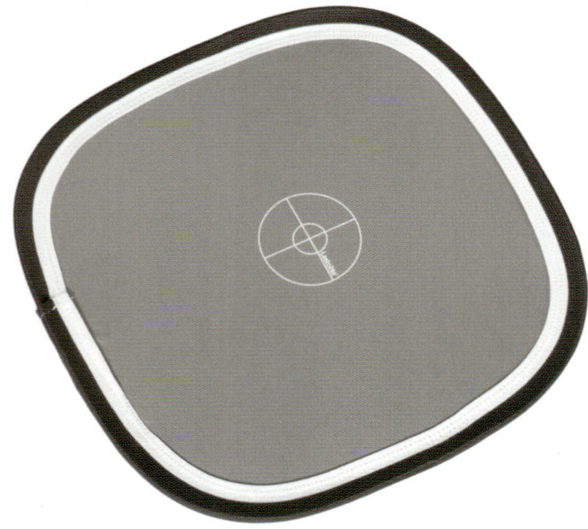

Above: This version of a gray card has a similar design to a pop-up reflector, so it can fold down to a much smaller size, making it much easier to drop in your camera bag.

Tips

- If you're using center-weighted or multi-area metering you need to make sure that the gray card fills the frame, so the exposure reading isn't affected by anything else; spot metering is a more precise option.

- With a handheld lightmeter you need to hold the meter fairly close to the card to get an accurate reading, but take care not to cast any shadows on the card as you do so.

- Your gray card doesn't need to be in the same place as your subject, just under the same lighting conditions, so if you want to photograph a distant sunlit landscape, for example, you simply need to ensure the gray card is in a similarly sunlit area.

- Sunlit green grass has approximately the same reflectance as a gray card.

Below: A light reading taken from a gray card won't be affected by a subject's brightness, allowing you to more accurately determine the amount of reflected light. The main thing to ensure is that the card is in the same light as your subject and that your metering pattern isn't larger than the card (spot metering is the ideal option).

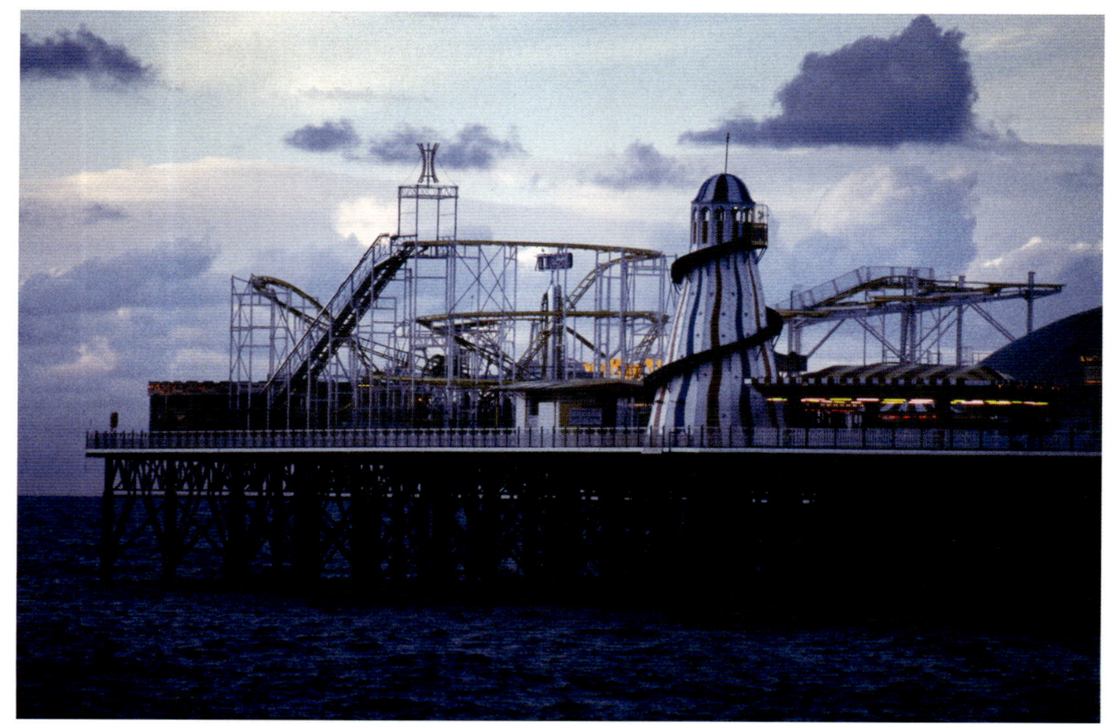

"Digital" Polaroid

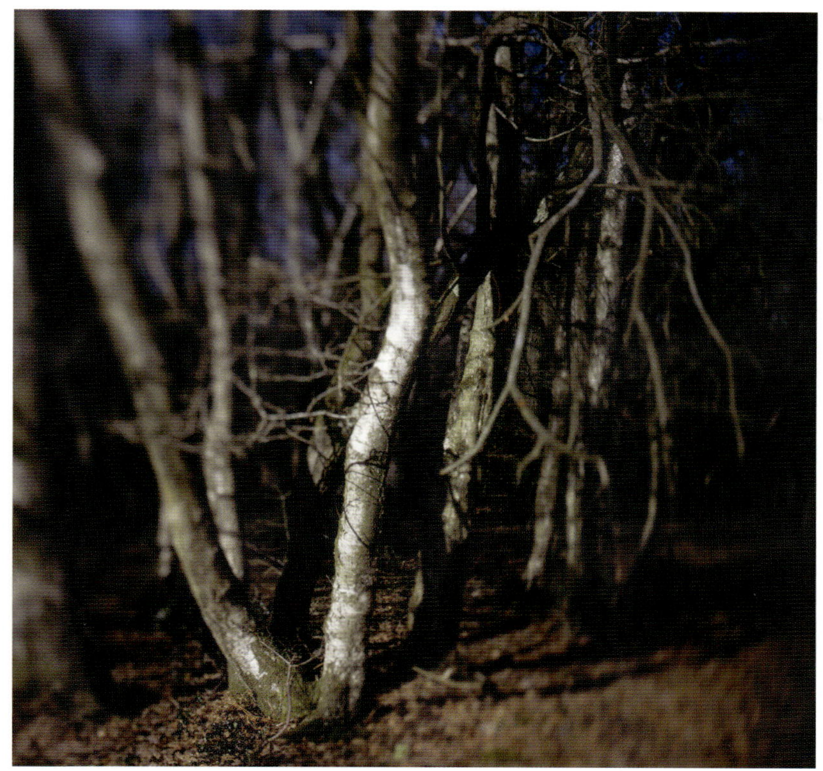

Left: Using large-format film is expensive, especially since the peel-apart film from Polaroid and Fujifilm was discontinued, preventing photographers from proofing their shots. In this instance, the simple solution was to use my digital SLR as a lightmeter, using playback and the histogram to ensure that I got the exposure I wanted.

In the past, a lot of pro photographers shooting medium- or large-format transparency film would use instant Polaroid (or Fujifilm's FP-range of instant packfilm) to check the exposure, lighting, focus, and framing of a shot before committing to film. This meant that when the (more expensive) film went to the lab the photographer could be pretty confident they had nailed the shot.

Today, peel-apart film has been discontinued by both Polaroid and Fujifilm, but a handful of diehard fans are trying to bring it back. For now though there is an alternative: use a digital camera instead. It's not a perfect replacement—you won't be able to check the focus or framing, for example—but if you've got a DSLR or mirrorless camera you can at least use it to check your lighting and take advantage of the histogram to guide your exposure. Simply fit a comparable focal length to the lens on your film camera, set the same ISO as you're using for your film, and use your "digital Polaroid" to set up your shot. Finally, transfer the settings to your medium- or large-format camera and go ahead and shoot your film.

Of course, some hardcore film shooters will say this is cheating, but it's not that different to shooting half a dozen Polaroids to get things right: it's simply using the tools that are available to you to ensure that you get the shot you want.

Tips

- If you're shooting transparency film, set your digital camera to a high-saturation, high-contrast picture mode to better emulate the dynamic range of your film.

- If you're going to use filters, fit them to your digital camera so that the filter is taken into account when you make your exposure reading. When you do this you don't have to concern yourself with things like filter factors (see page 110).

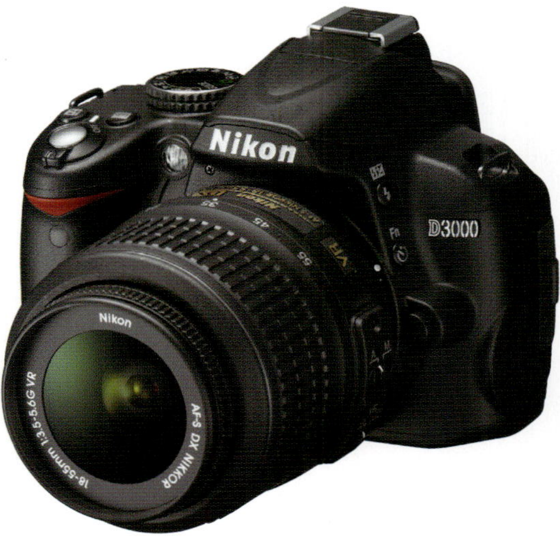

Left: Older entry-level DSLRs make great lightmeters: a pre-owned D3000 like this will cost you less than a good handheld meter, but offers spot, center-weighted, and multi-area metering, as well as instant playback and a histogram. The only downside is it can feel a bit like cheating when things become so easy; it's not really in the spirit of shooting film.

Reciprocity Failure

Exposure is usually based on the reciprocal relationship between the shutter speed and the aperture, which is measured in stops. Increasing either one of these controls by 1 stop doubles the amount of light reaching the film, while decreasing either by 1 stop halves the amount of light. Having this "rule" in place tells you that if you increase the shutter speed by 1 stop you need to decrease the aperture by 1 stop to maintain the same exposure overall, and there's a direct, and consistent, relationship between the two. In this way an exposure can be made and you can tweak your settings to get the shot you want.

Or can you? The problem with film is that this reciprocal relationship only holds true to a certain point. When exposure times become very long, the film effectively becomes less sensitive, because of the small amount of light reaching it. And when this happens, the exposure required increases exponentially, rather than following the "normal" rules of reciprocity. Consequently, long exposures need to be even longer and the usually sound theory of stops and doubling heads out of the door. This is known as reciprocity failure.

The issue is compounded by the fact that reciprocity failure affects different films at different exposure times, and will require different exposure increases—so there's no single formula that can be applied across the board. Fujifilm's Provia 100F doesn't need adjusting for reciprocity failure until exposure times reach 4 minutes, for example, but the same company's Fujicolor Pro 400H color negative film is affected at just 4 sec. Therefore you need to look at the manufacturer's data sheet to find out when reciprocity failure occurs and how to overcome it for your film. With black-and-white film, the solution is usually to extend the exposure time by a certain amount (and possibly reduce the development time), whereas color film will often require an increase in exposure and the use of color correction filters (see page 114), particularly if you're shooting transparency film.

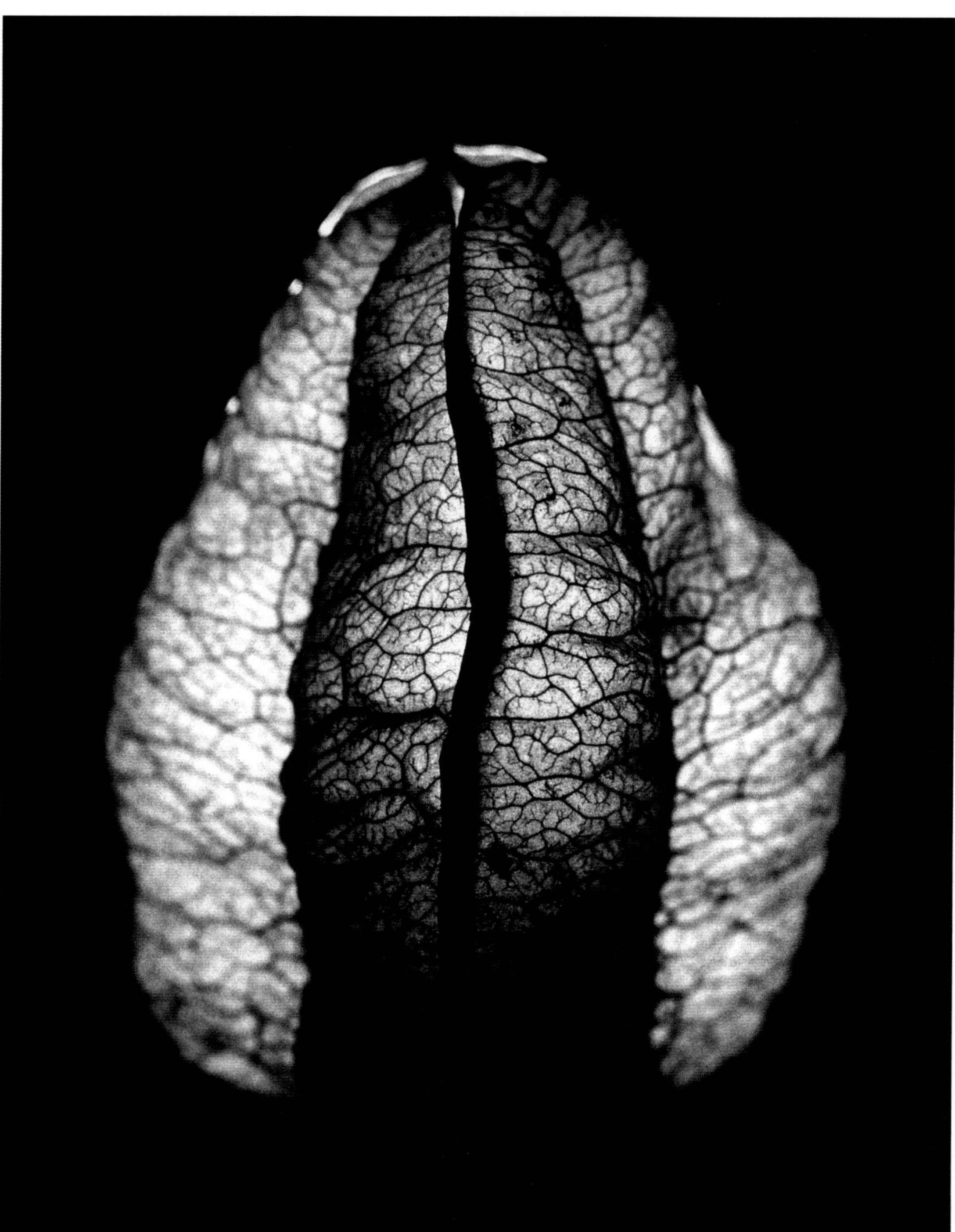

- Reciprocity failure is not a problem with digital camera sensors, only film.

- Reciprocity failure can also happen when exposure times are very short. But exposures that are measured in ten thousandths of a second tend to be restricted to specialist scientific imaging and are unavailable on "normal" cameras.

- Pinhole photography is often affected by reciprocity failure, due to the inherently long exposure times.

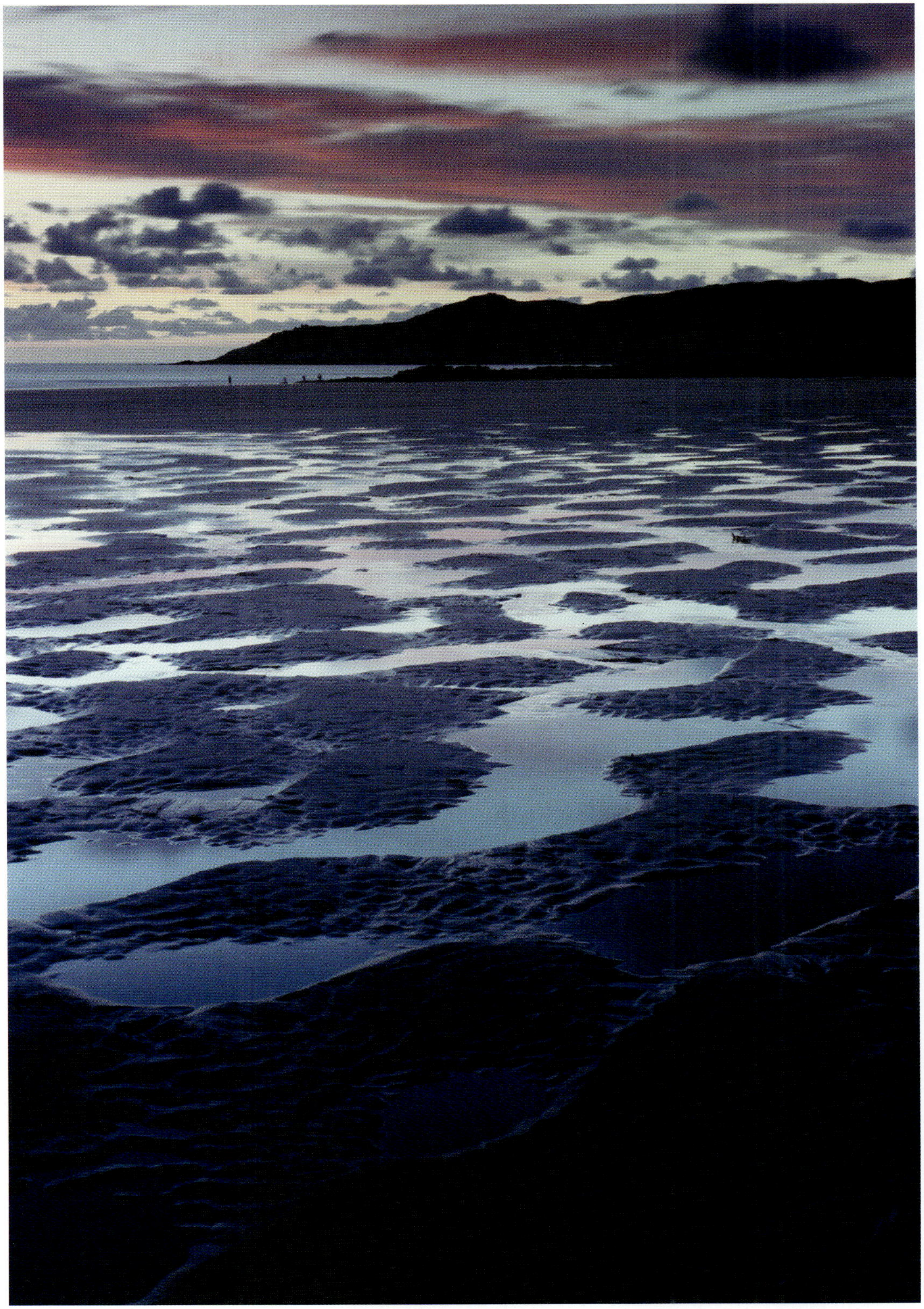

Right: This exposure was made just after sunset, with only a small amount of light in the sky. Using a small aperture of f/16 and a slow-speed film led to a long exposure time, which in turn led to reciprocity failure.

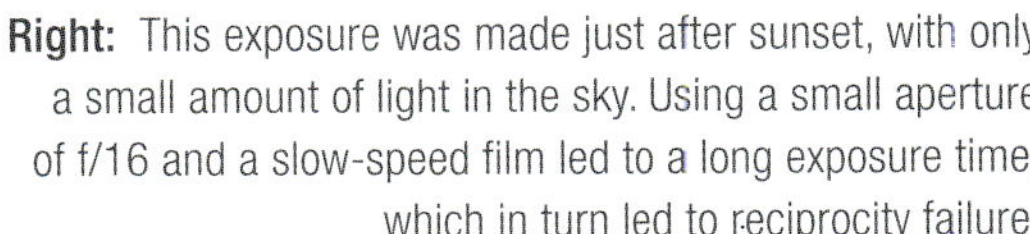

Left: Reciprocity failure isn't just encountered when you shoot at night; depending on the film it often needs to be considered whenever exposure times are longer than a second or two. In this instance I had placed this seedpod over a small hole cut in a sheet of black card, which was placed on a lightbox. To make the pod "glow" from the weak light source required an exposure time of several seconds, which was then extended to combat reciprocity failure.

Profile: Paul Thompson

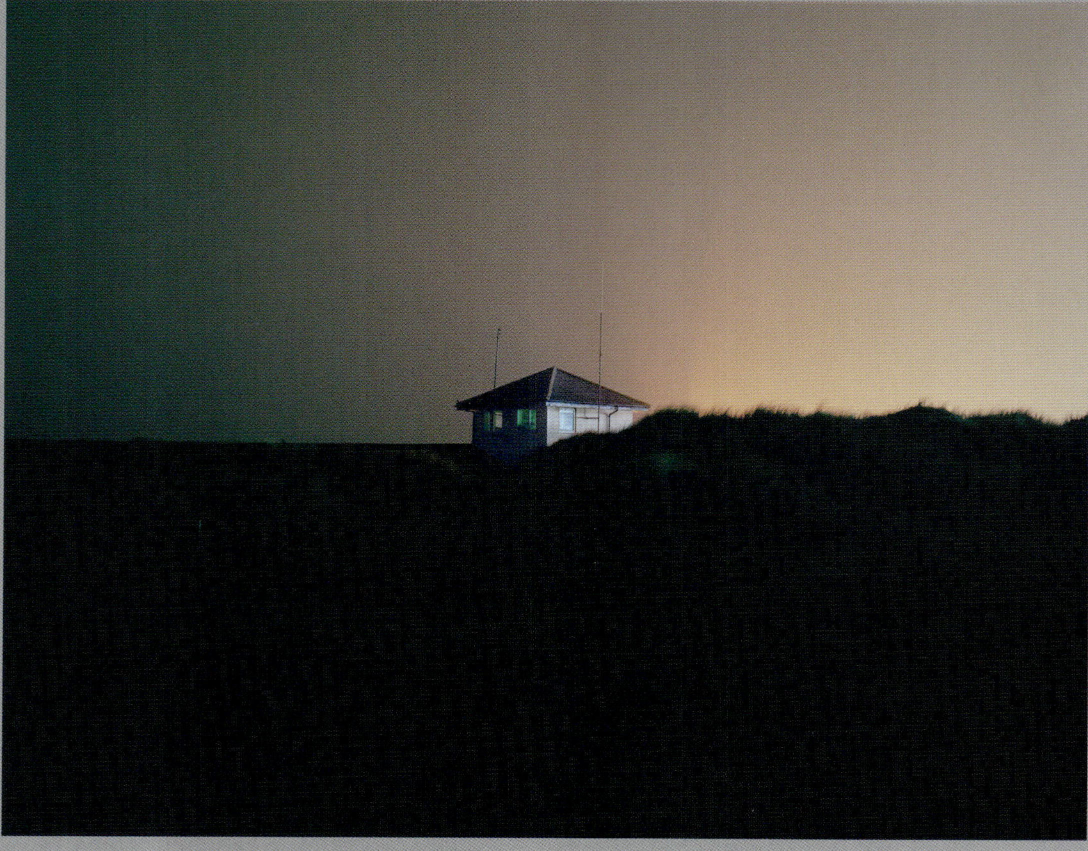

Right:
Southport #01
12:04–02:36

Q) How would you describe your *Moonlight* series?

A) *Moonlight* is a lonely labor of love. I have spent more than four years venturing to the English, Italian, Scottish, and Welsh coasts on dark nights, with only the moon to light my way. These are photographs of places, but they are also images of time passing. I only shoot my *Moonlight* pictures during the full moon, so I have to wait each month for its arrival, and over the course of these pivotal midnight hours the tides come and go, the clouds shift positions, and the skies might grow stormy at any moment.

The shutter remains open, and the camera records all the details that are too short-lived for the human eye to register. I use large-format film, and I am lucky if I get one image in a month.

Q) What camera do you use?

A) A 5x4 Wista field camera.

Q) Why shoot on film?

A) When I was studying photography and working as an assistant it was at the "crossover" stage between film and digital: my college years were spent shooting film and printing in the darkroom, but when I started assisting photographers they were starting to switch over to digital. Part of the reason I shoot film is because it was one of the factors that attracted me to photography in the first place; to be honest, I have no connection with or love for digital cameras.

Shooting on film makes you consider what you're doing, but it also encourages you to use your gut instincts while you're on location. If I was shooting on a digital camera I'm sure I would be tempted to shoot multiple options, which for me normally ends up in a weaker image. For example, I shoot all of my personal work on 5x4 film and

when I'm shooting a portrait I'll shoot 10 sheets of film at most, so I either get it right or I get it wrong. When I shoot portraits commercially with a digital camera I'll shoot hundreds of images per portrait to make sure I get the shot, but I'm not sure it makes for a better image. I guess my final answer would be why not shoot on film! That's what photography is all about after all.

Q) What film do you use? Is there a particular reason for this choice?
A) I shoot Kodak Porta 160 and 400, because I think the fine grain on it is fantastic.

Q) How do you determine your exposures?
A) Getting the exposures right requires a lot of trail and error. You can meter it to a certain extent, but there are still a lot of factors that affect the end result, mainly because the exposure times are so long. I can start with overcast conditions and decide the exposure based on that, but the cloud might break midway through, and I can have moonlight shining directly on the scene, so I need to modify my exposure or even cover the lens for a while. I never have the actual moon within the frame, but it still affects the exposure. Obviously, reciprocity failure comes into play, so I also have

to take that into consideration; I usually end up with an exposure time somewhere in the region of one to three hours.

Q) What would be your top tip for anyone looking to shoot long night exposures on film?
A) Wrap up warm!

Multiple Exposures

Multiple exposures have had something of a renaissance in recent years, largely thanks to image-editing software making it exceptionally easy to combine different shots, and digital cameras having increasingly sophisticated in-camera multi-shot options with on-screen previews of how your combinations will look. However, you could argue that digital tools make it too easy to create multiple exposures, and that the results are too slick, too polished, too perfect. That's definitely not the case with film, which is perhaps why shooting multiple exposures on film is so much more rewarding: the challenge is greater, but so too is the sense of achievement when things eventually come together.

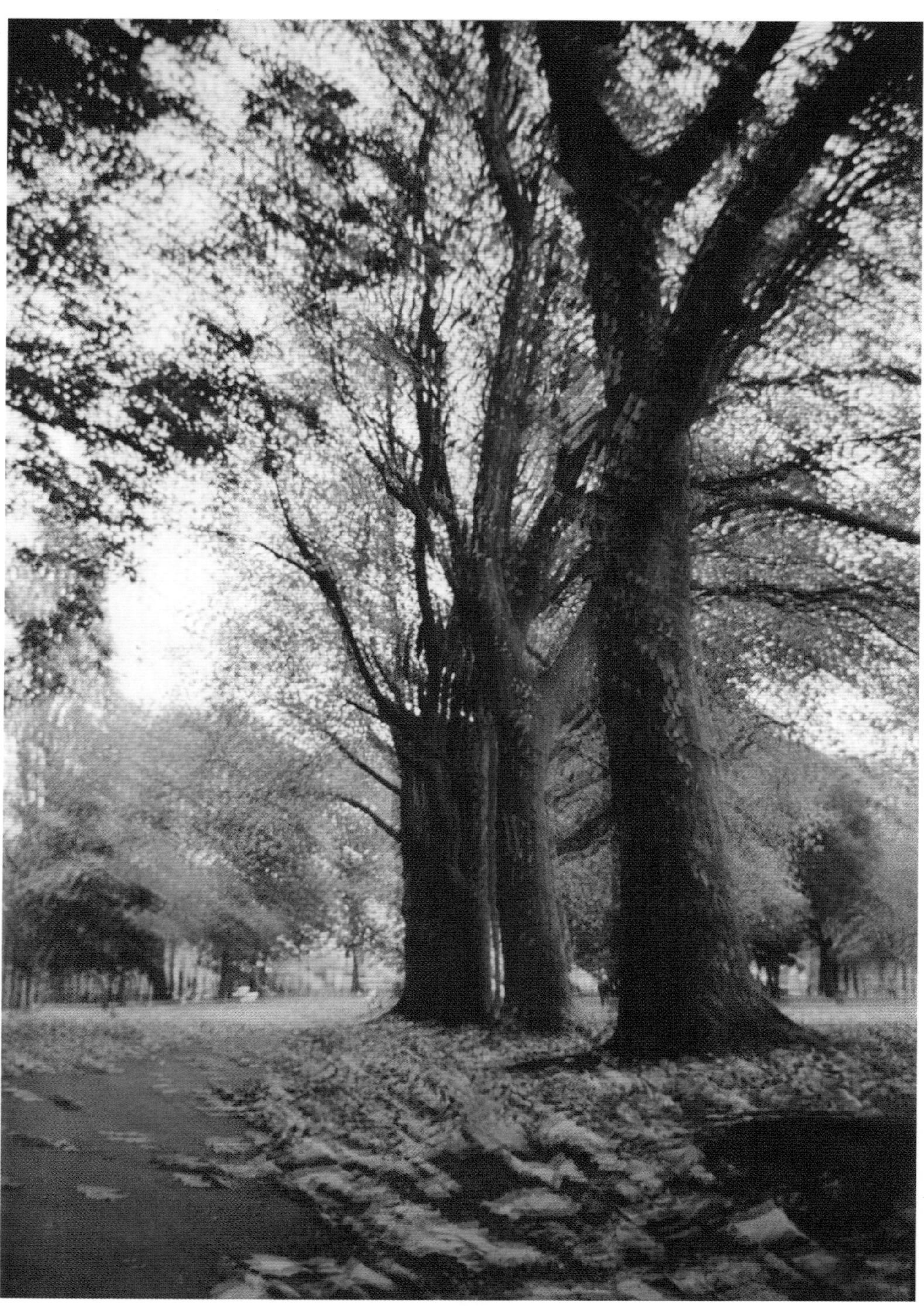

Right: This was taken on a box camera with a fixed shutter speed of around 1/100 sec. and a fixed aperture of f/16. The ISO 400 film I had loaded wasn't fast enough so I used multiple exposures to build up to the correct brightness, firing the shutter four times to lift the exposure by 2 stops. Shooting handheld gave the image a "jittery" look.

Tips

- With a lot of small- and medium-format cameras the film-winding and shutter-cocking mechanisms are interlinked, so to get the shutter ready to take a shot you need to wind the film on. For multiple exposures you ideally need a camera where the two processes are done independently, or there's a multiple exposure function (as in some advanced SLRs).

- It's possible to shoot multiple exposures with a manual SLR with a linked winding/shutter system. After exposing your first frame, hold the camera's film rewind button when you wind on: this releases the take-up spool, so you can wind on to cock the shutter, without pulling the film through the camera.

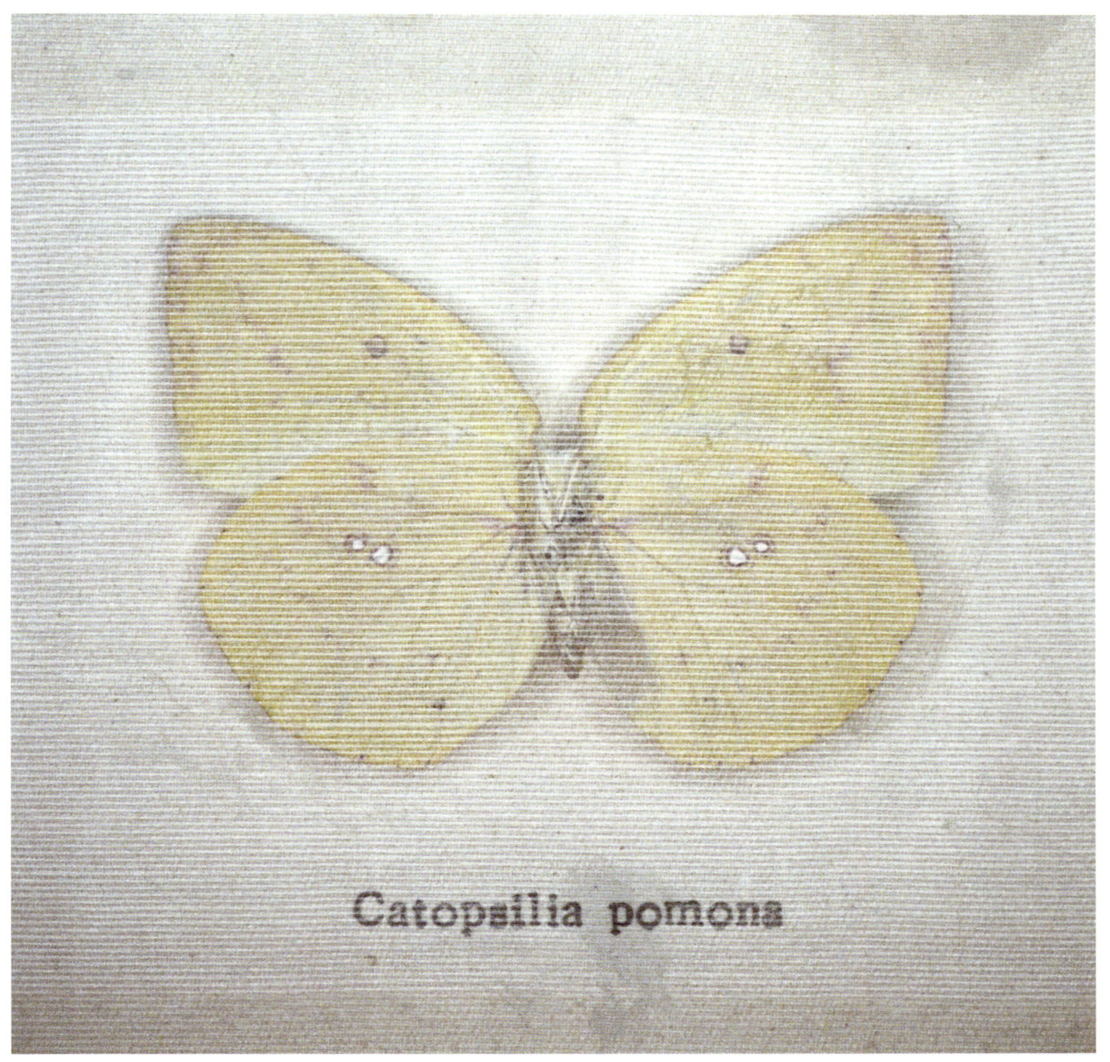

Same Frame Exposures

The classic approach to multiple exposures is to work a frame at a time, shooting multiple times on a single frame before moving on to the next one. This technique can be used in myriad ways, but the thing to remember is that you can only add to an exposure. Think of it as if you are starting with a black frame and adding light. As you add light, the exposure becomes brighter, both as a whole and for individual parts of the scene. If you keep adding light, then parts of the image will turn white, and any subsequent exposure to this area will not be registered; add enough light and the entire frame will be white. This means two things:

• Your second (and subsequent) exposure will only add to areas in the first (or previous) exposure that are darker than it. Your second shot can't add midtone detail to a bright highlight in the first exposure, for example, but it can add midtone detail to shadow areas.

• When your multiple shots are combined they need to reach the "ideal" overall exposure (the exposure that would be correct for a single shot). This means you need to make each exposure darker than you would normally, so they build up to the correct end result, as shown in the grid below.

Above: I'd tried shooting this disintegrating mounted common emigrant (*Catopsilia pomona*) butterfly a number of times, but a "straight" shot was just too clean. For this version I used my Nikon F100's multiple exposure mode to combine the butterfly with the fabric backing of an antique picture frame, which has added a textural layer.

Right: This grid shows the adjustment needed when you shoot multiple exposure images. You can use your camera's exposure compensation dial to make the adjustment, or manually adjust the aperture or shutter speed (depending on whether depth of field or motion control is most important). Remember that you need to make the exposure darker, not brighter, so set a smaller aperture or a faster shutter speed (or a combination of both).

ADJUSTMENTS FOR MULTIPLE EXPOSURES	
NUMBER OF EXPOSURES	EXPOSURE ADJUSTMENT (STOPS)
1	0
2	-1
3	-1½
4	-2
6	-2½
8	-3
12	-3½
16	-4

Double-Loaded Film

A fun multiple exposure exercise is to shoot the same roll of film more than once, so you run it through your camera from start to finish multiple times, with each pass adding another layer of exposures. Unlike the previous method, which relies on you concentrating on your multiple exposures a frame at a time, this one is more unpredictable and you will never be quite sure of the results you will get. The process is simple:

Tips

- You can reload and reshoot your film multiple times—just adjust the ISO by the number of stops detailed on page 87. However, be aware that it's easy to end up with a mess if you shoot too many times.

- Consider setting a theme for each of your "passes" of the film. This could be complementary, so you shoot your layers with a common color theme, for example, or it could be contrasting: hot and cold perhaps. In any case, creating a link between the images can strengthen your work.

- Although this method can be used with medium-format roll film, doing so means that you will have to manually re-spool your film when you've shot it for the first time. It's a lot easier to shoot on 35mm.

COLLABORATE

Shooting the same roll twice can make a great collaborative project, where one photographer shoots the roll and then another one shoots it. This can work particularly well if the photographers work "blind," so neither one knows what the other is shooting, although setting an overarching theme is a good way to connect the layers.

1 Load up your film.

2 If you're going to be shooting the film twice, set the ISO 1 stop faster than its actual speed (so rate an ISO 100 film at ISO 200, for example). Dial this into your camera or set it on your lightmeter.

3 Shoot your film at the revised ISO until you get to the end of the roll; at this point you will have a single shot on each frame, all 1 stop underexposed.

4 Rewind your film. Most automatic cameras rewind film all the way into the cassette, in which case you will need to use a film retriever to pull out the end. If you're using a manual 35mm SLR rewind the film until you hear the end of it click free from the take-up spool (the rewind crank will lose resistance). Don't wind any further or you will pull the film all the way back into the cassette.

5 Reload the film as if it's a fresh roll. Reshoot the film (again at an ISO that's 1 stop higher).

6 Once shot, process your film as normal. If you're using a lab, make sure that you tell them what you've done, so they don't think it's a mistake (this is especially important if you're asking for prints or scans!).

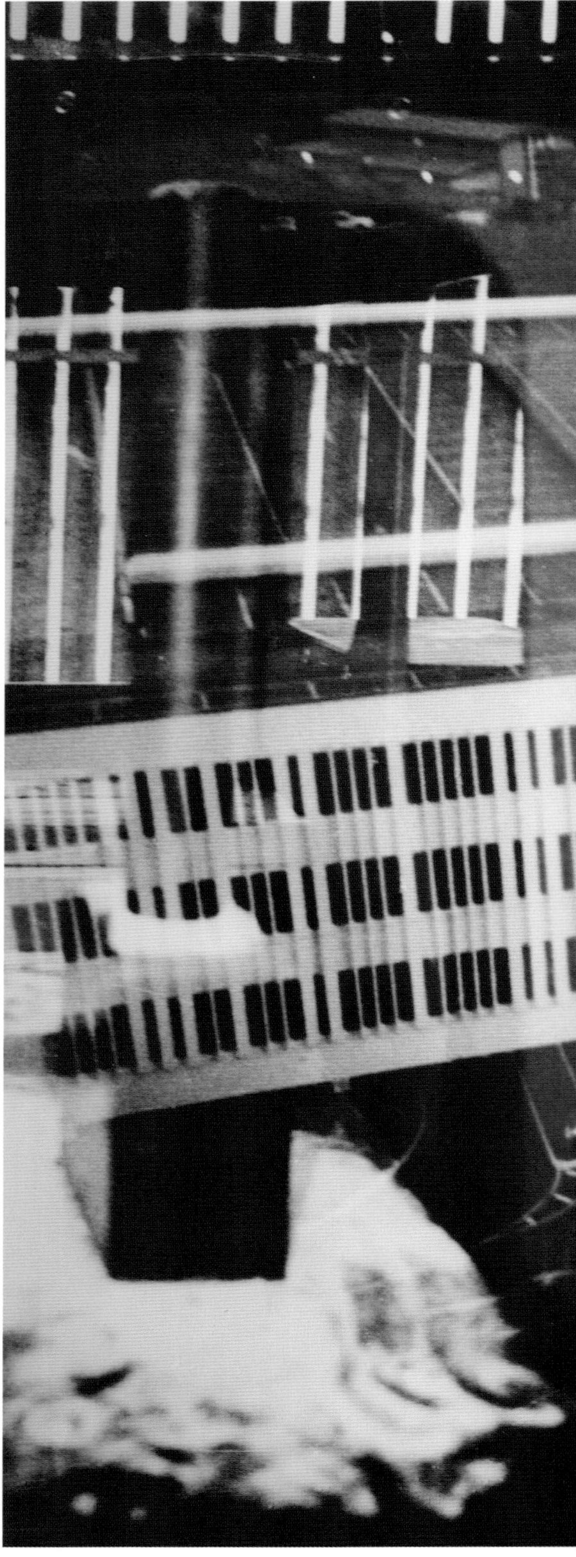

Right: Serendipity plays a huge part when you double-load film. From an entire roll of 35mm film this is the only frame that was "interesting," thanks to the juxtaposition of my son in a toy tractor and a parking lot; the fact that the frames are misaligned (the stripe down the center is the gap between two frames) adds to the graphic look, as does a monochrome treatment of the scanned multiple exposure.

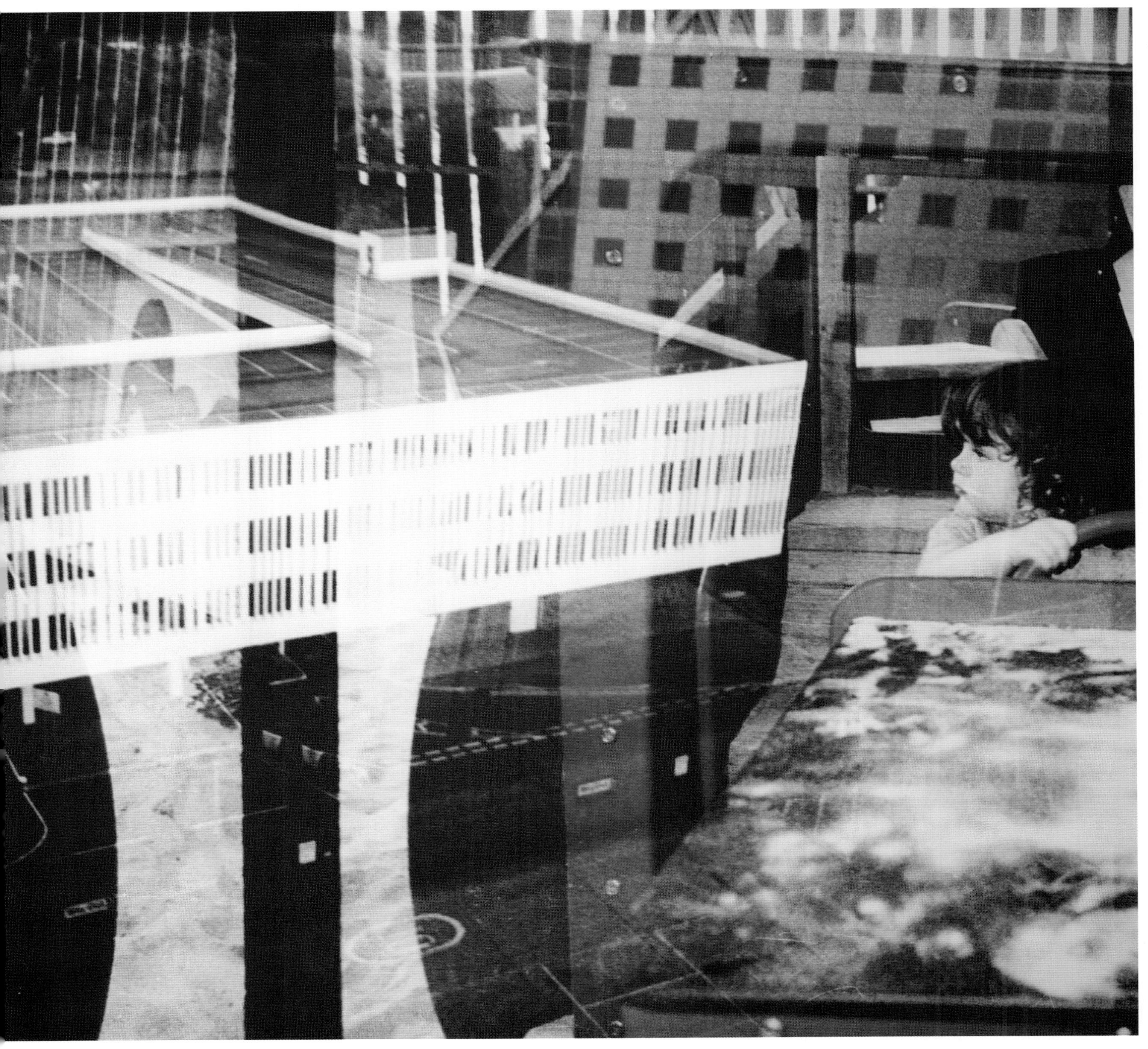

Profile: Wendy Laurel

BIOGRAPHY

Wendy Laurel is a film photographer based on Maui, Hawaii, who embraces the imperfect. She is more interested in the feeling you get when you look at an image than making sure that it is technically perfect. Wendy's work has been published worldwide and she is also the creator of *Seeing Double*, an in-depth PDF tutorial on creating double exposures, which is available to purchase via her website.

wendylaurel.com

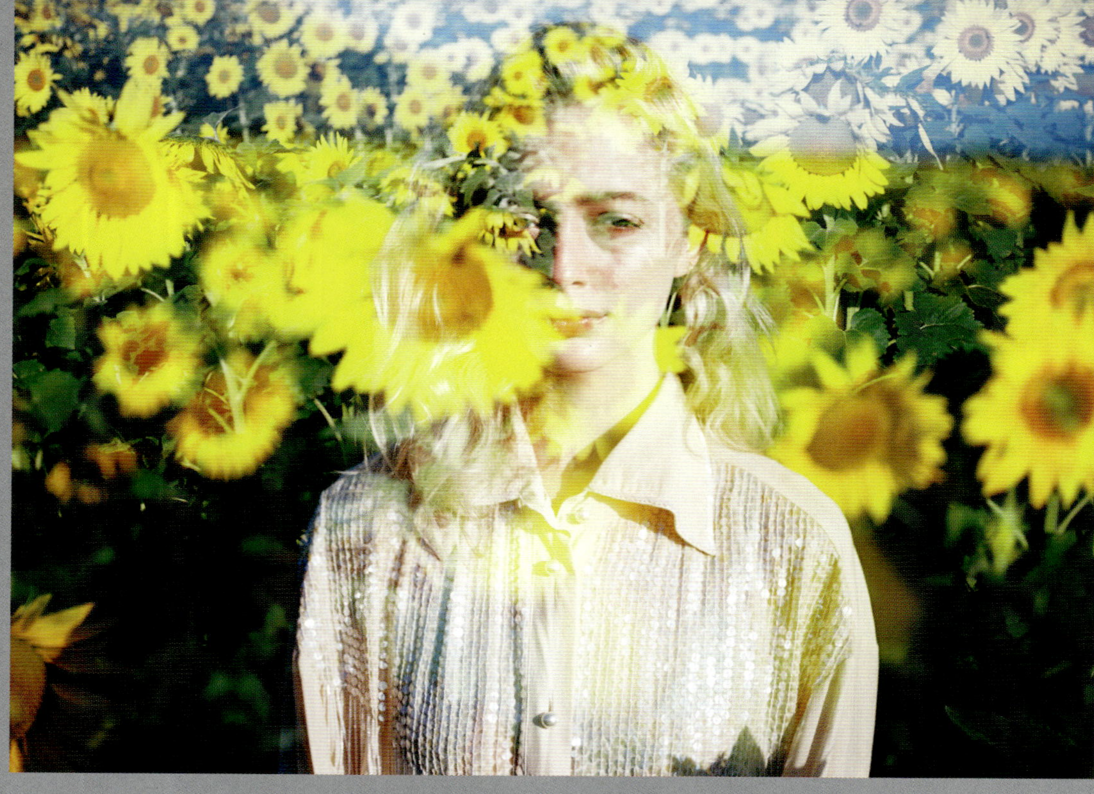

Right: I made this double exposure during a shoot for a swimwear and sportswear company, which took place in a sunflower field.

Q) How would you describe your work?
A) I shoot weddings, families, and commercial work, and use multiple exposures for all of them (although not all of the time). The overriding theme is "creative, colorful, honest, and joyful."

Q) What cameras do you use?
A) I have tons of cameras, including Contax 645, Pentax 645 and Mamiya 6 medium-format cameras, a Canon EOS-1V 35mm SLR, and Lomo LC-W and Fujifilm Klasse W 35mm compacts—and that's just a small selection of them! One of the great things about film is that there is such a wide choice of cameras available, and they are all different.

Q) Why shoot on film?
A) I love film because of how it looks. Film captures the colors as I see them and handles light really well, especially backlight. The colors look real and beautiful and I am able to capture a deep luminosity on film that feels true to me. Also, I love doing everything in-camera, in that frame, in that moment—I would rather be out shooting than editing photos on a computer.

Q) What film(s) do you use?
A) My favorite film is Kodak Ektar 100, which is a color negative film. I use it because the colors are amazingly vivid and really capture what a blue-sky day looks like here in Hawaii.

Q) How do you determine your exposures?
A) I use a lightmeter, although for sunny days (which is the norm where I live) I pretty much have those exposure settings memorized!

Q) What would be your top tip for anyone looking to shoot multiple exposures on film?
A) Don't be afraid to try new things, just experiment and remember to have fun.

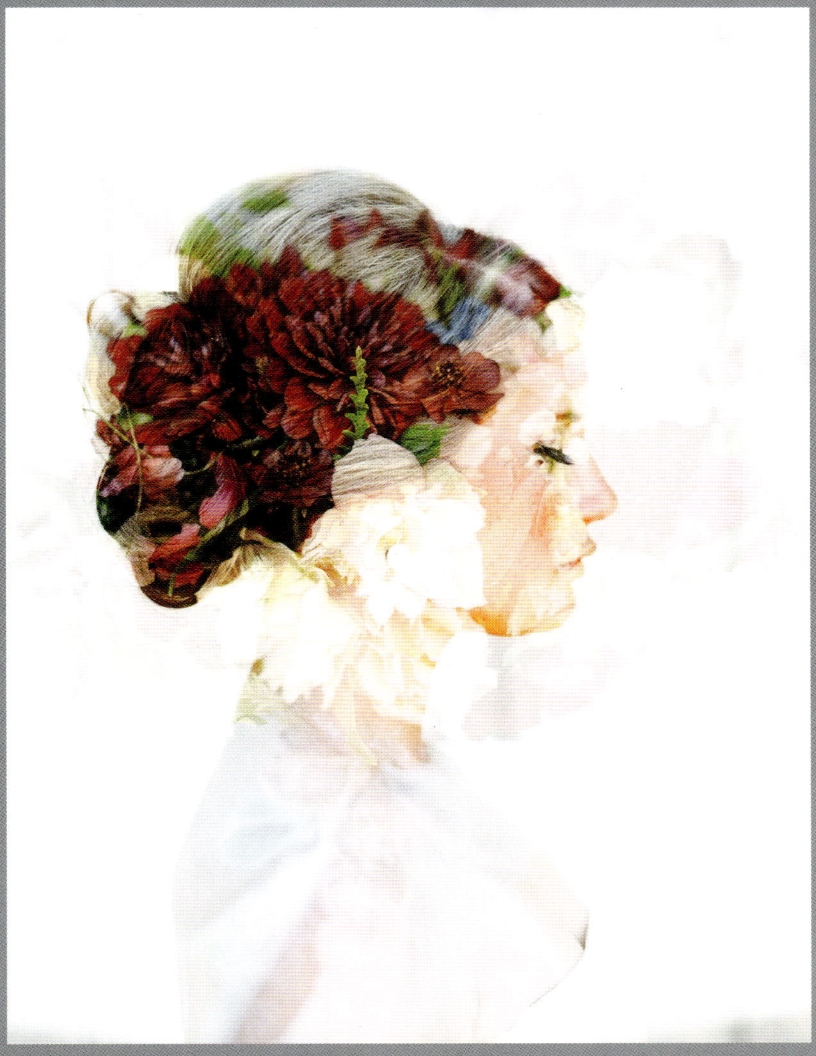

Above: I shot this double exposure during an editorial
wedding shoot. I filled the girl's profile with a shot of the
bridal bouquet flowers.

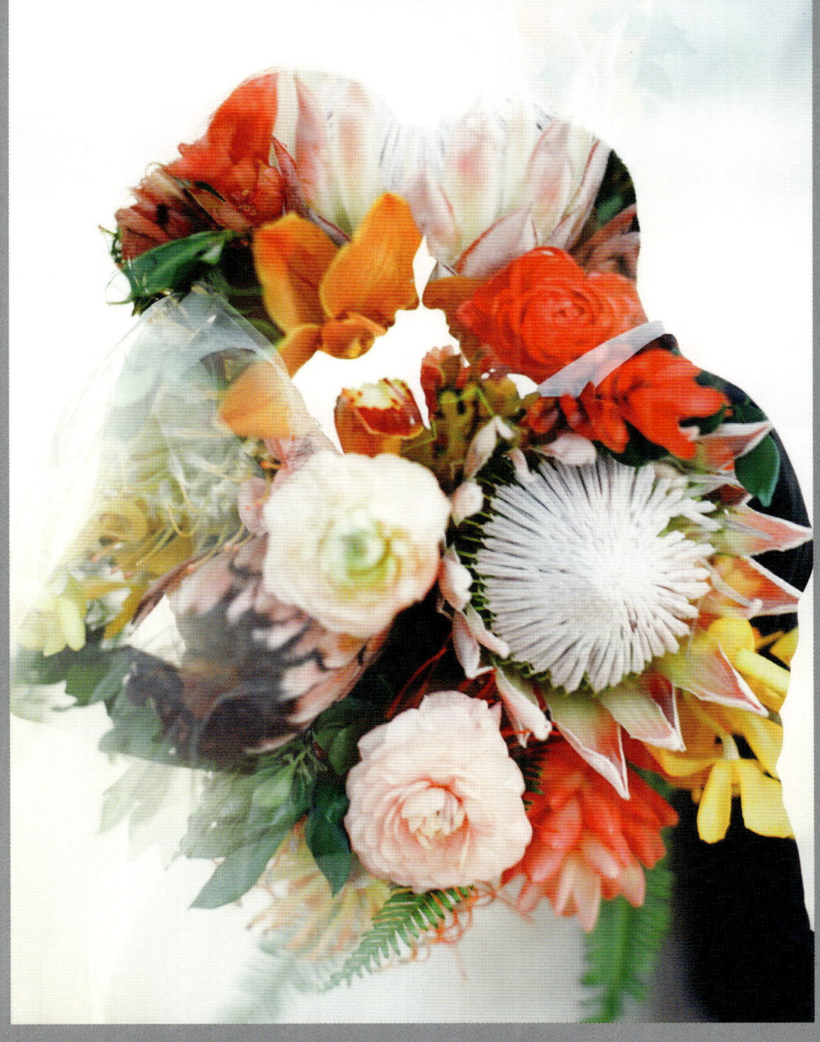

Above: I was taking pictures of a bride and groom on the
beach on Maui when I came up with the idea for this double
exposure. I shot the couple in silhouette first, then exposed
again with a close-up of her bridal bouquet.

Chapter 4
Flash

We've already seen how the lack of instant feedback makes exposing film accurately challenging, but it's doubly difficult when you're using flash. Unless you're shooting medium- or large-format film and using Polaroid to proof your shots you often cannot see what effect the burst of light is having on your subject, making it hard to know for sure how your final image will look, both in terms of where the light is falling and its impact on your exposure. It's hardly surprising that a lot of film photographers tend to shy away from flash, treating it as a mysterious "dark art" that should be avoided, rather than a technical or creative solution that should be embraced. In this chapter we will redress the balance.

Right: This close-up shot of a tiny skull was lit with a macro ringflash. However, rather than attach it to the lens I positioned the flash above the skull, where it acted as a soft top-light, and triggered it via a sync cord.

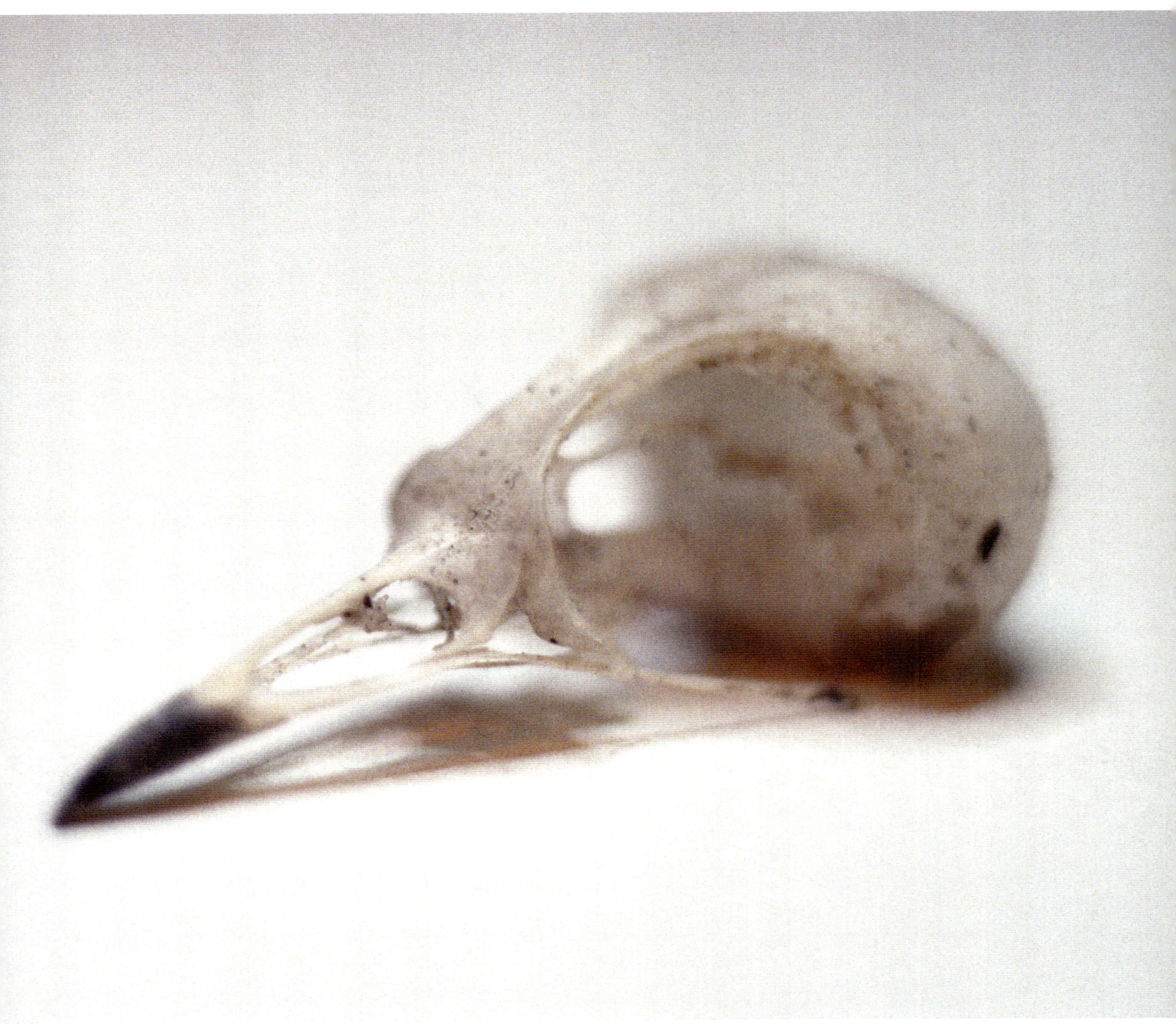

Flash Essentials

The first thing to appreciate when it comes to film photography is that there are lots more portable, battery-powered flash units available than there are for digital cameras. This is because the technology didn't necessarily need to be as sophisticated, so just like lenses, a host of third-party manufacturers stepped in to make a bewildering array of flashes. These generally fall into two categories that we'll focus on in this chapter: hotshoe-mounted units and larger, "hammerhead" flashes. We will explore the practicalities of using them—and the various levels of control on offer—on the following pages, but before we do it's worth running through a few fundamental flash properties. These include some important considerations if you're planning on buying a used flash for you film camera.

Dedicated Flashes

Most flashes designed for digital cameras are "dedicated" to a system, with TTL (Through The Lens) control making flash a point-and-shoot exercise. With film cameras, this is the exception, rather than the rule. While some of the later automatic 35mm SLRs offer this level of control with a compatible flash, most manual cameras—across all formats—do not. That isn't to say dedicated flashes don't exist for manual SLRs, just that they are not the integrated tools that we know and love today, so you often need to work a little harder and think a little more about what you're doing. But the beauty of film (and digital for that matter) is that you don't necessarily need this level of sophistication. A flash that's dedicated to your camera and offers some sort of automation is convenient, for sure, but a manual flash with a bounce and zoom head you can trigger either from the camera's hotshoe or via a sync lead can also be used creatively. These are not only in plentiful supply, but exceptionally cheap to buy.

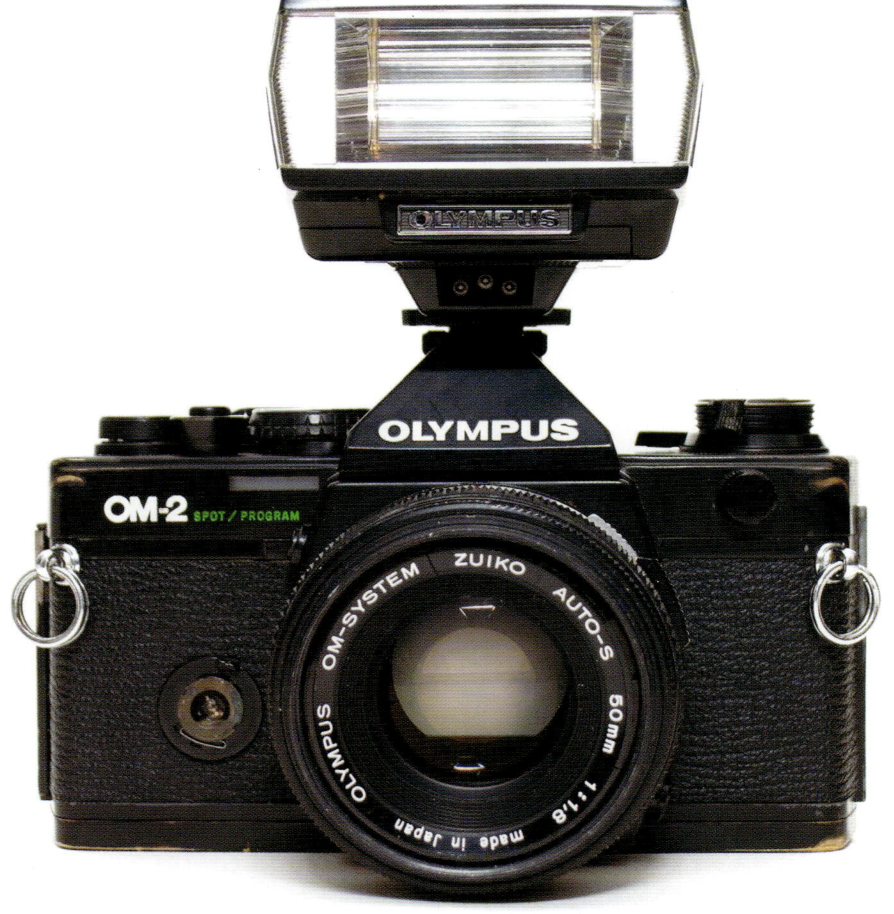

Right: The T20 was one of several flashes Olympus produced for its OM series of 35mm SLRs. With some of its cameras—including my bruised and battered OM2SP seen here—flash exposures could use "off-the-film" metering, which enabled the camera to end the flash exposure. Putting the camera in (partial) control was a forerunner to the TTL systems used today.

HAMMERHEAD FLASHES

Hammerhead flashes have almost completely disappeared in the digital age, replaced by powerful hotshoe-mounted units instead, but they were once the workhorse of professional wedding and portrait photographers the world over. Flashes such as the Metz 45 (seen below) are incredibly versatile for film photography, thanks to a combination of high power, wide-ranging control options, and off-camera positioning that gives the light a slight directionality. Because they aren't widely used for digital photography they are also a fraction of their original price.

However, be slightly wary about buying them online, as while the flashes themselves have stood the test of time, their NiCad (nickel cadmium) batteries almost certainly will not have and the modern NiMH (nickel-metal hydride) replacements are not cheap, so that bargain flash could quickly become expensive! Instead, look for a Metz 45 that comes with a battery cage that takes regular AA cells or even consider buying a flash bracket that can be used to transform any hotshoe-mounted flash into a similar off-camera tool.

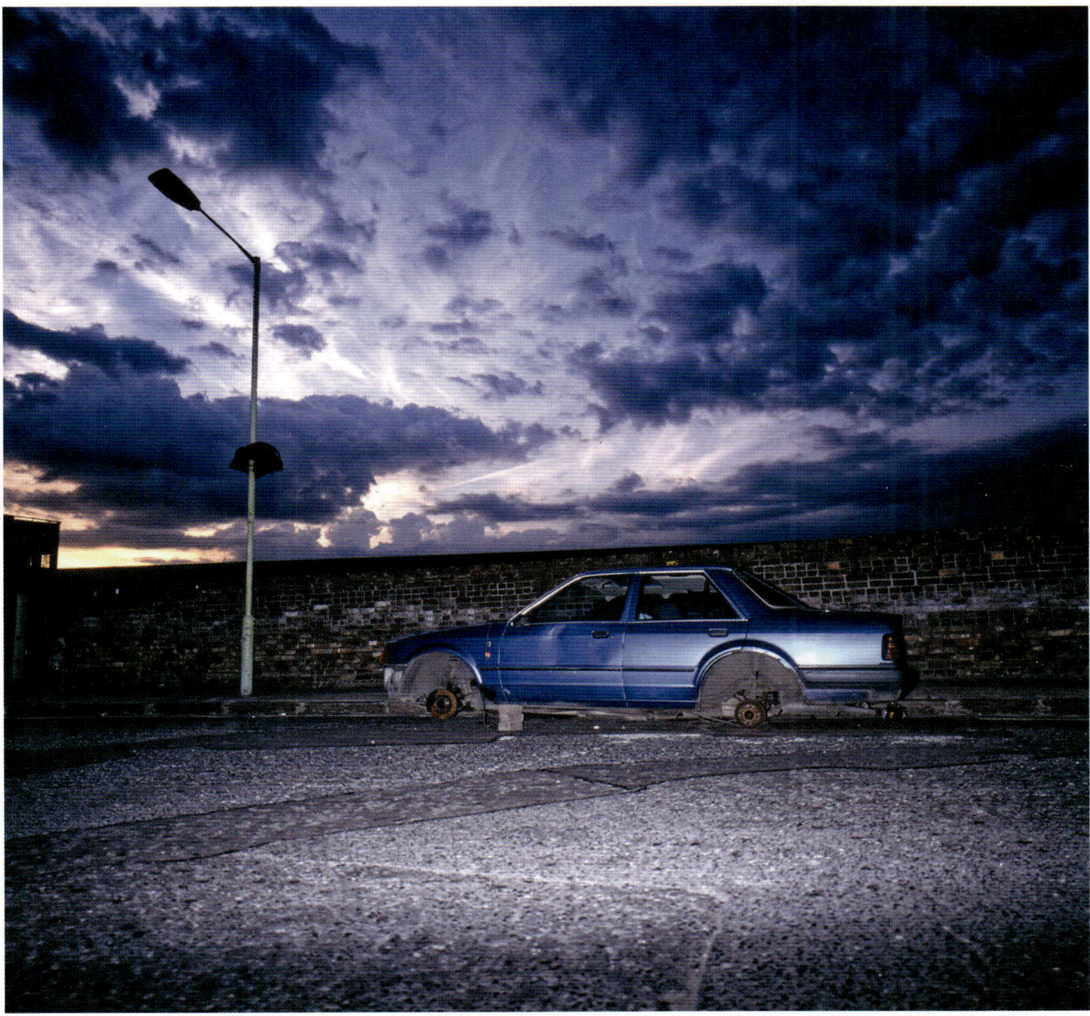

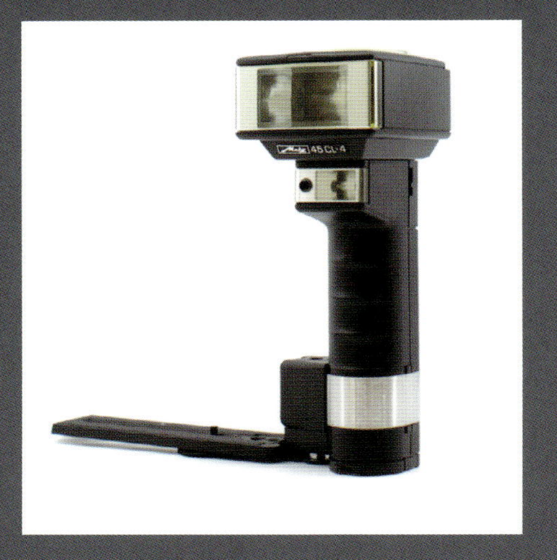

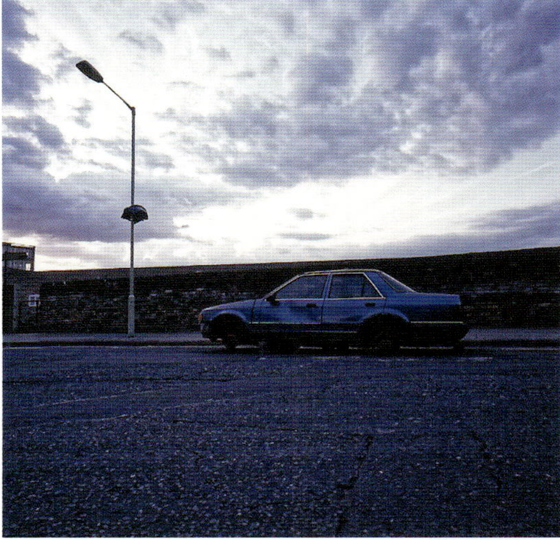

Left & above: Never underestimate how useful flash can be. Relying solely on the ambient light for this sunset shot resulted in a drab image with a washed out sky and flat contrast (left), but using a hammerhead flash meant that I could add plenty more drama and make the shot "pop" (above).

Flash Power

Every battery-powered flash has a guide number or GN. The technical purpose of this is to manually determine exposures, but more broadly it is used as an indication of the power of the flash. A GN usually comprises two parts: a distance (in feet and/or meters) and an ISO, so you might see a flash described as "GN 92ft/28m at ISO 100." We'll look at how that gets put to use on page 104, but for now just remember that the higher the GN, the more powerful the flash will be.

Tilt, Twist & Zoom

The "head" of the flash is the part with the plastic screen that the light comes out of. With some of the smallest and simplest flashes the head is a fixed, integral part of the flash body, so when you fit it on a camera it will point in exactly the same direction as the lens. However, get a flash with a bounce head and you can tilt it upward, to bounce the light from your flash off a ceiling or reflector held overhead, while a head that twists will allow you to turn your flash to the left or right and bounce the light off a wall. Some advanced flashes also feature a zoom head, which allows you to match the spread of light to the angle of view of your lens, optimizing the output of the flash.

Below: A flash with a head that can tilt and swivel lets you easily control the direction of the light, so that you can bounce it off a wall, ceiling, or even a reflector.

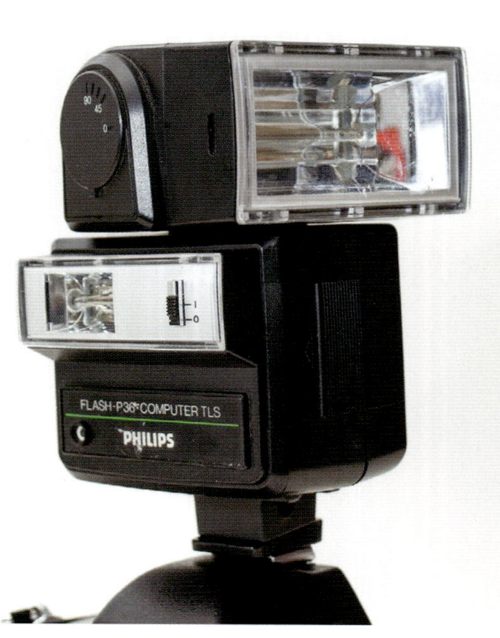

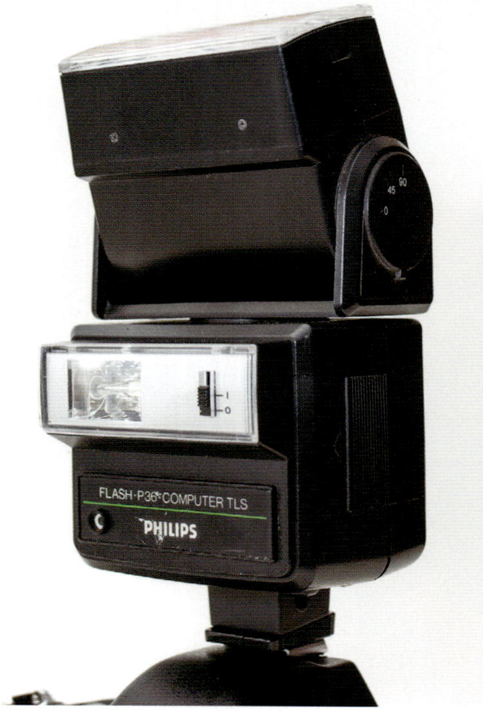

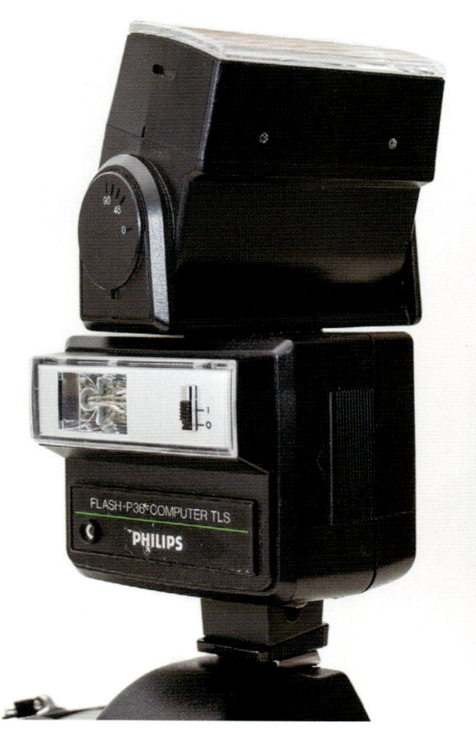

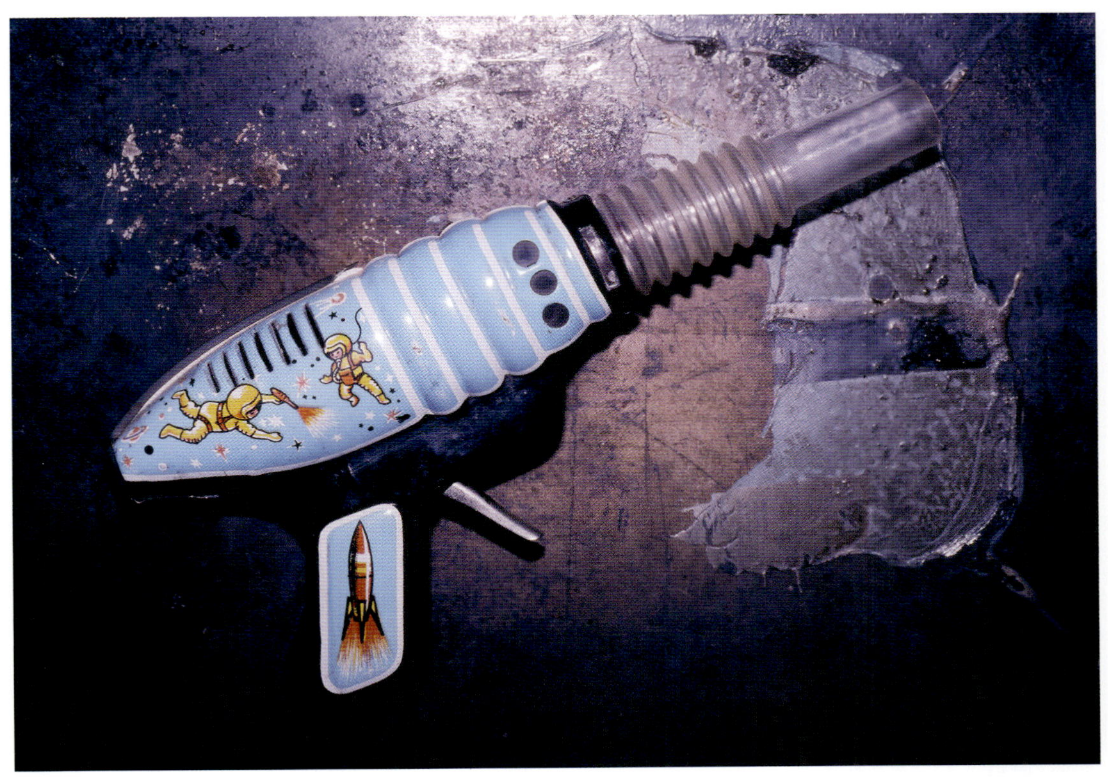

Bounce Flash

On-camera flash is a small, hard light source. Fitted to the camera's hotshoe, the light it produces will be direct and any shadows will be cast behind the subject making the light appear "flat." If you take the flash away from the camera (connecting it via a sync lead or remote trigger) you will be able to add some shadows to create a better sense of three dimensions in your subject, but because the flash is so small, the light it emits will produce dark, hard-edged shadows.

However, tilt it upward or turn it sideways to bounce it off a ceiling or wall and the light changes dramatically: not only does the direction change, creating much-needed shadows, but it becomes more diffuse, so those shadows are much softer. The only things you need to remember are to ensure that you bounce the light off a neutral-colored surface (white is ideal) to avoid coloring the light when it is reflected, and—if you are using auto or manual flash—to take into account the added distance the light needs to travel when it comes to determining the exposure.

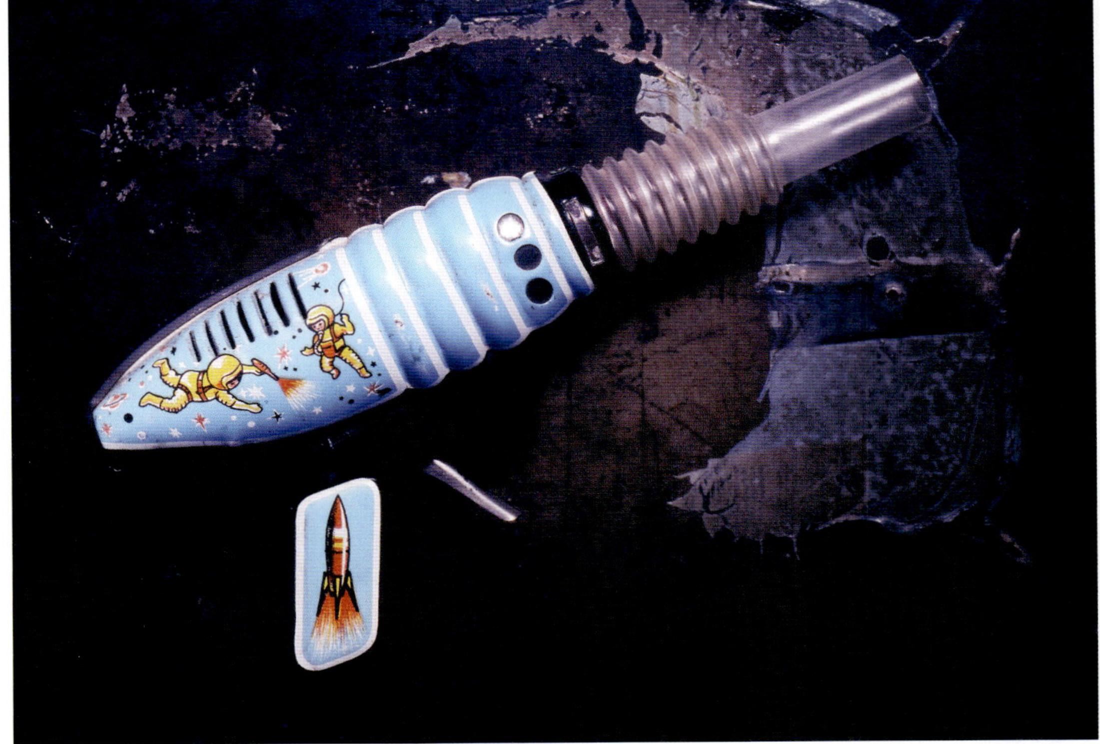

Left top: Direct flash. When the flash is aimed directly at the toy ray gun the light is harsh.

Left bottom: Bounce flash. Using a reflector to spread and soften the light produces a much better result.

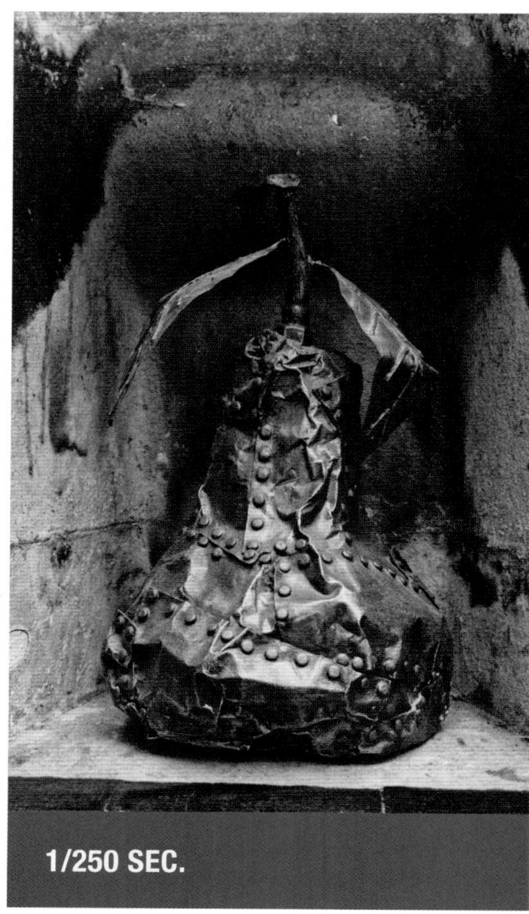

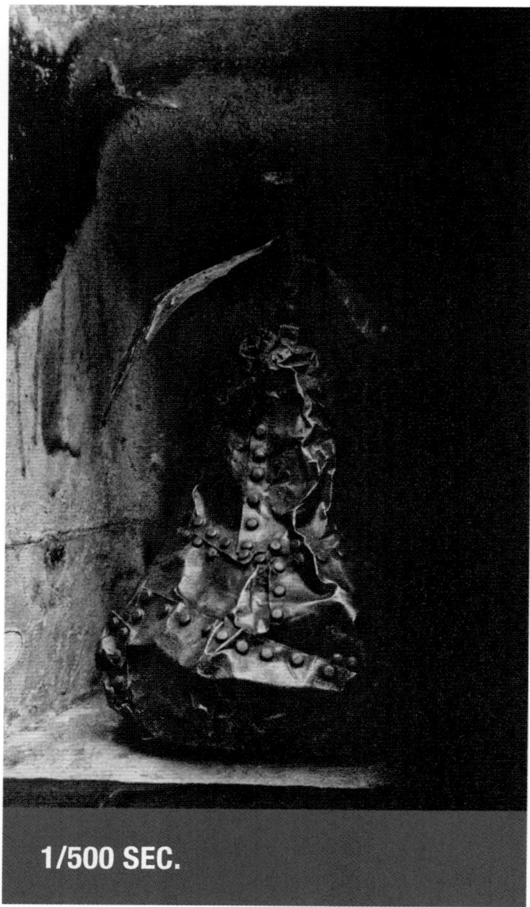

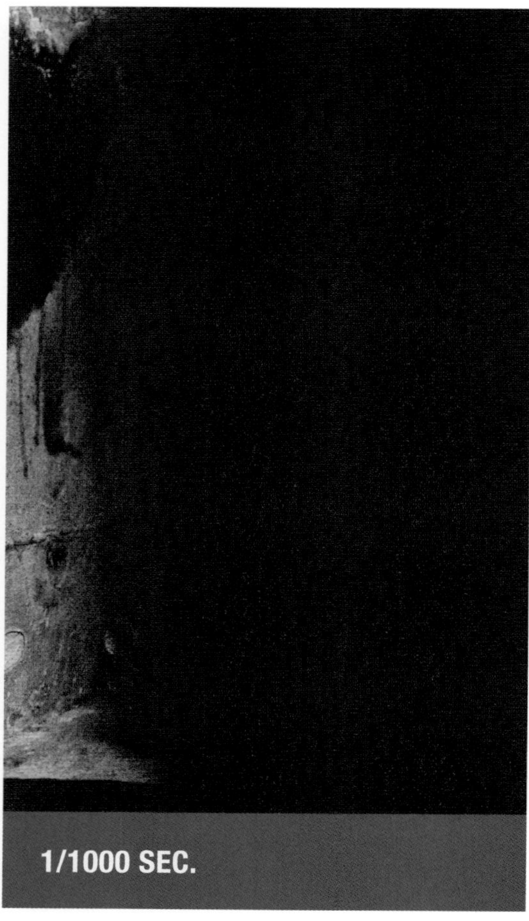

Above: As this sequence shows, it's important to be aware of your camera's sync speed when you're using flash. The sync speed of the Nikon F100 SLR I was using here is 1/250 sec., so setting the shutter speed at 1/250 sec. is "safe" and will give a full image. At faster shutter speeds, the image starts to get cut off, getting progressively worse as the exposure time reduces.

Sync Speed

Although the shutter speed doesn't affect the overall brightness of a flash image, this doesn't mean you can use any shutter speed. If you're using a camera with a focal-plane shutter (which is most 35mm cameras and some medium-format models) it will have a "sync speed," which is the fastest shutter speed at which the camera will synchronize with a flash. The precise sync speed varies between cameras, but it's usually in the region of 1/60–1/200 sec. If you exceed this, the closing shutter will cut off part of your image.

Tips

- If you are using leaf shutter lenses (some medium-format and all large-format cameras) you can safely shoot at all shutter speeds; there is no maximum sync speed.

- Flash can sometimes feel so complex that people shy away from it and rely on ambient lighting. This is perfectly understandable, but you don't have to restrict yourself to using natural light: there is an increasing number of battery-powered continuous LED lights that you can use instead of flash.

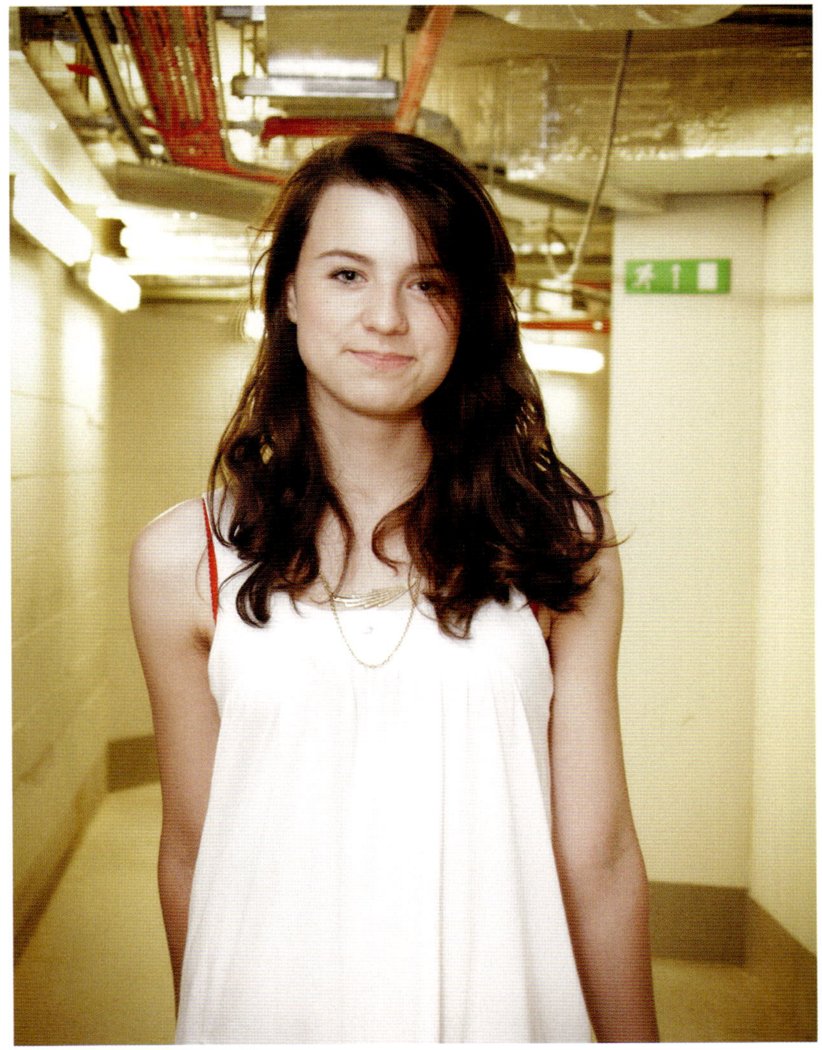

Left: This shot was taken using a single-flash setup. The exposure was set to balance the flash (bounced off the low white ceiling) with the ambient fluorescent lighting so the subject and background were exposed equally.

Flash, Shutter Speed & Aperture

Although you need to set the shutter speed and aperture for your flash exposures, one of the key things to appreciate is that the shutter speed will have little (if any) impact on an image where flash is the sole light source. This is because the duration of a flash—the actual flash of light—is much shorter than any shutter speed you will be using. The flash duration might actually be as little as 1/20,000 sec., for example, so it won't make any difference to the overall exposure if you use a shutter speed of 1/2 sec., 1/30 sec., or even 1/125 sec. In each case the flash will emit its full amount of light within the exposure time.

However, if there is any ambient light falling on your subject or scene then the shutter speed you choose will have an impact on the overall exposure, although it will only affect those parts of the image that are illuminated by ambient light, not those lit by the flash. If you want to shoot under mixed lighting conditions and balance your flash with the ambient light this is arguably one of the most important concepts to remember and often one of the most confusing, especially as the aperture has an impact on both the flash and ambient light exposures. We will explore how you can successfully mix the two later in this chapter.

TTL Flash

In the digital world, portable flash is typified by dedicated flash units that offer full TTL control. What this means is that you can set the exposure you want and the camera will set the flash to deliver a suitable burst of light, measuring its intensity through the lens, and often taking the focal length and the focus distance into consideration for added accuracy.

These modern systems were first developed for film cameras in the mid 1970s, and were a revelation to photographers who had previously had to rely on the auto and manual flash options we will explore shortly. However, the way in which TTL flash is implemented differs between the two technologies. With digital TTL a pre-flash is fired to determine how much light is needed for the main burst of flash, while in a film camera there is a sensor (in or on the camera) that reads the light and turns the flash off to end the exposure.

In both cases, the process boils down to the camera controlling the flash, and the biggest advantage of TTL flash is that this means the camera is doing all the work when it comes to setting the exposure. You can set the aperture you want to use (based on the depth of field you want) and as long as the shutter speed isn't too fast or the flash isn't too far away, the camera will generally deliver the correct exposure. Similarly, if you attach a softbox diffuser to the flash, take the flash off-camera, or bounce the light off a ceiling or wall the camera will take care of any added calculations for you.

There is a downside, though, and this is particularly important when you shoot on film. Just as your camera's regular ambient exposure metering can get things wrong with very bright and very dark subjects, so it can get the flash exposure wrong with similar subjects: a very bright subject will reflect more light, for example, so the camera may shut off the flash too early, resulting in slight underexposure. Obviously, the problem with film is that you won't know if this has happened until you get your film developed, so in these situations it can pay to use a less automated flash option.

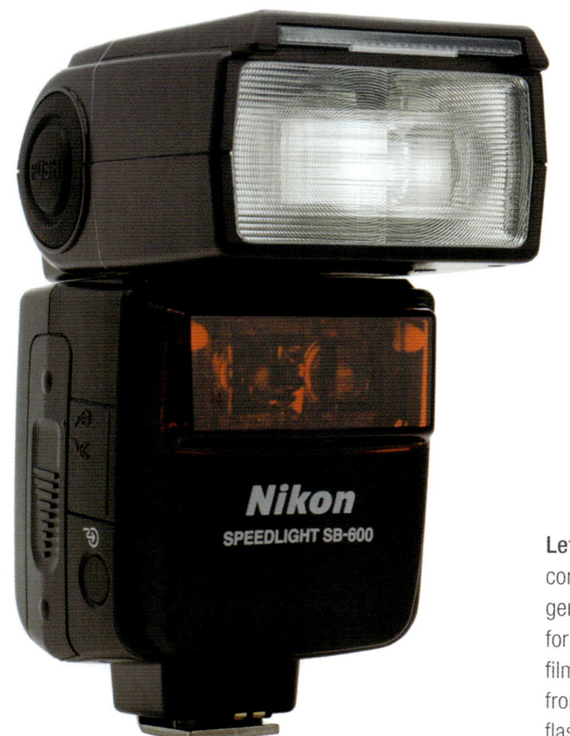

Left: Nikon's SB-600 Speedlight is compatible with the company's F6 35mm SLR, offering TTL control. However, generally speaking, a company's more recent "designed for digital" flash units are less likely to work with older film cameras, or at least may not allow you to get the most from the flash. Therefore, it's usually a good idea to use a flash of a similar vintage to the camera.

Right: Shooting in a stairwell, I used the small "pop up" TTL flash in the top of a Hasselblad H1 to light this shot, with the direct, hard, on-camera flash augmenting the high-contrast cross processing. To keep the background bright I had to use a wide aperture and long shutter speed, creating the shallow depth of field and a slight "double image" effect.

Tips

- You might be able to adjust your flash exposures using flash exposure compensation; this is an effective way of reducing the flash output to "fill in" any shadows on your subject without making the flash too obvious.

- Some third-party flashes—notably those from Metz—provide TTL control using dedicated adaptors and leads. These often appear on eBay and can expand the capabilities of a compatible flash, such as the Metz 45 hammerhead unit (see page 95).

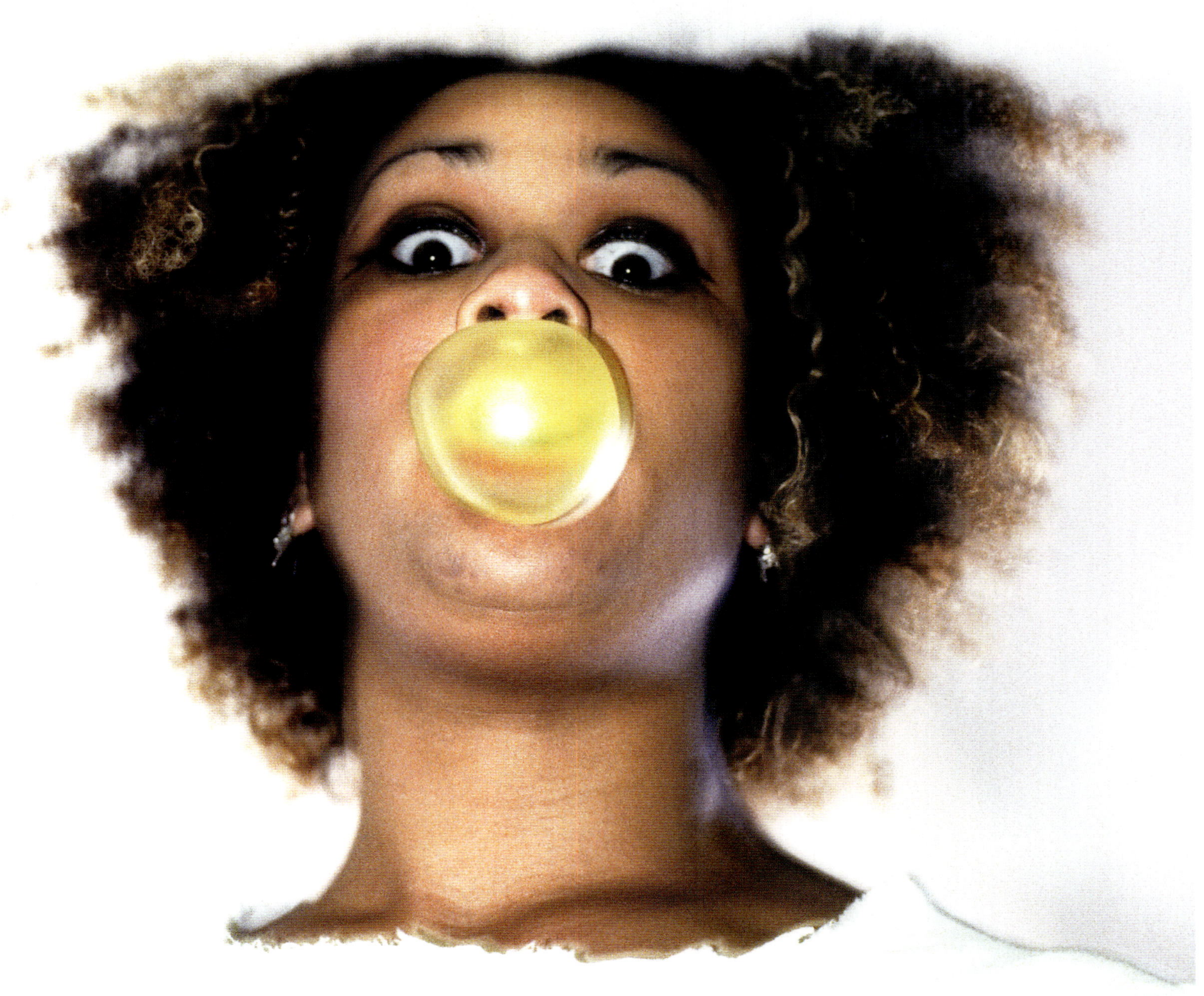

Auto Flash

Before flashes offered full TTL control and communicated with the camera, photographers looking to simplify their flash experience had to use automatic flashes instead. Unlike TTL flash, when an automatic flash fires the camera has no control over it. Instead, a sensor in the flash itself measures the light reflected from the subject and cuts the flash automatically when the correct exposure has been reached. In this way it is the flash, rather than the camera, that is controlling the exposure. Like TTL flash, this helps you get the right exposure without too much fuss, although you do need to make sure that both the flash and the camera are set correctly.

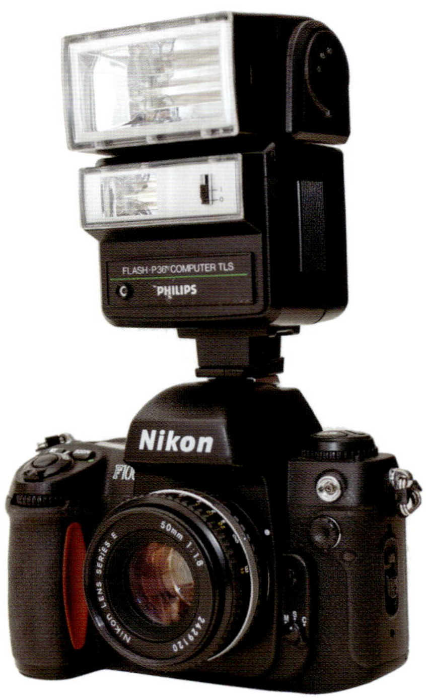

Above: This automatic flash cost me roughly $20, which is a bargain for a fairly powerful (GN118ft/36m at ISO 100), non-dedicated flash with a bounce and swivel head and three auto settings. It also has a secondary "fill" light that can be activated to add a weak pop of direct light when you bounce the main flash.

Using Auto Flash With Ambient Light

Automatic flashes typically have two or three automatic settings, which often use some sort of color-coding system to indicate a distance range and corresponding aperture. Different manufacturers explain the process in different ways, but my way of working is as follows:

1 Set the ISO on your flash unit so that it matches your film speed.

2 Choose a color-coded automatic option on the flash with a distance range that covers the flash-to-subject distance; if there are two or more options covering the same distance, choose which one you want to use based on the depth of field you want in your shot.

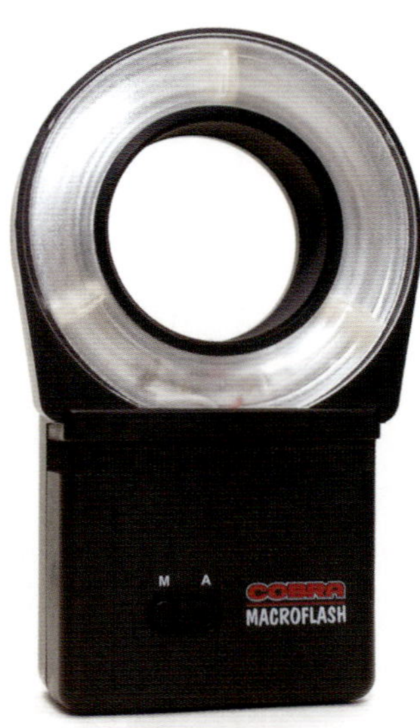

Above: A small ringlight or ringflash is great for macro work: this particuar model has an auto mode that works from 1-3ft (30-90cm), or it can be used manually.

3 Set the exposure for the scene you are photographing using Manual or Aperture Priority mode. Set the aperture to match the auto setting you have chosen on the flash.

4 Make sure the shutter speed does not exceed your camera's sync speed (see page 98). If it does, change your color-coded auto option to one that uses a smaller aperture setting (if possible) or adjust the flash-to-subject distance. In both cases you will need to change the exposure on your camera as well.

5 Shoot. As long as your subject remains within the distance range for your color-coded selection, and you don't change your aperture, the flash will deliver what it thinks is the most appropriate exposure, balancing the flash with the ambient light.

Tip

Sometimes you won't want it to be obvious that you've used flash; you'll just want a weak burst of light to lift heavy shadows on your subject, or perhaps to stop a subject turning into a silhouette if they are backlit. In either case, what you're looking for is "fill flash", which basically means the ambient light is stronger than the flash. To do this, in step 3 set the aperture on your camera 1 stop smaller than your color-coded auto option, and use that aperture setting to determine your exposure. So, if the auto mode on your flash says you should use f/11, you would set the exposure on your camera using an aperture of f/16 instead. The result will be that the flash is 1-stop darker than the ambient light, creating a less obvious "fill".

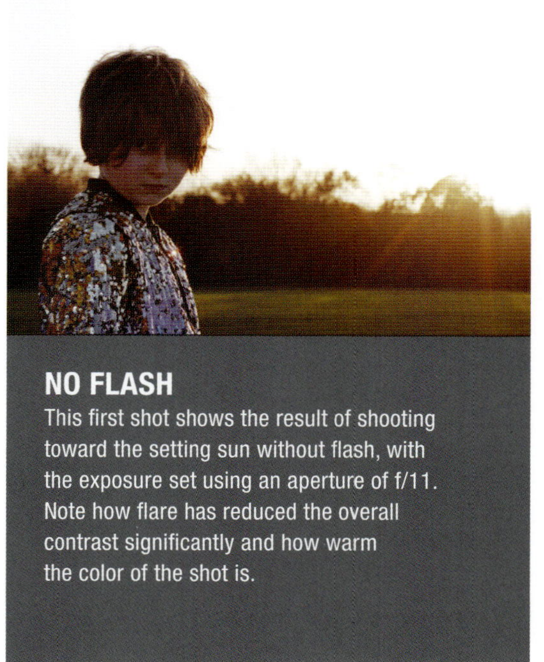

NO FLASH

This first shot shows the result of shooting toward the setting sun without flash, with the exposure set using an aperture of f/11. Note how flare has reduced the overall contrast significantly and how warm the color of the shot is.

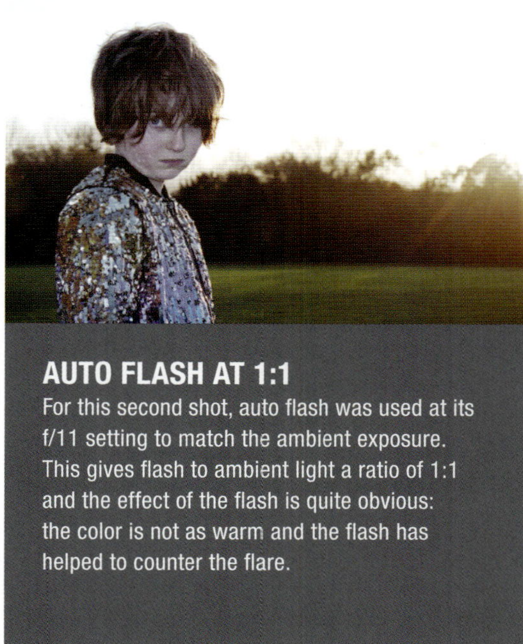

AUTO FLASH AT 1:1

For this second shot, auto flash was used at its f/11 setting to match the ambient exposure. This gives flash to ambient light a ratio of 1:1 and the effect of the flash is quite obvious: the color is not as warm and the flash has helped to counter the flare.

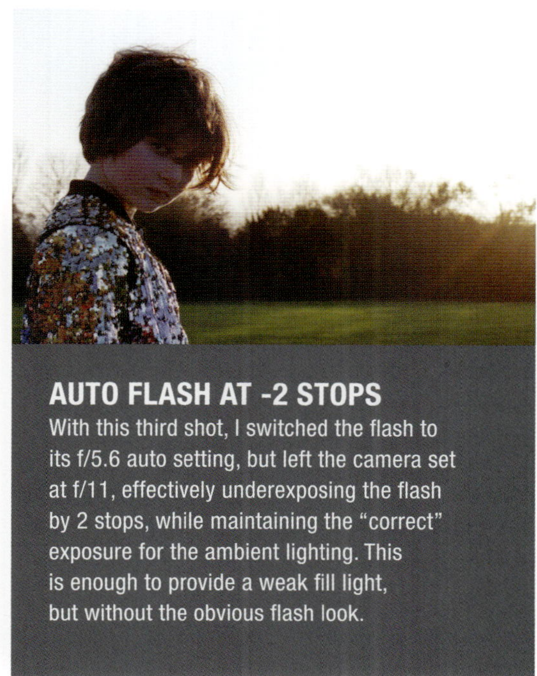

AUTO FLASH AT -2 STOPS

With this third shot, I switched the flash to its f/5.6 auto setting, but left the camera set at f/11, effectively underexposing the flash by 2 stops, while maintaining the "correct" exposure for the ambient lighting. This is enough to provide a weak fill light, but without the obvious flash look.

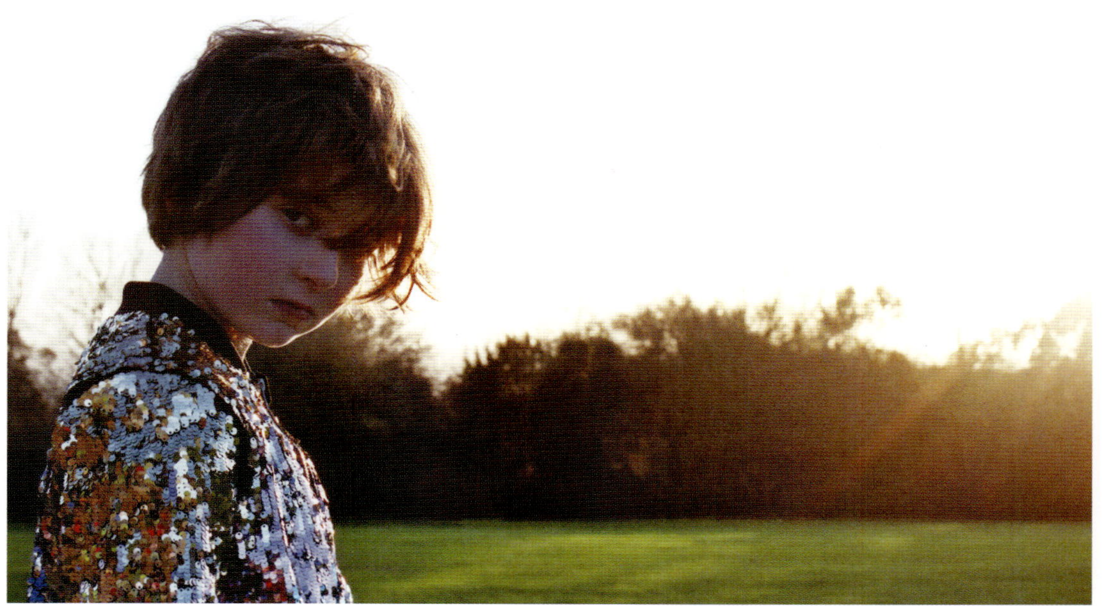

Tips

- You can vary the intensity of your fill light depending on how strong or weak you want the flash to appear and the type of film you are using: -½ stop might be enough for transparency film, while -2 stops might be preferable on negative film. However, start at -1 stop and take it from there.

- Negative film can often accommodate any slight flash exposure errors without them affecting the final image. However, transparency film is far less forgiving.

Above: The trio of shots (top) was taken using the camera and flash shown on page 102. Although I liked the warmth of the No Flash shot, the image I eventually settled on was this one taken with a weak burst of fill flash. During processing, I bumped up the contrast a little and gave it a warmer tone to shift it toward the ambient light exposure.

Manual Flash

Manual flash covers everything from the most basic hotshoe flash with no controls beyond "on" and "off," through to hotshoe-mounted and hammerhead units with multiple manual power settings, and studio strobes. It is basically any flash where you are taking full control over the exposure, and is perhaps the single most daunting aspect of using flash and film together. However, it needn't be a "dark art."

Guide Numbers & Exposure

As mentioned on page 96, battery-powered flashes have a guide number, which not only gives you an indication of their power, but enables you to work out the correct aperture setting or working distance when you're using flash. There are two equations that are important here, depending on whether you're looking to find the aperture or distance:

- Aperture = GN / Distance
- Distance = GN / Aperture

Tackling each of these in turn, if you want to work out what aperture to use, you simply need to divide the GN of your flash by the flash-to-subject distance. So, if your subject is 10ft (3m) from the camera and you're using a flash with a GN of 118ft (36m) the math you need is 118/10 (or 36/3), which gives you an aperture of f/12 (rounded to the nearest whole number). Your camera won't have this exact setting, but f/11 and f/13 are both reasonably close (and just ⅓ of a stop apart), so you can use either of those instead.

Alternatively, if you want to know the working distance for your flash, you divide the GN by the aperture you want to use. Let's say you're using a slightly less powerful flash with a GN of 92ft (28m) and want to shoot at f/4 because you want a fairly shallow depth of field. Using the formula above, the math is 92/4 (or 28/4), which gives you 23ft (or 7m): that's where your subject needs to be if you want to nail the flash exposure.

Simple eh? Or at least it is if you're using the ISO given with the GN of the flash (usually ISO 100); if you use a different film speed the math becomes more complicated. However, a lot of the time you don't need to worry about it, as many flash units have an ISO-related distance/aperture scale attached to them that cross references the two. Even if your flash doesn't have that, there are plenty of apps and online flash calculators that will automatically work out the optimum exposure at any given ISO, aperture, or distance. My advice is simple: just use one of those and move on. There's absolutely no need to make life difficult for yourself.

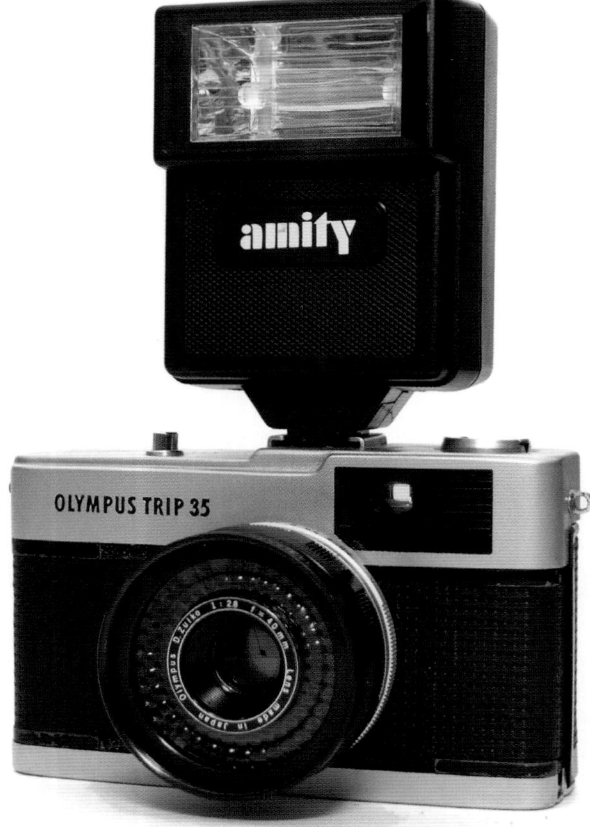

Left: This flash was made at least 20 years after my Olympus Trip 35, but the two work well together—I just have to remember to set the aperture on the camera!

EXPOSURE					TABLE
ASA ▶25	50	100	200	400	m. ▼
3	8	11	16	22	32	1
5	5.6	8	11	16	22	1.5
7	4	5.6	8	11	16	2
10	2.8	4	5.6	8	11	3
15	2	2.8	4	5.6	8	4.5
20 ▲	1.4	2	2.8	4	5.6	6
ft.	15	18	21	24	27 ◀DIN

Above: It might look primitive, but a flash exposure grid like this, printed on the back of the flash shown opposite, can be very effective if you are working without a lightmeter. All you need to do is cross-reference the film speed (given here as ASA/ISO or DIN) with the flash-to-subject distance (in feet or meters) to determine the aperture you need to use for the "correct" exposure. If you know the guide number of your flash it's pretty easy to make your own flash tables to carry with you in your camera bag.

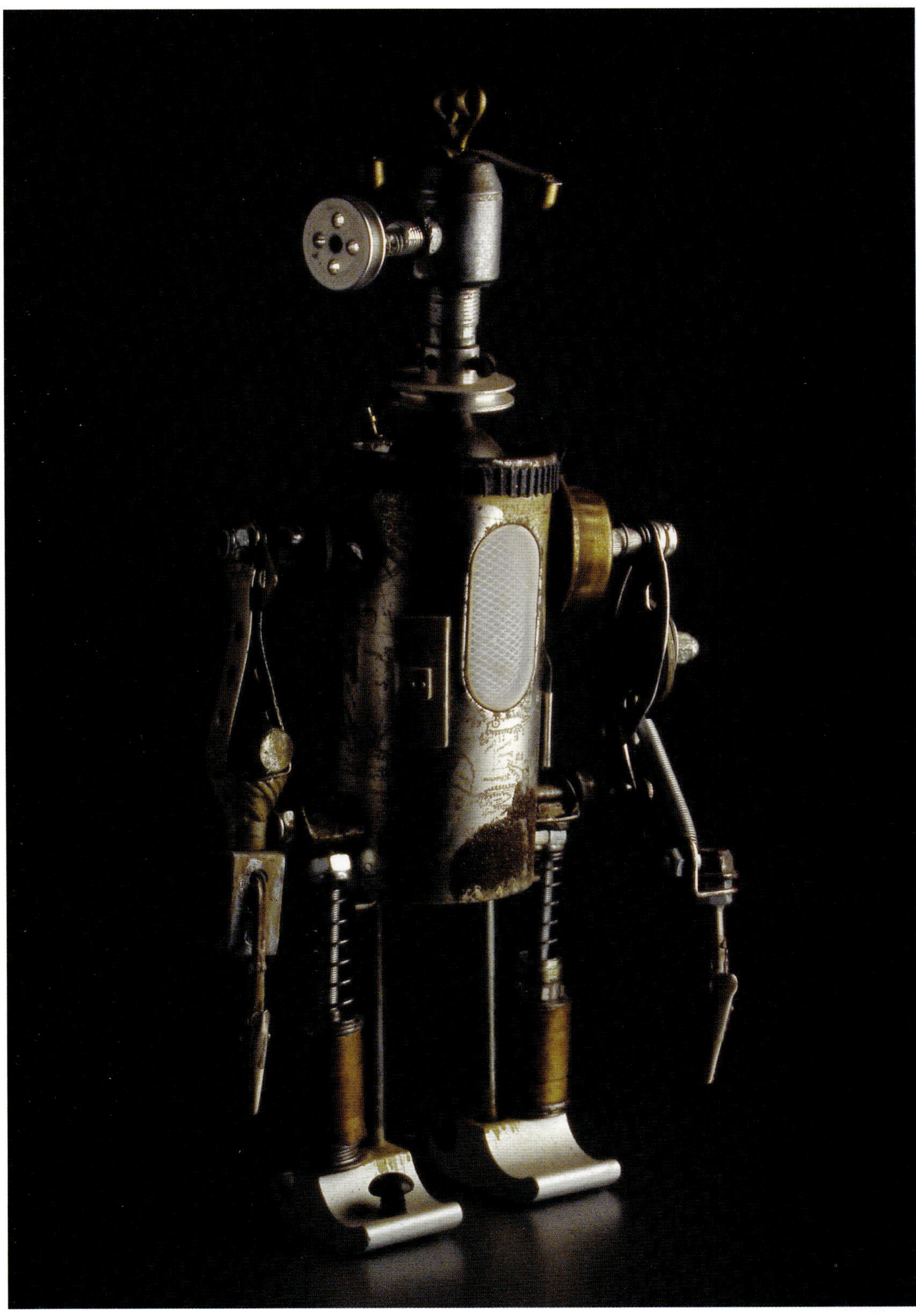

Left: For this still life I set up a small flash to the right of my subject, aimed away from the robot and toward a reflector. This made the light from the flash much softer, while a silver reflector on the opposite side added an even gentler fill.

Flash Meters

If you're going to use off-camera manual flash regularly (especially studio strobes, which have their power measured in watt seconds (Ws) or joules (J), rather than guide numbers, and/or multiple flash units) a flashmeter is essential. This is a feature found in some handheld lightmeters, which extends their capabilities so they can also take exposure readings for flash.

Generally speaking, most lightmeters will measure flash and ambient lighting separately, which means it is up to you to balance the two types of light in your shots. We're not going to get too heavily into this, as there are so many possible permutations, but the key thing to remember is that the shutter speed you use will only affect the ambient part of your exposures, while the aperture alters the exposure for both the ambient and flash lighting.

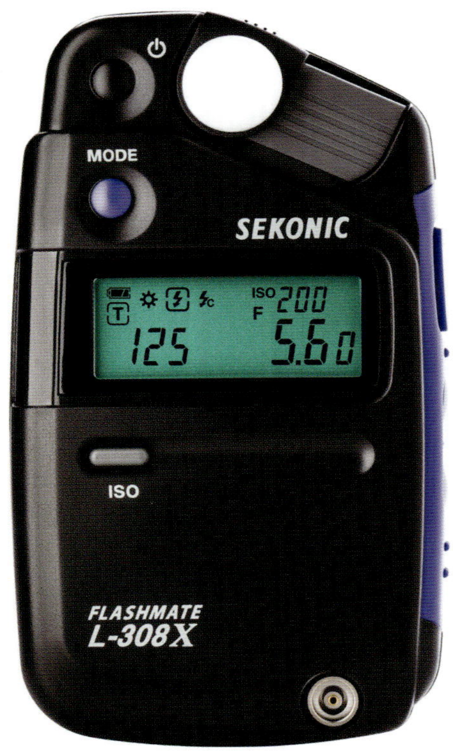

Left: I first used a Sekonic L-308 lightmeter almost 25 years ago, and have had one in my camera bag ever since. It's by no means a top-of-the-range model, but it's capable of taking incident and reflected light readings for both ambient light and flash, making it incredibly versatile.

Balancing Flash

With a flash meter it is relatively straightforward to balance flash with ambient light. Start by taking an ambient light reading, and use this to set the exposure on your camera. The aperture/shutter speed combination will depend on the shot you're taking, but you need to bear in mind two important things: your camera's sync speed (if applicable), and the fact that no matter what shutter speed you set, the flash part of the exposure will "freeze" any movement.

For the purposes of this example, let's say that our ambient exposure is f/8 at 1/125 sec. The next step is to set up your flash so it gives you the same exposure as your ambient light reading. You can do this by physically moving the flash to change the flash-to-subject distance and/or by adjusting the flash power, but the aim is to get the exact same aperture for your ambient and flash readings. When you do, the two light sources will be balanced perfectly in terms of their intensity.

Tweaking The Balance

Of course, sometimes you will want the flash to be less obvious, so the ambient light dominates your shot. In this case the flash needs to be weaker than the ambient light, so you want your flash reading to be suggesting a wider aperture than the ambient light reading. For example, if your ambient light reading is f/8 at 1/125 sec., you want the flash to be reading f/5.6 or f/4. The ambient exposure (f/8 at 1/125 sec.) would be the exposure you set on the camera, and this will effectively underexpose the flash.

At other times you might want the flash to overpower the ambient light, in which case you need the flash exposure to be giving you a smaller aperture. So, if the ambient light reading is again giving you f/8 at 1/125 sec., you want your flash reading to be smaller than that (f/11, for example). However, this time round, the exposure you set on the camera would be based on the flash reading (so it would be f/11 at 1/125 sec., for example). In this way, the flash will be correctly exposed and the ambient light will be underexposed.

From this basic theory you can adjust the balance or ratio of the flash and ambient light elements of a shot, to darken the (ambient) background exposure and make the flash the dominant light source, or simply use the flash to lightly fill any shadows. Just let your lightmeter guide you.

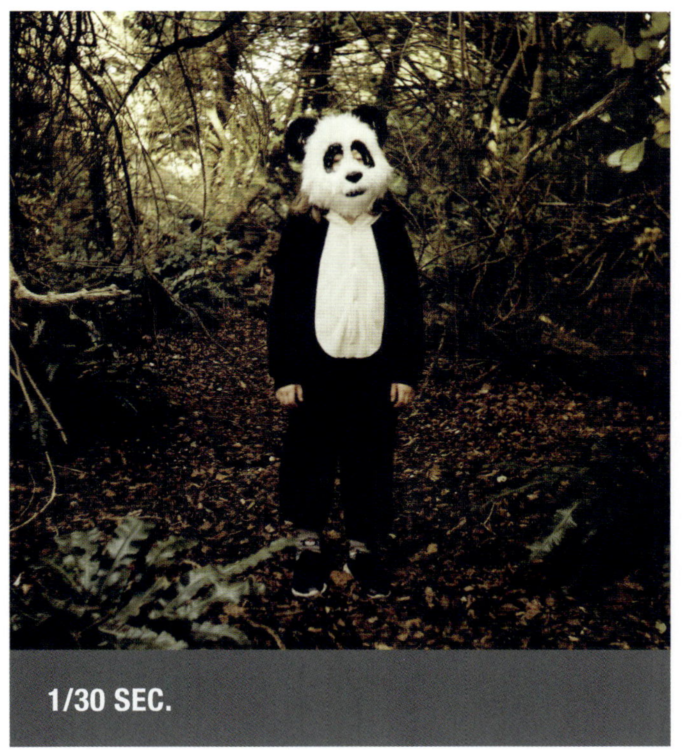

1/30 SEC.

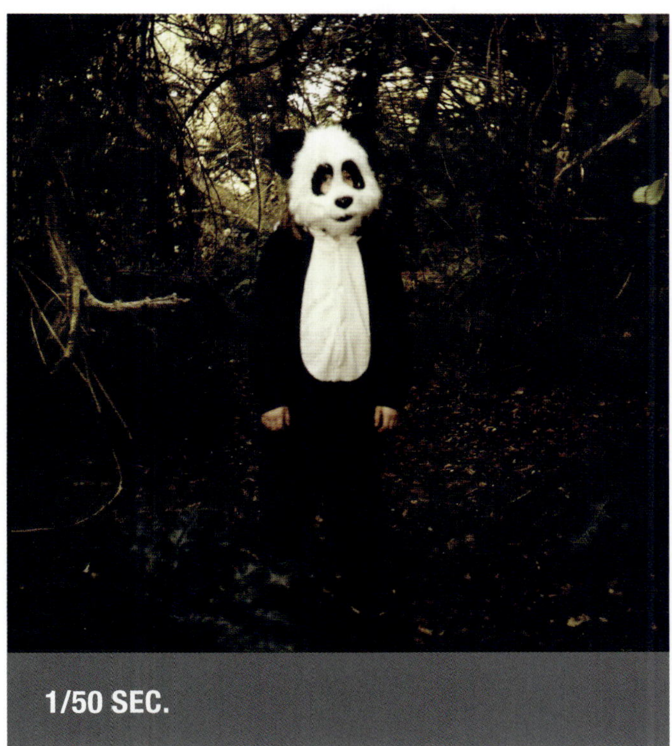

1/50 SEC.

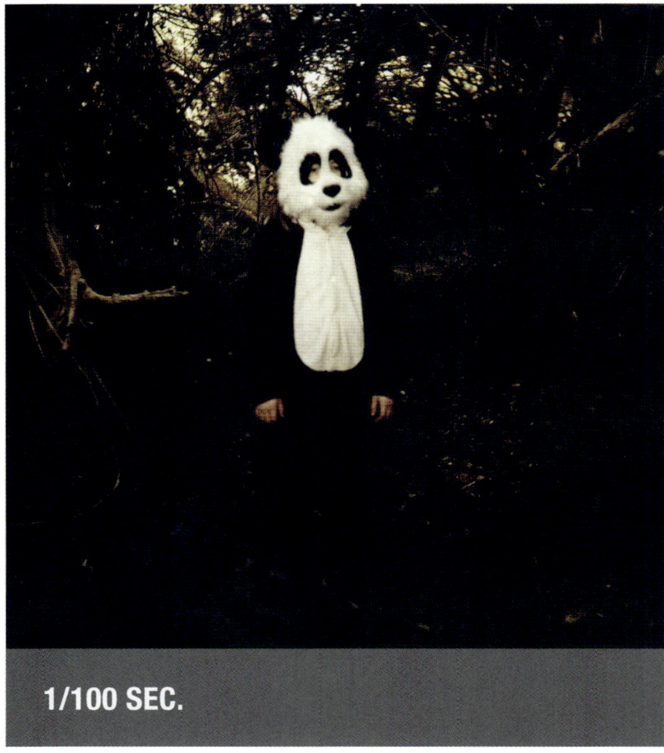

1/100 SEC.

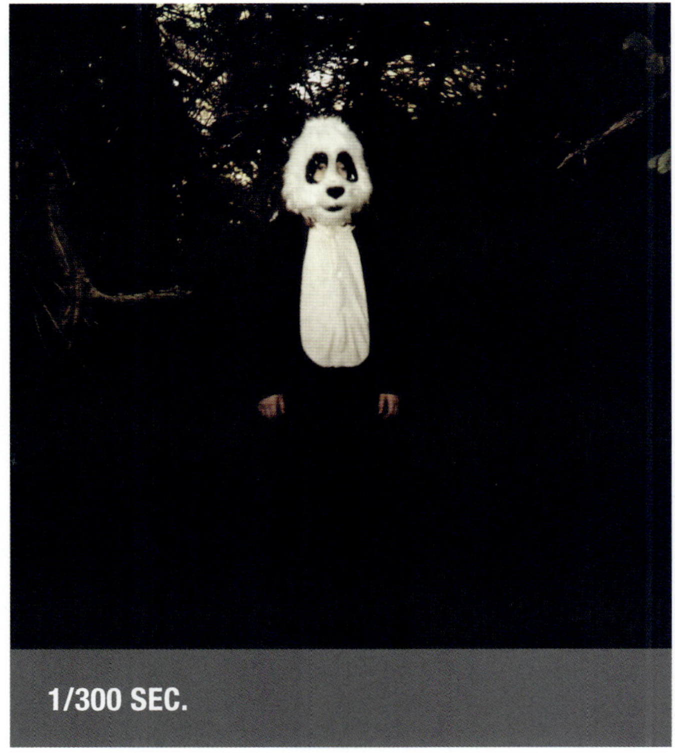

1/300 SEC.

Left: Shooting on ISO 100 negative film, the exposure for the ambient light in this woodland encounter was 1/30 sec. at f/5.6. I set my flash to give me the same aperture (f/5.6) and then shot a sequence of images at different shutter speeds. The flash exposure is maintained across the sequence because the aperture stayed at f/5.6 and the flash was set to deliver the right amount of light for that. However, the level of the ambient light changes depending on the shutter speed: the faster the shutter speed, the less ambient light is recorded.

Chapter 5
Filters

With digital photography the majority of filters are no longer necessary. There are so many ways to quickly and easily blend or manipulate images—either in-camera or during post-processing—that using a piece of resin or glass over the lens seems somehow primitive and out of touch. However, when you shoot film, filters become a much more important part of the process, and in many cases they can even be described as essential. This is because when you shoot film the options available to you post-capture are dramatically reduced. Even if you scan your negatives or transparencies, there is only so much you can do—both technically and creatively—to your film-based images, making it all the more important to get things "right" in-camera where possible.

Right: A filter is anything you put in front of the lens that modifies the light in some way, so as well as commercial photographic filters you can experiment with making your own; this beach shot was taken through some clear packaging, which softened the focus, reducing the image to two simple bands of color.

Filters & Exposure

Most filters block light to some degree. With neutral density (ND) filters (see page 118), reducing the amount of light passing through the lens is the main purpose, but with others it is a side effect. In either case, the density of the filter—which is given as a "filter factor"—needs to be taken into account when it comes to setting your exposure. If you fail to do this, you will underexpose your shot to some degree.

If you're using in-camera TTL metering, the effect of any filters (with the possible exception of extreme ND filters—see page 119) will be taken into account automatically, because the camera is reading the filtered light coming in through the lens. This is particularly helpful when you are using multiple filters or if you aren't quite sure of the actual density of a filter.

However, if you're using an external lightmeter of some kind you need to manually adjust your exposure to compensate for any filters. You can do this in a number of ways. If you're using filters on a shot-by-shot basis, and changing them as you go, the simplest option is to meter as normal, so the ISO of your lightmeter matches that of your film, and then adjust the aperture and/or shutter speed to compensate for the filter. So, if you fit a filter with a 2x filter factor, for example, simply open up the aperture by 1 stop or increase the shutter speed by 1 stop.

Alternatively, if you're shooting an entire roll with a filter attached—for example, if you're shooting black-and-white film and plan on using a red filter for all of your shots, or you're using a plain ND filter—you can take your light reading at an adjusted ISO setting that compensates for the filter. For example, if you were shooting with ISO 400 film and using a filter with a 4x filter factor (2-stop reduction in light), you could take all your light readings with the ISO set at 100 instead.

FILTER STACKING

It's possible—and often necessary—to use more than one filter at a time; you might want to lengthen an exposure with an ND filter (see page 118), but also use a polarizer (see page 124) for example. However, every filter you add has the potential to degrade the quality of your images, either by reducing the sharpness and/or by introducing unwanted artifacts such as flare and vignetting, so the simple rule is to keep filter stacking to a minimum.

CONVERTING FILTER FACTORS INTO STOPS	
FILTER FACTOR	**LIGHT LOSS (STOPS)**
1.25x	⅓
1.5x	⅔
2x	1
2.5x	1 ⅓
3x	1 ⅔
4x	2
5x	2 ⅓
6x	2 ⅔
8x	3
16x	4

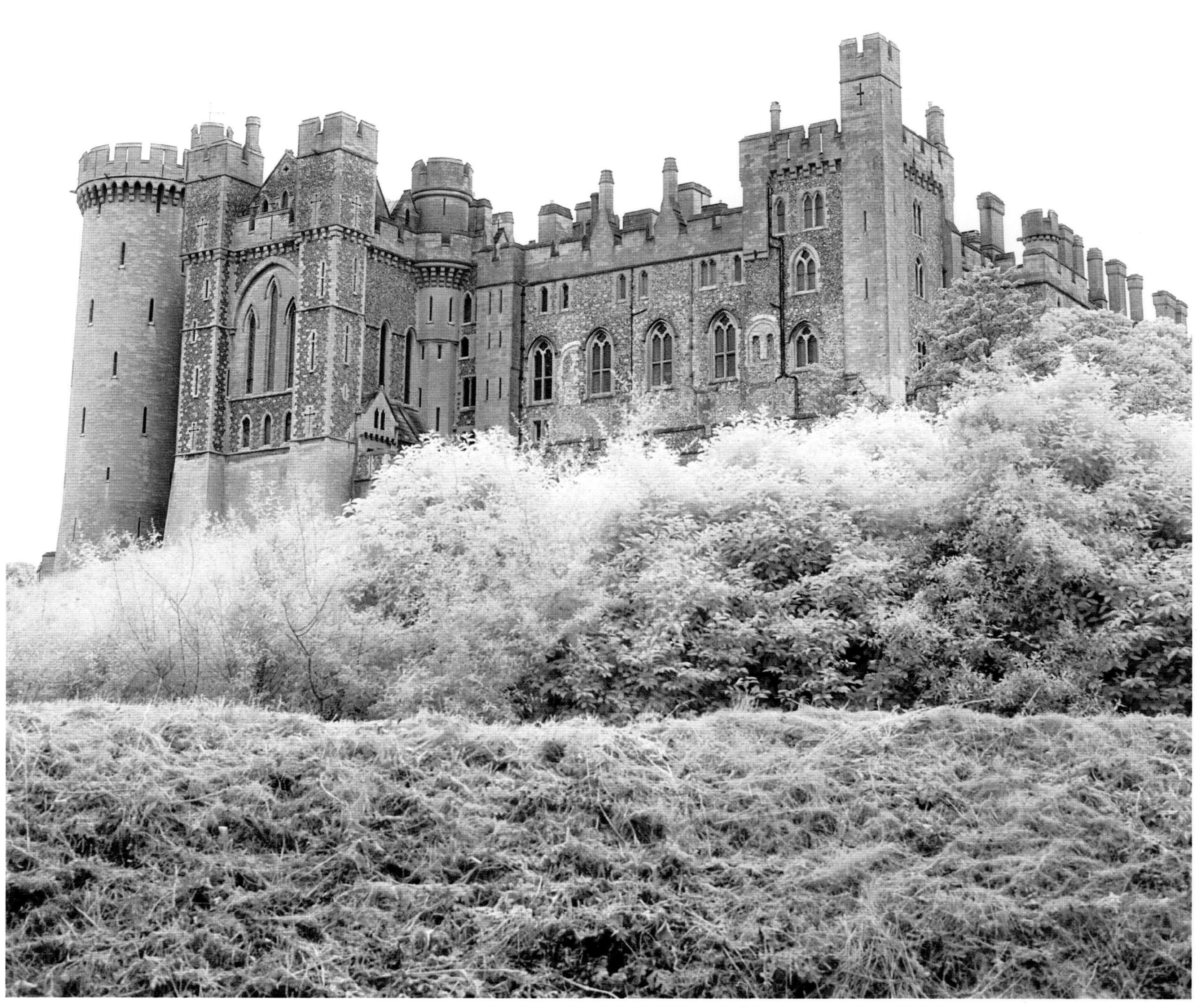

Color Control

As outlined in the opening chapter, most color film is daylight-balanced, which means it will take color-correct images under "blue sky" conditions or when you shoot with flash. Under any other light source—even on an overcast day—a color cast will be introduced into your shots because the color temperature of the light is different to the balance of the film. This is slightly less of an issue with color print film, as minor color casts can be removed at the printing stage, but with color transparency film it is far more important to correct any color shift using filters when you shoot. There are several types of color control filter to be aware of.

Warming & Cooling

The simplest color-correction filters are "warming" and "cooling" filters, which appear in various densities of amber/yellow and blue respectively. Although these filters can be used in conjunction with a color meter to perform precise color shifts up and down the color temperature scale, they are more often used intuitively to make minor adjustments; to warm a landscape on an overcast day, for example, add a warm glow to a portrait, or visually cool a snowy scene to make it look physically colder. The main filters falling into this category include 81 series (pale amber) and 82 series (pale blue) filters, which come in a variety of strengths, as well as filters with more esoteric names, such as coral and straw.

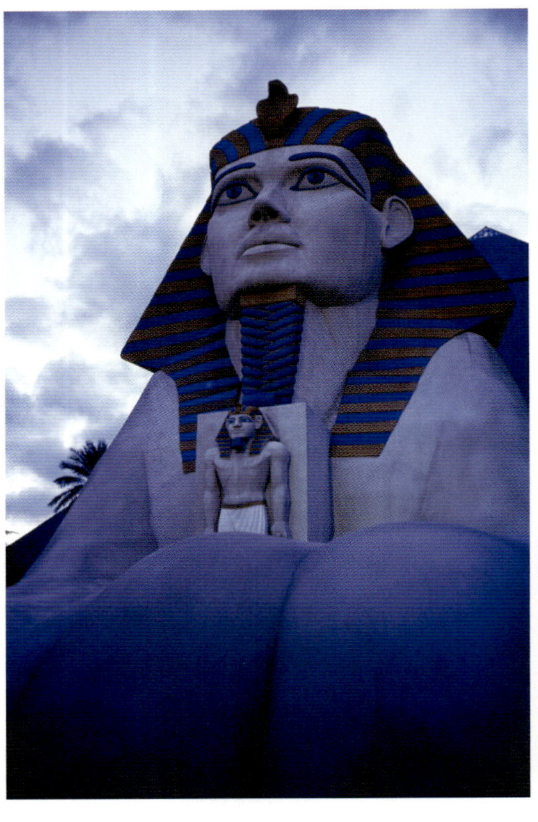

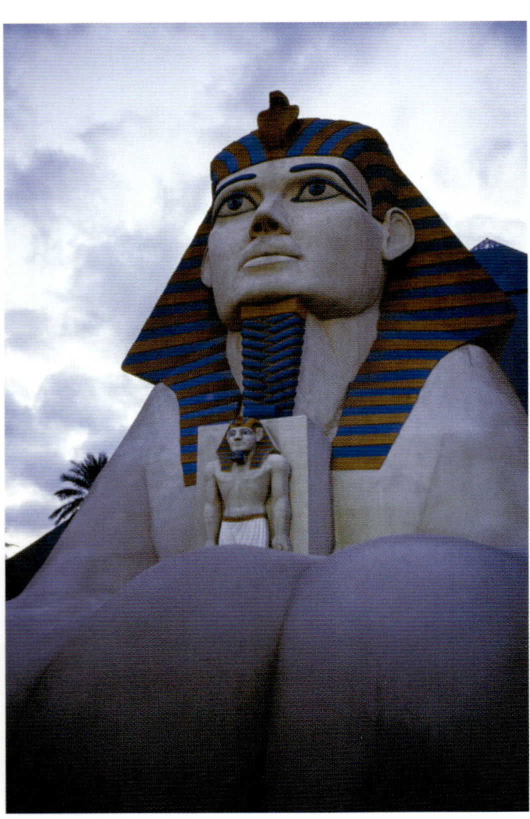

Above: How essential filters are to you depends on a number of factors, not least the film you use and your approach toward processing. Color transparency is far less forgiving than color negative film, but if you're happy to adopt a "hybrid" workflow and edit your film-shot images digitally, there's no reason why you can't adjust an image after the event. That's precisely what I did here with this overly-cool transparency.

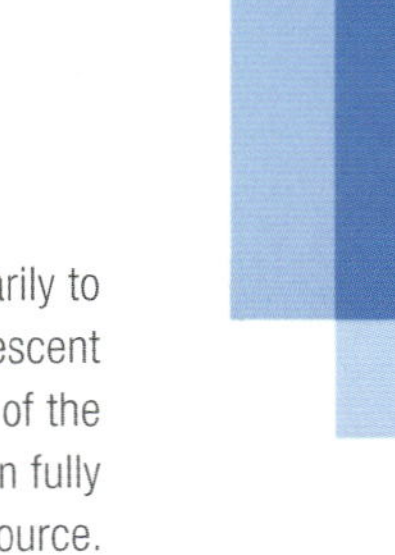

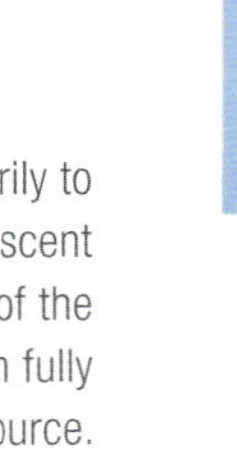

Right: The 80 series of blue filters are used primarily to shoot daylight-balanced film under tungsten/incandescent lighting; the blue of the filter counters the warmth of the lamp. There are various strengths of filter so you can fully or partially correct the light source.

Color Temperature

Color temperature filters have a greater impact on an image than warming/cooling filters, and are used to convert the color temperature of one light source to match another; an 80A (blue) filter might be used to neutralize the warm glow of tungsten lighting when you are using daylight-balance film, an 85 (orange) filter might be used to match daylight to tungsten-balanced film, or a specialist fluorescent filter (usually purple/magenta in color) might be used to balance fluorescent lighting with either tungsten or daylight film. As with warming and cooling filters, these filters come in a range of strengths for added precision.

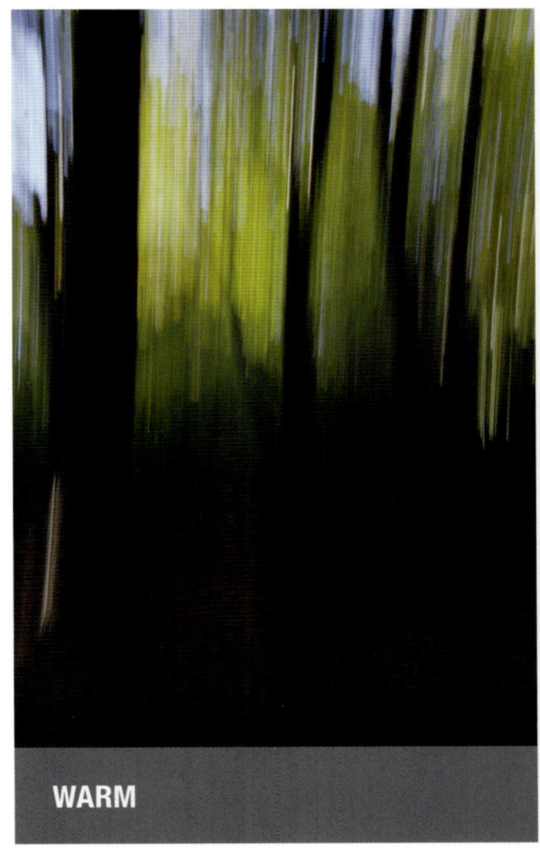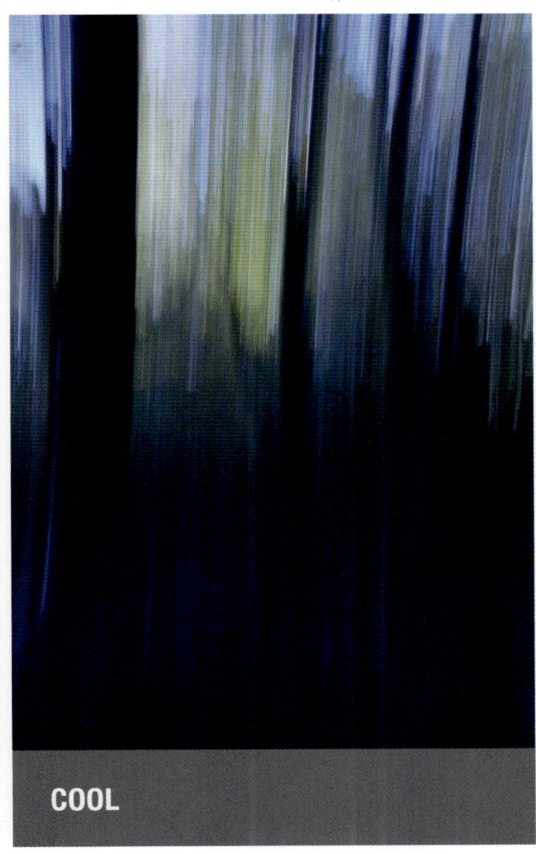

Right: Color filters can be used to create as well as correct. For these panning shots, taken in fall woodland, I tried both a warming and a cooling filter to deliberately introduce a color cast into the abstract shots.

WARMING & COOLING FILTERS					
FILTER NUMBER	**COLOR TEMPERATURE CONVERSION***	**MIRED SHIFT VALUE***	**FILTER NUMBER**	**COLOR TEMPERATURE CONVERSION***	**MIRED SHIFT VALUE***
85	5500K to 3400K	+112	80A	3200K to 5500K	-131
85B	5500K to 3200K	+131	80B	3400K to 5500K	-112
85C	5500K to 3800K	+81	80C	3800K to 5500K	-81
81	3300K to 3200K	+9	80D	4200K to 5500K	-56
81A	3400K to 3200K	+18	82	3100K to 3200K	-10
81B	3500K to 3200K	+27	82A	3000K to 3200K	-21
81C	3600K to 3200K	+35	82B	2900K to 3200K	-32
81D	3700K to 3200K	+42	82C	2800K to 3200K	-45
81EF	3850K to 3200K	+53			

* conversions and mired shift values based on Lee Filters' colored filters.

Color Correction

In addition to filters that shift the color along the Kelvin scale, making it warmer or cooler, you can also use color compensation or color correction (CC) filters, which can address other color issues, such as fine-tuning the many types of fluorescent lighting, or compensating for light reflecting off a colored surface that is affecting your subject. These filters are available in the additive primary colors of red, green, and blue, as well as the subtractive primaries of cyan, magenta, and yellow, with a range of densities for each.

However, using these filters really is entering into the realm of obsessive precision, and for most people the costs involved are simply prohibitive. To start with, a color meter is essential so you can accurately measure the color temperature of the light you are working in, and you will then (ideally) need a full set of filters of each color to ensure that you can make the correct adjustments.

Instead of this, consider shooting negative film or scanning your film, as minor color shifts can often be corrected digitally or when your negatives are printed. Shooting a frame containing a gray card, which you can then match in post processing, is often all you need to do.

FILTER TYPES

When it comes to color correction—and indeed any "plain" filter—you can choose between screw-in filters that attach to the lens or slot-in "system" filters that require a separate holder and adapter rings to fit your lenses. Screw-in filters tend to be a less expensive option, but if you have several lenses (or cameras) with different lens diameters it is usually preferable to go for a filter system as you can use the same filters across multiple lenses simply by buying a different sized adaptor ring; with screw-in filters you would need another filter in a different size (or stepping rings), negating the cost benefit.

You need to be careful with some camera designs, though, as a filter system's holder can partially block the viewfinder on a rangefinder camera or the viewing lens on a TLR, making it difficult to frame your shots. In this instance screw-in filters are a better option.

Above: A magenta color correction filter is typically used to correct fluorescent lighting, but you need a color meter to inform you of the exact filters you require. You will also need to buy multiple filters. This is simply too expensive for most photographers (including the majority of pros).

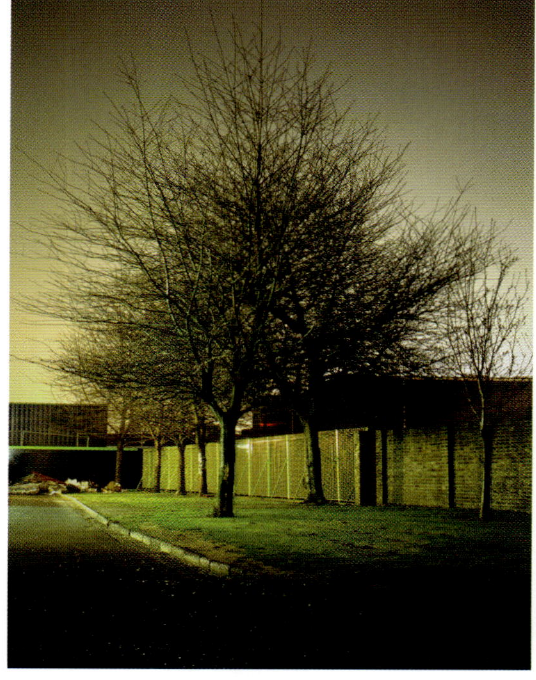

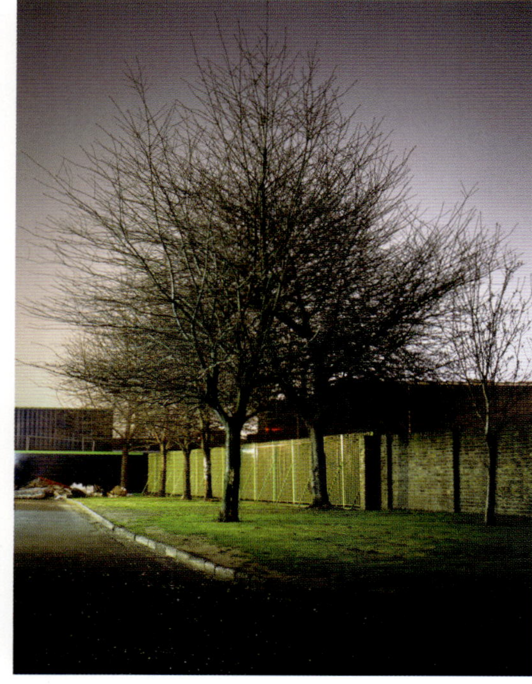

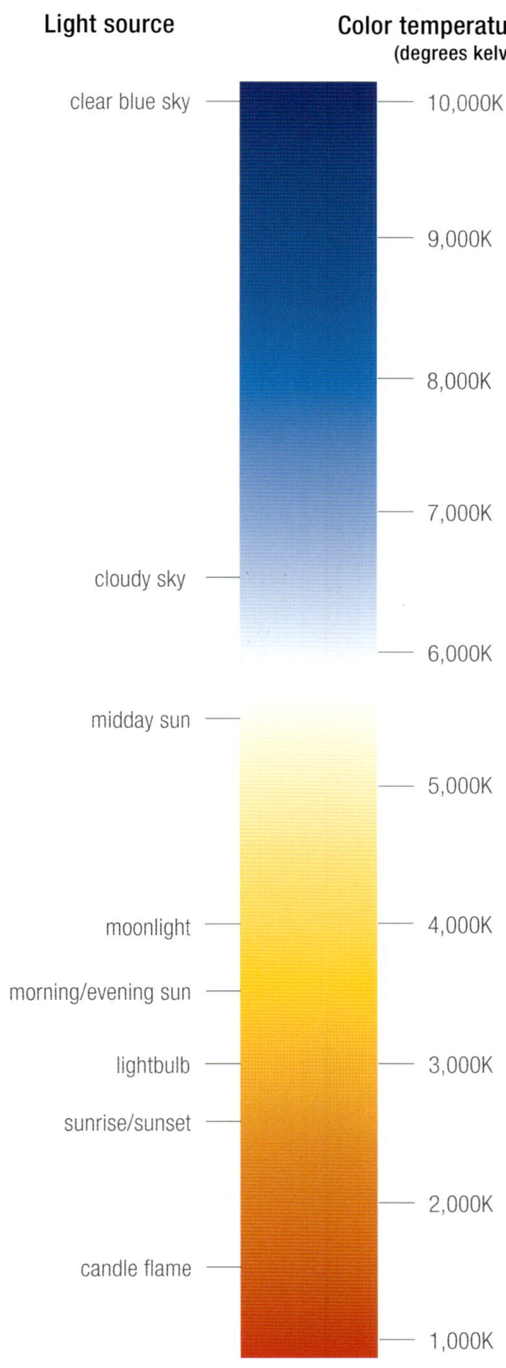

Above: As well as an intensity, or brightness, light also has a color temperature, which indicates how warm (orange) or cool (blue) it is; the lower the temperature the warmer the light source. Most film is balanced to 5500K (the temperature of daylight/electronic flash) so to balance the color temperature of a different light source you need to use filters.

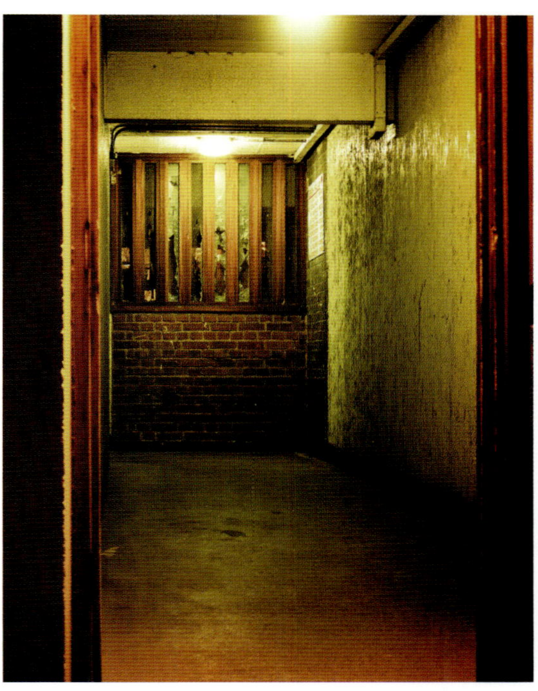

Above: You can buy fluorescent-to-daylight color temperature filters, but my advice is simple: DON'T! There are numerous types of fluorescent lighting, each with its own unique color temperature, so there is no guarantee the filter and light will match, leaving you with partial correction. Instead, keep the strong color cast (as here) and use it as part of the image.

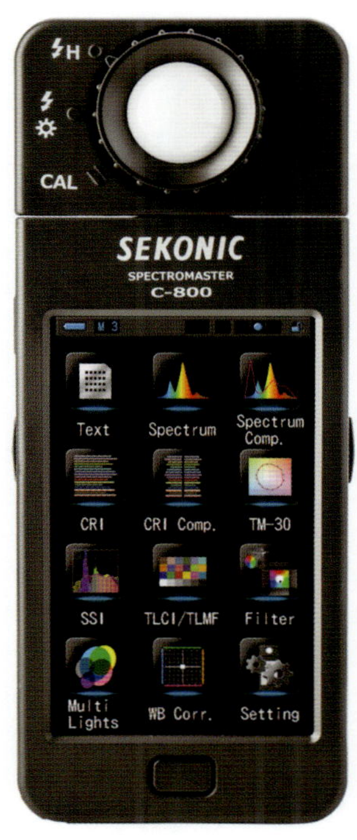

Above: A color meter like Sekonic's C-800 looks similar to a handheld lightmeter, but rather than measuring the intensity of light it measures its color temperature. A basic color meter will tell you which filters you need to convert the measured temperature to another value (usually 5500K if you are shooting daylight-balanced film), but the Sekonic C-800 can do so much more.

Tips

- The effect of color-correction filters is usually given as a "mired" value (short for micro reciprocal degree), rather than a color temperature measured in degrees Kelvin (which will be familiar to digital photographers). Although you can convert one to the other, this is rarely practical or necessary: the only reason why you would be working in mired shift values is if you are using a color meter and color correction filters, in which case the meter will indicate the relevant mired shift/filters to use.

- Dedicated color meters are very expensive, but there are apps that allow you to use a smartphone to measure the temperature of light. The Cine Meter II app, in conjunction with a Luxi For All lightmeter attachment, will turn an iPhone into a light- and color-metering tool for around $50.

- If you're using artificial light (flash or continuous) color-correction can often be applied to the light, rather than using filters over the lens. Lighting gels can convert tungsten lamps to match daylight, for example, or warm the light from a flash to use it with tungsten-balanced film. This is usually a better way to work, as it means that there are no filters over the lens to potentially degrade the image quality.

Tonal Control

Talking about colored filters in reference to black-and-white photography might seem slightly perverse (after all, we're not shooting color), but solid-color filters have been used to create stunning monochrome photographs for almost as long as black-and-white photography has existed. And it's a tradition that continues today.

The reason they are so important is because black-and-white film reduces whatever you are photographing to shades of gray. With panchromatic film (see page 19) this is a relatively "straight" conversion, so every element in the frame is translated into a gray shade based purely on the amount of light it reflects (its apparent brightness). In some instances this isn't a problem—yellow will almost always appear bright, for example—but you will find that some colors (particularly midtone reds and greens) will appear the exact same gray tone in black and white, which can make it hard to "read" the image.

To avoid this you need to use colored filters. These plain filters transmit light of the same (or similar) wavelength, while blocking others, so a red filter transmits red wavelengths, while blocking blues and greens, for example. In this way a colored filter effectively lightens similar colors and darkens opposing ones, creating tonal separation in your black-and-white shots.

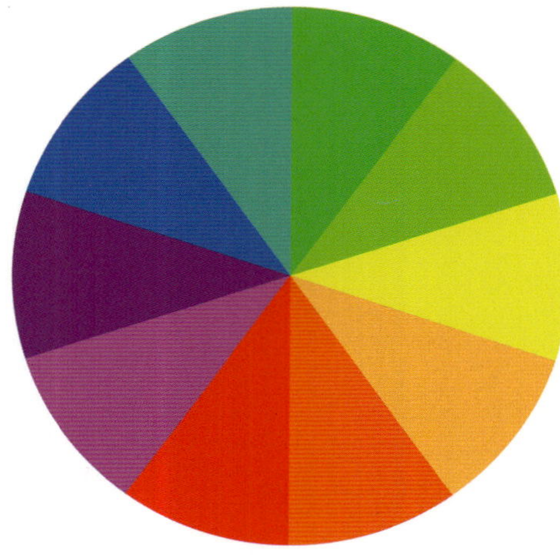

Above: The basic rule of colored filters is that they make the same (and similar) colors lighter in tone, and make opposing colors darker. A basic color wheel shows these relationships: red and orange are close to one another, but opposite blue and green, so an orange filter would lighten oranges and reds, and darken blues and greens.

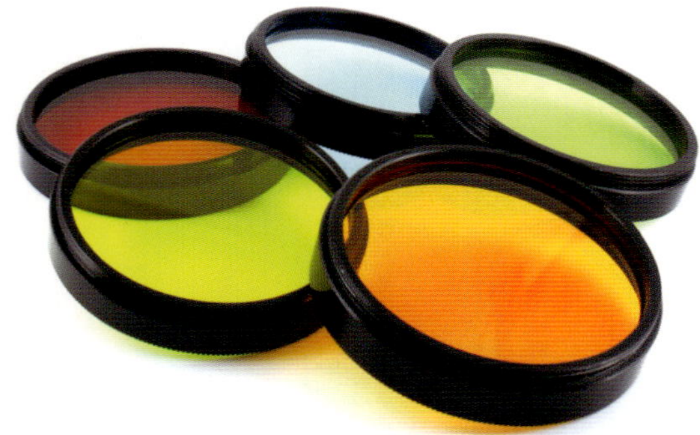

Above: There are five filters commonly associated with black-and-white photography: red, orange, yellow, green, and blue (although blue is used less frequently). Each one of these will have a different effect on the way that the colors in a scene are translated into black and white.

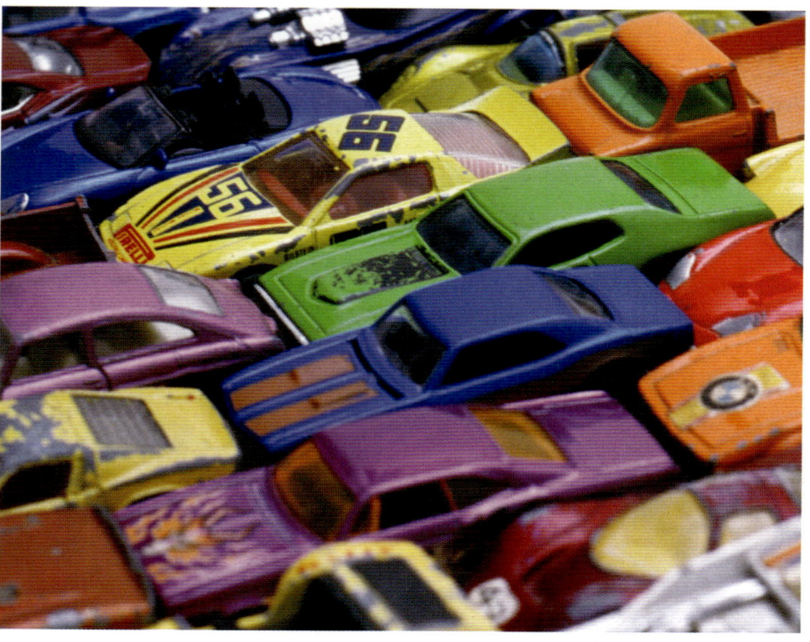

Right & opposite: In color, this scene contains a wide range of hues and it's easy to tell them apart. However, things can become slightly more complicated when the same scene is shot in black and white, making it important to select the most appropriate filter. The images opposite show the effect of using different colored filters, as well as shooting without a filter.

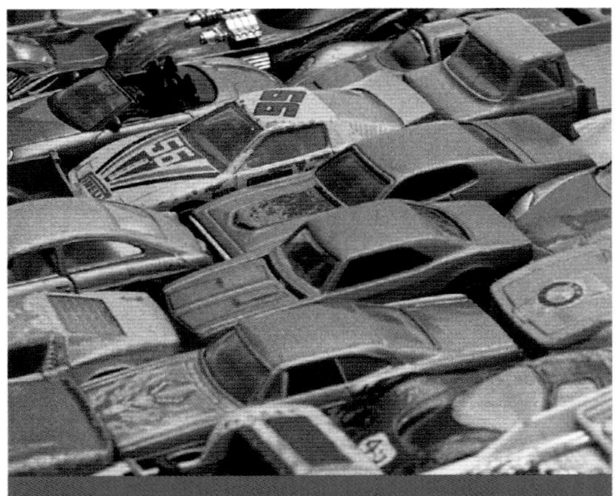

NO FILTER

Without a filter, all colors are converted equally into shades of gray. This can lead to colors that have a similar brightness (but a very different hue) appearing the same shade of gray, and black-and-white images that appear "flat" and lacking in contrast.

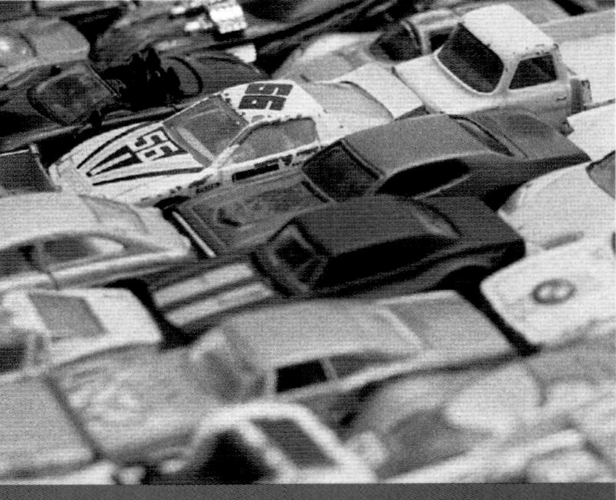

RED FILTER

A red filter lightens reds, oranges, and yellows, while darkening blues and greens. This is good for landscape photography when you want to create a dramatic sky: a blue sky can become near-black when a red filter is used, while white/light clouds will contrast strongly.

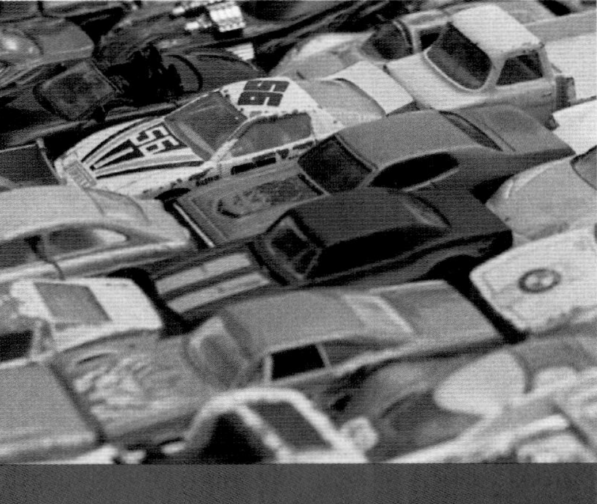

ORANGE FILTER

An orange filter lightens oranges and yellows (and some reds), and darkens blues and greens. This can be useful for reducing the appearance of freckles and blemishes in a portrait, giving bricks a pleasing tone in architecture shots, or darkening the sky in a landscape.

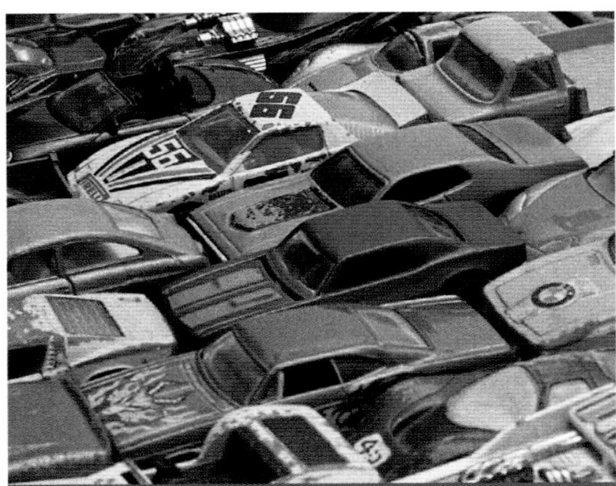

YELLOW FILTER

Yellow filters lighten yellows (and some oranges and reds) and darken blues and greens. This can be a less extreme option for landscape photography than a red or orange filter; a blue sky will be darkened slightly, increasing contrast between it and any clouds, but the effect is more natural looking.

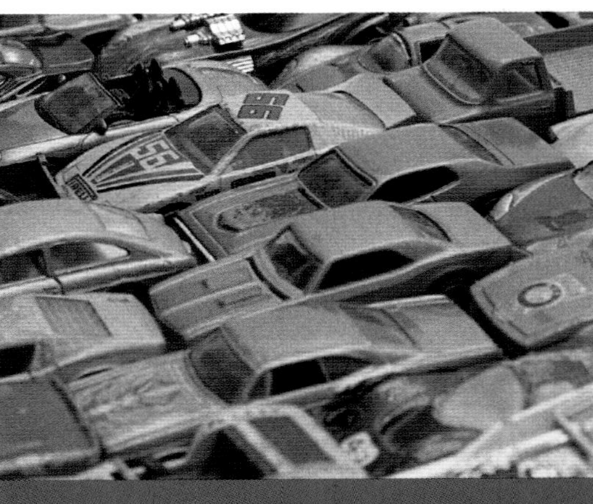

BLUE FILTER

A blue filter will lighten blues (and some greens), while darkening reds, oranges, and yellows. This can reduce contrast in an image, although blue filters are seldom used in any genre.

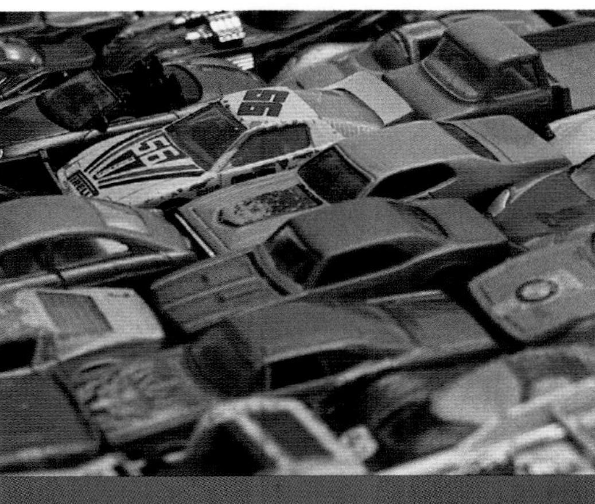

GREEN FILTER

Green filters lighten greens (and some blues) and darken some reds and oranges. Although not as widely used as the "warm" filters (red, orange, and yellow), a green filter can be useful for landscape work when you want foliage to stand out, although it can also lighten the sky.

Exposure Control

Digital cameras have revolutionized the way in which photographers can use ISO as an exposure control, adjusting it on a shot-by-shot basis in the same way as the aperture or shutter speed can be altered for creative or technical control. This is not the case with film, though, as you will typically pick your film to match the conditions you are shooting under, your subject, and/or the look you're after. Once you have set the ISO, that's generally the ISO you will use for the entire roll (if you want consistent exposures). This places greater emphasis on filters if you need to regulate the exposure, with neutral density (or ND) filters used most often for creative or technical reasons.

Above: ND filters come in a range of strengths, which are measured in a variety of ways. However, the number of stops of light they block is the most practical measurement; these filters (from top to bottom) block 1, 2, and 3 stops of light respectively.

Plain ND Filters

A plain ND filter reduces the amount of light passing through the lens (the "density" of the name), without affecting the color (hence "neutral"). In practical terms this has a similar effect to decreasing the ISO of the film: if you use a plain ND filter that blocks 2 stops of light with ISO 400 film, you will effectively be setting the aperture and shutter speed as if it were ISO 100, for example. This type of filter is most commonly associated with landscape photography—especially blurring water and clouds—but can also be useful for other subjects, such as taking outdoor portraits with a wide aperture and fast film on a bright day.

ND filters are available in a range of strengths, from those that reduce the light by 1 or 2 stops (which is great for portraits, or any other time when you want a slightly wider aperture), through to 10-stop and 15-stop "extreme" ND filters, which can turn a split-second exposure into one lasting minutes or hours. However, if you're using an extreme ND filter (or stacking multiple lower-strength ND filters) it can be impossible to focus automatically or manually with the filter in place, and the metering system on your camera may not be able to "see" through the filter either. The solution is to set the focus and take your light readings without the filter in place, and then adjust the exposure manually.

In addition to fixed-strength filters, there are also variable ND filters that allow you to "dial in" the filter's strength (typically from 2-8 stops). Although they can be more expensive than regular ND filters, the advantage is that you only need to use one of them. However, this convenience is countered by their usability: they tend not to be as neutral as single-strength filters. Obviously, this isn't a problem if you're shooting black and white, but it can be an issue for color work, especially if you are shooting with transparency film.

Tips

- There are numerous apps available to help you determine your filtered exposures with ND filters; one that allows you to combine multiple filters would be particularly useful.

- When you stack ND filters together, add the number of stops of light reduction together to find the overall effect. For example, stacking a 2-stop and 3-stop ND filter together will give you a 5-stop reduction in light.

- Don't forget to take reciprocity failure (see page 82) into account when you are using long exposure times.

- Extreme ND filters are rarely perfectly neutral, which can be problematic if you're shooting in color; stacking multiple low-strength ND filters will also emphasize any slight color shifts.

- A common buying mistake with ND filters is confusing filter factors with stops. A filter marked ND8 has a filter factor of 8, reducing the light by 3 stops: it is not a more extreme 8-stop filter. Make sure you know exactly what you are buying.

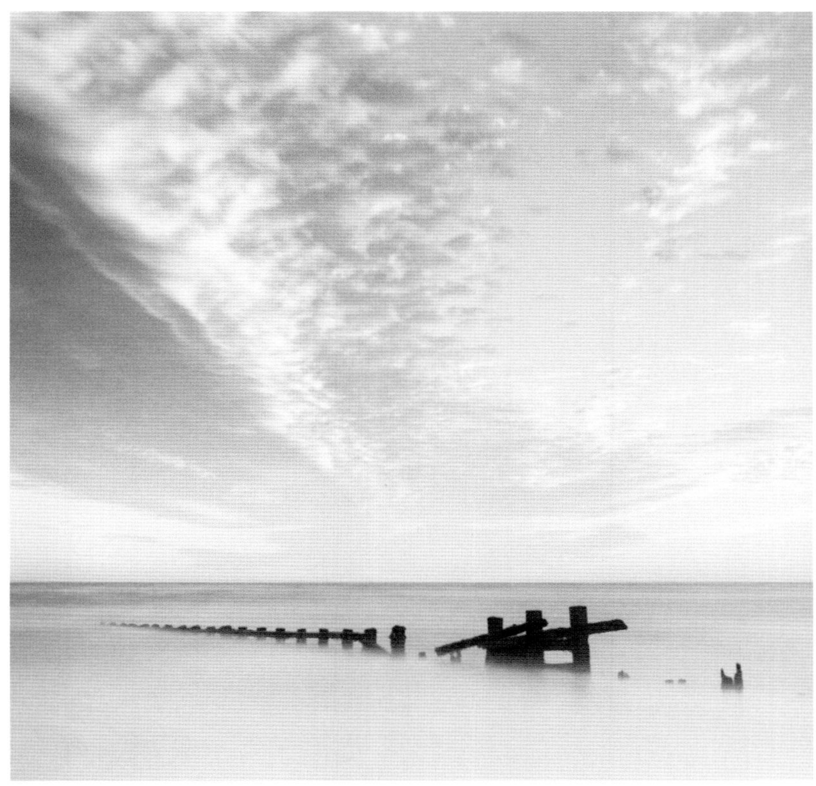

Above: The classic use for an ND filter is to extend the length of an exposure, often to increase the amount of motion blur in an image: seascapes and landscapes containing flowing water are the most common subjects, especially for more extreme ND filters.

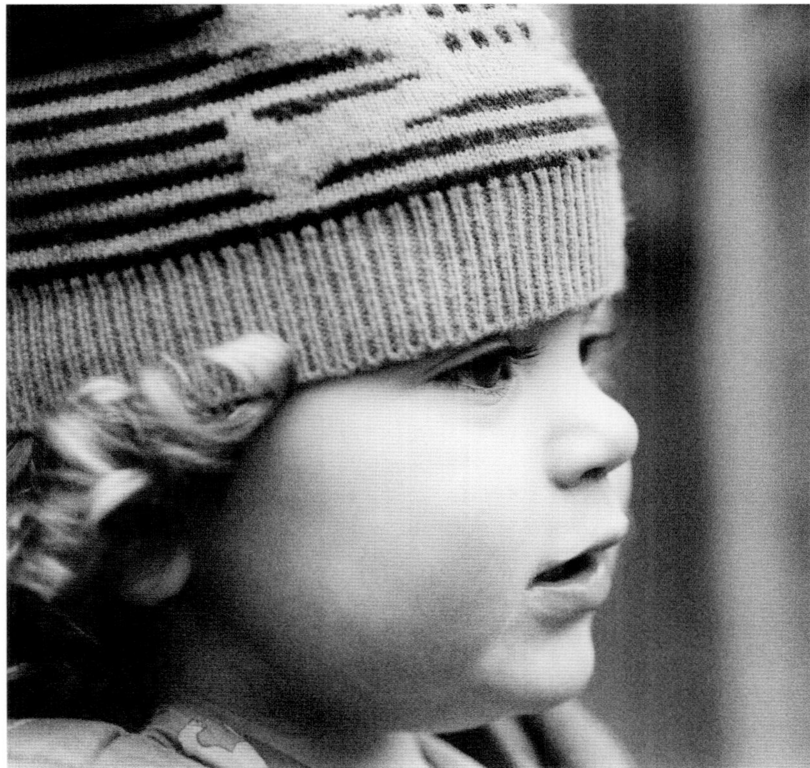

Above: My Olympus OM2SP 35mm SLR was loaded with black-and-white film rated at ISO 1600 when the batteries failed. Luckily, the camera has a mechanical 1/60 sec. shutter speed, so could still be used (albeit at a fixed shutter speed). Although the high ISO would have meant using a small aperture in the relatively bright conditions, fitting a 3-stop ND filter let me "open up" and shoot with a much wider aperture for a shallow depth of field.

ND FILTER STRENGTHS			
OPTICAL DENSITY	FILTER FACTOR	STOPS	TRANSMITTANCE (%)
0	0	0	100
0.3	ND2	1	50
0.6	ND4	2	25
0.9	ND8	3	12.5
1.2	ND16	4	6.25
1.8	ND64	6	1.5
3.0	ND1024 (or ND1000)	10	0.1
4.5	ND32768	15	0.003

Left: The strength of an ND filter can be expressed in a number of ways, including optical density, filter factor, stops, or transmittance. Different manufacturers use different systems, but this conversion grid shows how they all compare.

Graduated ND Filters

Graduated ND filters—or ND grads—are largely the preserve of landscape photographers looking to balance a bright sky with a darker ground. With an ND grad, half of the filter is clear and the other half is neutral density, which gets darker toward the top of the filter. ND grads come in a range of strengths (usually from 1-3 stops), and a variety of "transitions," which indicates how the neutral density and clear halves of the filter meet.

- **Soft:** A soft ND filter has a wide transition area from density to clear, so the join between the two areas is not obvious. This type of filter is ideal when the light and dark areas in the scene you are trying to balance are irregular; when the horizon is undulating, for example, or broken by mountains, trees, or some other element.
- **Hard:** The transition area on a hard-edged ND filter is narrow, and the move from clear to coated areas is more obvious. This type of ND grad is best suited to scenes with a relatively straight and level horizon line, or one that is broken by elements that you don't mind darkening.
- **Ultra hard:** Sometimes known as razor, the transition from the clear to coated areas on the filter is abrupt. This is ideal for the clearly defined horizon line in a seascape or a linear landscape.

Obviously, it's impossible to know which combination of strength and transition you will need for any given shot, and there are lots of possible filter permutations. The simplest answer would be to buy them all and cover every option. However, this is not only going to be expensive, but could also mean you end up with filters that you never use. Instead, think about your preferred landscape subject and use that to pick the most appropriate transition type; razor or hard if you shoot seascapes, for example. Then, think about when you like to shoot: if it's at the start and end of the day, when the sun is low in the sky, you will most likely need stronger ND grads, especially if you want to include the sun in the frame.

Selecting An ND Grad

When it comes to choosing how strong your ND grad should be there are several schools of thought. Some people like the sky to remain a little brighter than the ground; some prefer to match the two; and there are (a few) who like to bring the sky right down for dramatic effect. Whatever the case, the process starts with spot meter readings:

1. Take a spot meter reading from a midtone area on the ground. A patch of grass, a rock, or a nearby road lit by the sun are ideal. Alternatively, use a gray card.

2. Take a second spot meter reading from the brightest part of the sky in the scene you intend to photograph (but not the sun or its surrounding area).

3. Compare the two light readings to determine how many stops are between them, and then choose your filter strength based on your preferred result:

- To keep the sky brighter, fit a filter that will reduce the difference between your two readings to 1 stop (½ stop on transparency film). So, if the difference between your readings is 3 stops, use a 2-stop filter.

- To balance the sky and the ground use a filter equal to the difference in your meter readings: use a 3-stop filter for a 3-stop difference, for instance.

- To overpower the ground and create a moody sky, use a filter (or multiple filters) that exceeds the difference in meter readings; so use 4 or more stops of filtration for a 3-stop difference.

4. Take your shot, setting the exposure based on the light reading you took from the midtone area on the ground; the filter will adjust the exposure for the sky.

Left: Like regular ND filters, ND grads come in a range of strengths, but they also have a range of transitions from soft to very hard. These filters are 2- and 3-stop hard ND grads, although "neutral" is a little misleading, as they have a distinctly warm color bias.

Right: Measuring the difference between the sunlit grass and the brightest areas of cloud showed a 2-stop difference. On color transparency film I decided to use a 2-stop ND grad filter to ensure that the highlights were preserved, but for black and white I'd usually go a stop darker for added drama; in this instance using a 3-stop grad for my monochrome shot.

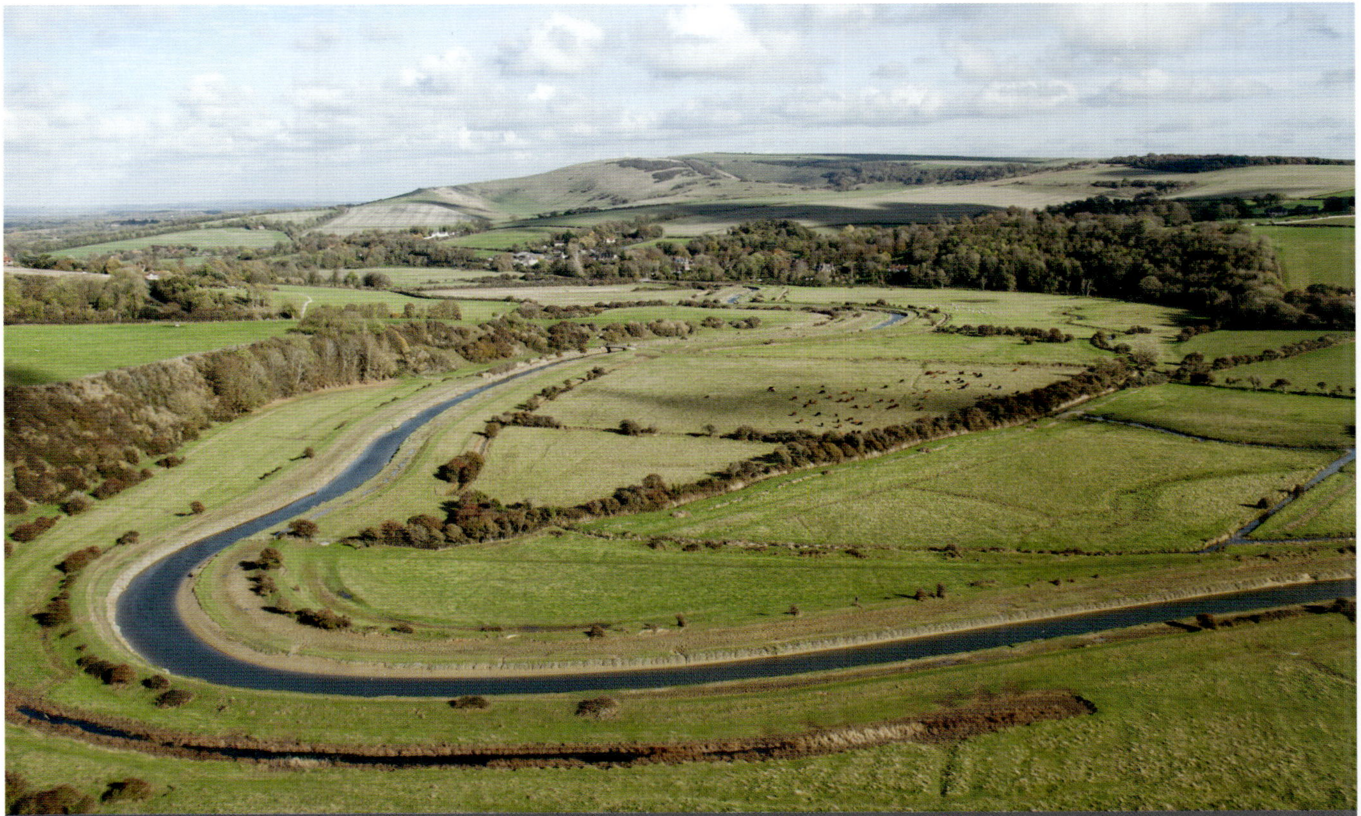

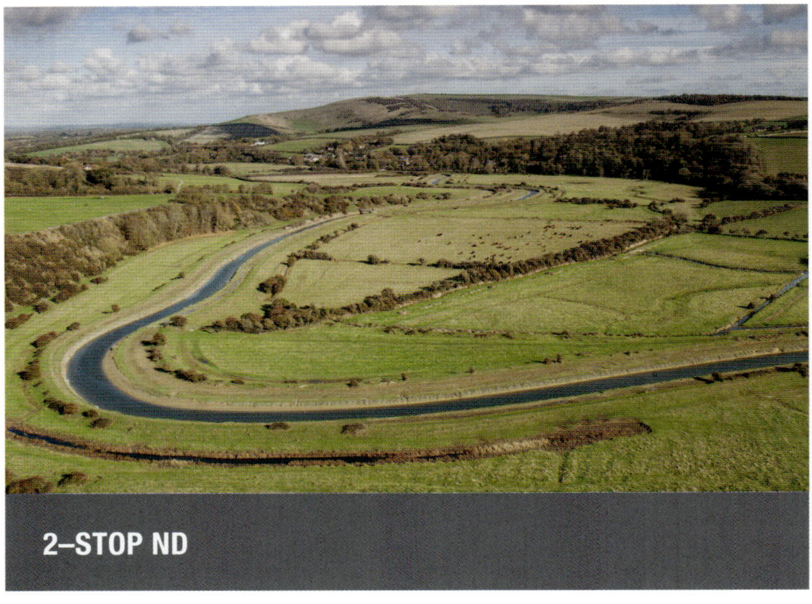

2–STOP ND

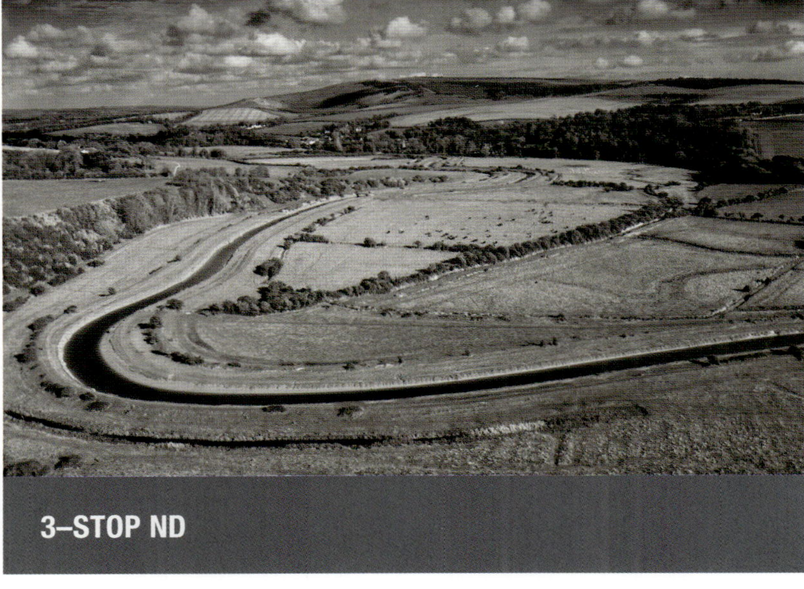

3–STOP ND

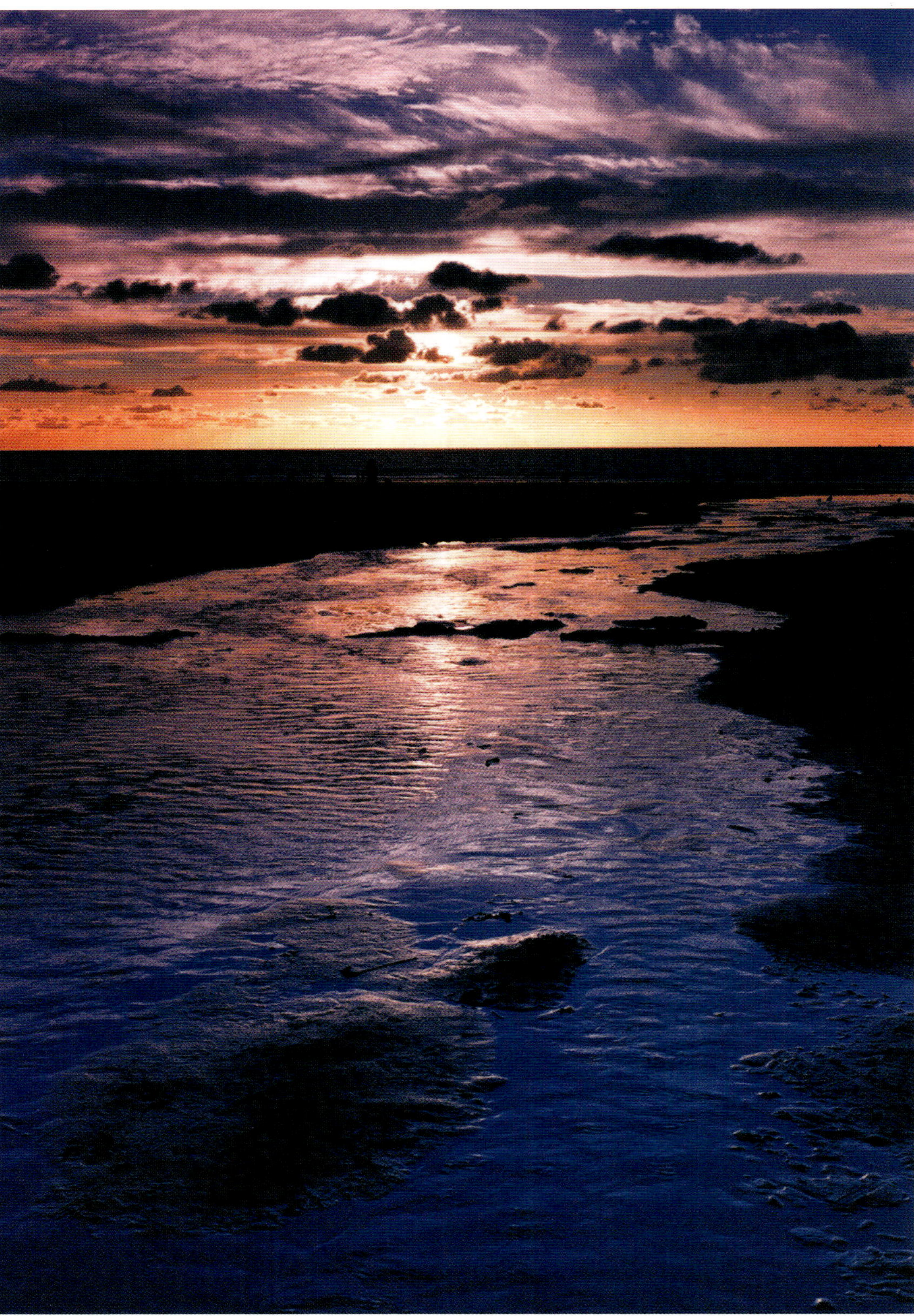

Tips

- A filter holder system and slot-in filters are essential for using ND grads, as you need to be able to precisely position the filter.

- If you scan your film, an alternative to ND filters is to shoot the same scene twice, at different exposure settings: one for the sky and one for the ground. You can then scan both frames and blend them in your editing software. Naturally, this will only work if your camera is mounted on a tripod.

REVERSE GRAD

At sunrise and sunset, the sky is brightest at the horizon while higher areas are darker. Conventional ND grads aren't ideal in this situation because the filter is quite likely to over-darken the upper area of sky, while not having a strong enough effect on the horizon. To tackle this, some manufacturers have produced "reverse" ND grads. As with a regular ND grad, these filters are half clear and half coated, but the major difference is that the ND is darkest where the two areas meet and becomes less dense toward the top of the frame (the reverse of a standard ND grad). Because the most pronounced darkening happens at the center of the filter, this allows you to neatly darken a bright horizon as the sun rises or sets.

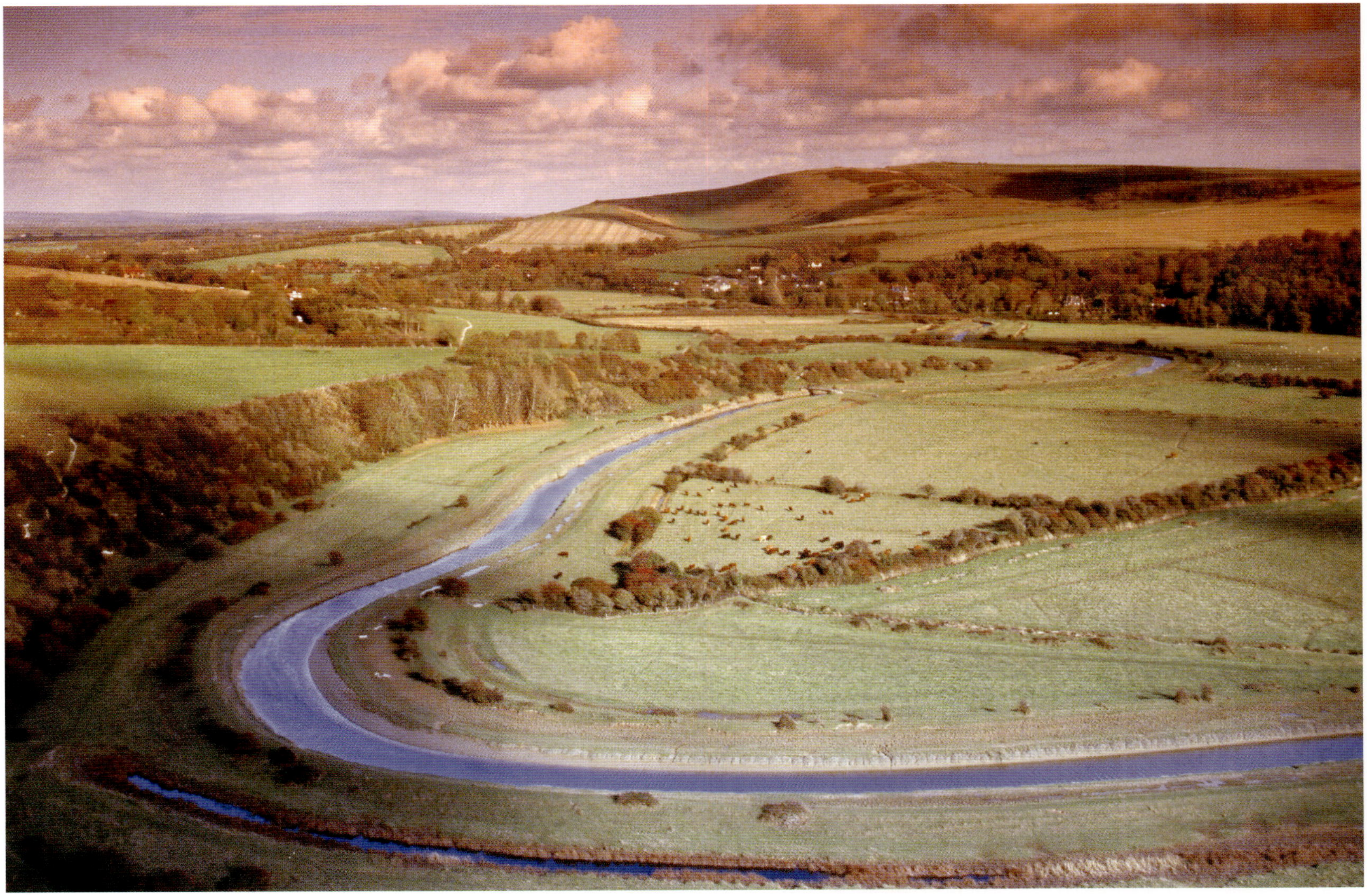

Left & above: As well as ND grads you can also get colored grad filters, which were once seen as a great way of injecting a little more atmosphere into color shots. This version of the scene on page 121 was taken through a "sunset" grad, but it's not that convincing…

Polarizing Filters

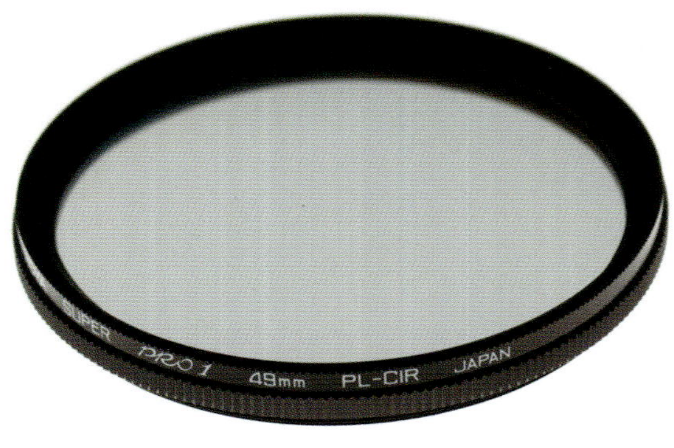

To understand polarizing filters you first need to understand what "polarized" light is. Wavelengths of light vibrate in different directions to each other, creating "unpolarized" light. However, when light reflects off a non-metallic surface, such as water, glass, or even wet leaves and rocks, it changes, and the wavelengths all vibrate in one particular direction: in doing so, the light becomes "polarized." The sky on a sunny day is also polarized, due to the light scattering as it travels through particles and moisture.

A polarizing filter only allows wavelengths that are vibrating in one direction to pass through it, which enables you to filter out polarized light. In doing so you can remove reflections from glass or water (to see beneath the surface, for example), intensify the color of wet leaves (again by removing the glare of reflected light), and deepen the blue of a sky, making clouds "pop," among other things.

To control how much polarized light is allowed to pass through the lens, a polarizing filter is designed so that it can be rotated. This changes the angle of polarization and therefore the intensity of the filter's effect. The angle between the filter and light source is important, though, as the polarization effect is strongest when the light source is at 90° to the camera, so finding the "sweet spot" will usually involve moving both your camera (or subject) and adjusting the filter. But don't simply look for the strongest effect. A fully polarized shot can sometimes look slightly odd, as it's not how we see the world with our own eyes. Retaining a slight reflection on water or dialing back the intensity of a blue sky can often make an image look more natural.

Above: A polarizing filter is designed so that it can be rotated in front of the lens to control the polarizing effect, but this is also determined by its angle to the sun.

Below: With this shot a polarizing filter had multiple effects. To start with it enhanced the color of the pale blue winter sky, but it also enriched the colors in the foliage, not only directly, but also their reflections, which were further improved thanks to the filter's glare-reducing properties.

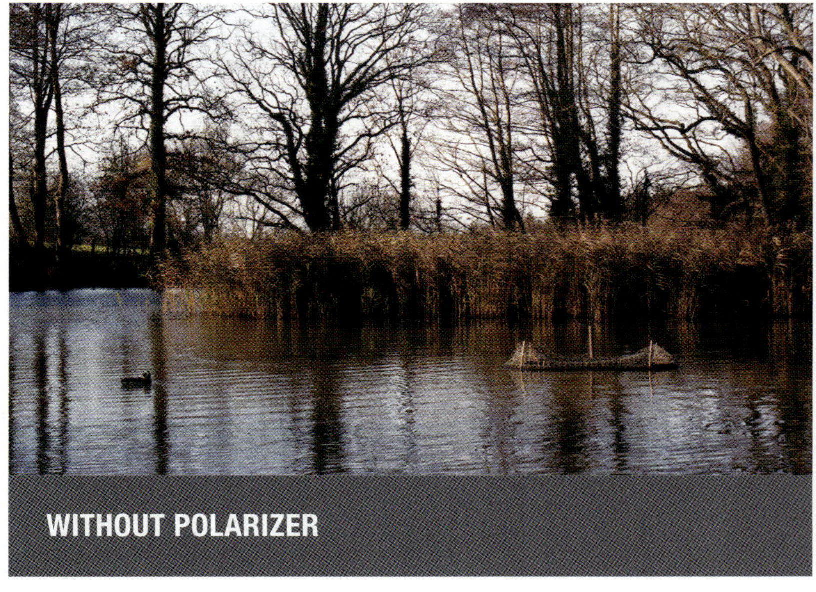

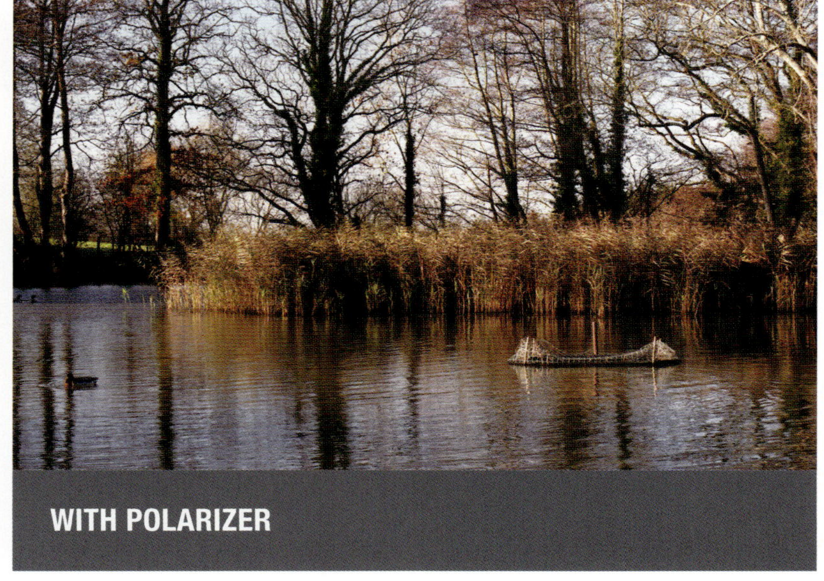

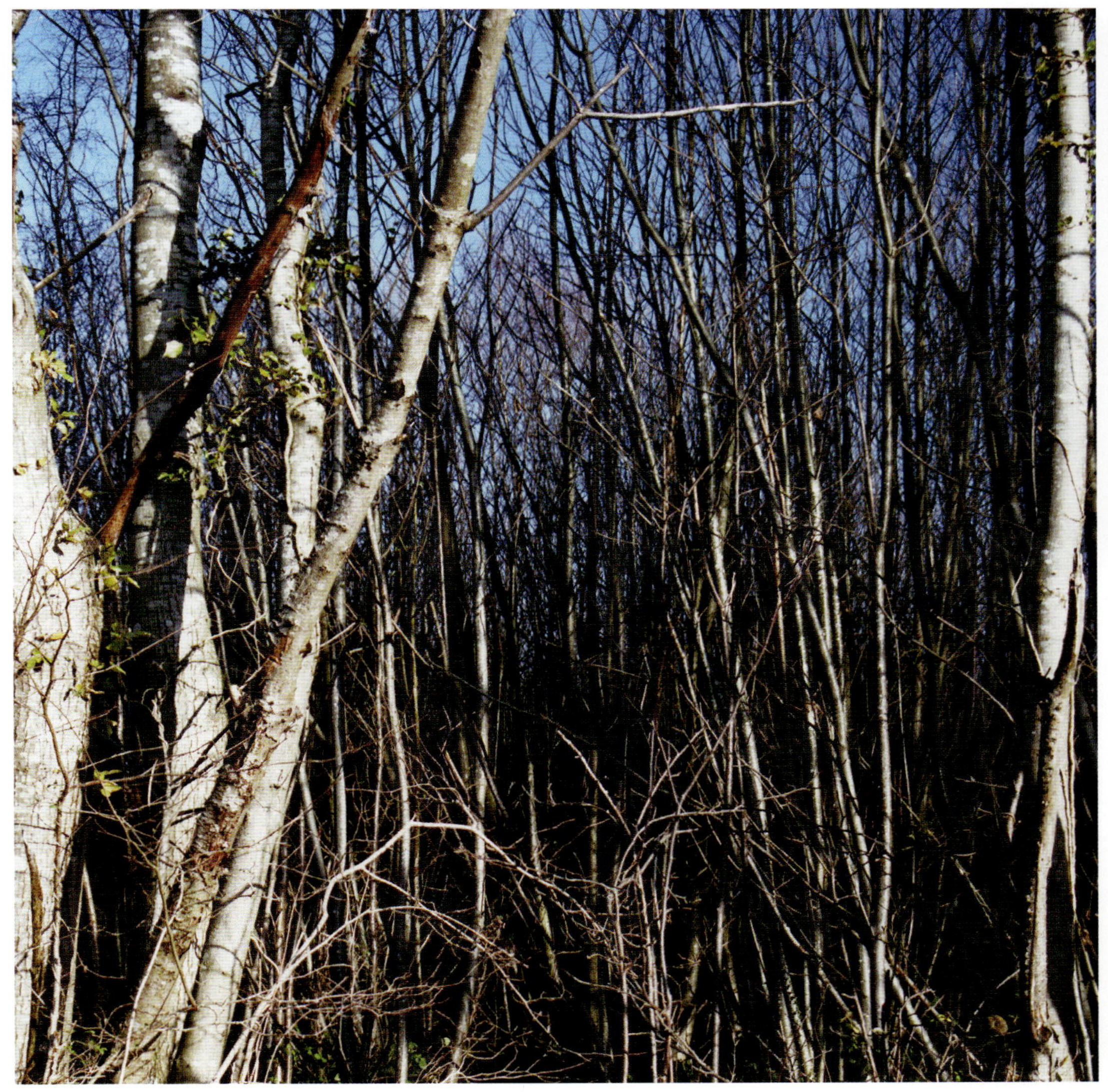

Above: The "classic" use for a polarizer in outdoor scenes is to intensify a blue sky, which was needed here to create some color contrast with the near-white, sunlit trees.

Tips

- Polarizing filters are closely associated with landscape photography, but they can also be useful for interiors (when windows appear in the shot), or still life images that include glass.

- Be aware that reflections off metal cannot be reduced using a polarizing filter.

- Polarizing filters reduce the amount of light passing through the lens by up to 2 stops, so they can also be used as mild ND filters.

- Reducing reflections with a polarizing filter also reduces contrast; but contrast is usually increased in a polarized sky.

Other Filters

The filters we have looked at so far can all be bundled into the category of "technical filters" as they are designed to overcome a specific technical challenge. There are, however, many other filters out there, ranging from those that are genuinely useful, to others that are more esoteric.

UV & Skylight Filters

A UV or skylight filter should be thought of as a "technical" filter, because its main purpose is to filter out any unwanted UV light. With color film, this can be important, because if you're shooting at high altitudes or on a sunny day when there is a lot of UV light, images can take on a slightly blue color cast without a filter attached. As always, this is much more noticeable on transparency film, as the shift tends to be neutralized when prints are made from negatives.

However, few people consciously use them for their intended purpose, and instead attach a UV or skylight filter permanently to their lens to protect the front element from damage. Although it's debatable how useful this will be if you drop the lens from a great height, it can help prevent the ingress of water and dust into the lens, and any damage from aggressive cleaning—not to mention filtering out UV light—so it's worth considering.

Effects Filters

There simply isn't space to cover all of the "creative" filters introduced over the years, or highlight the crimes against photography that have been committed by some of them. Some truly horrific photographs can be created using these decidedly unnatural filters, but don't let that stop you playing around with them: rainbow filters, sunset filters, colored grads, starburst filters, fog and mist, a bewildering array of soft focus and diffusion effects, and even the decidedly suspect "through the keyhole" cut-out filters can all add a retro look to your photographs.

Below: As well as using dedicated effects filters to transform your images you can also create a neat color effect by combining a regular polarizing filter with a polarizing gel designed to go over lights. Place transparent plastic objects above or in front of the lighting gel and then use a polarizing filter on the lens; adjusting the filter will reveal a vivid spectrum of color (actually stresses within the plastic) that is invisible to the naked eye. The subject of this shot is a plastic graduate I use to measure out my processing chemicals.

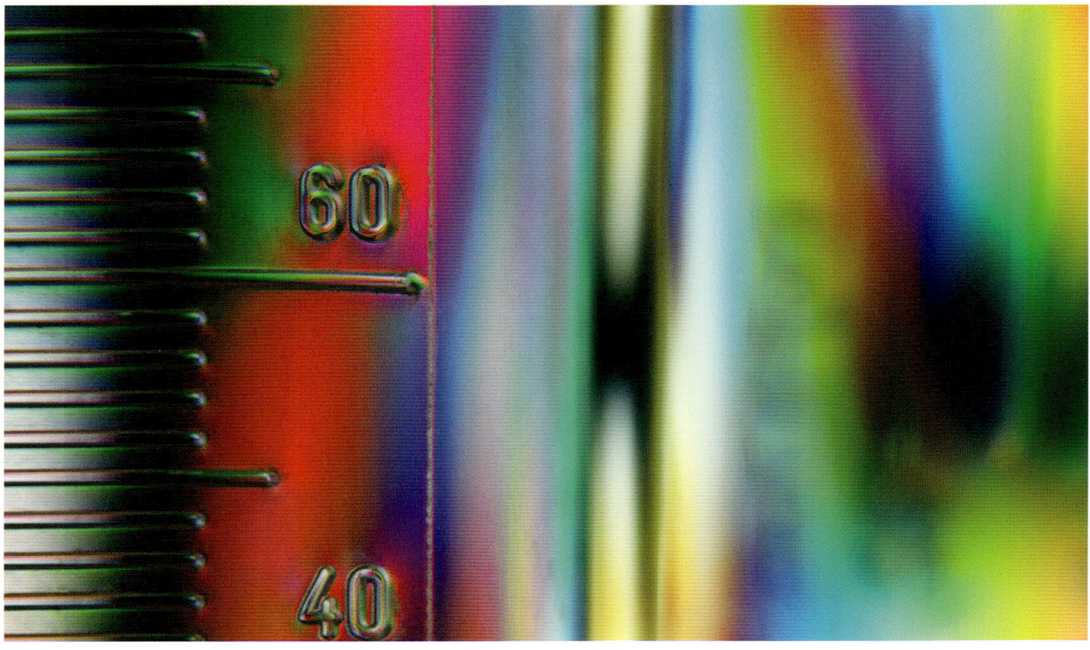

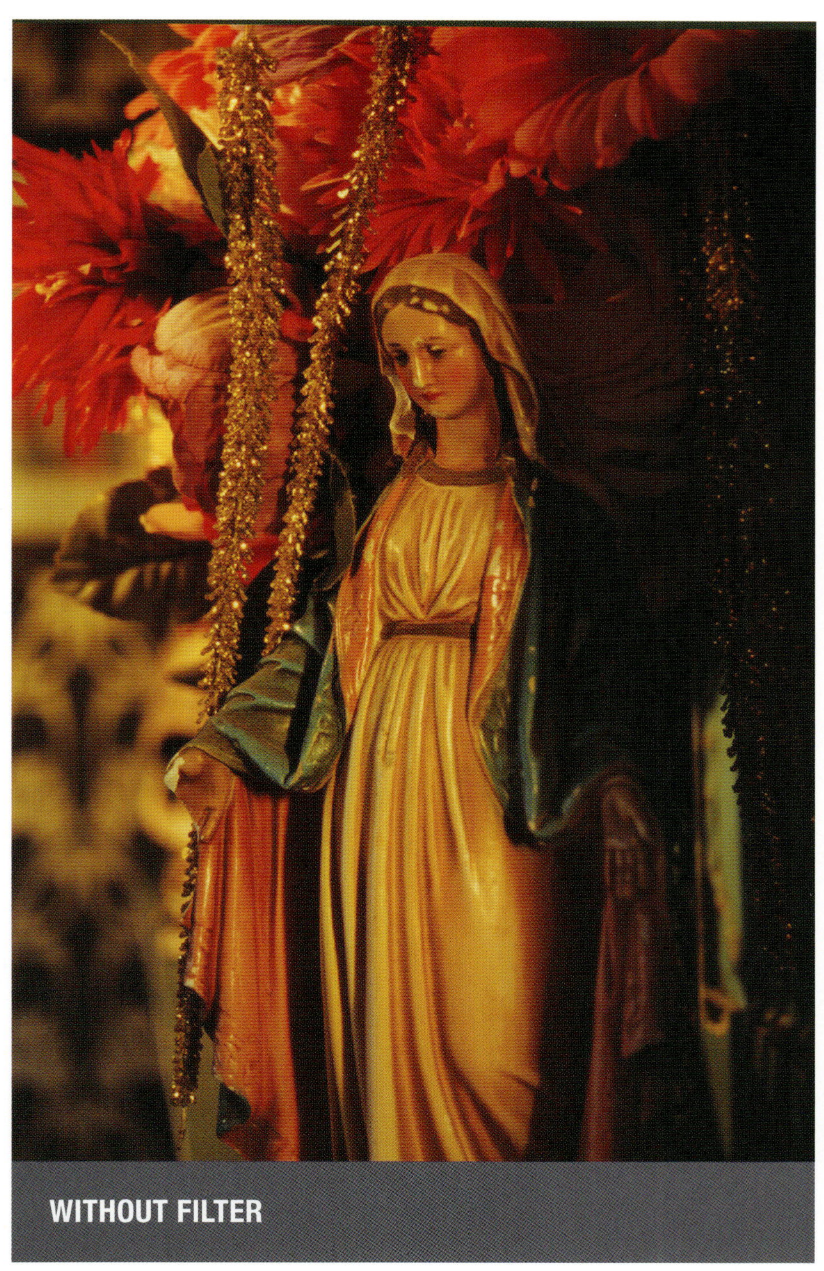

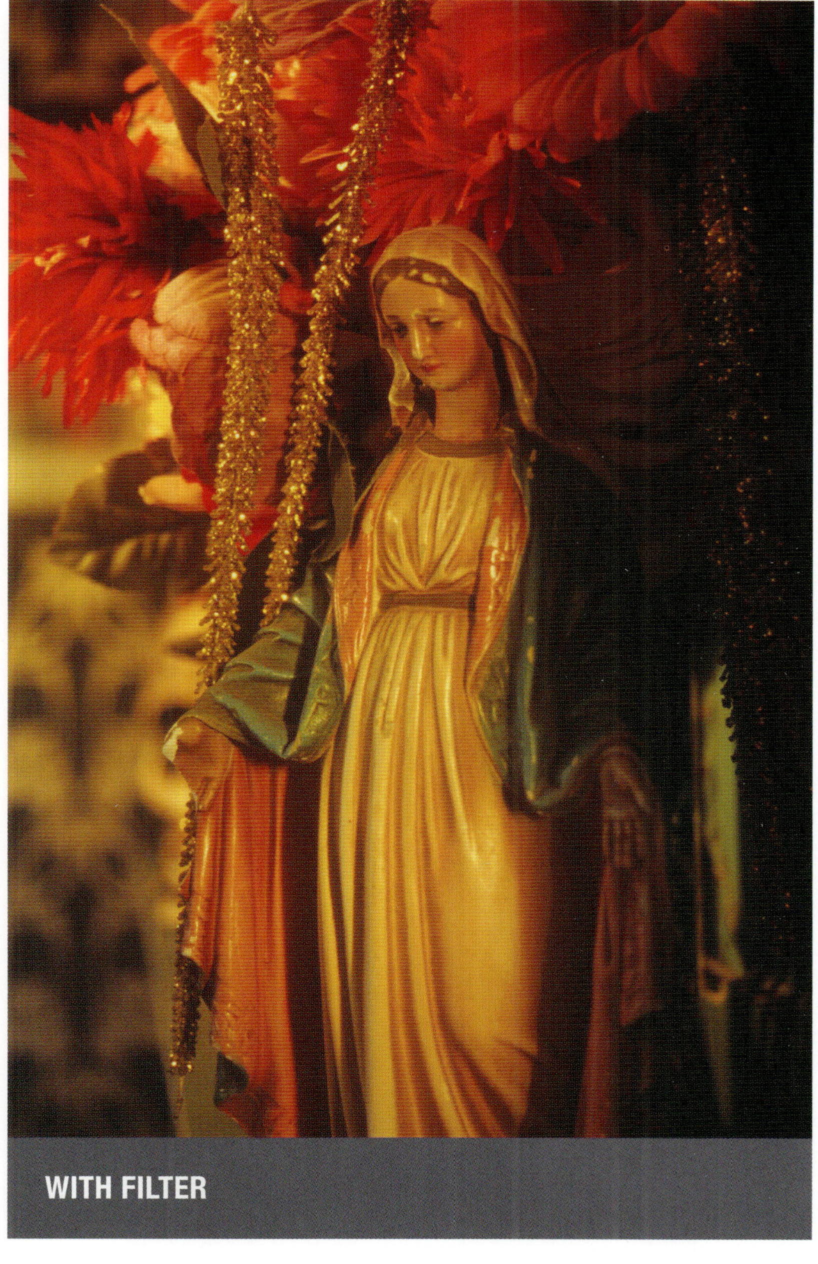

Above & right: A whole host of filters have drifted in and out of fashion over the years, and soft-focus filters often divide opinion. In some situations they can add to the atmosphere of a shot, though; this image was taken using tungsten lighting (on daylight-balanced film) to give it a warm color, with a "pastel" filter to add some diffusion.

Pinhole Photography

While mainstream photography has evolved around optical lenses designed to focus and sharpen the image entering your camera, the luxury of a glass lens is entirely optional. In its simplest sense, pinhole photography relies on nothing more than a light-tight box, a pinhole, and some film or photographic paper, and yet these three components are enough to make a camera that is capable of creating some truly unique and fascinating images. This is especially true if you make your own pinholes and/or cameras, which as you will see on the following pages is neither difficult, nor costly, and can be a whole heap of fun.

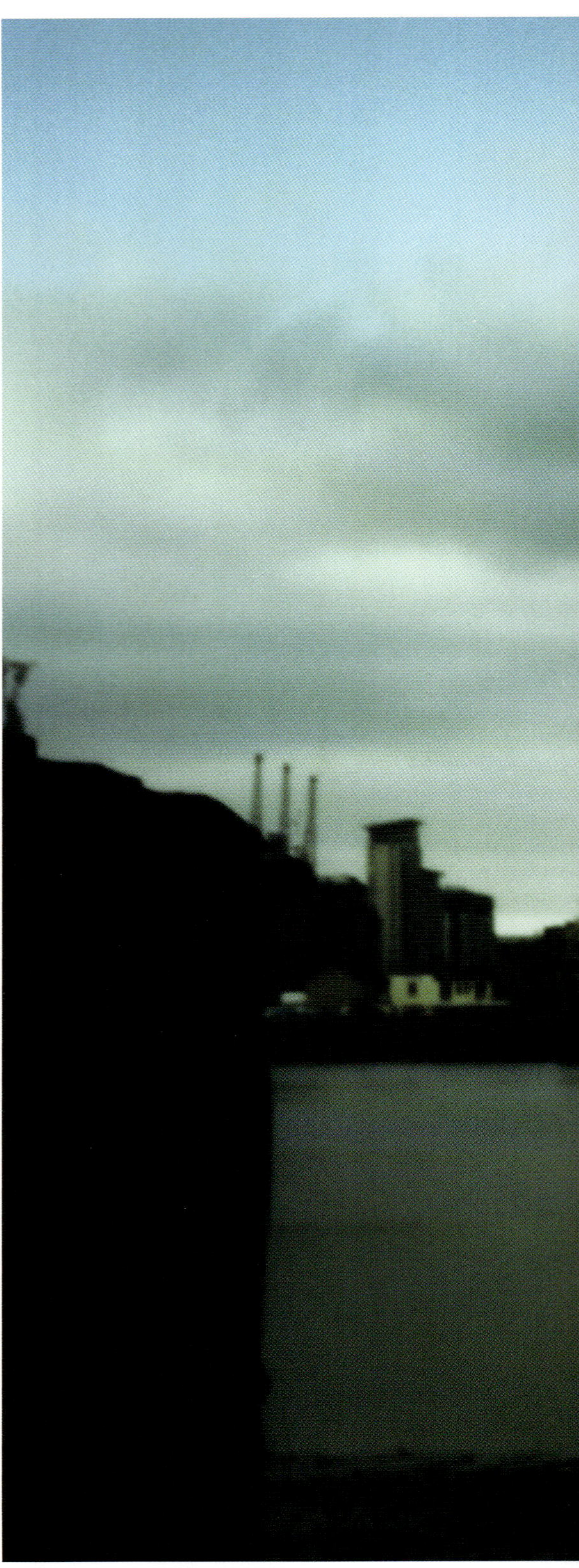

Right: London's Canary Wharf, as seen from Greenwich in 2003. For me, the beauty of pinhole photography is not its ability to record reality, but the power it has to capture mood and atmosphere by pushing film to its limits, and sometimes beyond.

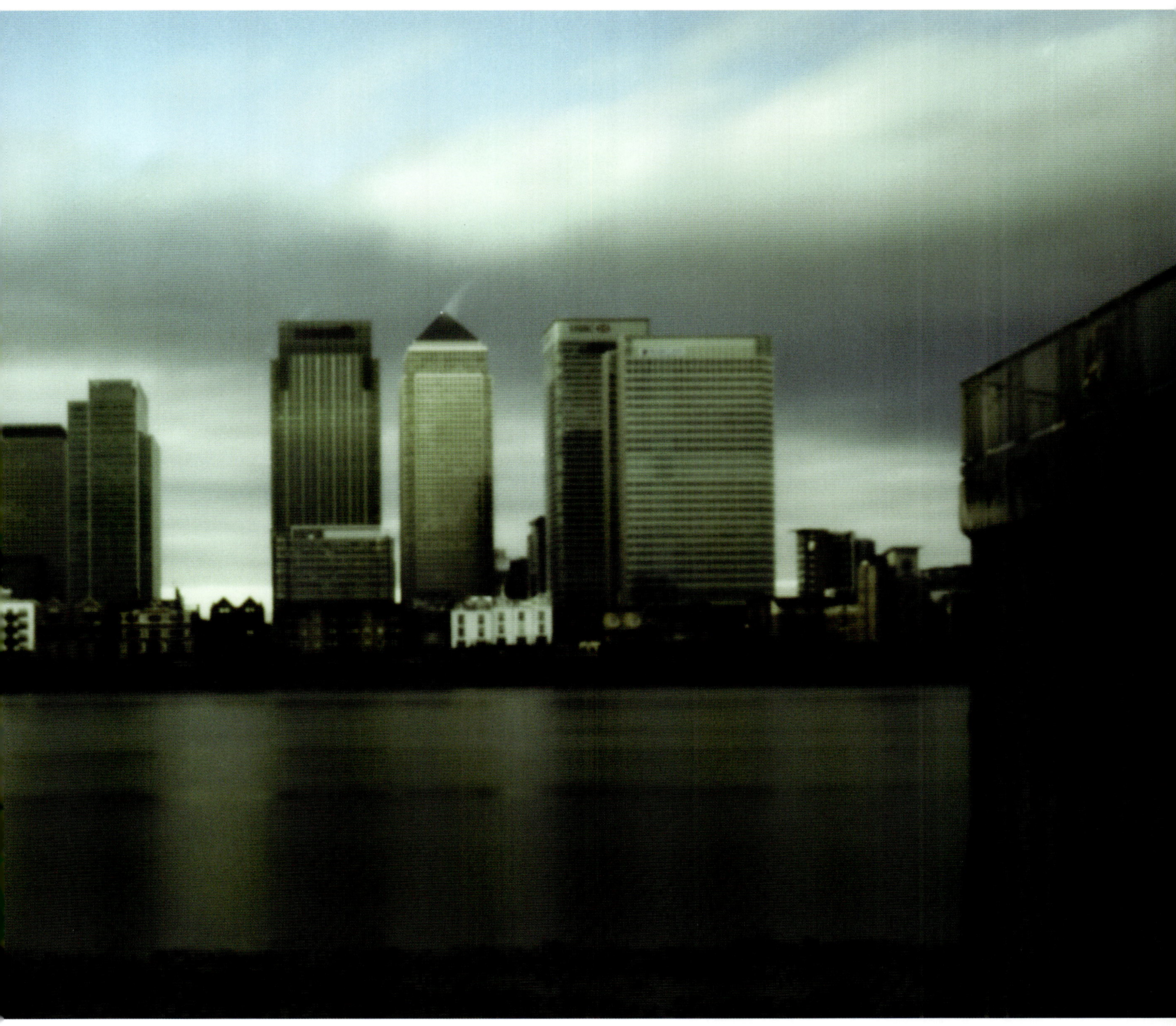

Pinhole Primer

Although people make and use pinholes with their digital cameras, this is one area of photography where film is definitely the better option. The reason for this comes down to the recording medium itself. With pinhole photography you are shooting through a tiny hole, which can give you a fixed aperture in the region of f/250 (or smaller). This means you will be dealing with long exposures. Really long exposures.

If there is one thing that digital sensors don't like it's being exposed for a long time, because this causes heat to build up on the sensor, which creates non-image-forming digital "noise" that can degrade an image. Film, on the other hand, doesn't suffer from this problem. Sure, you will need to take reciprocity failure (see page 82) into account when you shoot, but your images won't become any grainier as the exposure time increases: the grain is part of the film's emulsion and that doesn't change, regardless of whether you're making an exposure lasting 1/1000 sec. or one that lasts for an hour or more.

Commercial Cameras

The easiest way to get started with pinhole photography is to buy a pinhole camera. There are plenty of options out there, ranging from beautiful wood and brass boxes from the likes of Zero Image to the cheap-and-cheerful toy-camera based offerings of Holga, with lots of choice in between, covering formats from 35mm right up to 10x8in sheet film.

There are two main benefits to buying a readymade camera like this. The first is that the mechanical aspects of the film holding and transporting systems will have been worked out for you, so whether you shoot 35mm, medium-format roll film, or large-format sheet film, loading your film (and winding it on, where necessary) is usually as easy as it is with a regular camera.

The second benefit is that the pinhole is likely to be optimized for the camera, although this isn't guaranteed, especially with low-cost pinhole cameras. Some of the more refined offerings also use high-quality materials for their pinhole plates and precision-cut them to ensure the hole is a good match to the camera, allowing it to deliver the sharpest (in pinhole terms) results.

Below: The principle of pinhole photography is based on an observation going back thousands of years: namely, that light passing through a small aperture will project an inverted image. All that is needed to make a pinhole camera is a light-tight box with a pinhole in it and a light-sensitive medium (whether that be film, photographic paper, or a digital sensor) to record the projected image.

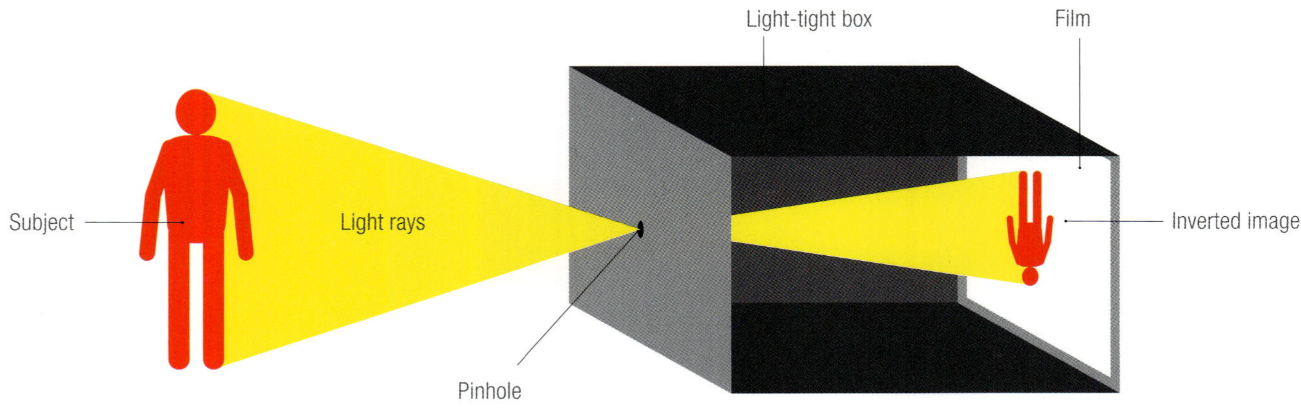

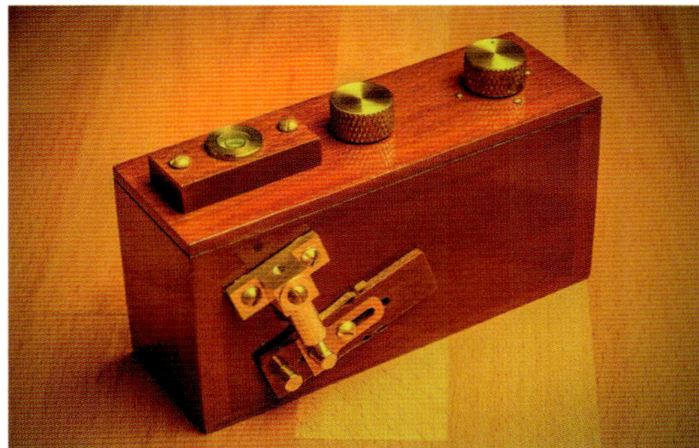

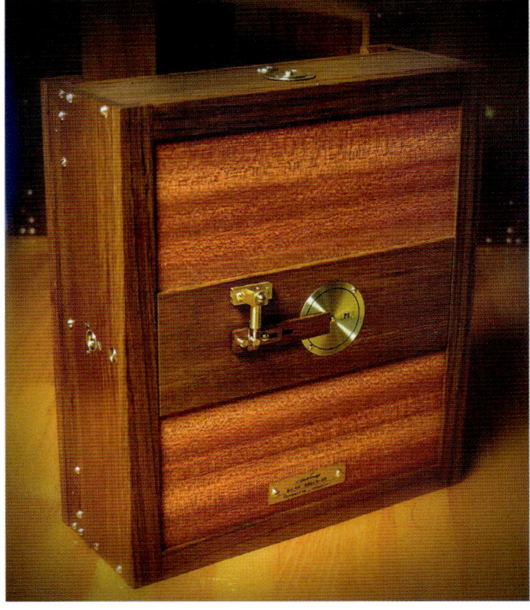

Above: Zero Image makes a wide range of wooden pinhole cameras covering formats from 35mm (top) all the way up to 10x8in (above). The benefits of a bespoke camera like this are a quality pinhole lens, a shutter mechanism, and—where applicable—a film transport mechanism, which all help to make shooting pinhole as simple as possible.

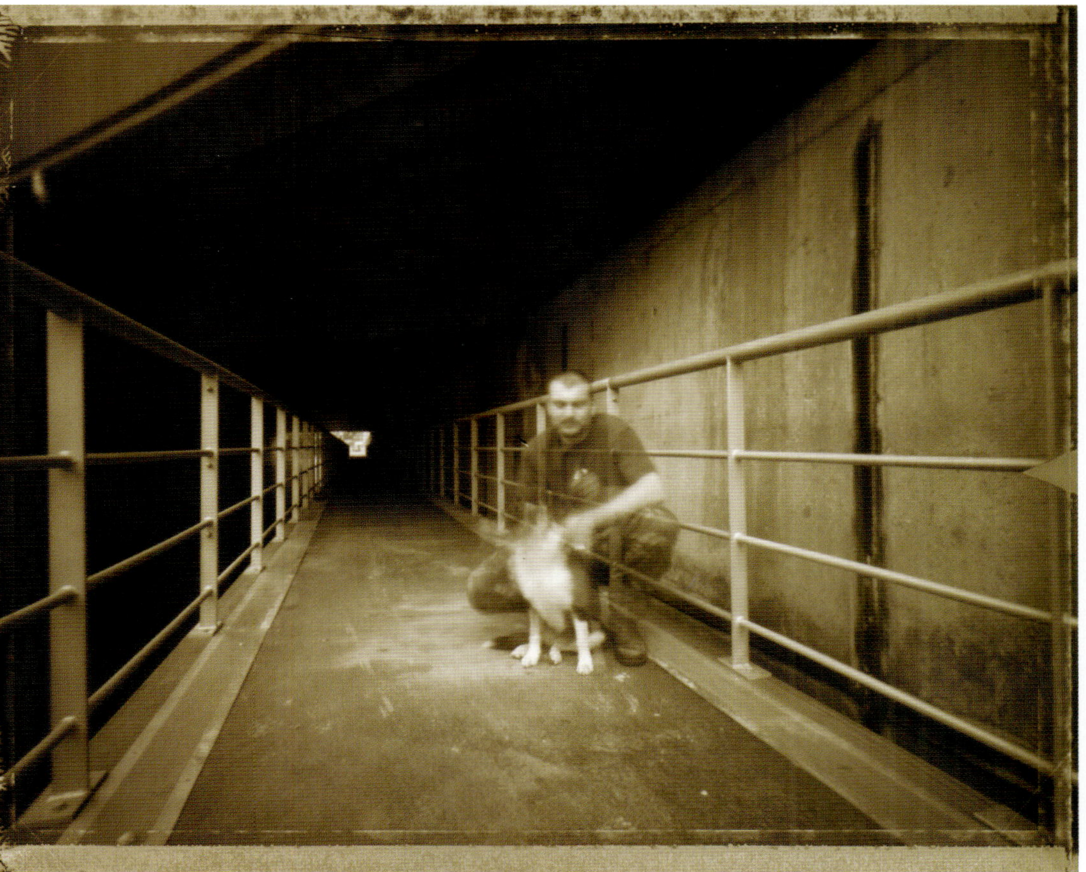

Above: This shot was taken using a Watkins Classic 50 pinhole camera, which is a mahogany 5x4in camera with a brass lens and an ultrawide 50mm focal length. I have no idea what the exposure time was for this "selfie," but I left midway through the exposure to create a "ghostlike" image.

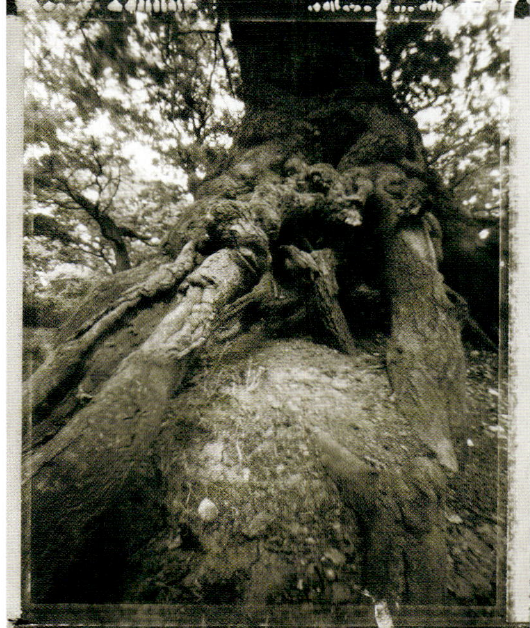

Left: For this pinhole shot I used Polaroid's Type 55 instant film, which gives a positive print and a black-and-white negative with a distinctive border. Unfortunately, like all Polaroid's peel-apart film it is no longer available, and attempts to resuscitate this particular film in the form of New55 have now ceased.

Homebrew Cameras

Although commercial pinhole cameras are great to use, pinhole photography—more than any other photographic genre—opens itself up to self-made camera designs and builds. In doing so, the regular rules of what a camera is and what it can be made of are turned on their head.

Any light-tight container (or container that can be made light-tight) has the potential to be transformed into a pinhole camera, and from a matchbox to a panel van, pinhole photographers the world over have exploited a wide array of high- and low-tech solutions in their pinhole endeavors.

Tips

- Brass shim with a thickness of 0.002in (0.05mm) is great for making high-quality pinholes. Try your local model-making store or look online for suitable sheets.

- Ideally, the pinhole should be perfectly round, as any deviation from this will affect image quality and introduce distortions.

The Pinhole

At the heart of any pinhole camera is the pinhole itself. You can buy these from specialist suppliers online, and this is a great option if you want a quality camera, as you can choose a pinhole with a close-to-optimum size for your camera.

Alternatively, you can make a pinhole plate yourself using nothing more sophisticated than an aluminum drinks can and a pin (see below).

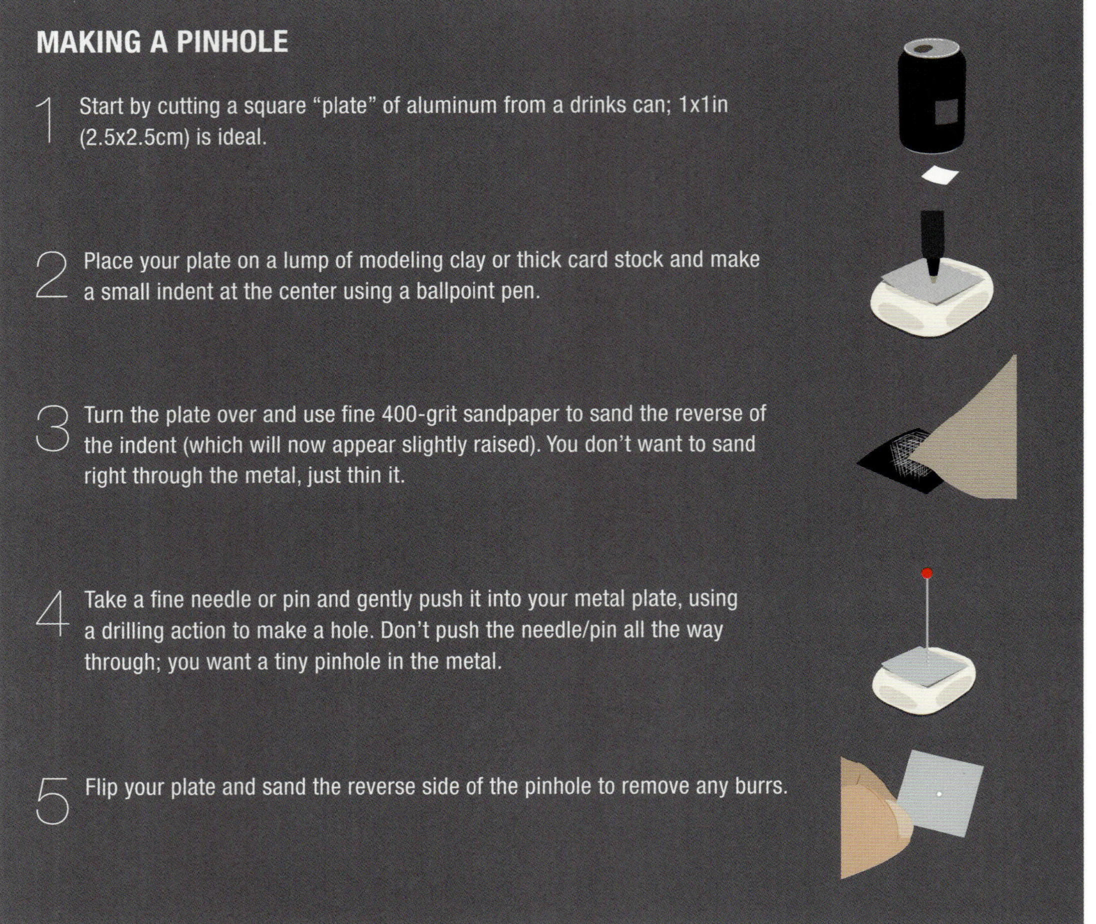

MAKING A PINHOLE

1. Start by cutting a square "plate" of aluminum from a drinks can; 1x1in (2.5x2.5cm) is ideal.

2. Place your plate on a lump of modeling clay or thick card stock and make a small indent at the center using a ballpoint pen.

3. Turn the plate over and use fine 400-grit sandpaper to sand the reverse of the indent (which will now appear slightly raised). You don't want to sand right through the metal, just thin it.

4. Take a fine needle or pin and gently push it into your metal plate, using a drilling action to make a hole. Don't push the needle/pin all the way through; you want a tiny pinhole in the metal.

5. Flip your plate and sand the reverse side of the pinhole to remove any burrs.

Right: How sharp (or otherwise) your pinhole images are has a lot to do with the hole itself: a round hole free from burrs and made in a thin material will create the sharpest images. However, this only holds true if the pinhole is then mounted at the optimum distance from the film.

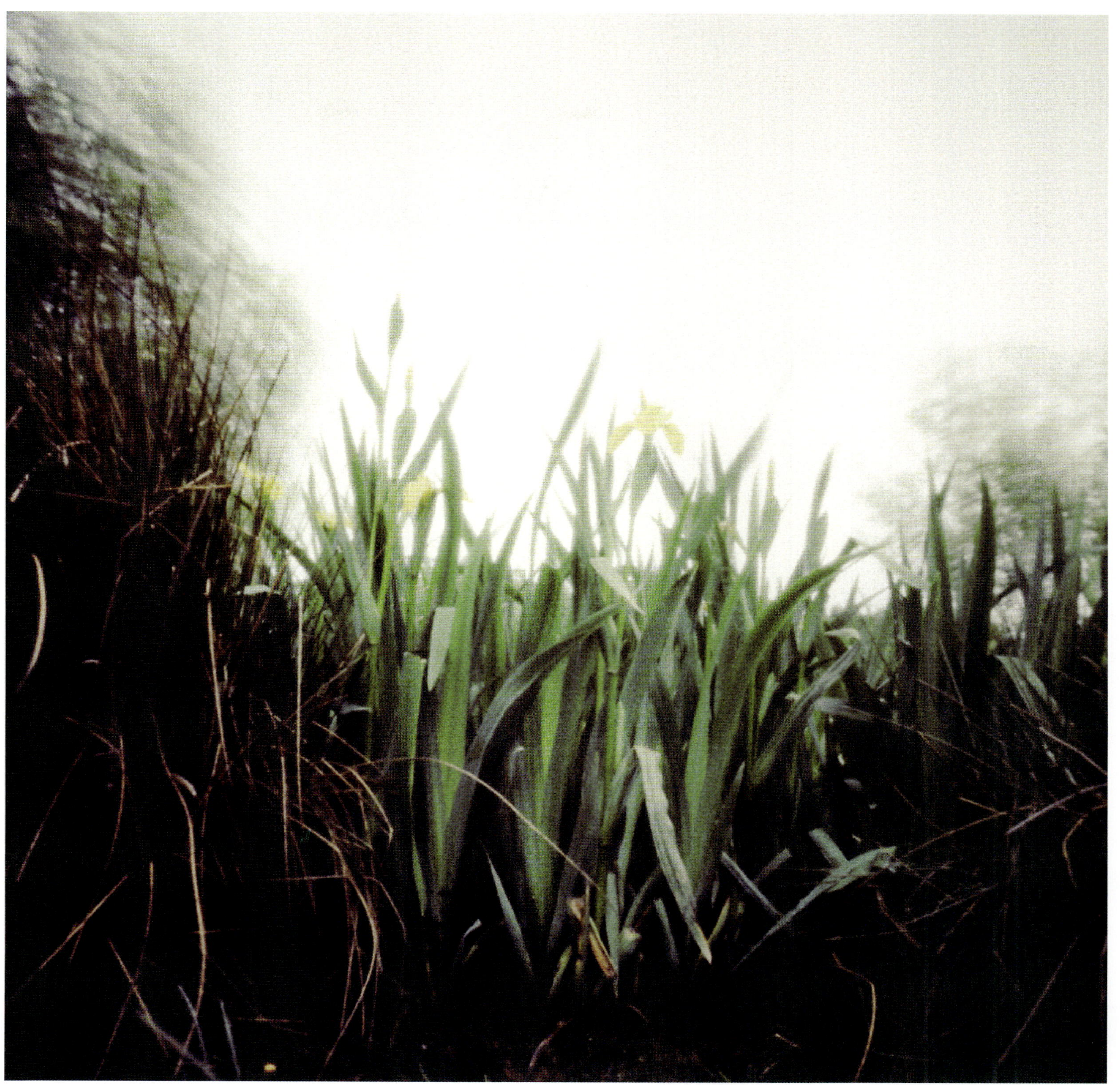

Converted Cameras

Once you've made (or bought) your pinhole you need something to put it in, and one of the easiest ways to get into homebrew pinhole photography is to convert an existing camera. This is a great first-time project, as it will take care of any issues regarding film holding/winding and making the box light tight, and most cameras have a tripod socket so that you can hold your camera steady when you shoot. Look out for an old camera with a broken shutter or lens and swap the lens out for a pinhole. There are piles of box cameras, folding cameras, and other vintage offerings online and in thrift stores that fit this description, although you will have to work out how to remove the lens so you can stick a pinhole in its place.

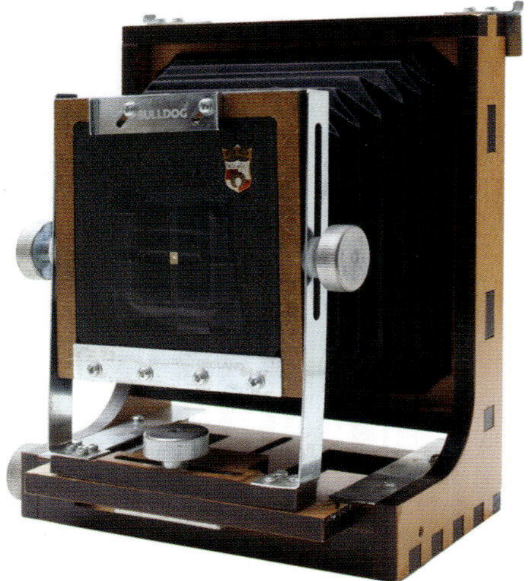

Below: Converting a large-format camera into a pinhole camera involves mounting a pinhole in a lens panel. This 5x4 camera came in kit form and had to be assembled; it's not solid enough to hold a heavy large-format lens, so I use it with a homemade pinhole plate instead. I made a selection of pinholes to choose from and the one I settled on measures 0.018in (0.46mm). This is about right for a 120mm focal length, which I've (roughly) marked on the camera's focusing rail to help me set up.

Focal Length & Pinhole Size

Over the years there have been numerous formulas suggested for working out the optimum pinhole size for a camera. Although they are all slightly different, they are all based on the focal length of the camera, and will allow you to either work out the optimum pinhole size for a particular camera (which is useful if you've got a camera and want to put the "best" pinhole in it), or determine the ideal focal length for a specific pinhole diameter (which is useful if you've made your own pinhole and want the "perfect" camera to fit it in). The various formulas will work regardless of the camera format, and apply equally to converted cameras and scratch-built ones.

Unless you really love the math involved with fairly complex formulas, the simplest option is to search online for "pinhole size calculators," which will typically let you enter a pinhole size or focal length, and then perform all the calculations needed to give you the optimum setting for the other variable. There are plenty of pinhole calculators out there—some more advanced than others—but they can give slightly different results, depending on the formula driving them. Because no one formula is accepted as definitive I would suggest trying a few online calculators and then averaging the results: this will be about as close as you can get to the "right" answer.

Tips

- If you shoot with a large-format camera, you can easily turn it into a pinhole camera by fitting a pinhole to one of your existing lens boards. Try using a piece of black electrical tape as a simple shutter.

- If you can find a camera with a working shutter (and Bulb mode), you may want to try and remove the lens and aperture, but not the shutter. You can then use the camera's Bulb setting to make your exposures.

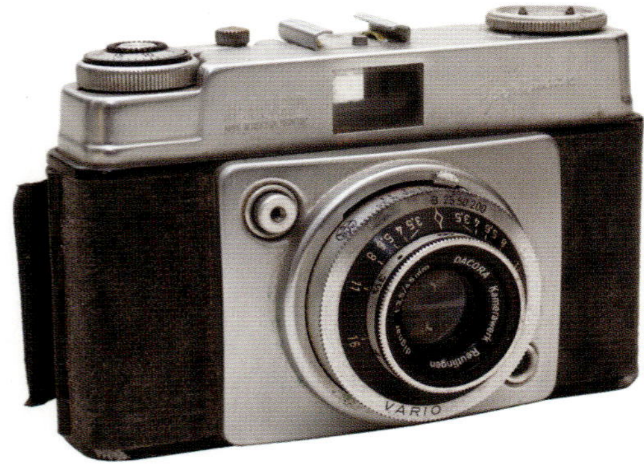

Below: When the shutter on this tired old 35mm camera stopped working there was no point fixing it, but the film winding mechanism was fine, so it had the potential for a great little pinhole camera. I removed the lens, replaced it with a homemade pinhole plate, and gave it a makeover with some wallpaper—the addition of a "step up" filter ring on the front now means it can take screw-in filters as well!

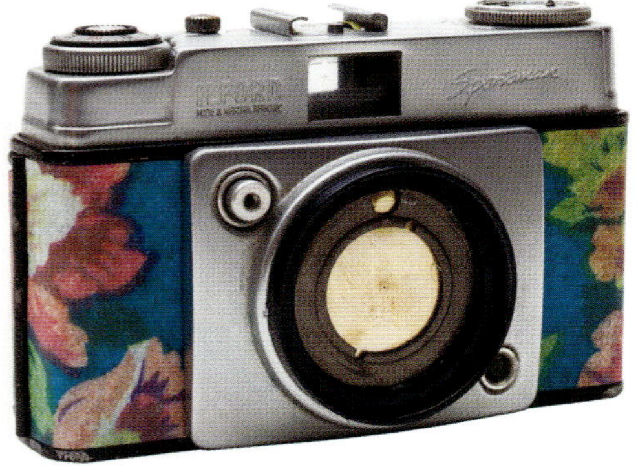

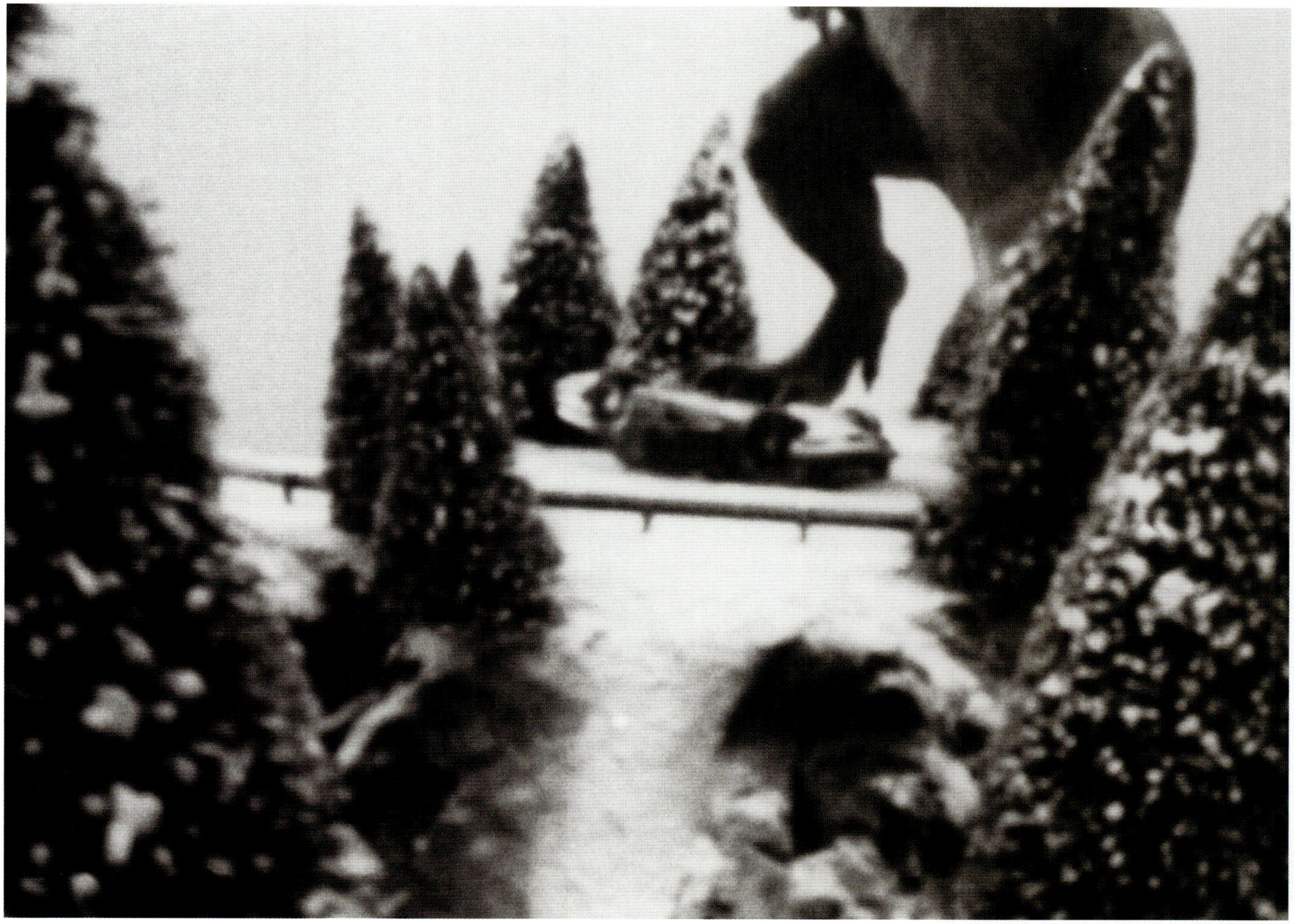

Left: I shot this B-movie themed "dino attack" with the converted Ilford Sportsman pinhole camera shown opposite. Its simple viewfinder helped me aim the camera, but I was so close to my subject (roughly 6in/15cm) that it was only a very rough guide. Even with ISO 400 film and a bright 800W tungsten lamp the exposure time was in the region of 30–45 minutes once reciprocity failure had been accounted for.

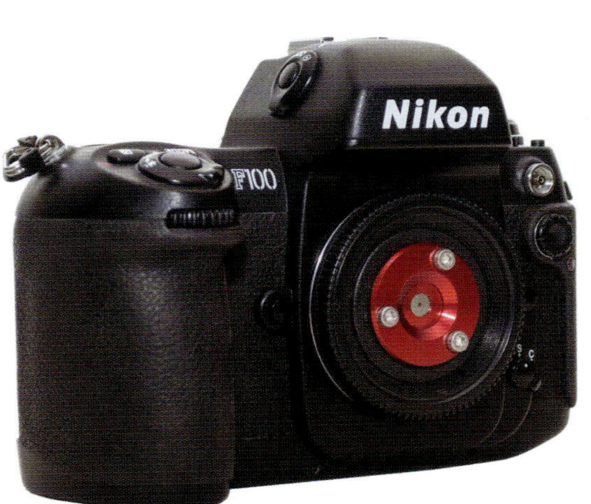

Left: An alternative to a dedicated pinhole camera is a "pinhole cap," which is essentially a pinhole plate mounted in a camera body cap that you attach to your SLR like a regular lens. You can buy these or make your own; in either case you need to set the camera to manual exposure mode and use the Bulb function to make your exposures.

PINHOLE FOCUS

Pinhole cameras don't focus in the traditional sense. Instead, the tiny aperture creates an expansive depth of field that stretches from a few inches in front of the lens to infinity, creating images that are sharp throughout the frame. However, "sharp" in pinhole terms is not the same as "sharp" when you're using a lens, as the pinhole is affected by the limiting effect of diffraction, which softens images slightly. This is part of the beauty of pinhole images.

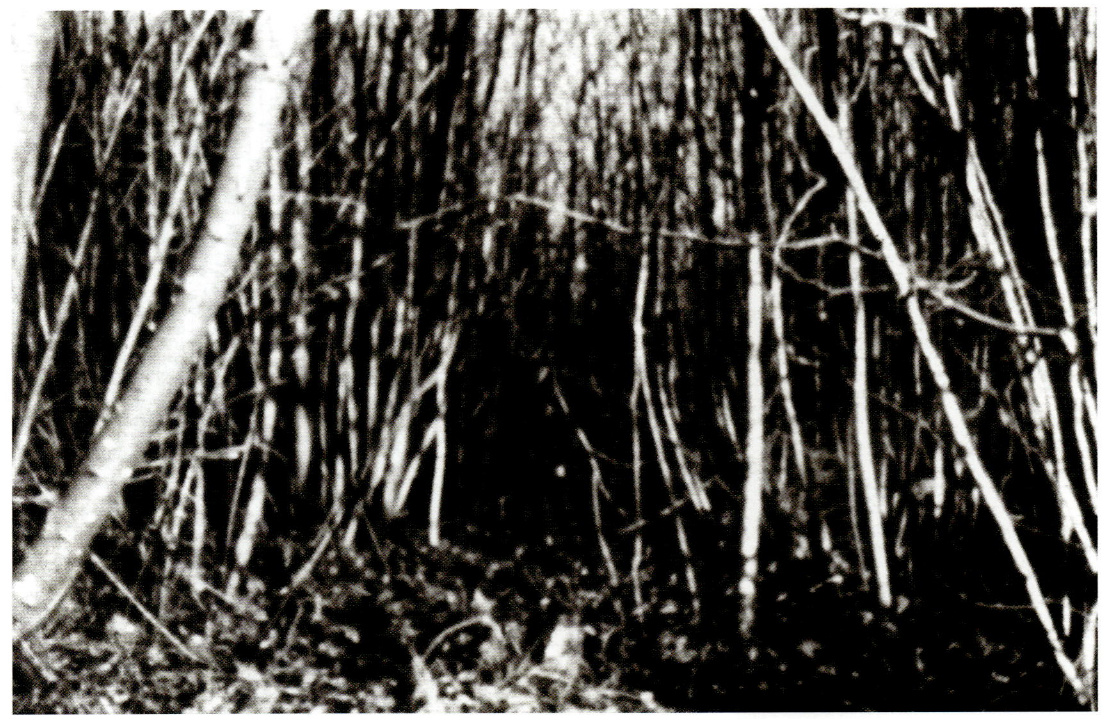

Scratch-Built Cameras

All you need to scratch-build a pinhole camera is a light-tight container of some description (or something that can be made light tight) and a pinhole plate. If you're just getting started, a small metal container with a tight-fitting lid—such as an empty coffee can or cookie tin—is ideal. Not only is the metal naturally light tight, but the lid can usually be sealed easily with black electrical tape, and the container will be rugged enough to be used over and over again. Wood is another popular material for pinhole cameras, for much the same reason, and for more sophisticated designs it can also be easier to work with.

Once you have your camera, mounting a pinhole is a very simple procedure. It doesn't matter if you've bought a laser-cut pinhole or made a plate yourself (as outlined on page 132): you just need to drill a hole in the side of your container and stick your pinhole panel over it using black electrical tape. An additional piece of black tape can then be used as a crude shutter: peel it off to start your exposure and then stick it back down to end it. What is more of a challenge is holding your film in the camera. Small magnets can work well with metal-bodied cameras, and adhesive tape will hold your film to almost anything, but this limits you to shooting a single frame at a time. This is fine if you're shooting large-format sheet film (especially as a large-format darkslide can be attached to most things using rubber bands and a bit of ingenuity), but if you want to shoot 35mm or medium-format roll film you'll need to develop some sort of winding mechanism. There really is no single way of working here, and no right or wrong answers: it's a good idea to look online for inspiration, throw a camera together, and experiment. If it doesn't work? Strip it down and use your pinhole elsewhere.

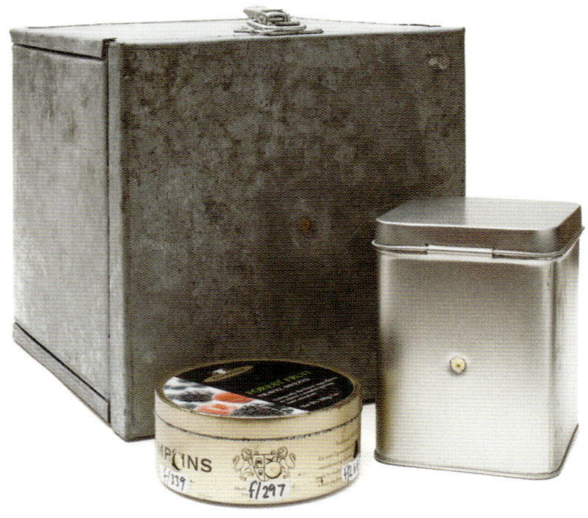

Below: This selection of homemade pinhole cameras includes a galvanized box (rear left) with a 230mm focal length and f/450 pinhole, which is designed to shoot an ultra-long exposure on photographic paper up to 7x7in; a silver tin (front right) with a 90mm wideangle focal length and f/225 pinhole that can shoot paper or cut down 120 film to give 6x10cm images; and a triple lens camera made from an old candy tin, which can shoot on cut down 35mm film or paper and creates a trio of images covering almost 180 degrees.

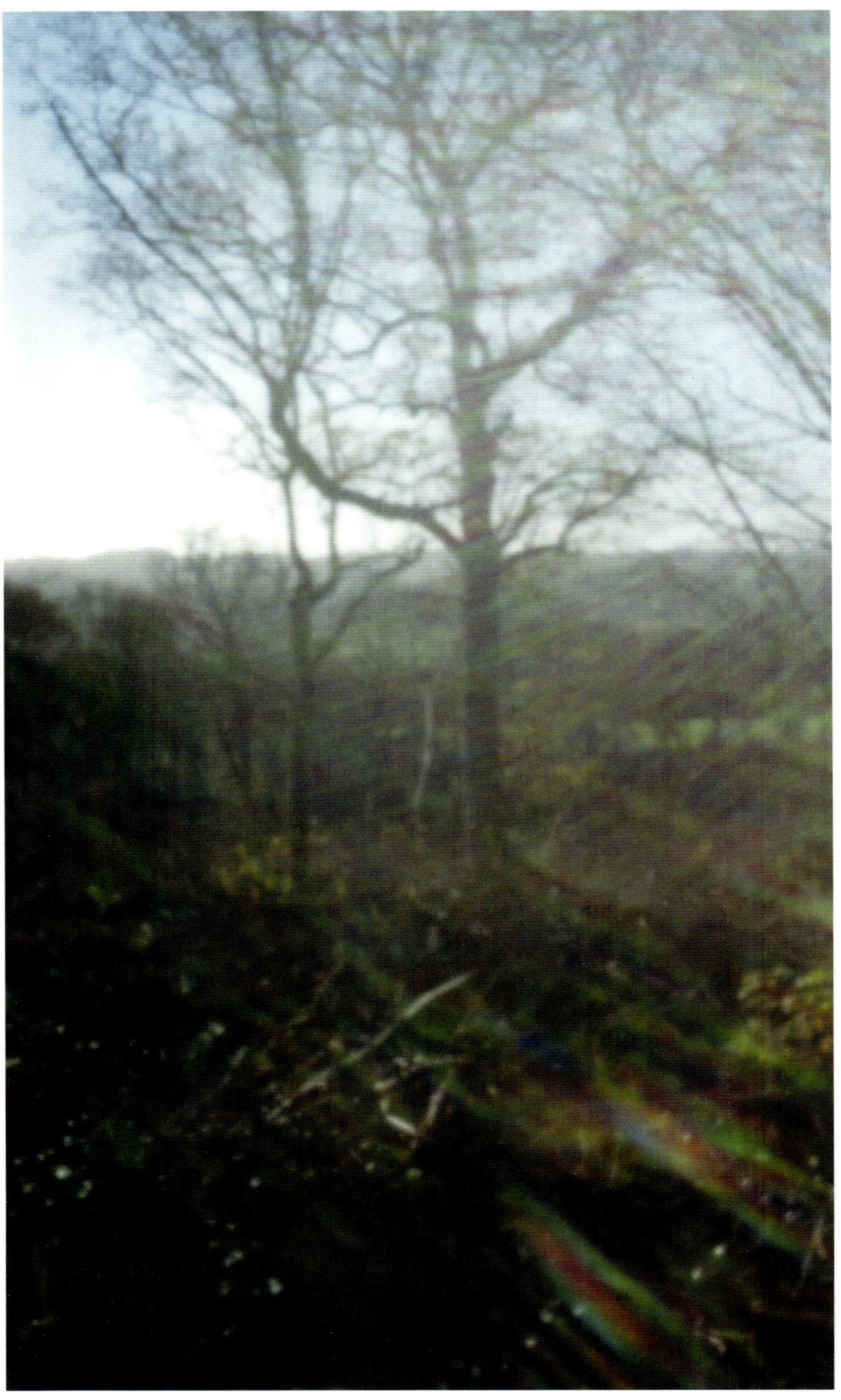

- Seal around any joins on your camera with black electrical tape to ensure it's light tight.

- Painting the inside of your camera with flat black paint will prevent any stray light from bouncing around during your exposure. This can be especially beneficial with metal containers that have a reflective interior.

- Don't limit yourself to making cameras with a single pinhole: there's nothing to stop you from experimenting with multi-pinhole designs.

SHOOTING PAPER

If you make your own camera from scratch it can be easier to make your exposures on single sheets of black-and-white photographic paper, rather than film. These can be loaded and unloaded in a darkroom (or changing bag) and developed like a normal photographic print to give you a paper negative that can be contact printed or scanned to make a positive image. The great thing with paper is that it's much cheaper than film and you can use large sheets; the downside is your exposures will be much longer, as paper typically has an effective ISO somewhere in the region of ISO 3–7.

Left: Pinhole photography creates fundamentally different images to lens-based imaging. Here, shooting into the sun using cheap color film in a homemade pinhole camera resulted in the light refracting and diffracting as it passed through the lens, revealing a rainbow of colors and unusual swirling patterns—it's "flare," but not as we usually know it.

Pinhole Exposures

When it comes to using a pinhole camera, almost everything you think you know about exposure goes straight out of the window, primarily due to the incredibly long exposure times you'll be working with. But before you can determine the exposure you need to know the pinhole's aperture, and how easy this is will depend on where your pinhole has come from.

If you have bought a pinhole camera readymade, there should be an indication of the aperture somewhere, so you just need to check the instruction sheet or manufacturer's web site. However, if you've bought a pinhole plate (to put in a homebrew camera) or made your own pinhole plate you will need to work out the effective aperture using this formula:

- aperture = focal length / pinhole diameter

As commercial pinholes are sold based on the diameter of the hole (0.1mm, 0.2mm, and so on), all you need to do is measure the distance between your pinhole and film (which gives you your camera's focal length) and then divide that by the pinhole's diameter. For example, if your camera's focal length is 4in (10cm) and your pinhole measures 0.016in (0.4mm), this gives you an aperture of f/250.

A bigger challenge comes if you have made the camera and the pinhole plate. Working out the focal length of the camera is easy enough, but working out the size of the pinhole means jumping through a few hoops, as outlined opposite.

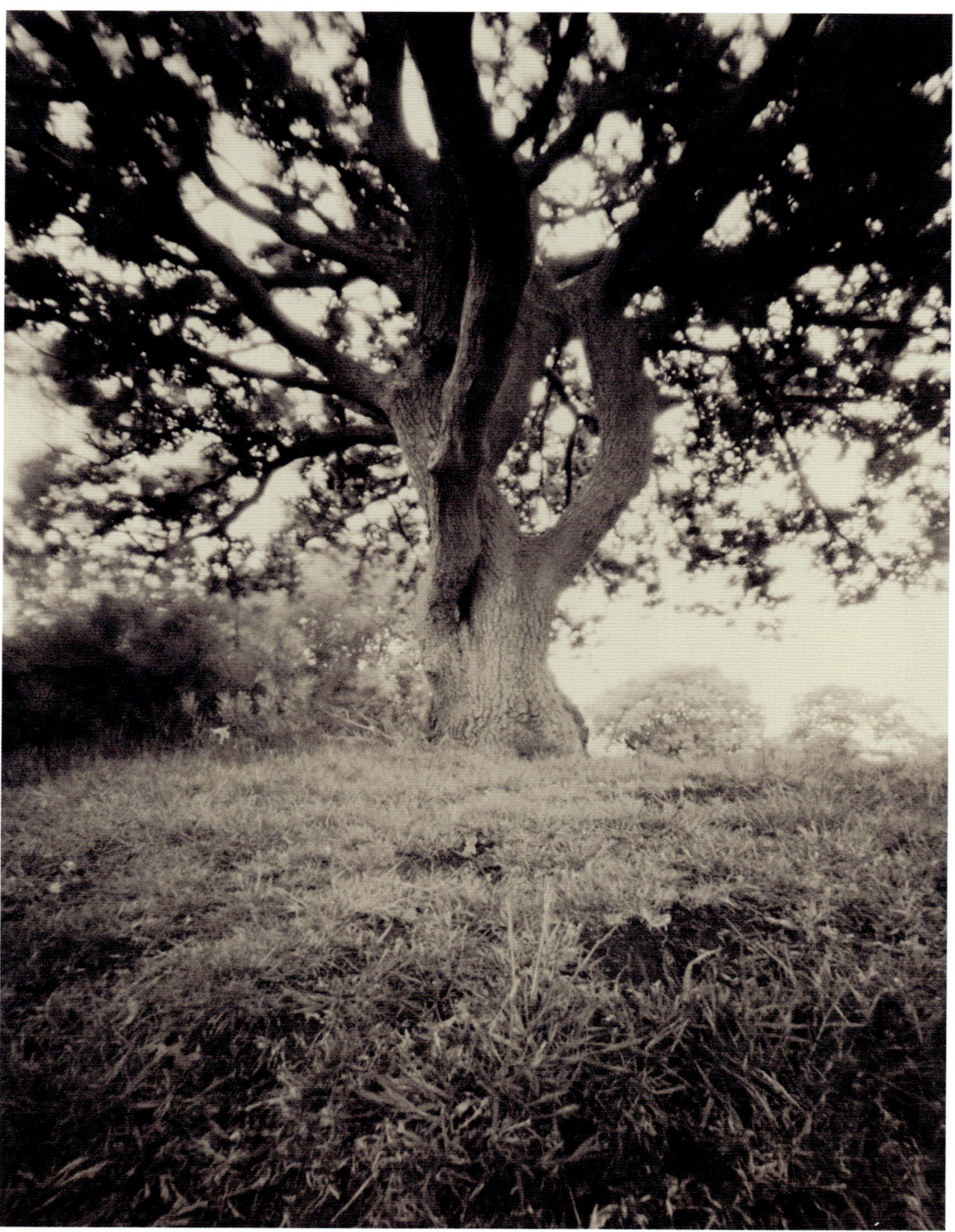

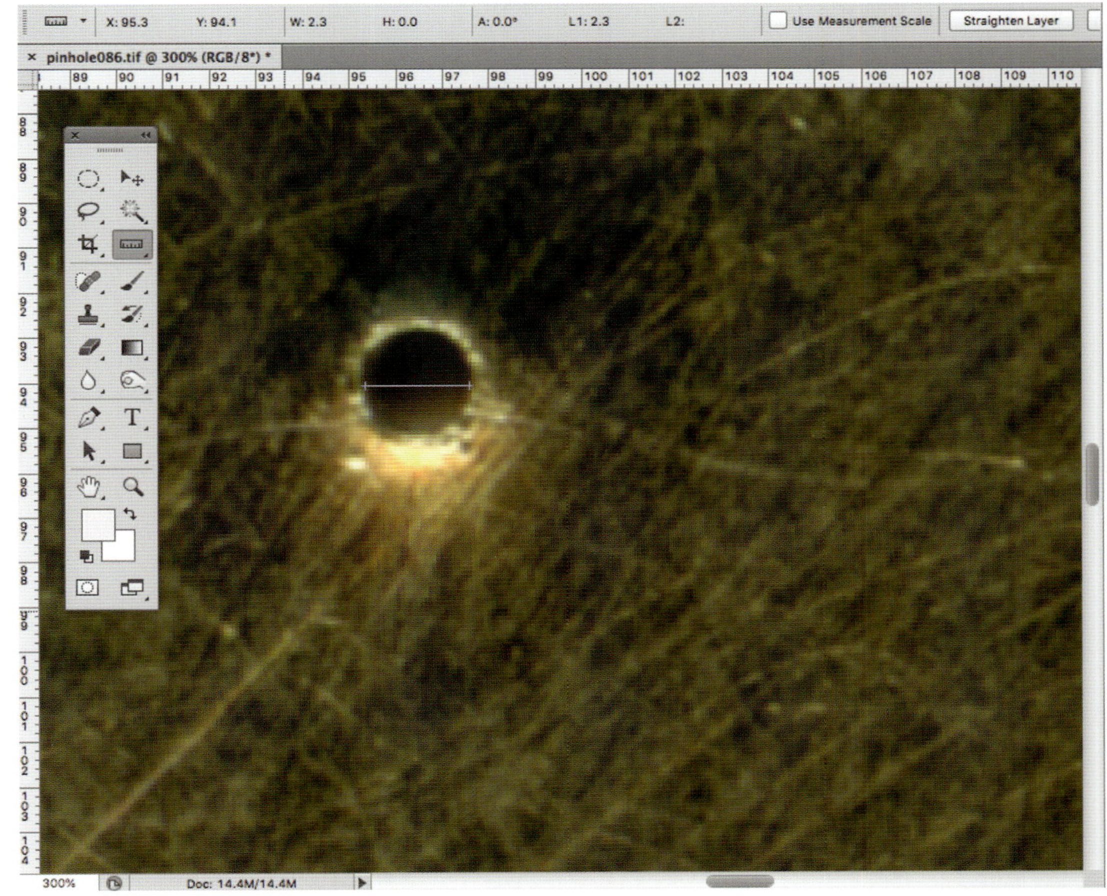

Above: When you zoom in on your pinhole you can not only measure its diameter, but also see how round and clean it is. This one doesn't look too bad!

Left: A pinhole will typically have a very small aperture, which creates two opposing effects: an incredible depth of field, where everything appears equally in focus, and a low resolution caused in part by diffraction. As seen in this image, this creates a visual paradox where everything is equally "almost sharp"—the grass in the foreground (which was maybe one foot from the camera) is just as sharp as the tree bark in the middle distance, and the distant trees beyond that.

Homemade Pinhole Aperture

The traditional way of determining the working aperture of a homemade pinhole plate is to put it in an enlarger or projector and project the image at an upscaled size, but you can do the exact same thing using a digital camera or scanner:

1 Take a digital photograph of your pinhole plate (or scan it) and then open it in your image-editing software.

2 Measure the size of the pinhole plate and view it on screen at 5x or 10x this size. So, if your plate measures 1x1in (2.5x2.5cm), enlarge it on your computer monitor to 10x10in (25x25cm). If you scan your pinhole plate you can simply scan it in at 500% for a 5x increase.

3 Zoom into the image and use your software's ruler tool to measure the diameter of the pinhole.

4 Divide the measurement by the enlargement factor (5 or 10) to find the hole's diameter. For example, if your on-screen hole measures 0.16in. (4mm), your actual pinhole is 0.016in (0.4mm).

5 You can now use the formula (see page 138) to convert your pinhole diameter into an aperture (f/stop).

Exposure Times

Once you know your aperture you can start to work out your exposure times, and by far the easiest way of doing this is to search online for "pinhole exposure calculators." As with pinhole size calculators, there are plenty of web sites and apps that allow you to generate a bespoke exposure grid based on your pinhole camera's aperture. What you want is something that gives you one or two "regular" photographic apertures (such as f/8, f/16, and so on) and your pinhole aperture, with a range of exposure times listed for each of them.

To use the grid you need to take a regular light reading with a camera or lightmeter and then read off the corresponding pinhole exposure time. For example, using the grid below right, a regular exposure reading of 1/30 sec. at f/16 would become an 8 sec. exposure for an f/280 pinhole (the ISO is set based on the film/paper you are using in your pinhole camera).

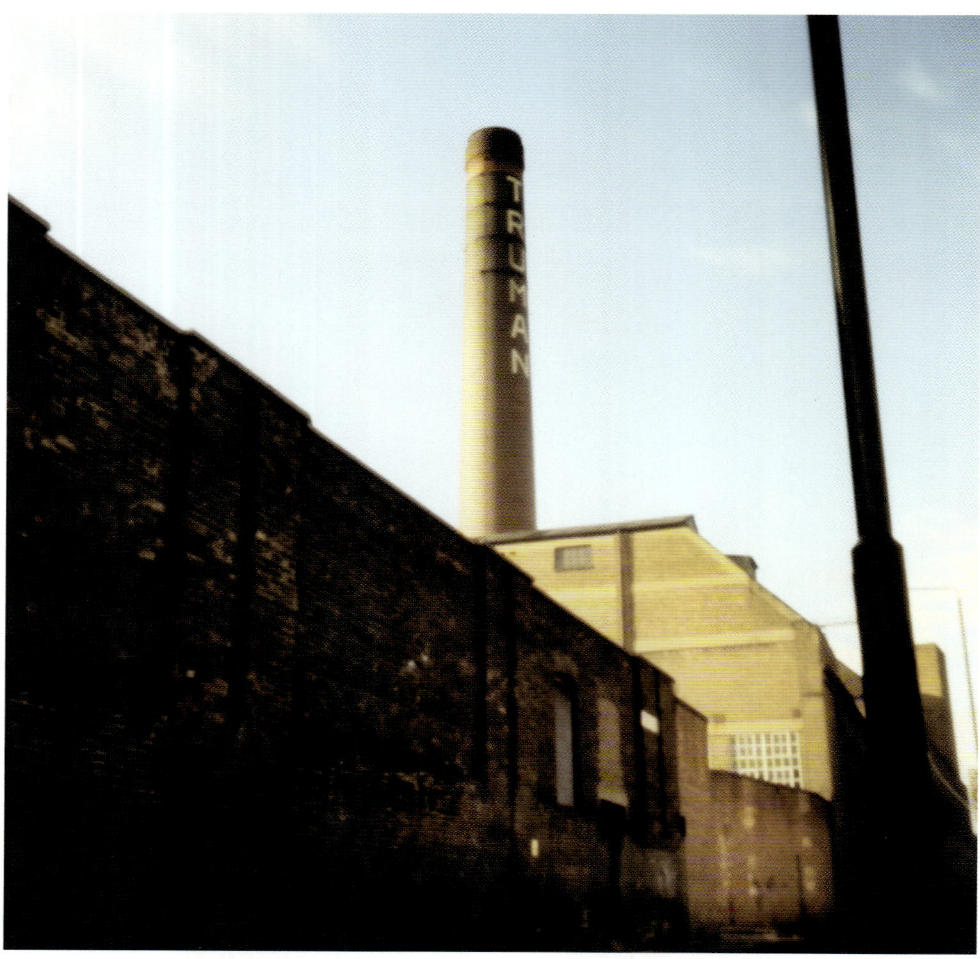

Right: In addition to getting the exposure right, one of the biggest challenges of pinhole photography is framing your shot to start with. Some cameras offer some form of viewing angle or "sight line" indicator, but more often it comes down to guesswork. This 5x4 image needed cropping heavily to "find" the composition within it (and processing heavily to finish it!).

Right: An exposure grid like this lets you use the exposure meter in a camera or a handheld lightmeter to determine your pinhole exposure times. Simply cross-reference the aperture/shutter speed with the pinhole aperture to find your new exposure time. Note, however, that pinhole exposure grids do not take into account reciprocity failure.

PINHOLE EXPOSURE GRID			
f/16	**f/140**	**f/280**	**f/560**
1/500 sec.	1/8 sec.	1/2 sec.	2 sec.
1/250 sec.	1/4 sec.	1 sec.	4 sec.
1/125 sec.	1/2 sec.	2 sec.	8 sec.
1/60 sec.	1 sec.	4 sec.	16 sec.
1/30 sec.	2 sec.	8 sec.	32 sec.
1/15 sec.	4 sec.	16 sec.	1 min.
1/8 sec.	8 sec.	32 sec.	2 min.
1/4 sec.	16 sec.	1 min.	4 min.
1/2 sec.	32 sec.	2 min.	8 min.
1 sec.	64 sec.	4 min.	16 min.

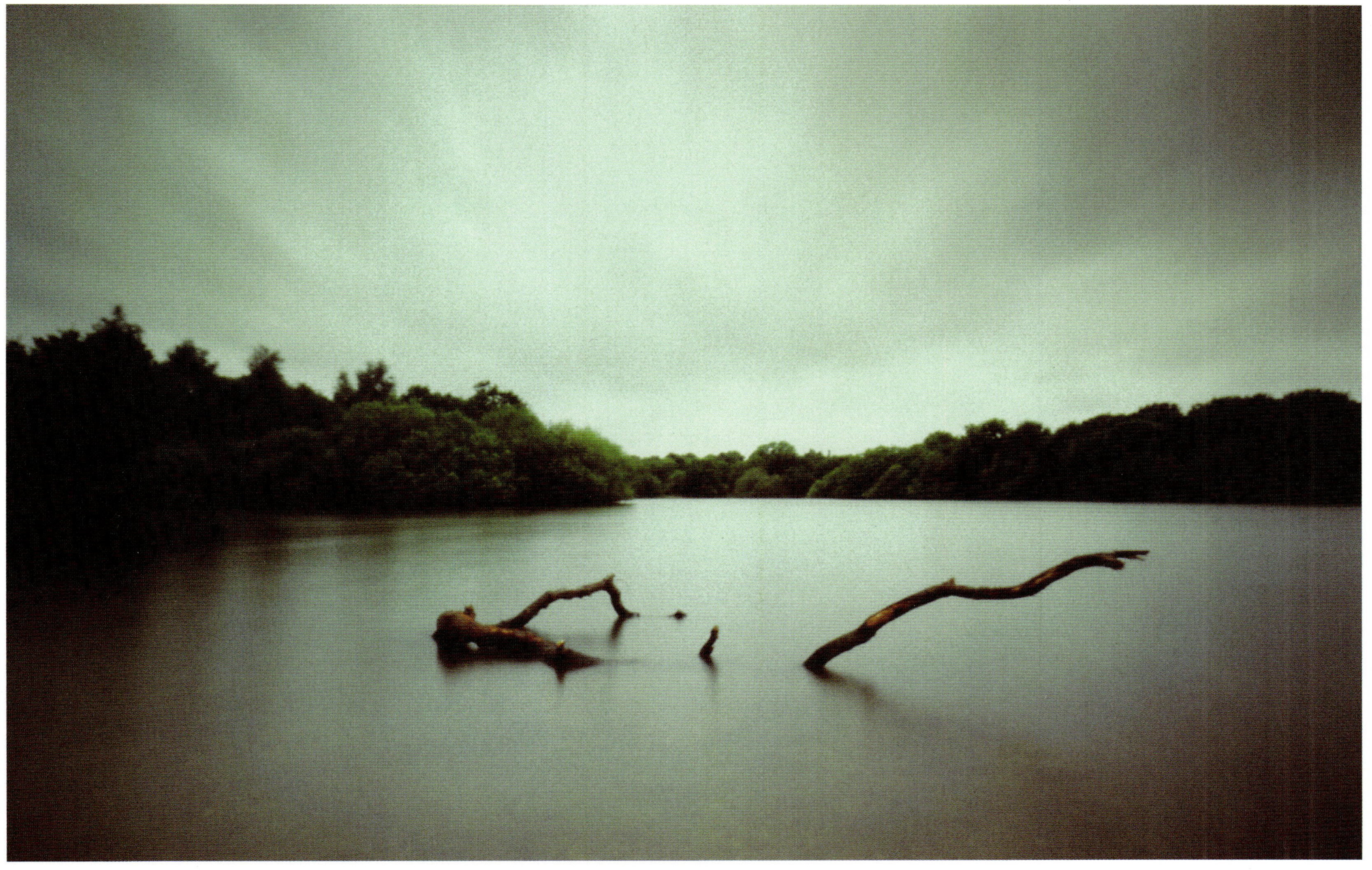

Tips

- The reciprocity data from most manufacturers doesn't extend to the exposure times necessitated by a pinhole aperture (although Ilford is a notable exception), so a huge amount of guesswork and practice is required to get things absolutely right. Alternatively, you can invest in an app such as Pinhole Assist, which will at least point you in the right direction.

- When it comes to ultra-long exposures it can be quite difficult to overexpose a pinhole shot taken on negative film. Increasing an exposure from 10 minutes to 20 minutes, for example, will make little difference overall, because of reciprocity failure (it certainly won't be a 1-stop difference).

- It is better to overexpose negative film than underexpose it, so don't be afraid to use much longer exposure times than you think you need, especially when your exposures start to be measured in minutes, rather than seconds.

Profile: Matt Pringle

BIOGRAPHY

Matt Pringle is a relative newcomer to photography, having started taking pictures in 2008 when he enrolled on a home-study photography course. Since then his work has featured in multiple magazines and websites, and has been exhibited many times. In an increasingly hectic and fast-paced world he aims to capture images that emanate stillness and reflection, placing greater emphasis on the mood and feeling of a shot than on the subject.

mpringle.co.uk

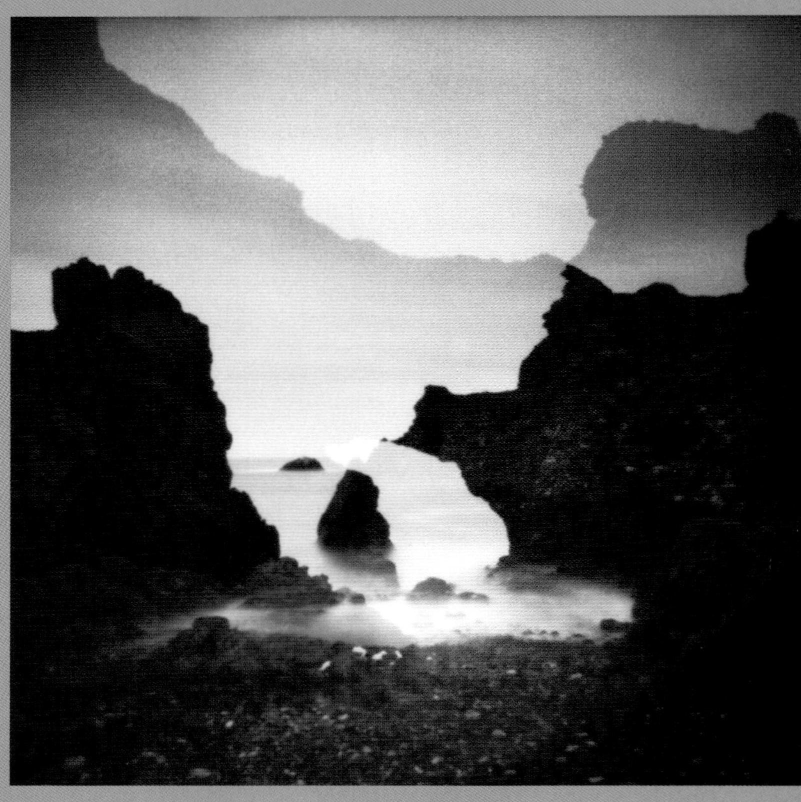

Right:
Dunbar, Scotland
The same rock formation shot from two different viewpoints creates an image with an almost otherworldly abstract feel.

Q) How would you describe your *Immersion* series (some of which features here)?
A) *Immersion* is a culmination of many things: my love of pinhole photography, my fascination with double exposures, and the sea. The concept behind the series was the creation of images of a more abstract nature, focusing mostly on form, shape, and texture. The use of double exposures allowed me to explore these themes much more creatively than shooting single exposures.

Q) Why shoot on film?
A) When I first got into photography, I shot with digital cameras and often found that I would instinctively add "grain" to my pictures in an attempt to offset the clinical nature of digital capture. After a while I decided to buy my first film camera—a Holga 120N—and instantly fell in love with the look and feel of film, particularly the grain and rich tonality. The financial cost of film also forced me to become much more disciplined with regards to how and what I shoot, so I inevitably found myself spending more time refining my compositions.

Q) What camera(s) do you use?
A) The two pinhole cameras I use the most are a Holga Pinhole and a RealitySoSubtle 6x6 pinhole, both of which are medium-format cameras shooting 6x6cm images. The shots here were taken using the Holga, although I now almost exclusively shoot with the RealitySoSubtle 6x6 due to its compact size and reliability.

Q) What film(s) do you use?
A) For black and white pinhole work I primarily use Ilford film—Ilford HP5 Plus is my favorite, as it's very flexible, and being ISO 400 it allows a lot of latitude. For longer exposures I tend to use Ilford FP4.

Q) How do you determine your exposures?
A) My exposure times are calculated using an old Sekonic lightmeter that I bought off eBay for around $5, in conjunction with a pinhole exposure

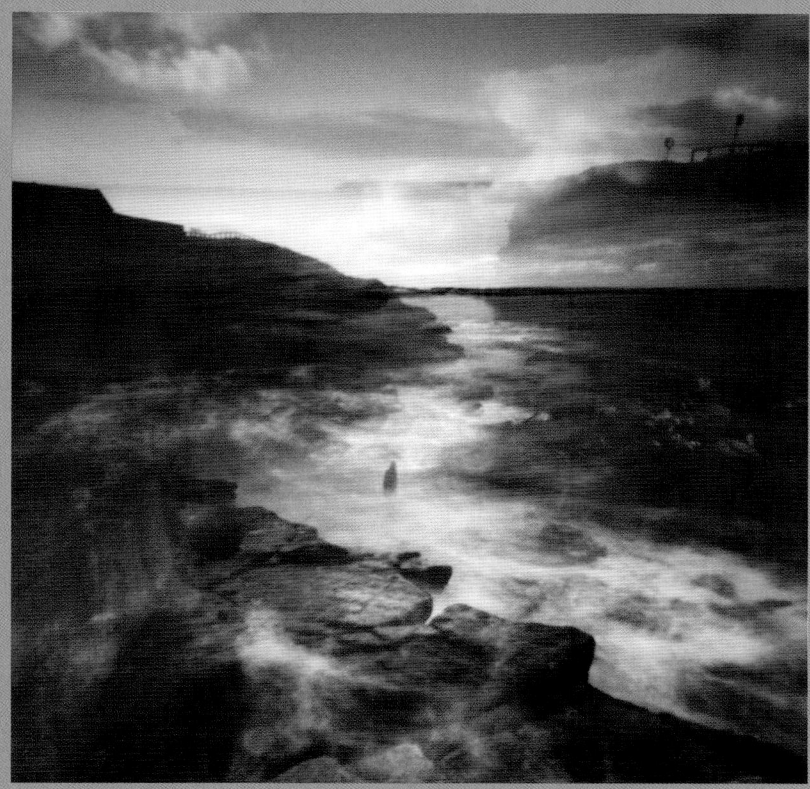

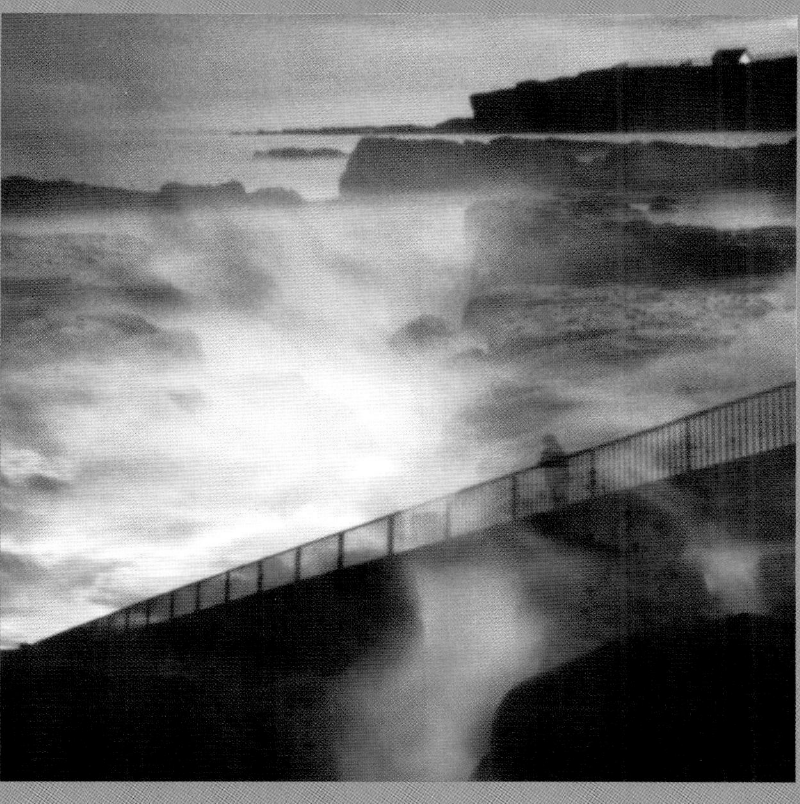

grid created through a program called Pinhole Designer. For double exposures I underexpose each shot by 1 stop to prevent the final negative from becoming overexposed.

Q) Are there any specific problems that you need to overcome?
A) Pinhole photography, by its very nature, can be quite unpredictable: You hope that you have your exposure set correctly and that the light doesn't change too much during the exposure. As I'm working with either a very inaccurate viewfinder (Holga Pinhole) or no viewfinder at all (RealitySoSubtle 6x6), composing can be difficult as well. Combine this with taking two images on the same negative in-camera and hoping that they work well together, and it makes things even more tricky. However, when it works, it feels fantastic and can result in some truly magical and otherworldly images!

Above left:
Seaton Sluice, England
This was the pinhole double exposure that inspired me to start the *Immersion* series. One shot was taken with the camera pointing up the coast, the other down.

Above right:
Cullercoats, England
Sometimes it is difficult to visualize how a double exposure is going to turn out, but I was delighted with the result here. The motion of the sea adds drama and the contemplative lone figure appears engulfed within this dreamscape.

Chapter 7
Processing

Until digital photography came along the idea of a "workflow" didn't really exist in the photographer's vernacular. Film was processed and then it was printed or projected: there were no other stages. Today, however, we have a bewildering array of options when it comes to deciding what happens to our carefully exposed and filtered frames once that roll or sheet of film leaves the camera. Rather than explore every scenario, in this chapter I'm going to cover my own personal way of working—in both color and black and white—and the core skills I believe are necessary for anyone working with film. You may prefer to work differently, or disagree with my philosophy, and that's fine; only you know which path is right for you.

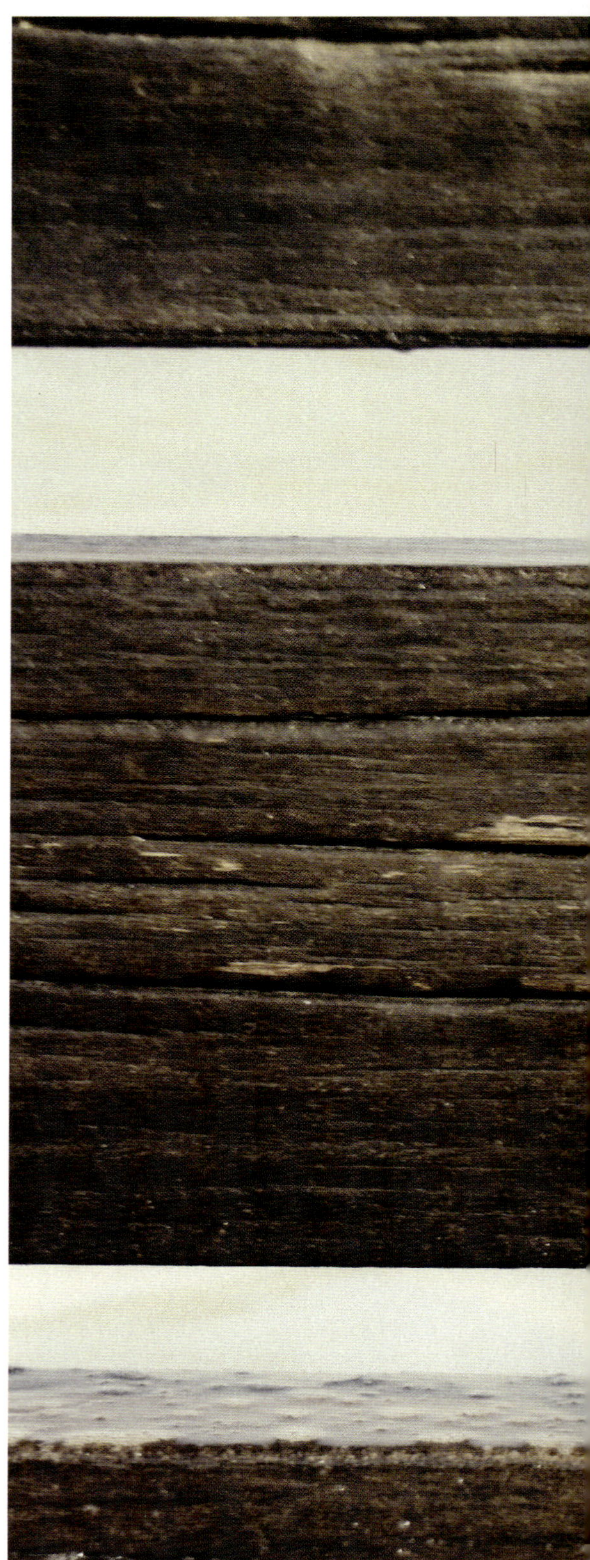

Right: What happens to your exposed film once it leaves your camera is entirely up to you: today's options range from the fully traditional darkroom to a hybrid approach that accepts digital editing as part of the process.

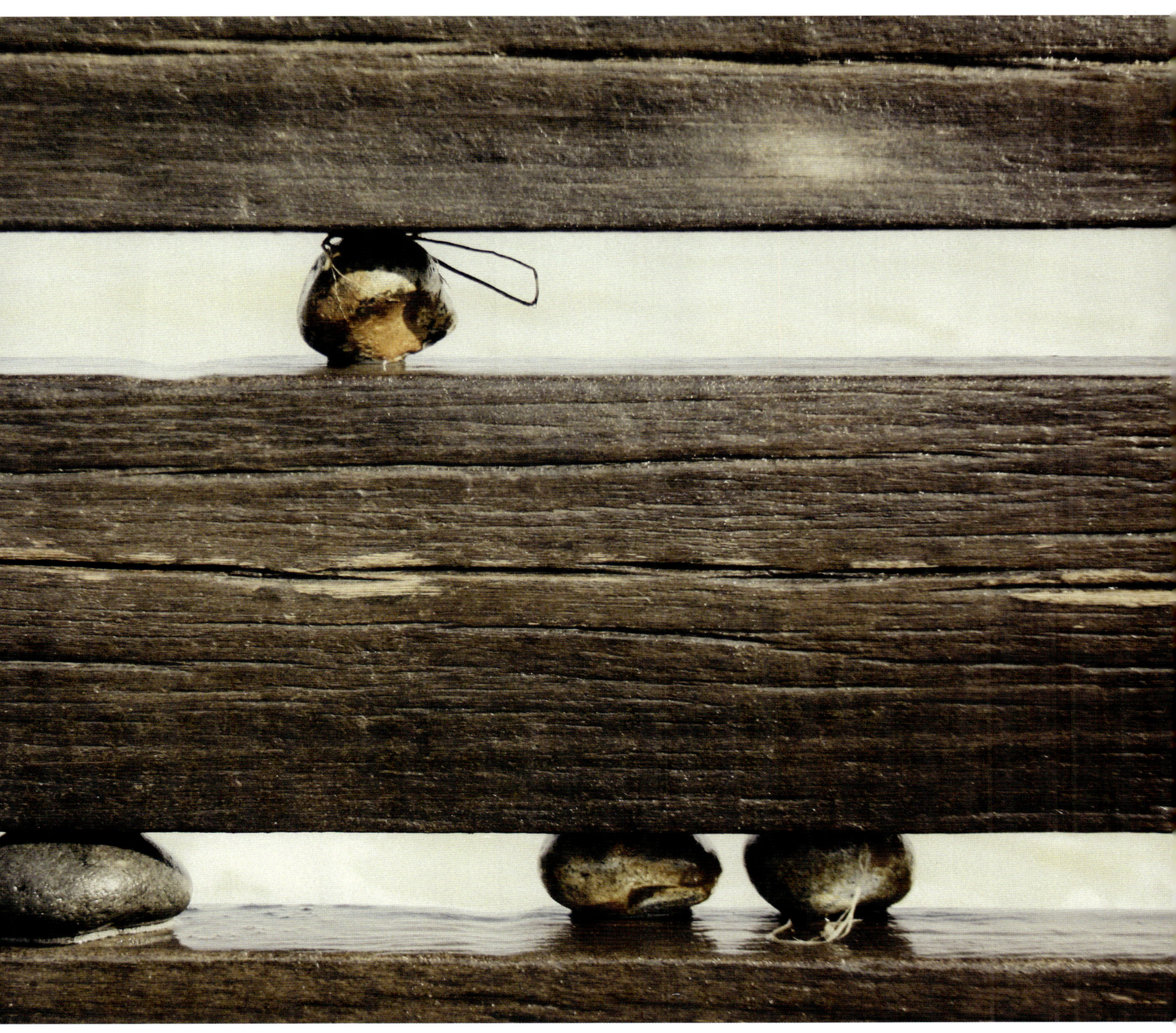

After The Shot

When it comes to film photography there are far more answers to the question "what next?" than there are in the digital arena. This might sound strange when you consider how a Raw file from a digital SLR is open to broad interpretation, thanks to image-editing software, but the latent images on your exposed film can be revealed and exploited in many more ways, from traditional "wet" processes through to anything you wish to undertake in the digital darkroom. The only limitation is how far you are willing, or able, to go down any one route.

Black & White

I was introduced to black-and-white film processing when I was 17, and to this day (more than 25 years later) I have processed every single roll of black-and-white film I have shot. By doing this, I have full control over the developer I use and the time that I give it—enabling me to have a fundamental say in the overall "look" of my images. There's also the sheer convenience of knowing that I can shoot all day and have my film processed before nightfall, then dry and ready for whatever I choose to do with it the following morning. As you will see in this chapter, you don't need a lot of expensive equipment (or indeed a lot of equipment) or a lot of space to process your film—I do mine at the kitchen sink—so, as far as I'm concerned, there is no reason not to process your own black-and-white negatives.

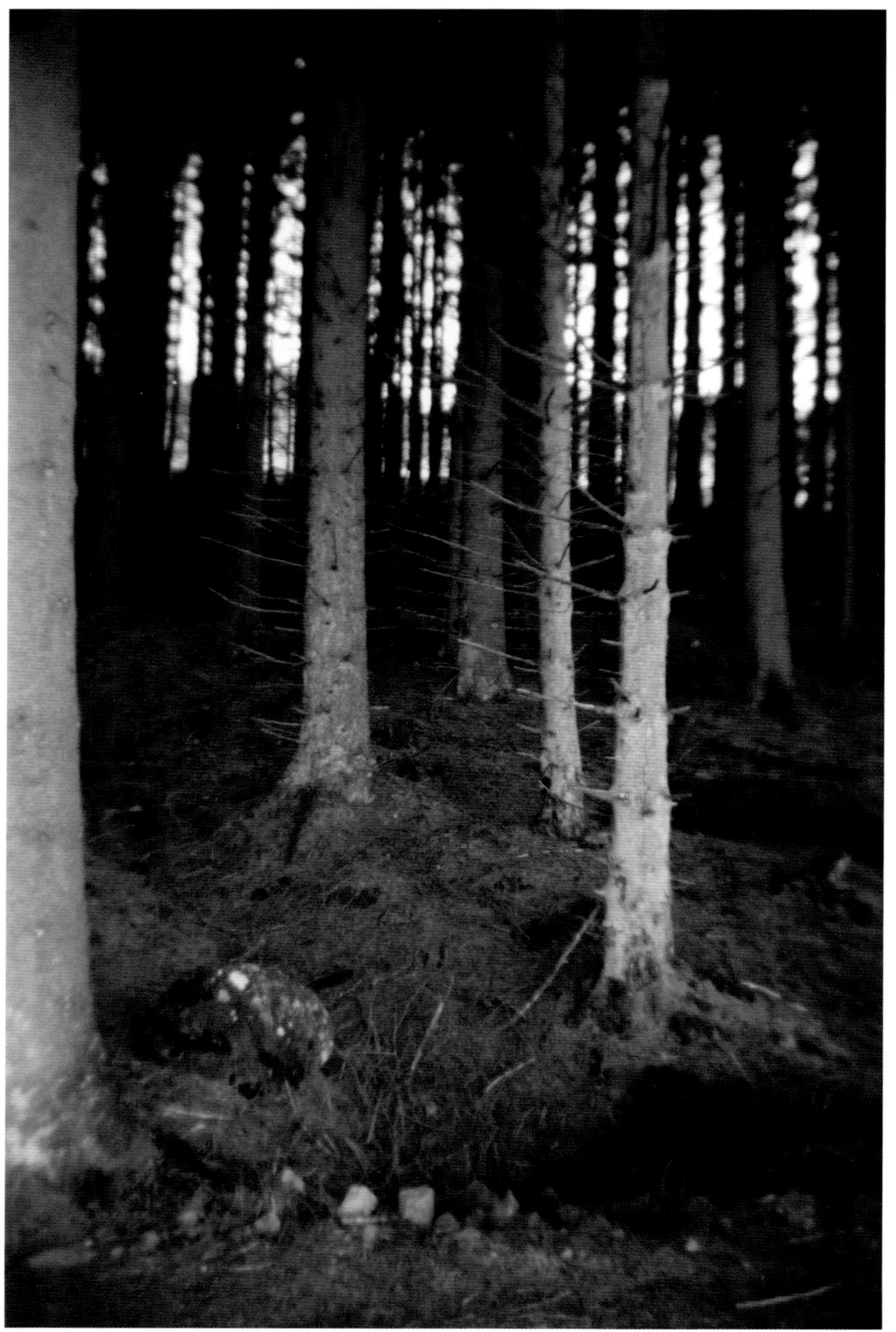

Right: I've lost count of how many black-and-white films I've developed over the years, but whether it's film from a Hasselblad or (as here) a vintage folding camera, the process is exactly the same. Perhaps one of the best investments I made was in a large processing tank that could take multiple films; it will seriously speed up your workflow if you can develop several (or more) rolls of film at the same time!

Color

While I've always processed my black-and-white film, when it comes to color I always hand my rolls in at a lab. There's no single reason why I don't process it myself, but I can give you plenty of niggles that all add up. Perhaps my biggest excuse is that—to my mind at least—processing color film isn't a particularly creative exercise. Sure, you can introduce color shifts (usually by mistake, rather than through intent), and you can experiment with cross processing, but unlike black-and-white processing there aren't dozens of different developers to explore, so when it comes to a "straight" process—E6 or C41—it's simply a mechanical exercise that's about getting the job done, rather than injecting some unique personality or character into the images.

If lab-processing costs become prohibitively expensive, perhaps I'll change my mind, but for now, the lab costs for color are far more appealing than the thought of spending time and effort on a task that doesn't "stir my soul." Black and white? Yes, absolutely. Color? I'll pass thanks!

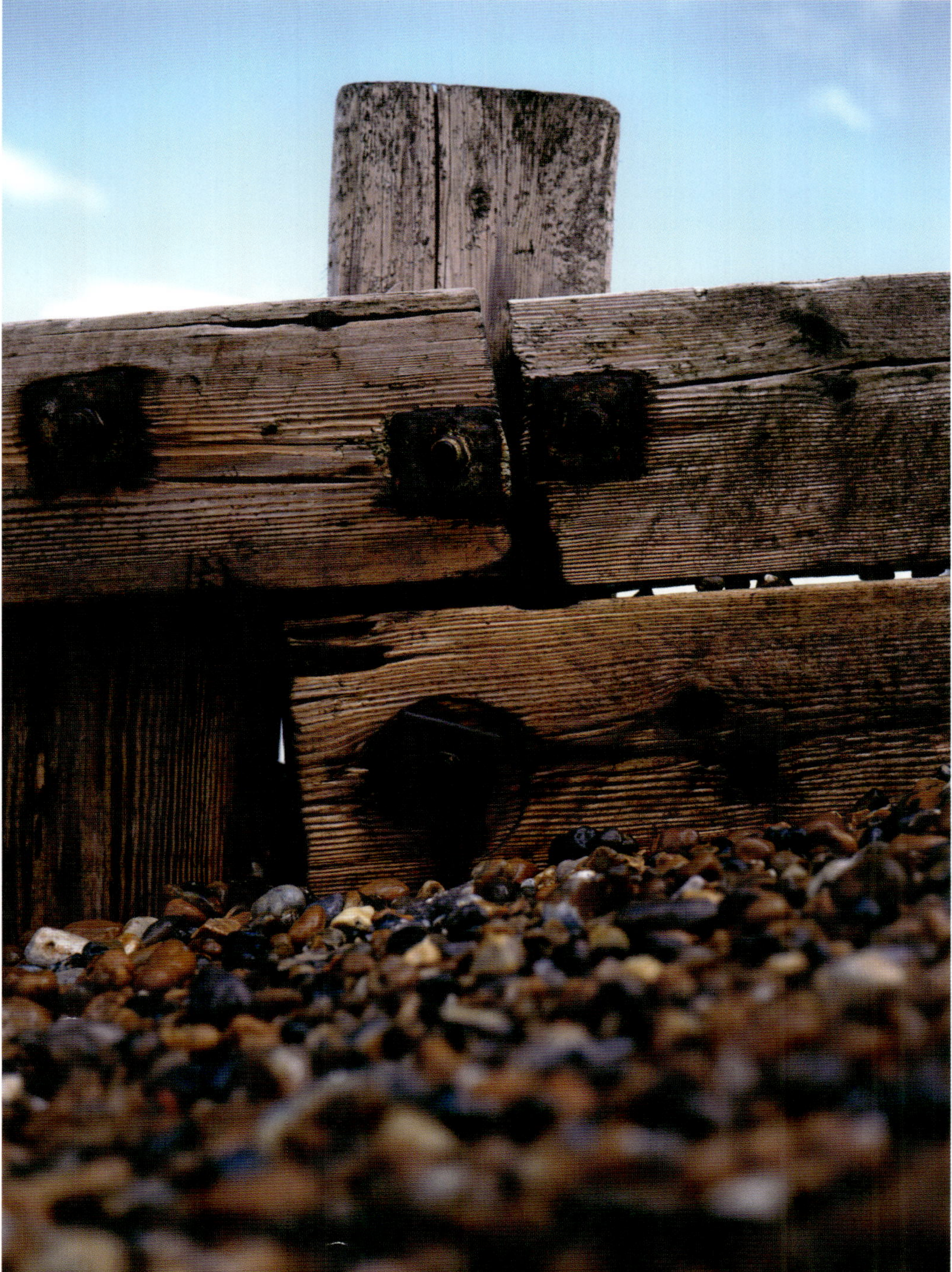

Right: I have very little incentive to process my own color film: my local lab does a decent job and isn't hugely expensive. Until color processing costs become prohibitively expensive I'm happy to let someone else perform this task.

Printing

Regardless of whether you process them yourself or get a lab to do it for you, once you have your negatives or transparencies in hand the options of what to do with them are vast. There are, however, two broad paths you can walk down: one leads to the traditional darkroom and the other to a computer. It would be impossible to cover every possible permutation here. Working in a traditional darkroom would require an entire book just to cover "straight" print making, with yet another volume (or perhaps two) needed if you want to start exploring alternative and vintage processes. To compound it all, for a lot of photographers there is likely to be little, if any, overlap between the disciplines: digital practitioners tend to have little desire to immerse themselves in the gloom of a wet darkroom, while those who love the smells and solitude of a chemical environment may balk at the thought of pushing pixels around a computer screen.

However, if you see a chemical darkroom and "silver prints" as the only option, you need to be aware that it requires effort and commitment to have your own private printing space. Not only do you need room for an enlarger and print trays (either temporary or permanent), but you also need to be able to dedicate time to printing. This is massively underestimated, because if you don't print negatives regularly your chemicals will expire, your enlarger will quickly gather dust, and getting ready for a print session will become an increasingly uphill struggle.

A potential alternative is to see if there are any darkrooms to hire in your local area. As interest in film grows again, an increasing number of public darkrooms are popping up in major cities. For a fee you can book an enlarger for a few hours (or days) and all you need to take with you is printing paper and your negatives: the enlarger and chemicals are usually supplied and ready to go. These places can also be a great starting point if you've never printed before, as they often run printing classes and workshops, where you can learn the craft of making a "real" photographic print, and also hang out with likeminded people.

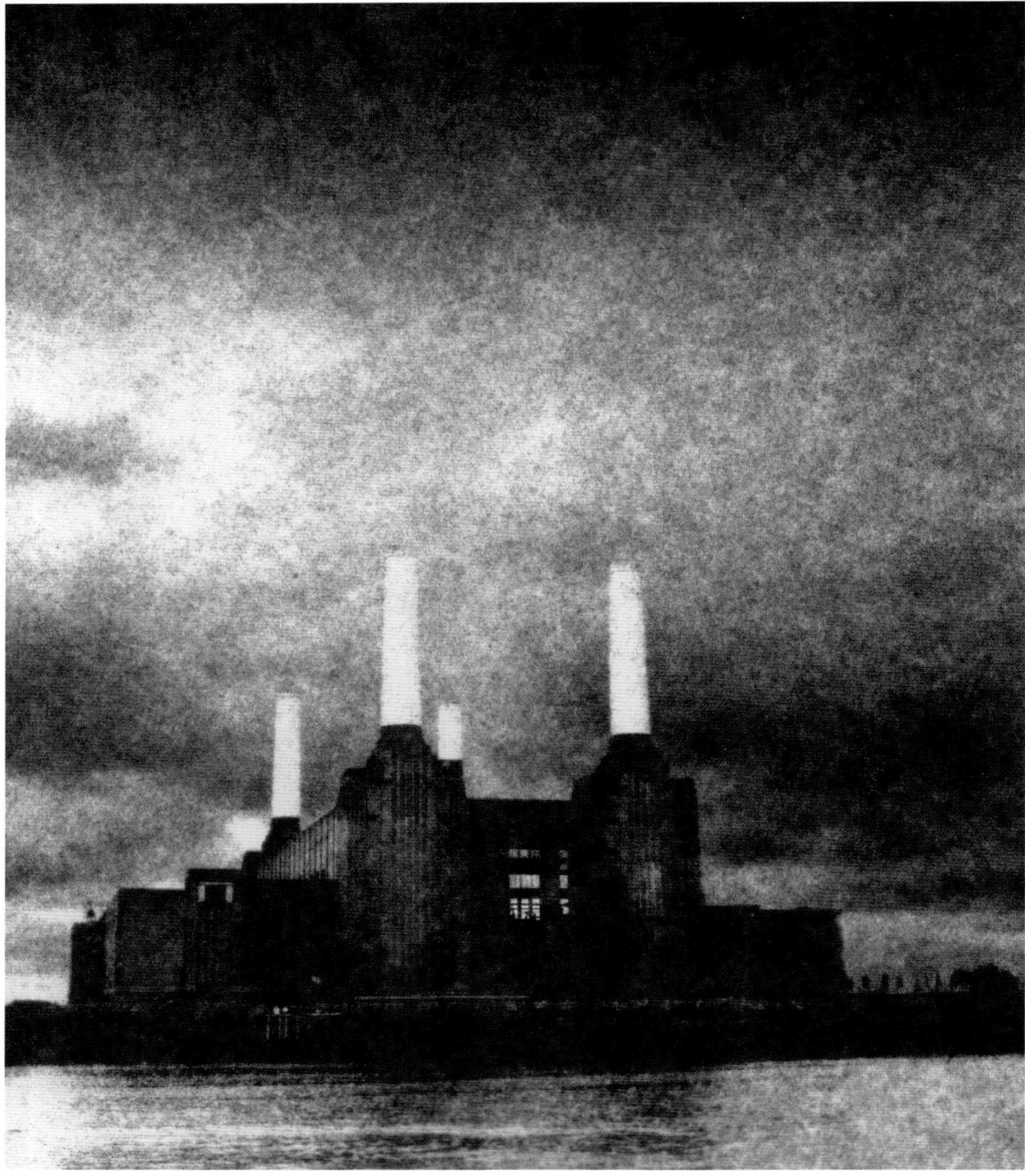

Of course, working in the dark isn't for everyone and for a variety of reasons a lot of people now adopt a hybrid approach to their work, where film is processed, scanned, and taken into the digital realm. There are plenty of advantages to working in this way, as images can be digitally worked on before they are printed at home on an inkjet printer or sent to a lab, assuming of course, that a print

Above: This is a real "hybrid" image. The shot was taken on black-and-white film, scanned, and printed onto thin copier paper as a negative image using an inket printer. I then took the paper negative into the darkroom and used it to make a contact print on photographic paper. Each of the stages was designed to add texture to the final image.

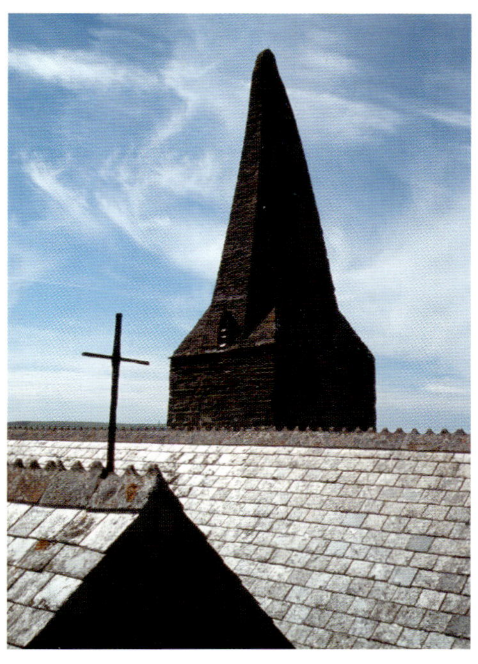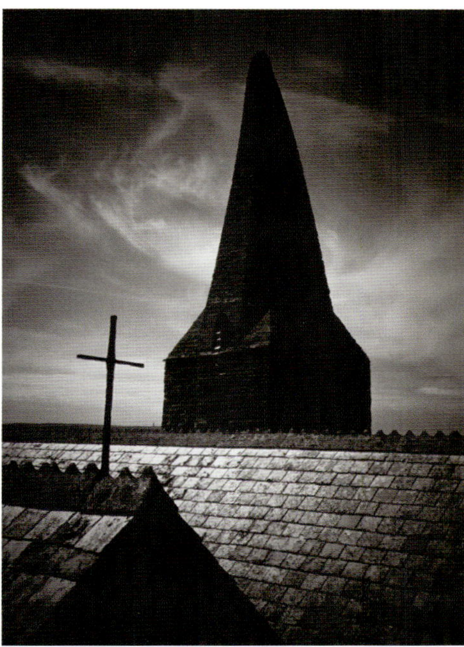

remains the desired end product: once digitized, images can be delivered directly to clients, or displayed in an online, on-screen context. In either case the image still originates on film, but then ends up as 0s and 1s.

You can happily argue the pros and cons of both approaches (and some online forums are home to quite extreme advocates of one or the other), but I'm not going to dwell on them here. The tools are there and it's really up to you which ones you decide to use. If you choose to take the digital route then it's also entirely up to you how far you go with your digital processing. Some people limit themselves to replicating darkroom tools. As a result, they have a set of personal guidelines that say dodging and burning are OK, getting rid of dust and scratches is fine, and contrast (and color) tweaks are acceptable, but they might draw the line at layered composites and heavy filtering: it's your call.

In any case, the first thing you need to do is to get your film processed, so let's take a look at how you can get started.

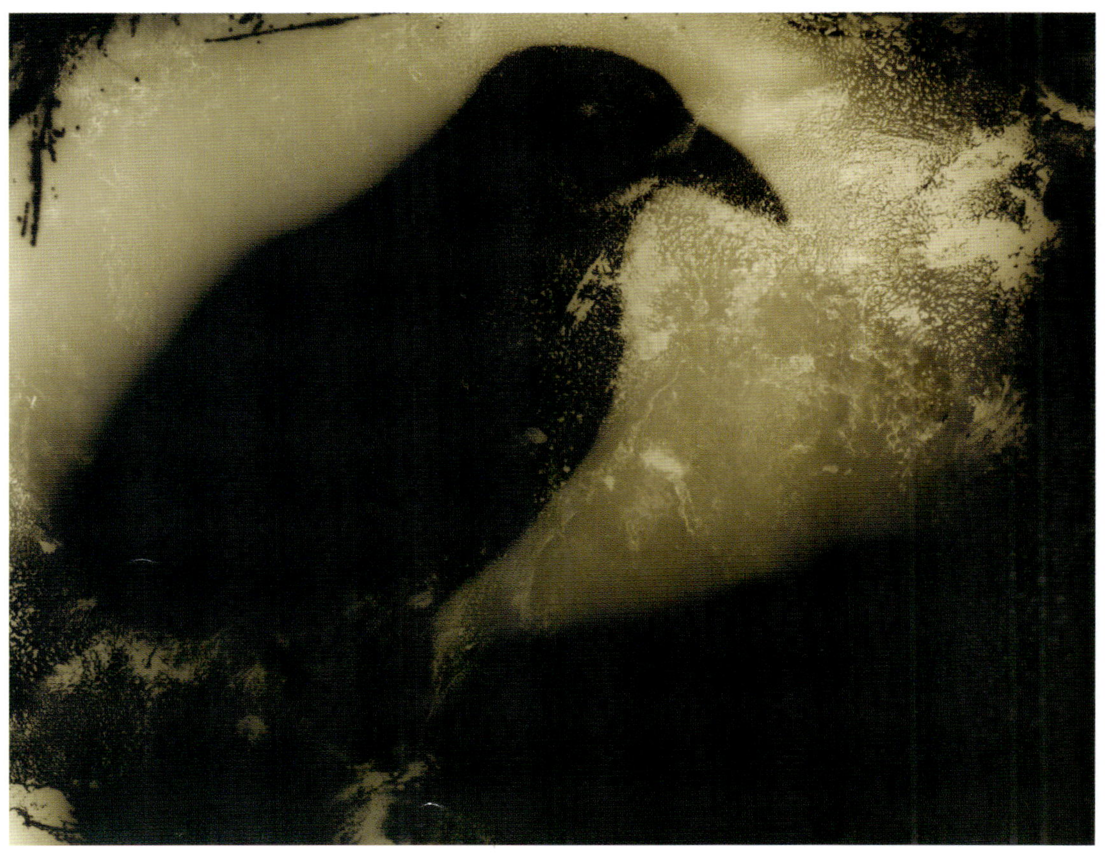

Processing Black & White Film

Now, as I explained earlier, I process all of my black-and–white film, and it's hard to come up with a good reason not to (other than it takes a bit of time). One of the great things about developing black-and-white film is that it doesn't require a lot of specialist equipment, and the items it does require can be purchased relatively easily from online auctions and photo stores. If you're lucky, you may even find old processing items in yard sales or thrift stores. The key items to look for are a developing tank (complete with light-tight lid and one or more spirals to load film onto), graduated measuring cylinders of various capacities, and light-tight bottles (if you want to reuse your chemicals). Other items, such as measuring jugs, a thermometer, bottle opener, and timer are more universally available.

You will also need the chemicals necessary for processing your film. The essential chemicals are developer (to bring out the latent image) and fixer (to make it permanent), but you might also want to use a stop bath and wetting agent. In all cases there are multiple options available from different brands, but perhaps the one that has the biggest effect on your film is the developer, as this ultimately determines how you want your latent images to be drawn from the emulsion.

Developers

Even in this digital age there are still dozens of different developers to choose from for processing your black-and-white film. Your choice will initially depend on the "type" of developer you want to use, as not all of them are equal: some are designed to minimize grain, others to maximize film speed (at the expense of a slight increase in grain), there are high- and low-contrast options, some aimed at specific films or film types, and good all-round "standard" developers. Just remember that virtually any developer will develop almost any film, so your choice largely comes down to one thing: personal preference. This will be driven in part by the type of developer you think is best suited to your film and/or images, the look you're after, and partly by experience.

Below: Unlike traditional film developers that require a separate fixing stage, CineStill's Df96 is an all-in-one processing solution that develops and fixes almost any film in under 10 minutes, making it an ultra-convenient choice for anyone looking for a "general" film-processing option.

Below: German manufacturer ADOX produces a range of film chemicals, including powdered and liquid film developers. Its Rodinal liquid developer is the modern incarnation of Agfa's classic developer of the same name, which was originally patented in 1891.

Tips

- All film-processing chemicals degrade over time, but storing them in airtight and light-tight bottles will increase their usable life.

- If you're in any doubt about whether your chemicals are still "good" or not, err on the side of caution. It might cost a bit of money to replace them, but that's preferable to an undeveloped or inadequately fixed roll of film. Better still, add a label when you first open the bottle or mix your chemistry so that you know how old it is.

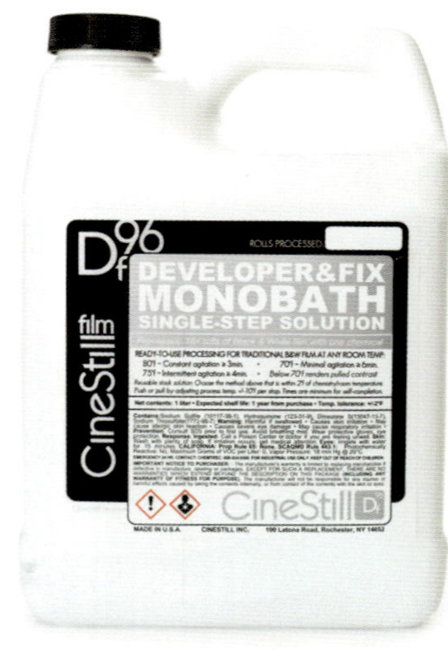

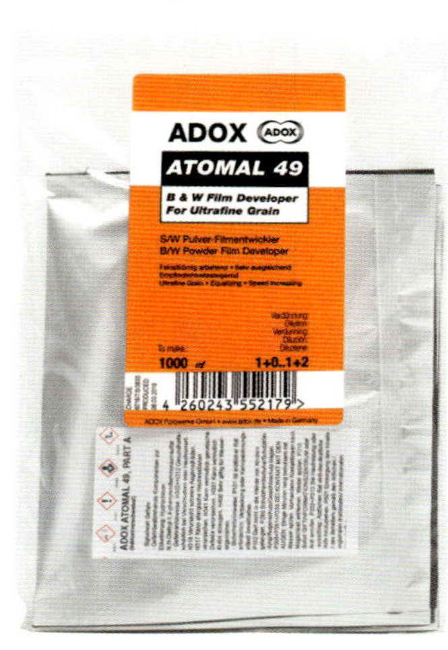

Loading Your Film

The first stage in developing a film is to load it into your developing tank. There are various tank designs on the market but the most common type use "self-loading" plastic spirals, as shown here. Getting your film from its light-tight cassette, or off its plastic spool is one of the most nerve-jangling parts of processing film, because this is when it's at its most vulnerable. At this point film can be scratched, creased, or even exposed to light, which can potentially ruin your shots.

To compound the issue, loading film needs to be done in total darkness, so you either need a room that can be blacked out entirely or a film-changing bag. The latter is convenient as it means you can load your film anywhere, but I prefer to head into a blacked-out room, simply because there is more space. In either case it's worth practicing a few times with a scrap roll of film, just to familiarize yourself with the process. The steps on the right relate to 35mm film.

Tips

- If you're loading film in a blacked-out room in your house or apartment check for any devices with LEDs in them; these can be bright enough to affect your film. If you can see anything, your room is not completely dark.

- Whether you use a darkroom or a changing bag to load your film in, it's a good idea to have a spare spiral on hand in case the one you're trying to load jams or refuses to load smoothly (which can occasionally happen).

- If you're shooting medium format (120) roll film, the loading process is similar, but you need to separate the film from its backing paper in the dark.

- Orthochromatic film (see page 19) is not sensitive to red light, so can be loaded in a darkroom with the red safelight on; panchromatic film must be handled in total darkness.

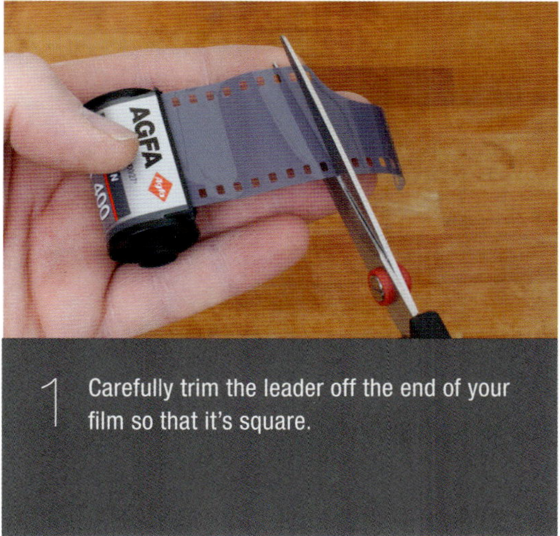

1 Carefully trim the leader off the end of your film so that it's square.

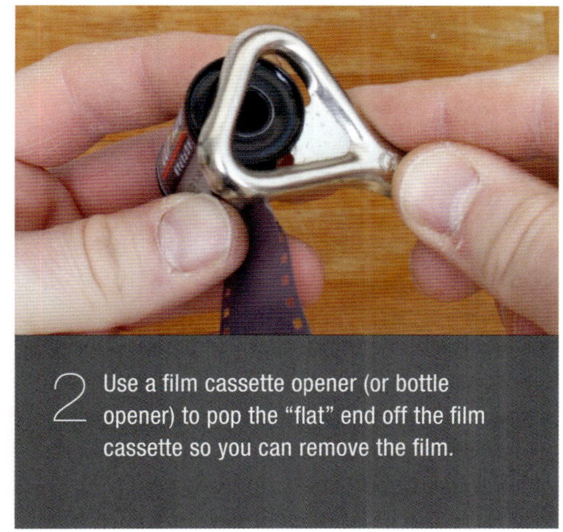

2 Use a film cassette opener (or bottle opener) to pop the "flat" end off the film cassette so you can remove the film.

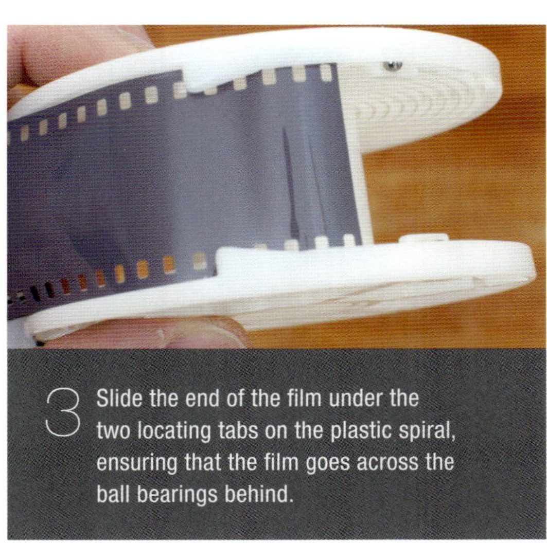

3 Slide the end of the film under the two locating tabs on the plastic spiral, ensuring that the film goes across the ball bearings behind.

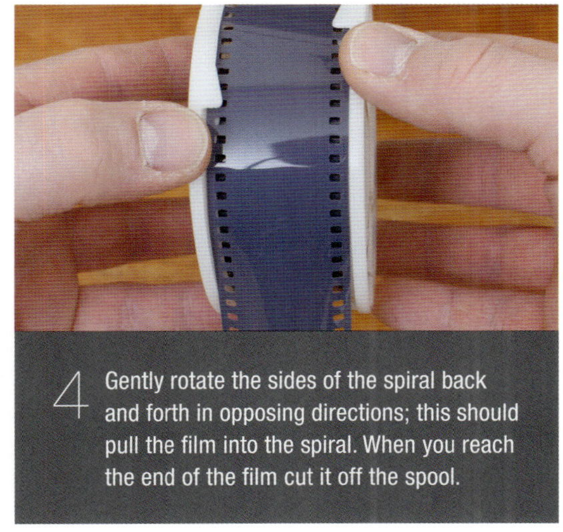

4 Gently rotate the sides of the spiral back and forth in opposing directions; this should pull the film into the spiral. When you reach the end of the film cut it off the spool.

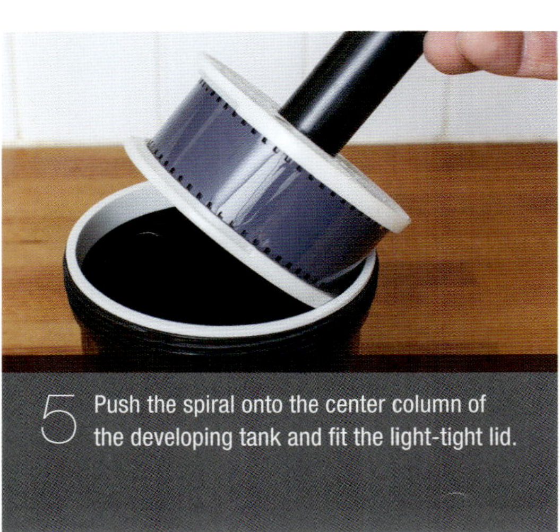

5 Push the spiral onto the center column of the developing tank and fit the light-tight lid.

Warning

All the steps here should be carried out in total darkness, as any light source will affect the film.

Mixing Chemistry

Once your film is safely in the developing tank and the light-tight lid is on, you can turn on the lights and begin the wet process. Start by mixing your chemicals; your developer, stop bath (optional), and fixer. In each case, follow the manufacturer's advice when it comes to the dilution ratio (this is usually printed on the bottle or packet) and match the overall volume of chemistry to the number of films you are processing (this is usually stamped on the underside of the developing tank). If you get stuck on the math, consider downloading the Massive Dev Chart Timer app (see page 155).

It's also important that you get the temperature right for your chemicals, especially the developer. Most developer timings are given at a temperature of 68°F (20°C), but again, it pays to check the manufacturer's recommendations, especially if you're using a developer you haven't tried before. The stop bath (if you're using it) and fixer are less temperature critical, but it's still a good idea to maintain a similar temperature throughout the process; you can control the temperature using hot and cold water baths.

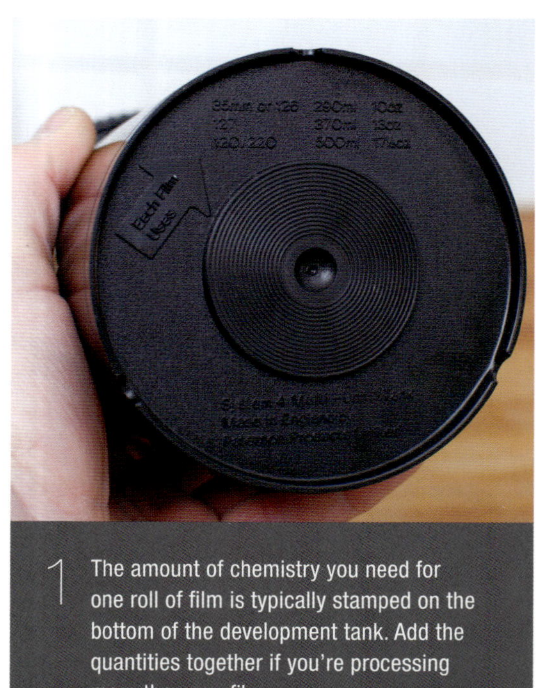

1 The amount of chemistry you need for one roll of film is typically stamped on the bottom of the development tank. Add the quantities together if you're processing more than one film.

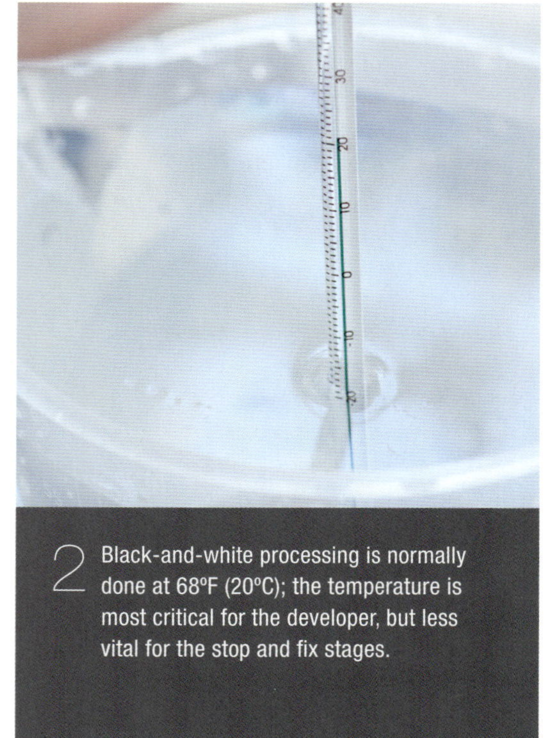

2 Black-and-white processing is normally done at 68°F (20°C); the temperature is most critical for the developer, but less vital for the stop and fix stages.

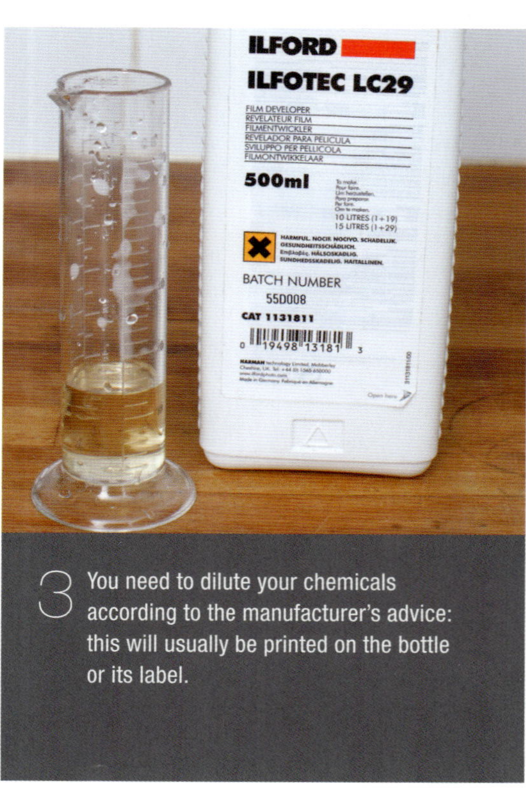

3 You need to dilute your chemicals according to the manufacturer's advice: this will usually be printed on the bottle or its label.

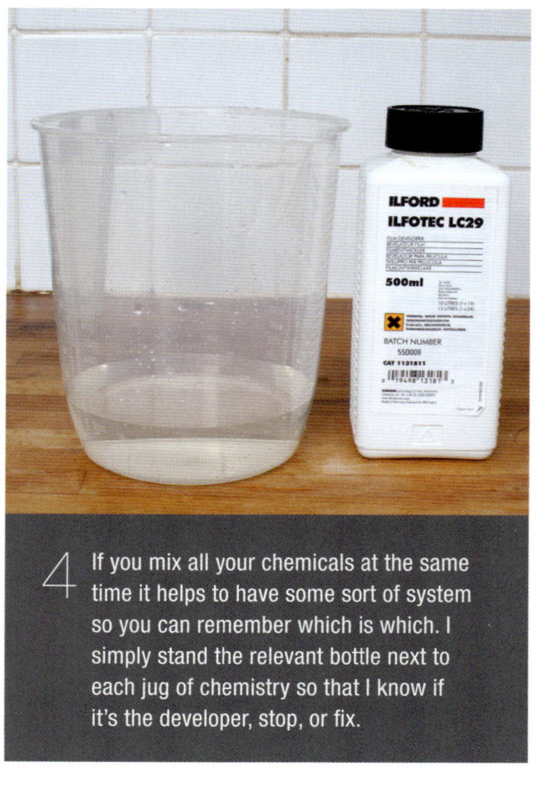

4 If you mix all your chemicals at the same time it helps to have some sort of system so you can remember which is which. I simply stand the relevant bottle next to each jug of chemistry so that I know if it's the developer, stop, or fix.

Develop, Stop, Fix

The process itself involves three consecutive stages: development, stop (or wash), and then fix. You can find the development time on the packet or bottle of the developer, or on the Massive Dev Chart (or similar). The first step is to pour in your developer and start your timer. At each stage of the process you will need to agitate the developing tank. Instructions vary, but with developer I agitate for 30 seconds at the start of the process and then for 5 seconds every minute. This means inverting the tank a couple of times every minute, and then giving it a sharp tap on a solid surface to dislodge any air bubbles that may have formed.

Just before the development time comes to an end, pour out the developer and pour in your stop bath. You can substitute this for a wash with plain water if you prefer, but the benefit of a chemical stop is that it will halt development immediately. This stage is pretty quick—maybe 30–60 seconds—at which point you can pour out the stop and pour in the fixer. Again, agitate the fixer intermittently and for at least the recommended time: this tends to be quite long (10 minutes is not uncommon), but do not be tempted to cut the time to speed things up, as insufficiently fixed negatives will fade over time.

Once it's fixed, your film needs to be washed, which can be done in one of two ways. The easiest method is to put the developing tank under a tap (with or without a specialist film-washing hose) and simply let the water run for 10–20 minutes. Obviously, this will use a lot of water, so a less wasteful option is to fill the tank with water (ideally at 68°F/20°C) and agitate constantly for 10 seconds. Pour the water out, replace with fresh water, and agitate for 20 seconds; then pour out, replace, and agitate for 45 seconds, and repeat the process once more for 90 seconds.

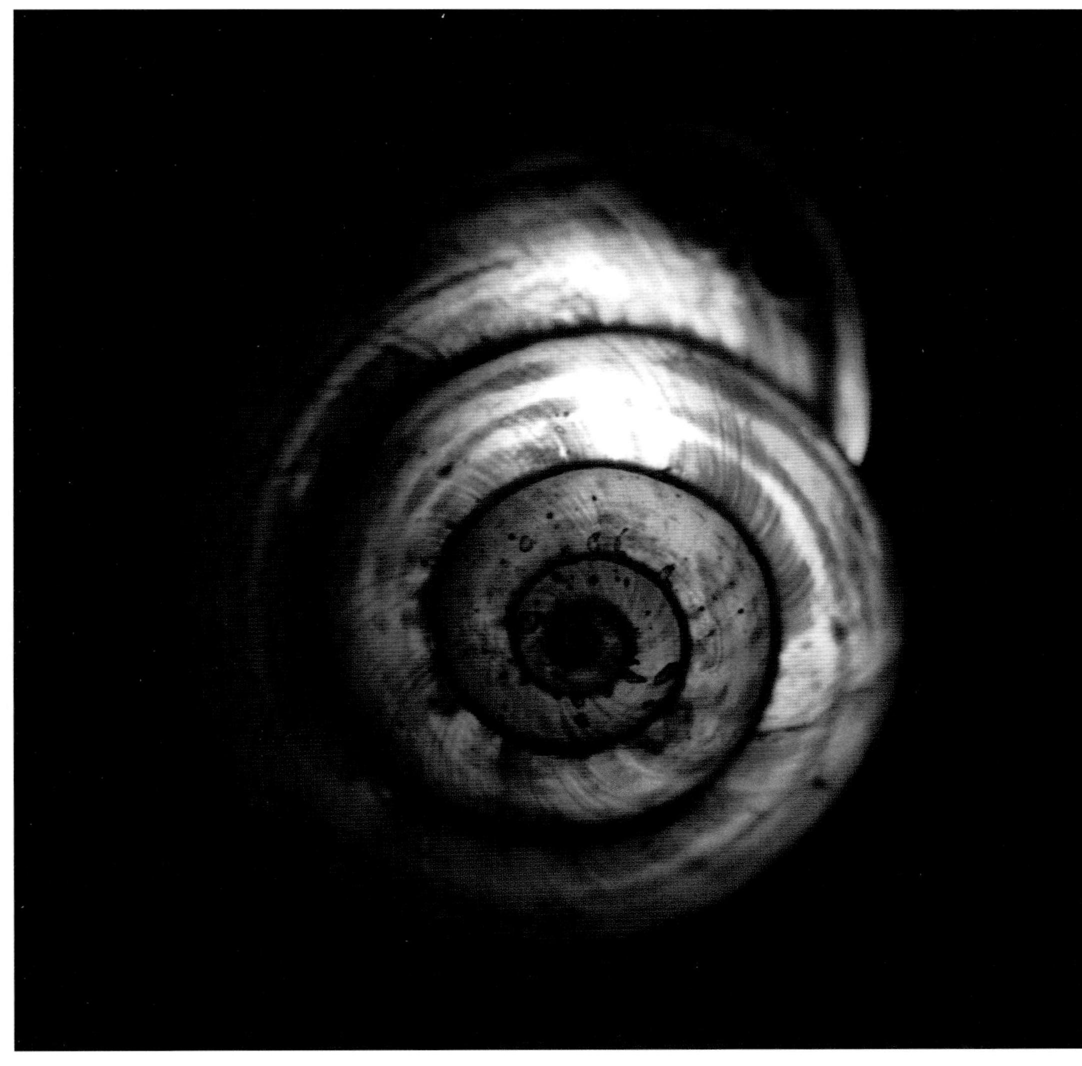

Above: You don't need to process films of the same format together: you can happily process 35mm and medium format simultaneously, just as long as your tank will hold them and you make sure you add the correct amount of chemistry. For example, I shot this snail shell on 35mm and medium format, and processed both rolls at the same time.

When your film has been washed—and with the developing tank still full of water—add a couple of drops of wetting agent or dishwashing soap, give it a very gentle stir, and lift the spiral out of the tank. Carefully pull the film from the spiral and hang it up to dry in a dust-free environment. Run your forefinger and middle finger from the top to the bottom of the film to remove excess water, but be careful not to scratch the film in the process.

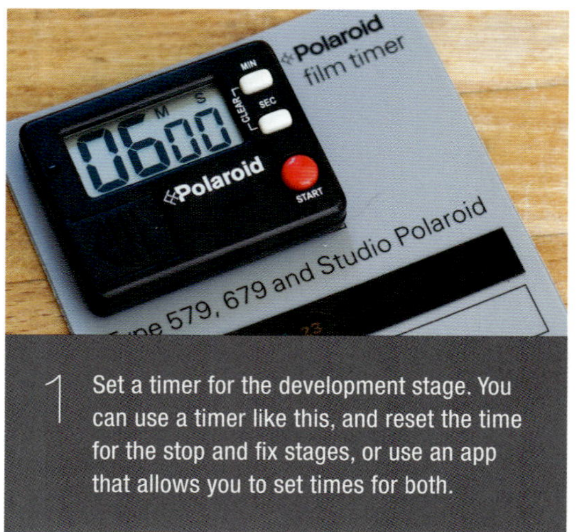

1 Set a timer for the development stage. You can use a timer like this, and reset the time for the stop and fix stages, or use an app that allows you to set times for both.

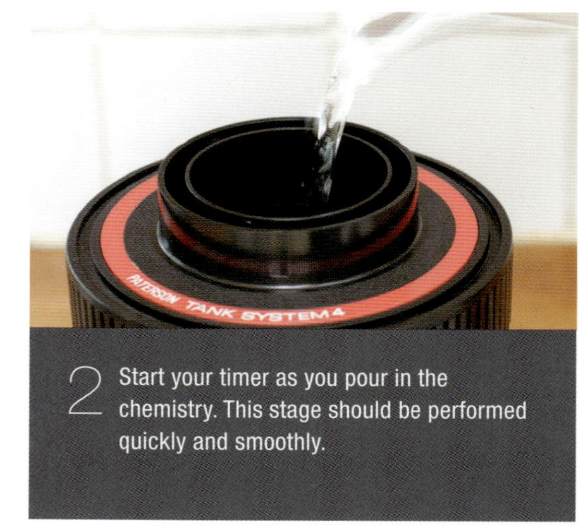

2 Start your timer as you pour in the chemistry. This stage should be performed quickly and smoothly.

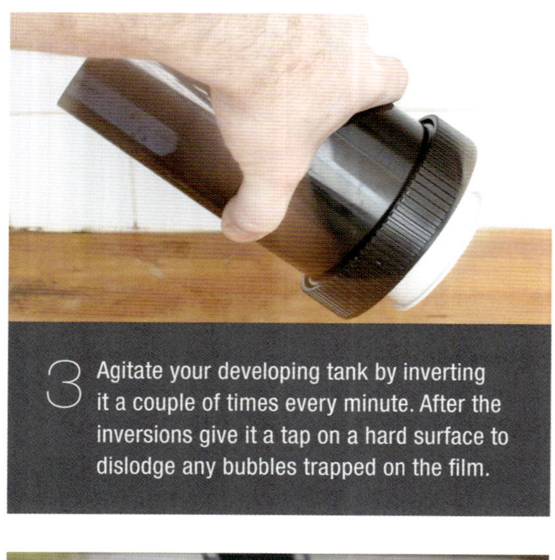

3 Agitate your developing tank by inverting it a couple of times every minute. After the inversions give it a tap on a hard surface to dislodge any bubbles trapped on the film.

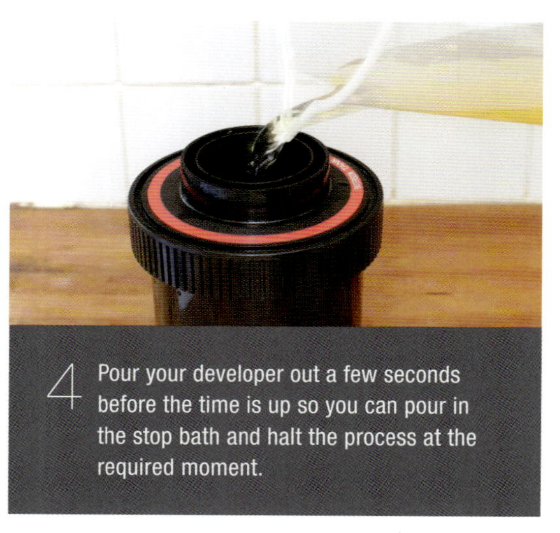

4 Pour your developer out a few seconds before the time is up so you can pour in the stop bath and halt the process at the required moment.

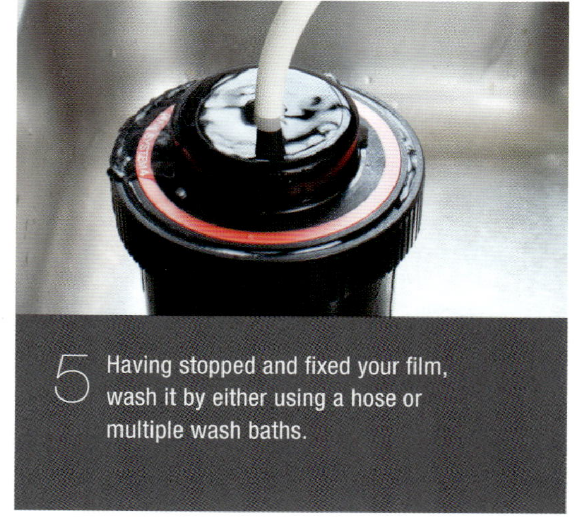

5 Having stopped and fixed your film, wash it by either using a hose or multiple wash baths.

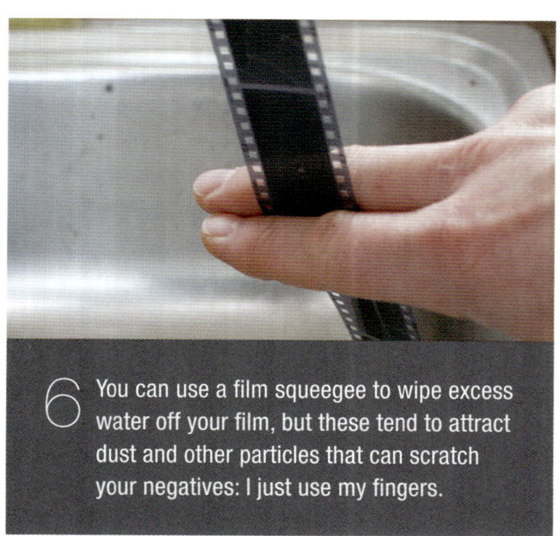

6 You can use a film squeegee to wipe excess water off your film, but these tend to attract dust and other particles that can scratch your negatives: I just use my fingers.

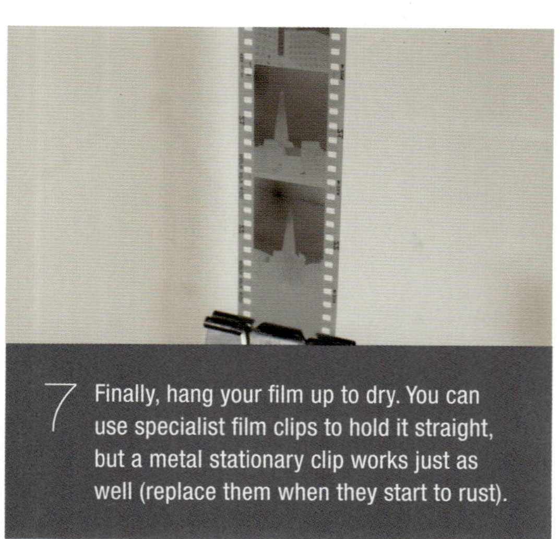

7 Finally, hang your film up to dry. You can use specialist film clips to hold it straight, but a metal stationary clip works just as well (replace them when they start to rust).

Tips

- Some chemicals (especially stop and fix), can be used to process numerous films, while others (particularly some developers) are "single shot" and should be thrown away after they have been used. Always check the instructions to avoid confusion.

- If your chemicals can be used repeatedly, check if you need to compensate for additional uses by extending the time of the process. Also, keep a note of how many films the chemistry has worked on: a simple checklist stuck to the storage bottle will be sufficient.

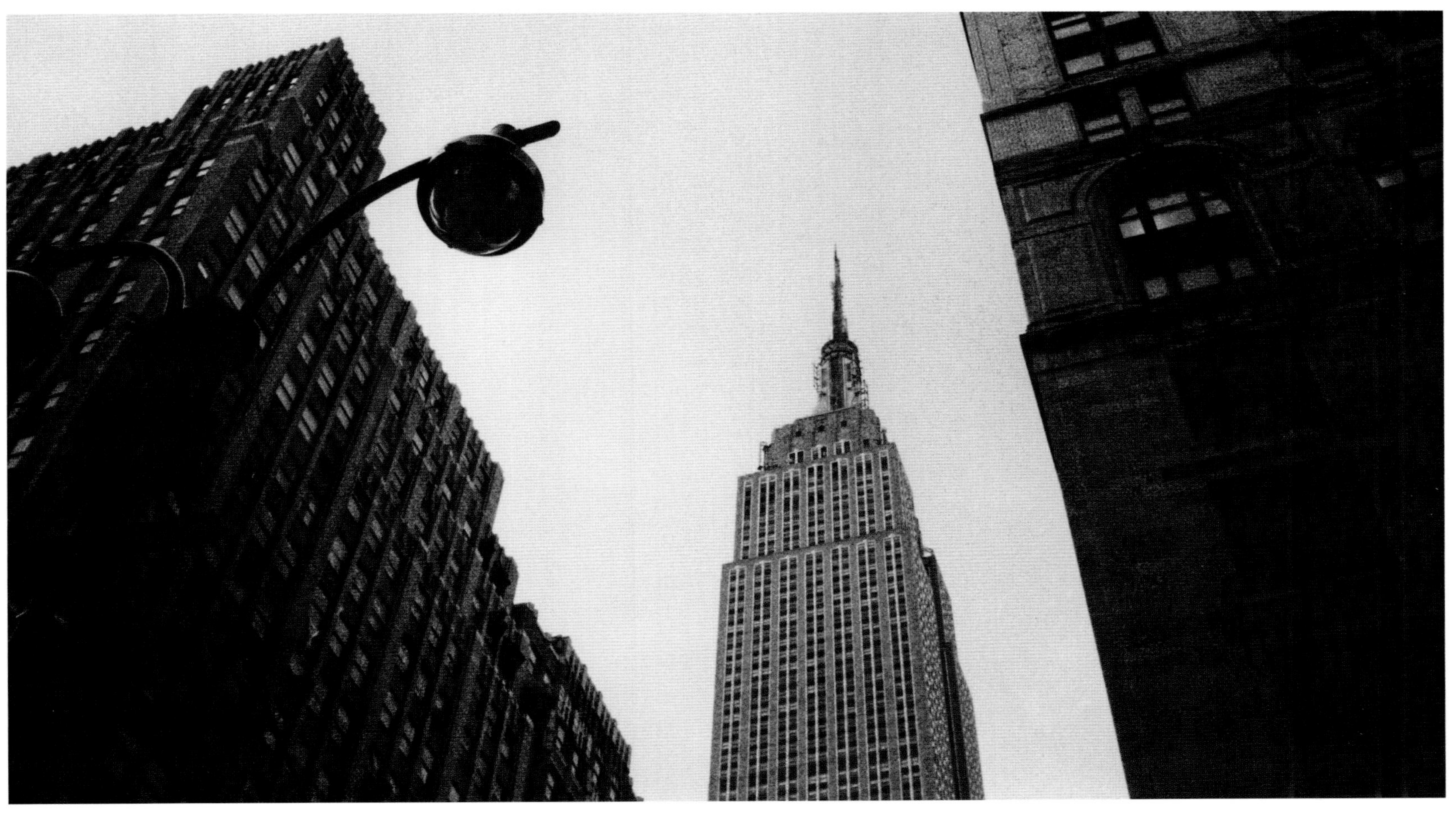

MASSIVE DEV CHART

If you want to take a lot of the pain out of processing black-and-white film head over to digitaltruth.com and locate the aptly named Massive Dev Chart (and its associated Massive Dev Chart Timer iOS/Android app).

This vast online resource can provide development times and mixing ratios for more than 18,000 developer and film combinations, while the app also adds a super-useful timer for each of the processing stages.

STAND DEVELOPMENT

While normal film development requires regular agitation, stand development—which dates back to the late 19th century—requires the exact opposite: little or no agitation. The process uses incredibly dilute developer and the film is left for an hour or more to slowly develop. The benefits of this process are reduced grain (and improved sharpness), and increased shadow detail; the downside is that negatives may be developed unevenly.

CAFFENOL

Mixing water with instant coffee, vitamin C, and washing soda makes the classic version of this alternative film developer. It may not sound like a classic photographic brew, but it's capable of replacing the chemical developer in your process and delivering great results. But agitation needs to be done carefully to prevent the solution from "frothing up," and you should use two or three washes between the developer and fixer, rather than a chemical stop bath.

Push & Pull Processing

Although film is given a single ISO rating, there's nothing to say you have to stick to that; in fact a lot of film photographers don't. Black-and-white film in particular is forgiving when it comes to being shot at a higher or lower ISO setting, as long as you compensate for this with the development. For example, you could rate an ISO 400 film at ISO 800 or ISO 1600 (effectively underexposing the film by 1 stop and 2 stops respectively) and then develop it for longer—known as "push" processing. This can be useful when you are in low-light conditions and effectively want to shoot with a more sensitive film, or it can be used for creative effect; push processing tends to increase grain and contrast. In either case, monochrome films that are well suited to "pushing" will often have different development times supplied by the manufacturer for different ISO settings, or an indication will be given as to how much of an increase you need to give to the development.

The opposite technique is known as "pull" processing, which is when you rate a film at a lower ISO—effectively overexposing it—and then reduce the development time. However, this is far less common than push processing as it generally leads to flat, low-contrast, and "muddy" images.

Below: Ilford HP5 Plus (an ISO 400 fim) rated at ISO 200, ISO 800, and ISO 1600.

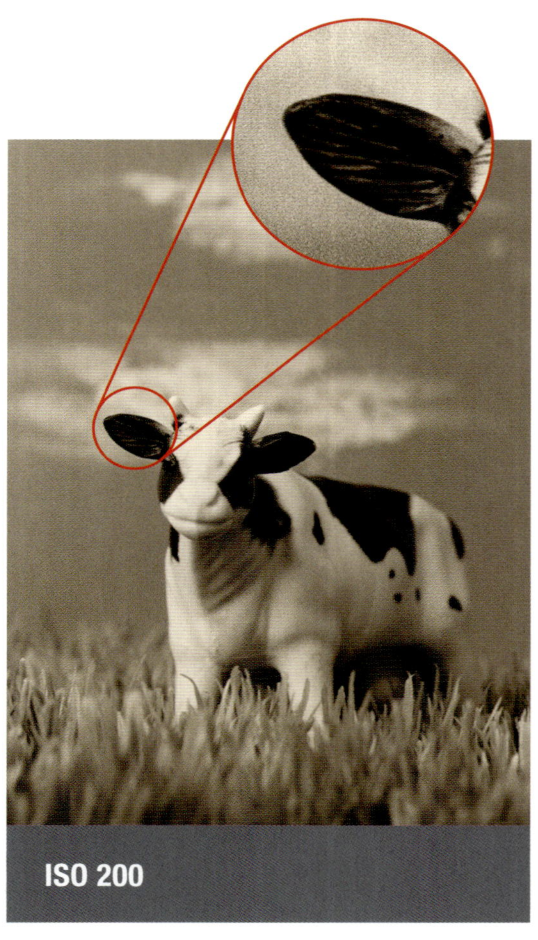

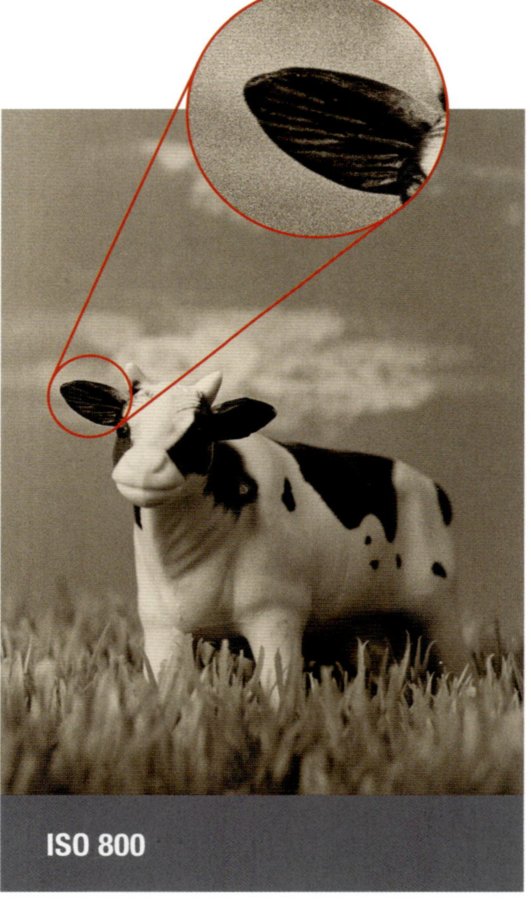

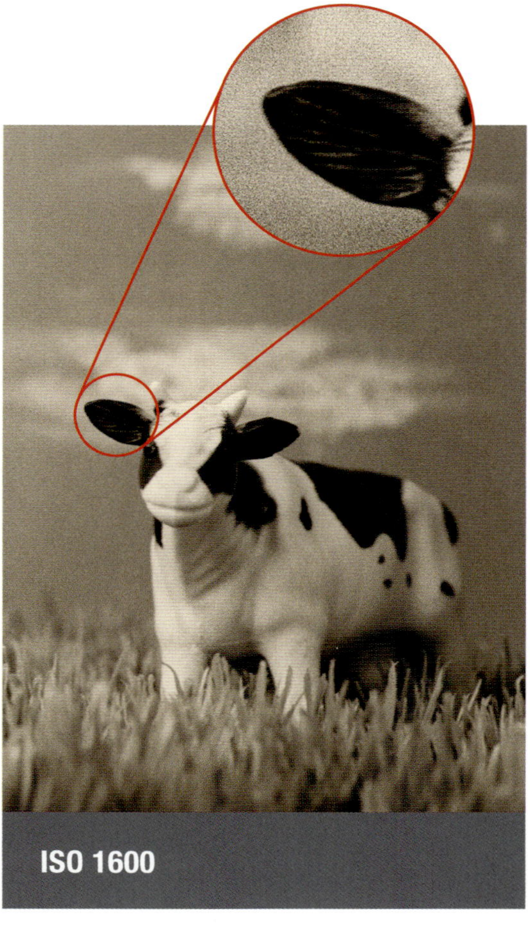

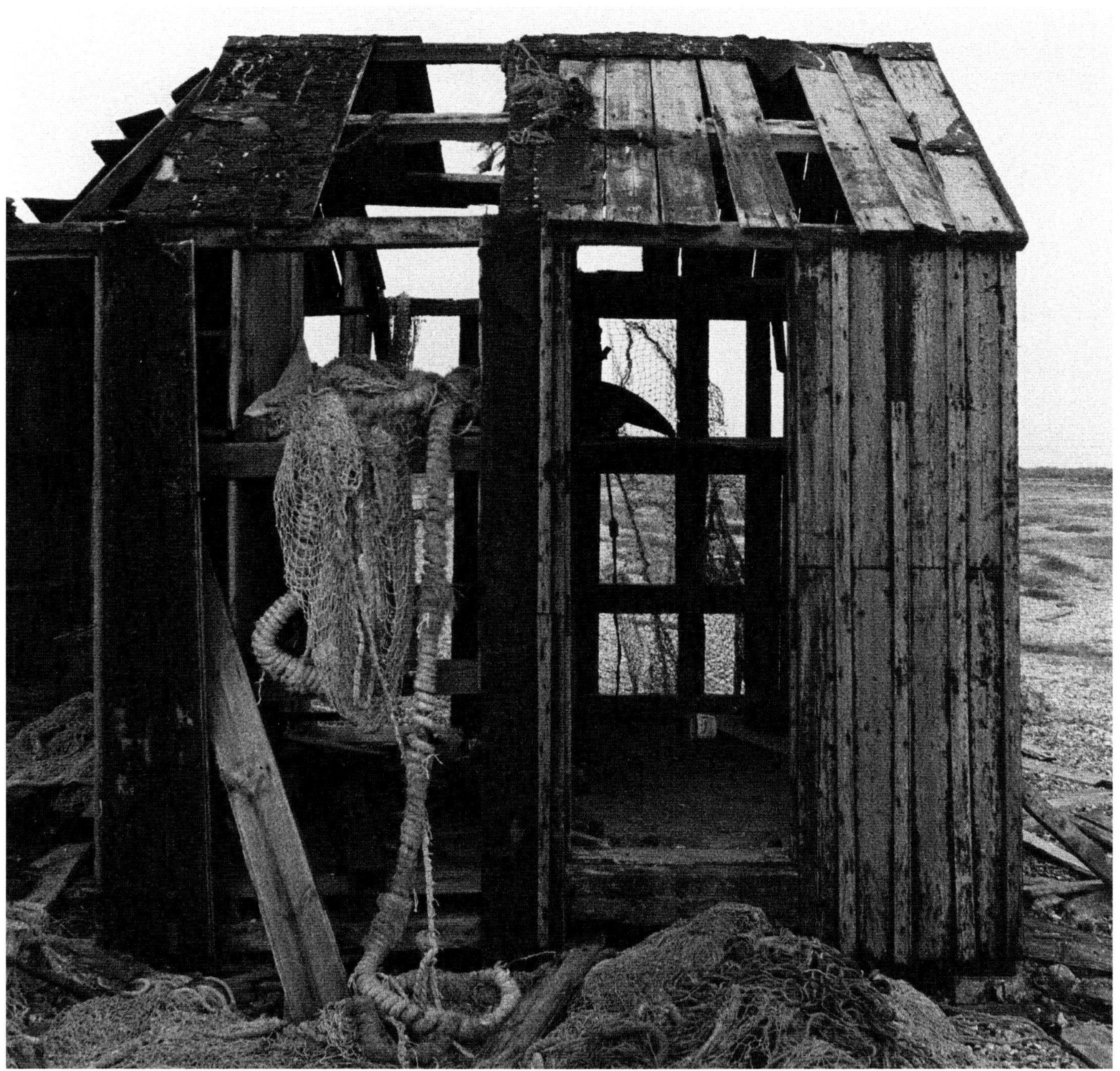

Above: Pushing and pulling film only works for the whole roll, so you need to decide whether to do it before you start shooting. On this occasion I got caught out with a film that was slightly too slow to handhold in the overcast conditions. I should have "uprated" it and push processed it, but instead I had to accept very slightly soft images due to a small amount of camera shake.

Processing Color Film

When it comes to processing color film at home, there aren't a lot of chemical options. However, Tetenal continues to manufacture and supply its C41 and E6 Colortec kits, while CineFilm's Cs41 "color simplified" kit claims to make color negative processing as straightforward as possible.

As I said before, I choose not to process my color film, but you might feel differently. If you do, there are several processing kits available for both color negative and color transparency film, and unless you want to cross process your film it's important that you choose the right one: C41 for negatives or E6 for transparencies.

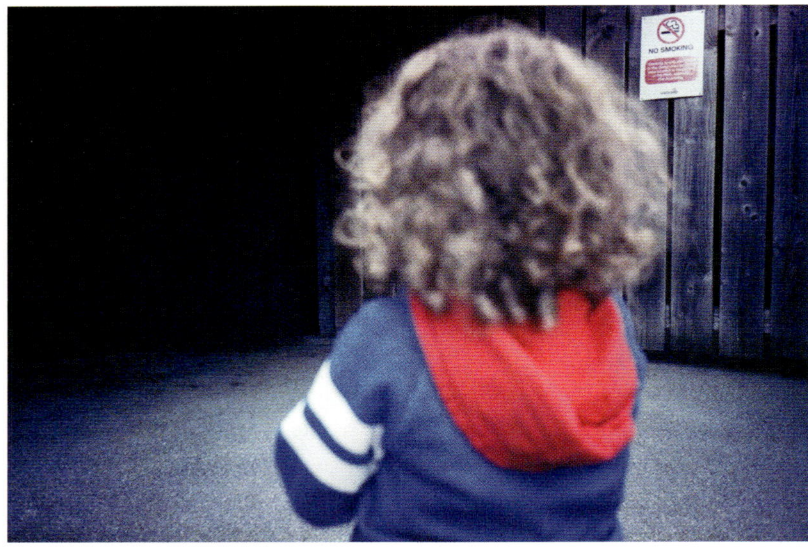

Right: Cross processing (see page 160) is something you can experiment with more fully if you hand-process your own film, as you will easily be able to vary the development times you use.

C41

Home-processing color negative film is easier than most people think. Although there are some differences between processing kits, it boils down to three chemical steps, which isn't too dissimilar to processing black-and-white film. Aside from the chemicals themselves, one of the biggest differences is perhaps the temperatures involved. Whereas black-and-white negatives are usually processed at 68°F (20°C), color negatives are processed at around 102°F (38.8°C). So, the first step is to get your film loaded and your chemicals mixed, up to temperature, and into a water bath that will keep the temperature consistent. It is then a case of pouring the solutions into your developing tank in the right order and for the right amount of time (just like processing black-and-white film).

1 **Developer** The standard development time for color negative film is 3½ minutes, regardless of the film you're using. Unlike black-and-white processing, this means that you can process different speed films simultaneously.

2 **Blix** A contraction of "bleach" and "fix." This removes undeveloped silver halide generated during development, and fixes the film.

3 **Wash** A short rinse that gets rid of any chemicals.

4 **Stabilizer** This gives the film a final clean and helps to prevent watermarks.

5 **Rinse** A very quick (and optional) rinse.

6 **Hang** Allow to dry!

E6

I'm not going to dwell on home-processing E6, as it's a broadly similar experience to developing C41: if you can process C41 you can process E6 (and vice versa). The main difference in terms of the process is that E6 requires an additional developer and extra wash stages, and there is also a greater need for accuracy when it comes to temperatures and timings. This is because your processed transparency film is effectively your finished work, so any color or contrast shifts introduced during processing will be there in your final images (with color negatives there will always be a printing or scanning stage where things can be tweaked).

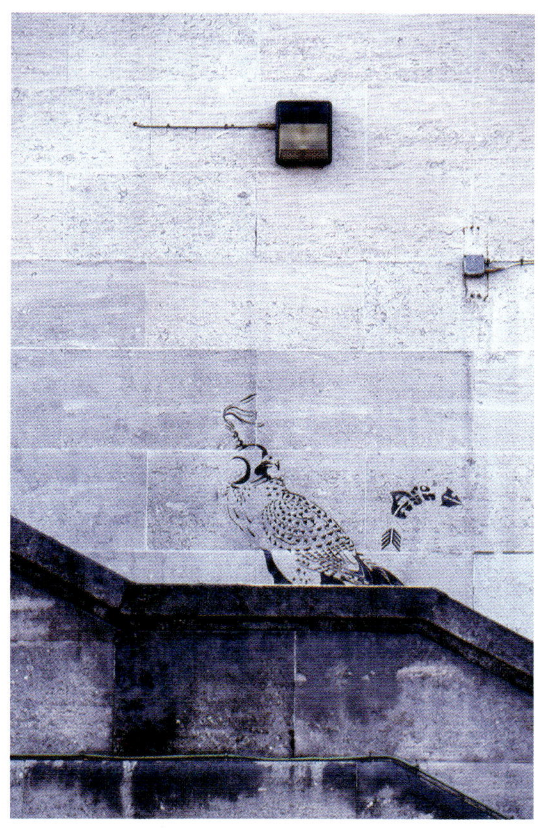

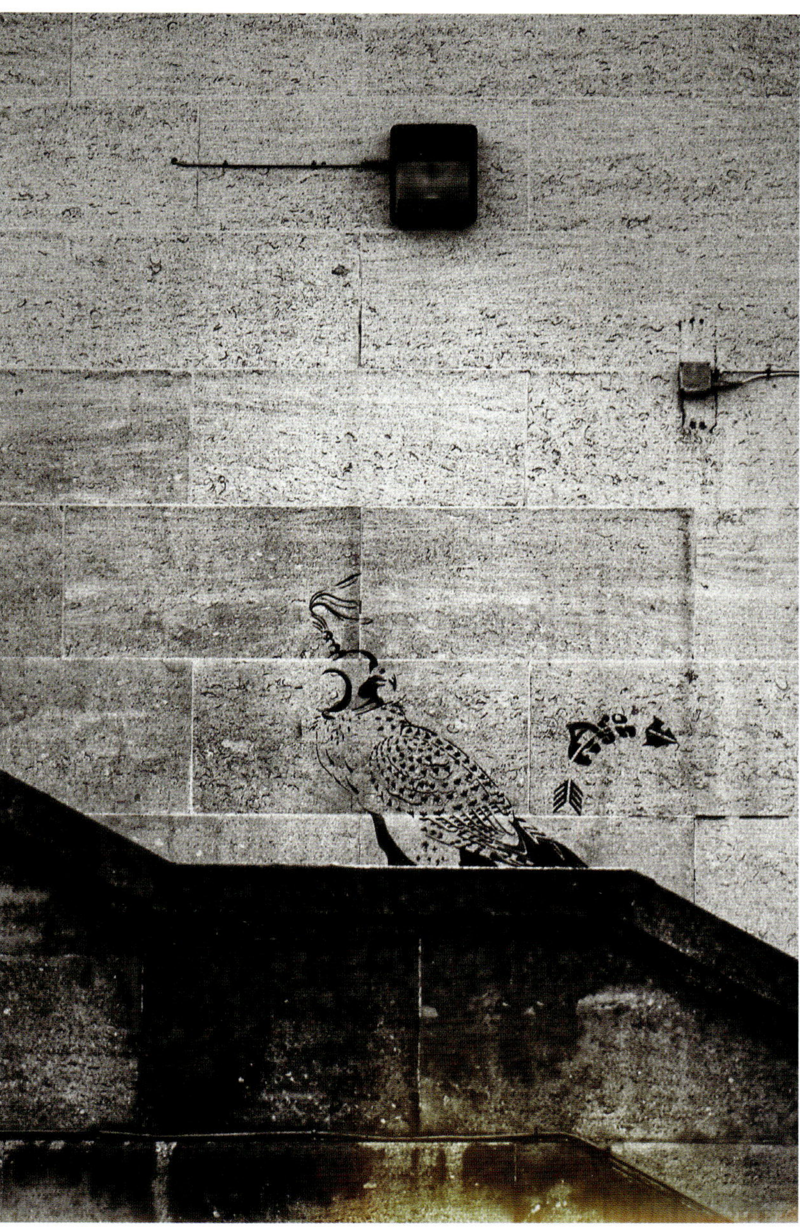

PUSH / PULL

You can push and pull color film in the same way as black-and-white film (see page 156), enabling you to change the film's speed and compensate with the development. Most labs will push and pull transparency film without any problem (although there may be an additional charge), but negative film can be more of a challenge. The problem is, a lot of labs use automated machines for their C41 processing, and to push (or pull) a film the machine needs to be recalibrated and the film run through on its own. In a commercial environment it's not worth the time and effort to do this for a single roll of film. However, if the lab uses "dip and dunk" tanks, or can hand process C41, pushing and pulling may be an option (or you can process it yourself). Be warned, though, if you choose to go down this road you may experience adverse color shifts that are very difficult to correct.

Tips

- Some processing kits recommend a pre-wash before using the developer.

- Push processing a C41 film involves increasing the development time; pulling a film means you have to reduce the development time.

Cross Processing

Over the years, cross processing has been particularly popular with fashion photographers looking to give their work an edge, studio photographers looking to make product shots "pop," and portrait photographers looking for a more crisp, contemporary vibe. However, this is a technique that drifts in and out of fashion, and—perhaps more pertinently—is limited by the choice of films available.

Simply put, cross processing involves running color film through the "wrong" color process, so color negative film gets processed through the E6 process and transparency film goes through C41. In each case the result matches the chemistry, so you will get a negative image on your cross-processed transparency film, and your color negative film will deliver positive images. In both cases the look of the images will be radically different to normal.

The most popular option is to run transparency film through C41 chemistry. This will typically give the contrast a dramatic boost and also introduce some wild color shifts. The appearance of these shifts will depend on a range of things, including the film you use, the exposure you give it, and the lighting: this is one area where experimenting is essential.

The opposite cross process—color negative film through E6 chemistry—also results in strong color shifts, but this time contrast tends to be reduced. Rather than eye-popping color, things tend to be more pastel and muted, which can lead to quite drab-looking results (this is part of the reason why this is seen as the weaker cross processing option). However, don't let this put you off: push-processing film by as much as 3 stops can often help, although again, it's really a case of trial and error until you find that perfect combination of film, exposure, and processing.

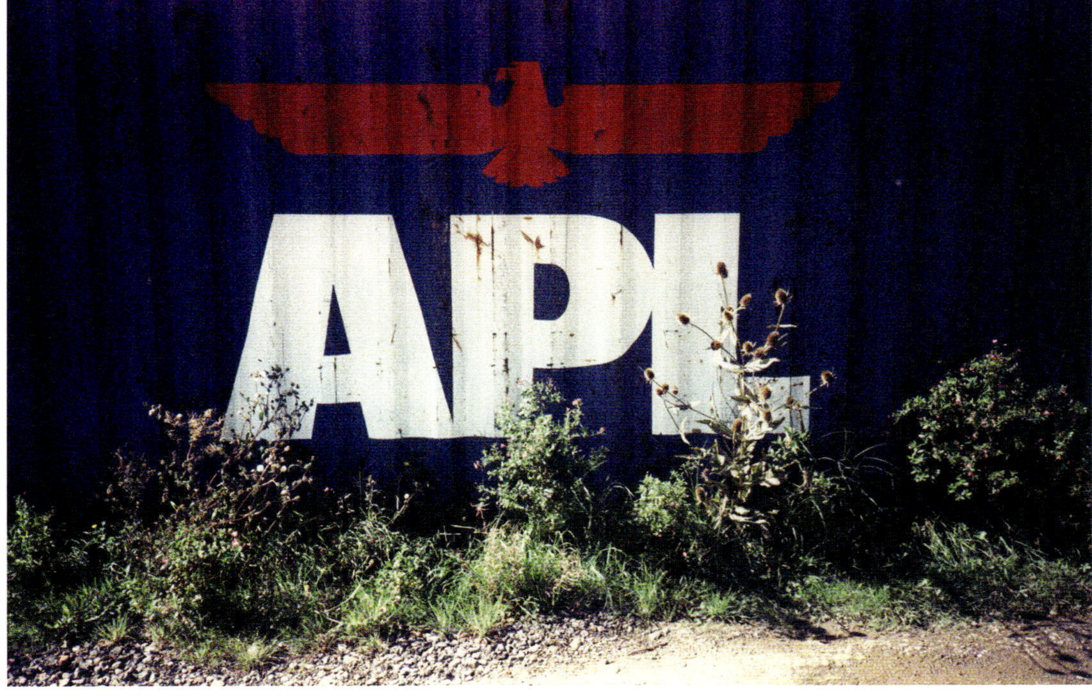

Left: Cross processing can be unpredictable when you use a film for the first time because you don't know how the color and contrast will respond to being developed in the "wrong" chemicals. Testing your film (see page 24) can be useful here, as it will help you see what might happen, but generally speaking if you run transparency film through C41 chemicals you can expect an increase in contrast and color.

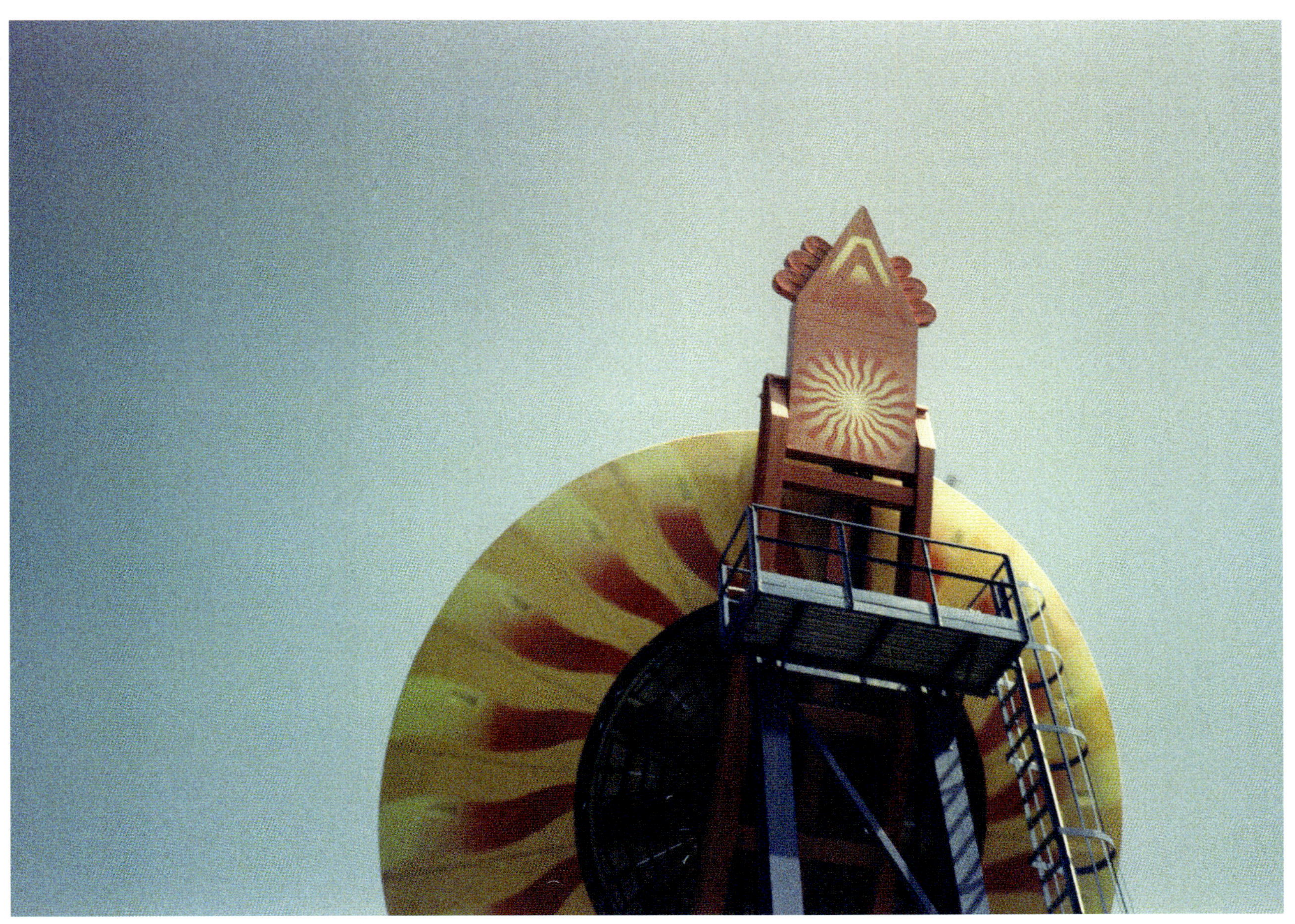

Above: This shot was taken on my last roll of out-of-date Kodak Ektachrome 160T (EPT), which was my "go to" emulsion for cross processing. Through testing I learned that when you shoot this tungsten-balanced film in daylight (and cross process it), the tungsten balance helps keep the colors in check, rather than introducing a heavy blue color cast. I also discovered that it responded best if it was rated at ISO 100, effectively overexposing it by ½–⅔ stop, and given a "standard" process through C41 chemicals.

Scanning

If you want to digitize your film the traditional option is to scan it. You can pay a lab to do this for you (it's often cheaper to get it done when they process your film), but it's just as easy to do it yourself, and the outlay doesn't have to be huge. There are plenty of new scanners available that will scan film, ranging from ultra-cheap flatbeds to dedicated film scanners. Most of these will do a good job with black-and-white negatives, and as long as you've got a scanner with a high DMax you should be fine scanning transparencies as well; the main thing is that the film holders actually hold your film flat. Scanning color negatives can be a slightly different matter, though, not because of the scanner, but because of its software. We'll look at a way to overcome this on the following pages, but for now let's look at what you need to get started.

Hardware

When we talk about hardware we're talking about the scanner itself. There are some great scanners out there today (Epson's V850 Photo, for example), but in my opinion the best scanners for film are the dedicated film scanners from almost two decades ago. It might sound rather counterintuitive, but 15–20 years ago scanning was at its peak and the likes of Canon, Konica Minolta, Nikon, and Polaroid were all producing dedicated high-end film scanners designed to meet the needs of the most demanding professionals. These weren't multifunctional devices that could scan, print, and copy, but single-purpose units designed for one task, and one task only: extracting every last bit of detail from a film frame.

It's not necessarily a straightforward ride, though. High-end dedicated film scanners were pretty expensive when they came out, and have held their prices surprisingly well (especially the relatively rare medium-format models). This has been compounded by the fact that there is only a limited supply of used models, so as more people look to explore film photography and the demand increases, so too do the prices. However, if you get a good one it is likely to be every bit as good today as it was back in the day.

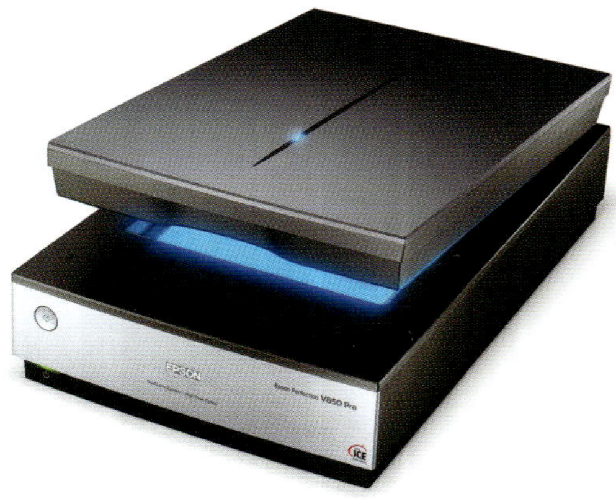

Above: There are still some great scanners available, such as Epson's V850 Pro, which will scan virtually every film format up to 10x8in sheet film, as well as prints. I use its predecessor—the V750 Pro—for all my medium- and large-format scans, although for scanning 35mm I prefer to use a dedicated 35mm film scanner.

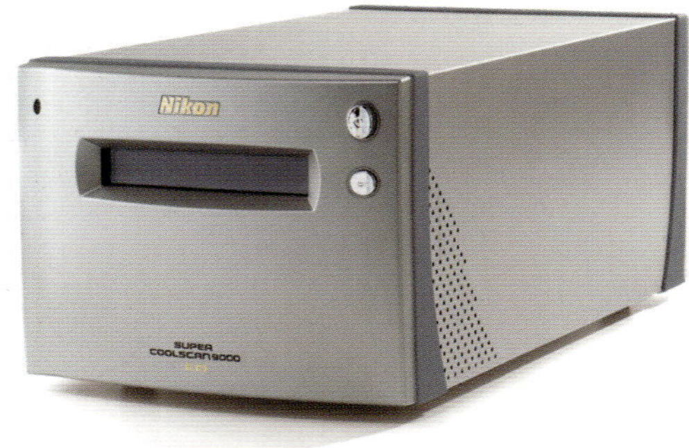

Above: A dedicated film scanner is perhaps the ultimate solution for scanning film at home, but the high-end models that were once commonplace are now only available used and prices are slowly increasing as demand outstrips supply. Medium-format scanners, such as Nikon's Coolscan 9000ED, are particularly sought after.

Software

One of the fundamental problems of buying a vintage scanner is getting it to "talk" to your computer. These devices were designed to run on versions of Windows and Mac OS that are long out of date, so the software that came in the box won't work on your current computer, and the manufacturer won't have an updated version that you can download.

However, this doesn't make these "orphaned" scanners redundant. VueScan is a one-of-a-kind scanner driver from Hamrick that runs on all modern operating systems and is compatible with virtually every scanner made. You'll have to pay around $100 for the "pro" version of the program, but I can't recommend it highly enough: not only will it save an older scanner from the digital scrapheap, but it can also be used with modern scanners to extend their capabilities (VueScan offers multi-pass scan, for example). I use it to keep my Canon FS4000 film scanner running, and with an Epson V750, which means I can use the same scanning routine with each (the Canon is fantastic for 35mm film; the Epson does everything else).

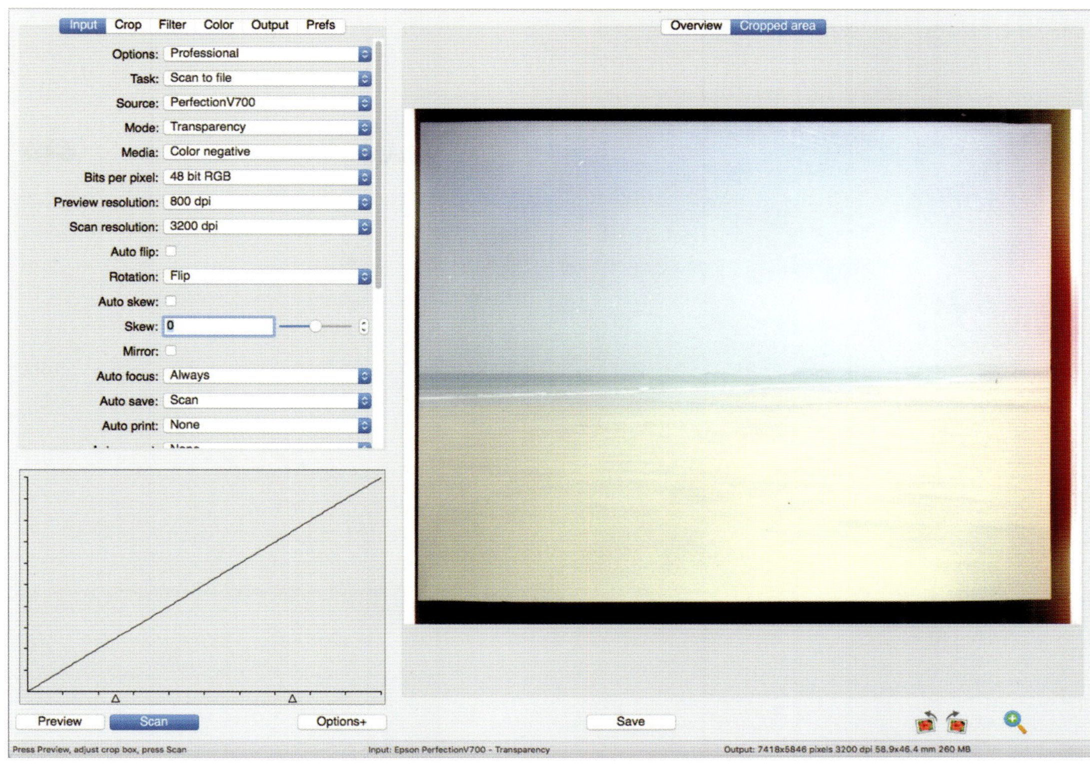

Above right: It's hard to get excited about scanner software, but VueScan is a one-of-a-kind app that deserves to be celebrated. Not only does it unlock the full potential of virtually any scanner, but it prevents the hardware from ending up as landfill after its manufacturer abandons it. So in a small way this unassuming program is actually helping to save the planet from our electronic detritus!

Right: Scanning film will let you work on it digitally, which is far easier (and cheaper) than making a print in the darkroom, especially if you're working in color and/or need to get rid of a lot of dust on your film. However, printing in a darkroom is a more organic and Zen-like experience, which—like using film to start with—is more open to happy accidents. There is no right or wrong approach.

Scanning Color Negatives

Different negative films have a different colored base when they're processed: some are almost bright orange, while others are close to brown, with myriad shades in between. However, most scanner driver software has just one color negative option on its dropdown menu, and then relies on automatic algorithms and/or manual adjustments to get the color right from there. This isn't that different to shooting with your camera on auto: it can do a decent job some of the time, but not all of the time. In this instance, when the scanner fails to deliver the result you're after, it can mean hours of painstaking color correction to get things close to right, or just accepting slightly odd colors from time to time. However, ColorNeg—a nifty little utility from ColorPerfect—contains profiles for more than 300 color negative films, making it much easier to obtain color-accurate results from your scans. Like VueScan, it costs a few dollars to buy a licence, but that quickly pays for itself with the time you save messing about trying to get your colors right. As I said before, I use VueScan to drive my scanners, so my approach to scanning negatives is the same, regardless of whether I am scanning 35mm on the Canon FS4000 or 5x4 on the Epson V750. I then work on the scanned files in Photoshop (ColorNeg works with Photoshop Elements as well).

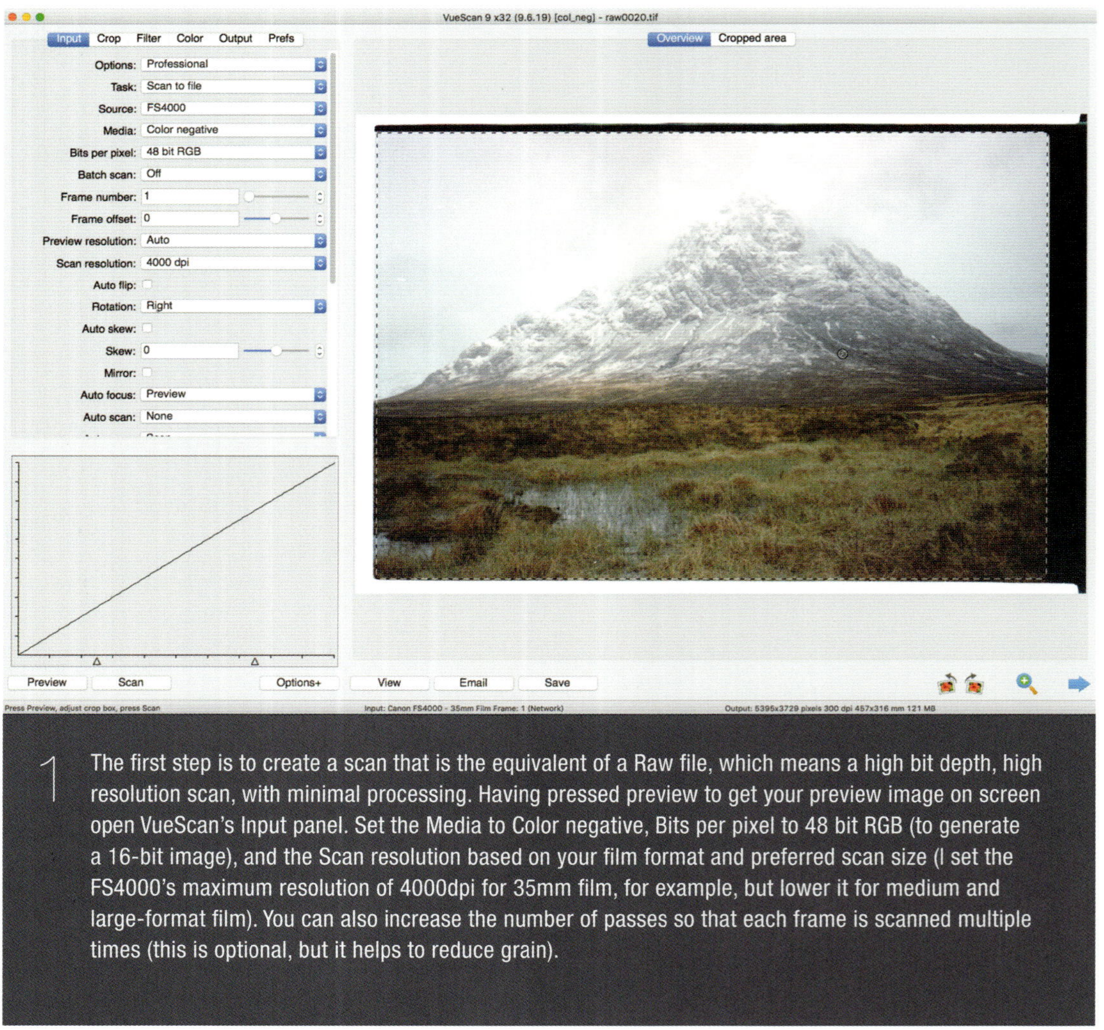

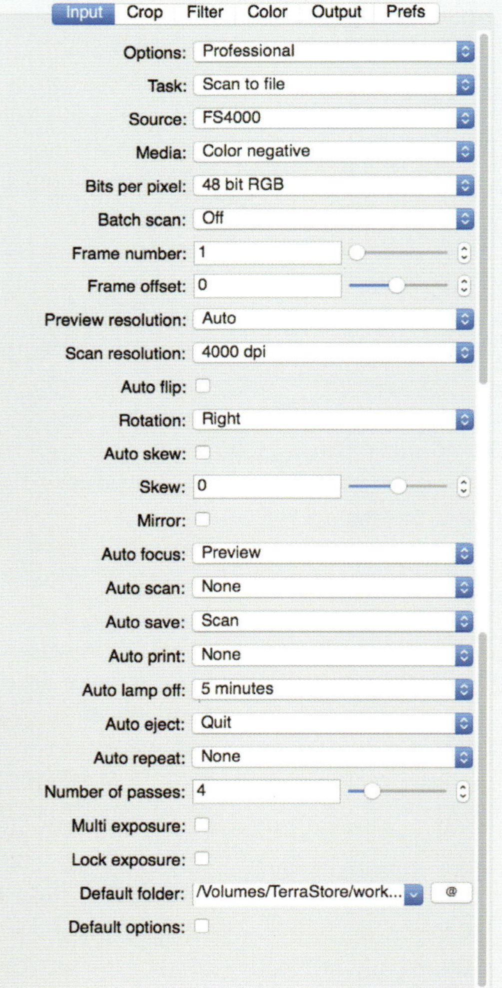

1 The first step is to create a scan that is the equivalent of a Raw file, which means a high bit depth, high resolution scan, with minimal processing. Having pressed preview to get your preview image on screen open VueScan's Input panel. Set the Media to Color negative, Bits per pixel to 48 bit RGB (to generate a 16-bit image), and the Scan resolution based on your film format and preferred scan size (I set the FS4000's maximum resolution of 4000dpi for 35mm film, for example, but lower it for medium and large-format film). You can also increase the number of passes so that each frame is scanned multiple times (this is optional, but it helps to reduce grain).

2 In the Filter panel I keep everything turned off, so there is no grain reduction, sharpening, color restoration, or anything else applied to the image. These are jobs best left to Photoshop.

3 The Color options can be left at their default settings with one exception: set Output color space to AdobeRGB.

4 A few settings need to be checked, and possibly changed, in the Output tab. At the top of the panel you can set your Default folder, which is where your scans will be saved, and also choose a Printed size: I always set this at 300dpi (my "go to" print resolution). Next, make sure that the only file type checked is Raw file at the bottom of the list (not TIFF, JPEG, PDF, or Index). Set the Raw file type to 48-bit RGB (to output your 16-bit image), switch Raw compression to Off, and uncheck Raw DNG format. Press scan and wait for your scanner to do its thing (which may take a while if you have opted for multiple passes), then save the file.

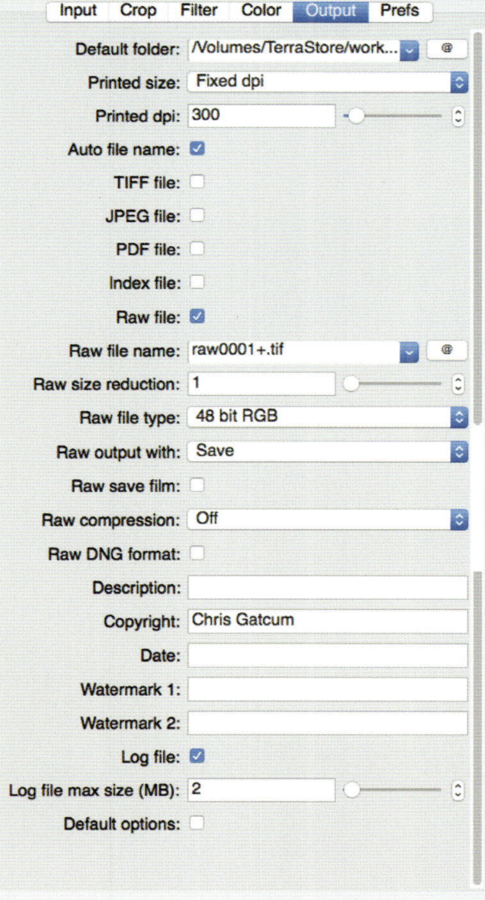

5 Open your scan in Photoshop. What you should be looking at is an orange negative that looks exactly the same as the film: this is your Raw image. Once you've installed it, you will find ColorNeg in Photoshop's menu (Filters > CFSystems > ColorPerfect). Be warned, though, this is not some cuddly app with an intuitive interface: this window is full of buttons, dropdowns, and values that might not immediately make sense.

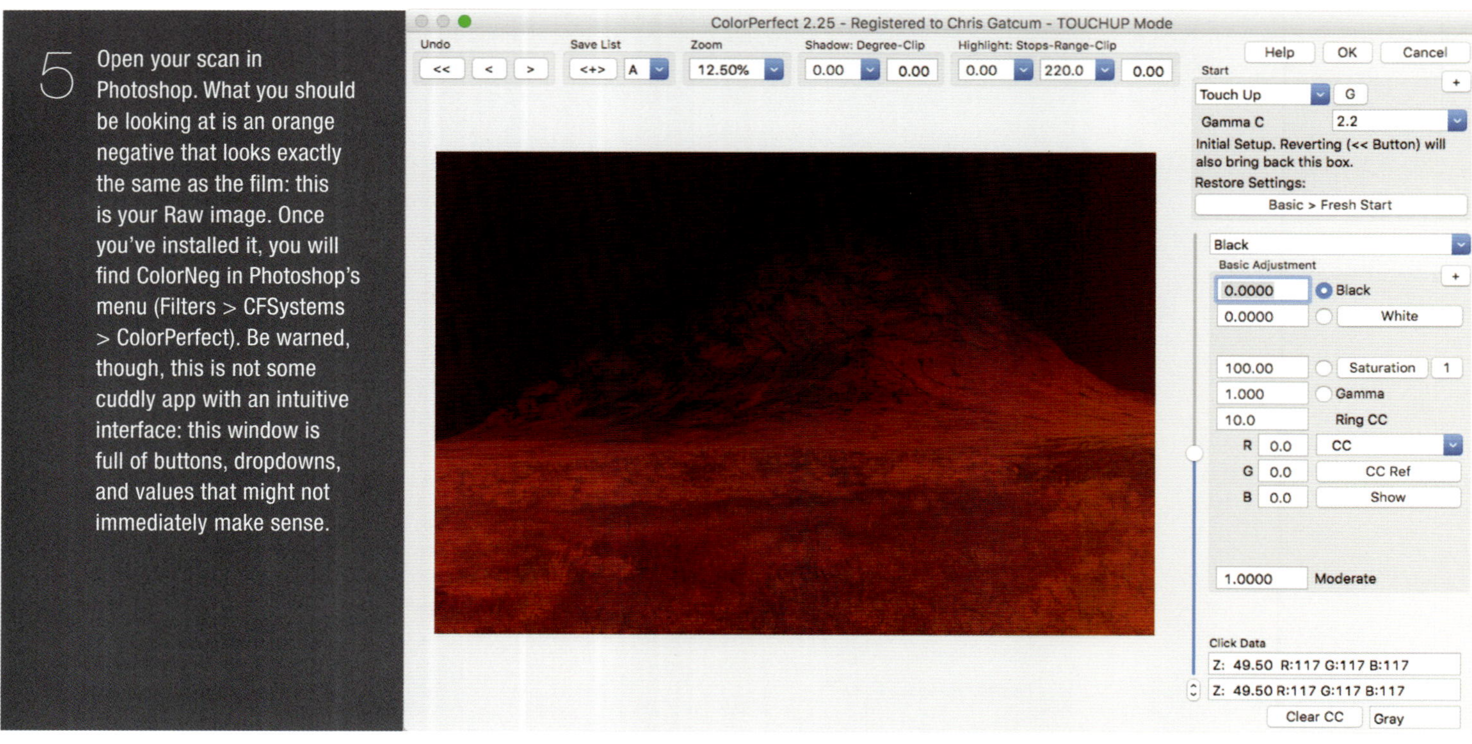

6 To start with (and just under the word "Start" at the top right of the dialog window), choose ColorNeg from the drop-down menu. Then, to its immediate right make sure that the check box says L (clicking on it toggles between L and G), and beneath that set Gamma C to 2.2 (this basically sets the gamma to match the AdobeRGB setting you gave your scan). Finally, set Restore Settings to Basic > Fresh Start, to ensure that each time you open the dialog it doesn't automatically apply any previous adjustments.

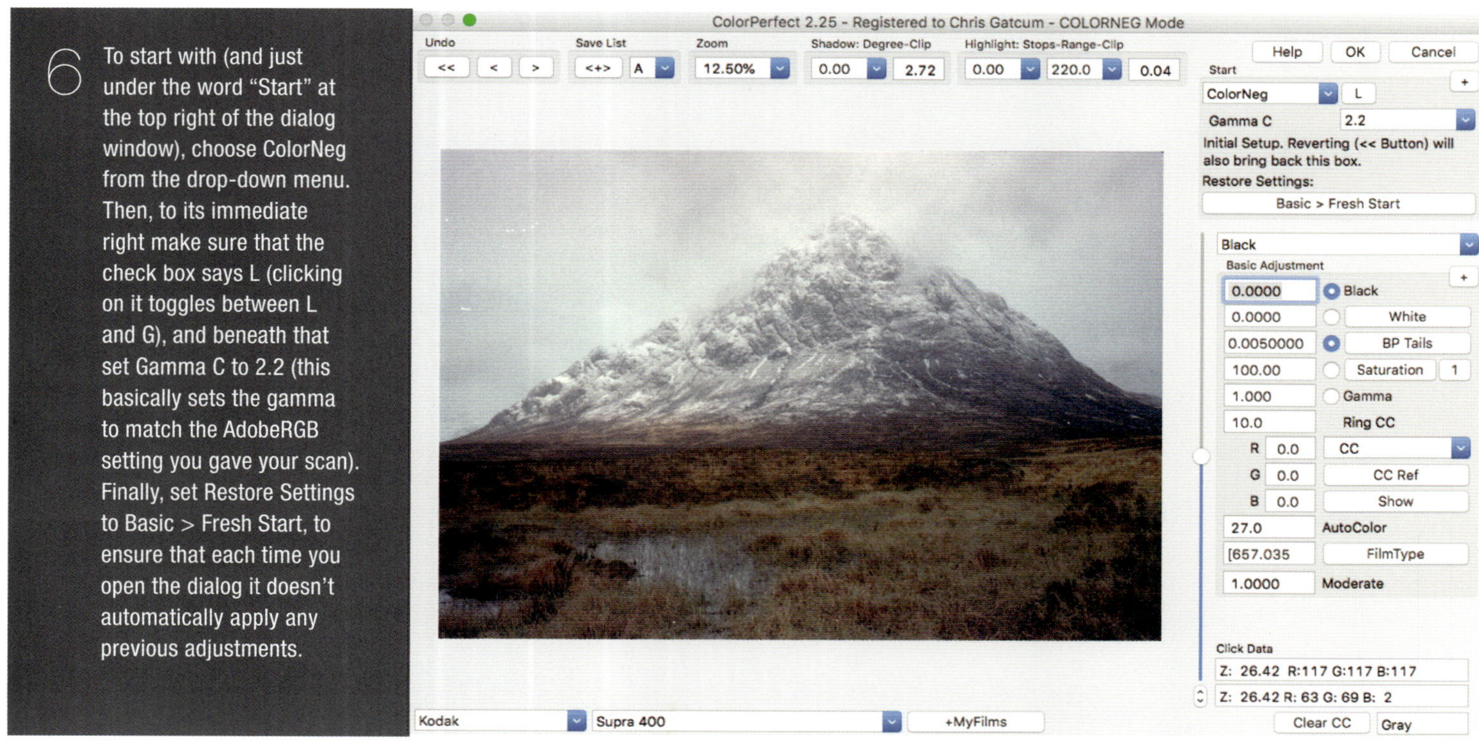

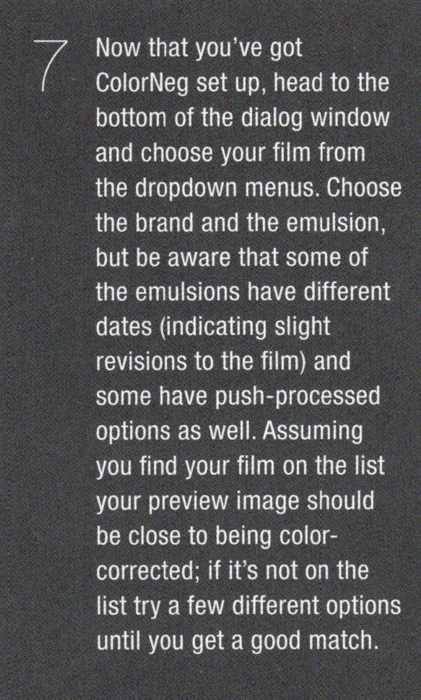

7 Now that you've got ColorNeg set up, head to the bottom of the dialog window and choose your film from the dropdown menus. Choose the brand and the emulsion, but be aware that some of the emulsions have different dates (indicating slight revisions to the film) and some have push-processed options as well. Assuming you find your film on the list your preview image should be close to being color-corrected; if it's not on the list try a few different options until you get a good match.

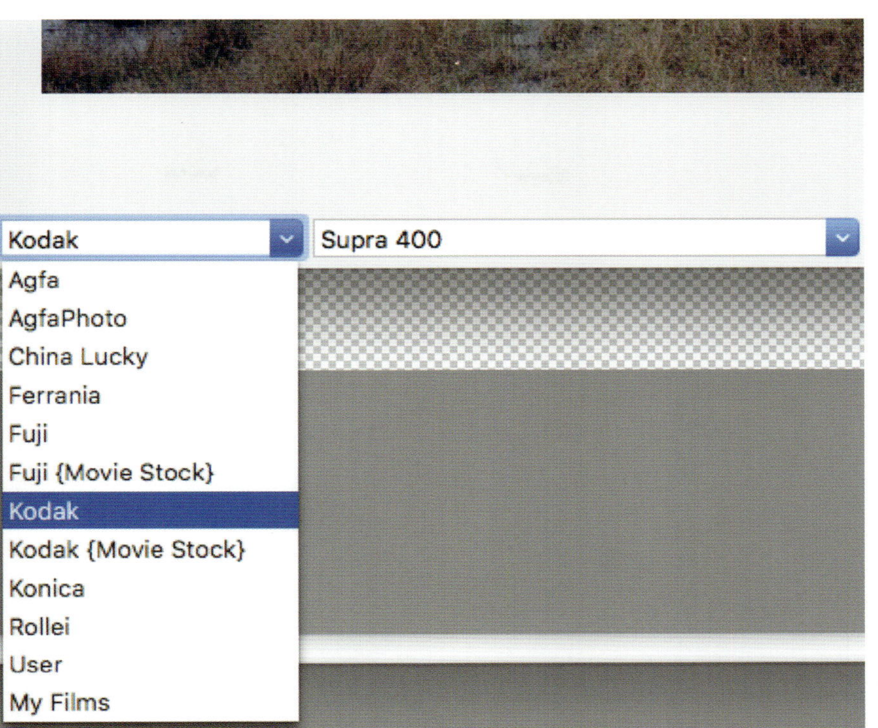

8 There's not space here to fully appreciate everything that ColorNeg will allow you to do, but the dropdown list at the upper right (above the "Basic Adjustments" label) gives you access to a host of controls, most of which can be changed using the vertical slider to the right of the image preview. A useful option is Film type: simply select it from the list and then click anywhere on the image to set that point to a neutral gray, guaranteeing instant "white balance."

Right: It took a bit of work to clean all the dust off this old negative, and tweak the color and contrast, but it was definitely worth the time and effort.

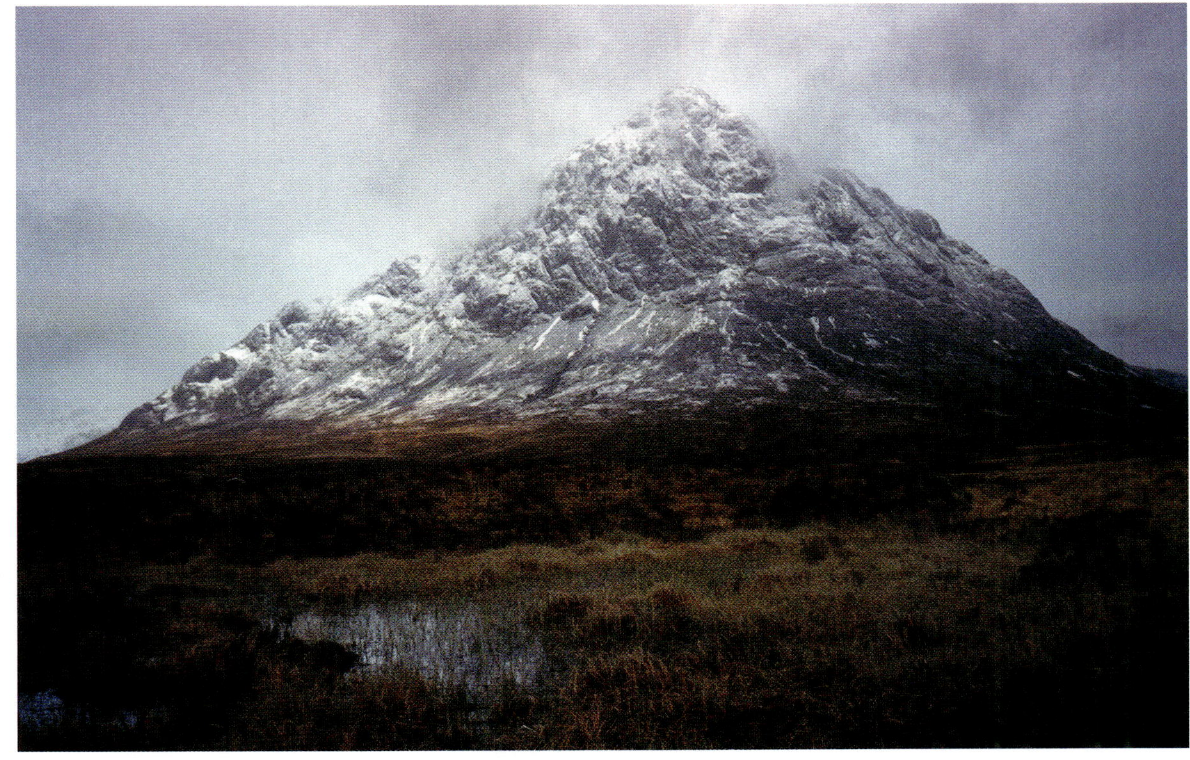

Profile: Elizabeth Opalenik

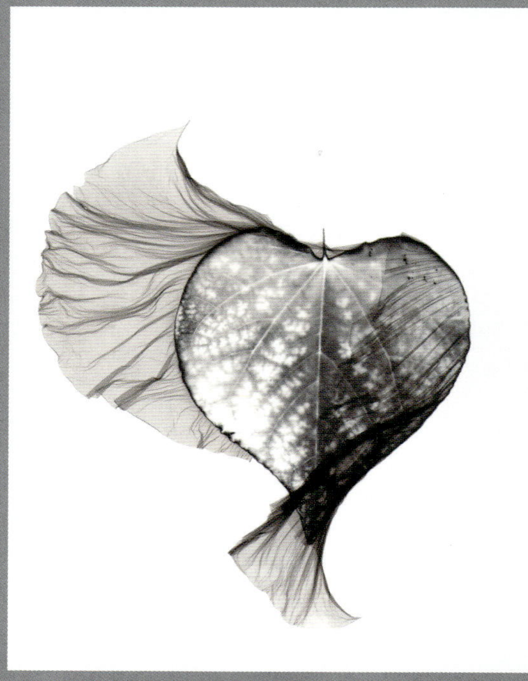

Above:
I'll Fly Away
Simple and elegant, less is more.

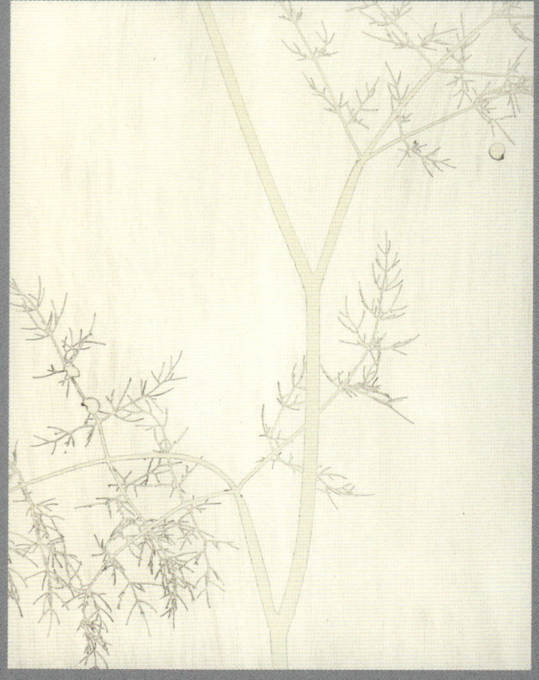

Above:
Le Fenouil #4, 1991
Creating texture like rain.

Q) When did you first become aware of the mordançage process?

A) In 1983 I was assisting a Maine Photographic Workshop in Provence, and we took the class to visit Jean-Pierre Sudre. After a workshop with this master in 1991, I discovered the possibilities of mordançage for myself and continued—even after his death in 1997—to visit his atelier and share his work with my students.

Q) What is the mordançage process? How does it work?

A) Mordançage is a darkroom process that alters a silver gelatin print by bleaching the photograph before redeveloping it. Its history began with the old bleach-etch process. Starting with a high-contrast silver gelatin print, the photographic silver emulsion is chemically lifted in the shadow areas and either removed or rearranged and dried back onto the print. Where the emulsion is removed, it will appear to be in relief.

Q) What challenges do you face when creating a mordançage image?

A) As artists, we must each find our way and hope to leave something of value behind. The "draped spidery veils" in my mordançage images are my contribution to this process, which are accomplished by using my breath or drops of water to preserve and alter the delicate floating silver skin. If left, the veils must add, not detract from the final image as they give new life to the subject. Those fragile veils can just as easily float away after long hours of working on an image.

Q) Is the choice of paper important?

A) Yes. Many of today's darkroom papers have less silver, thus saving veils is more difficult. Also, every paper/developer combination and redeveloper or toner choice alters colors in the print.

Q) Are the images created usng this process repeatable, or are they all one-offs?

A) No two will ever be exactly alike because of the removal or rearranging process, but if you are not saving veils, you can achieve a certain level of repeatability as long as you keep good notes. In my case, although I keep good notes it is never my intent to duplicate an image, although I may use the same negative or leaf (when creating a photogram). As such, each piece is unique and truly made by hand.

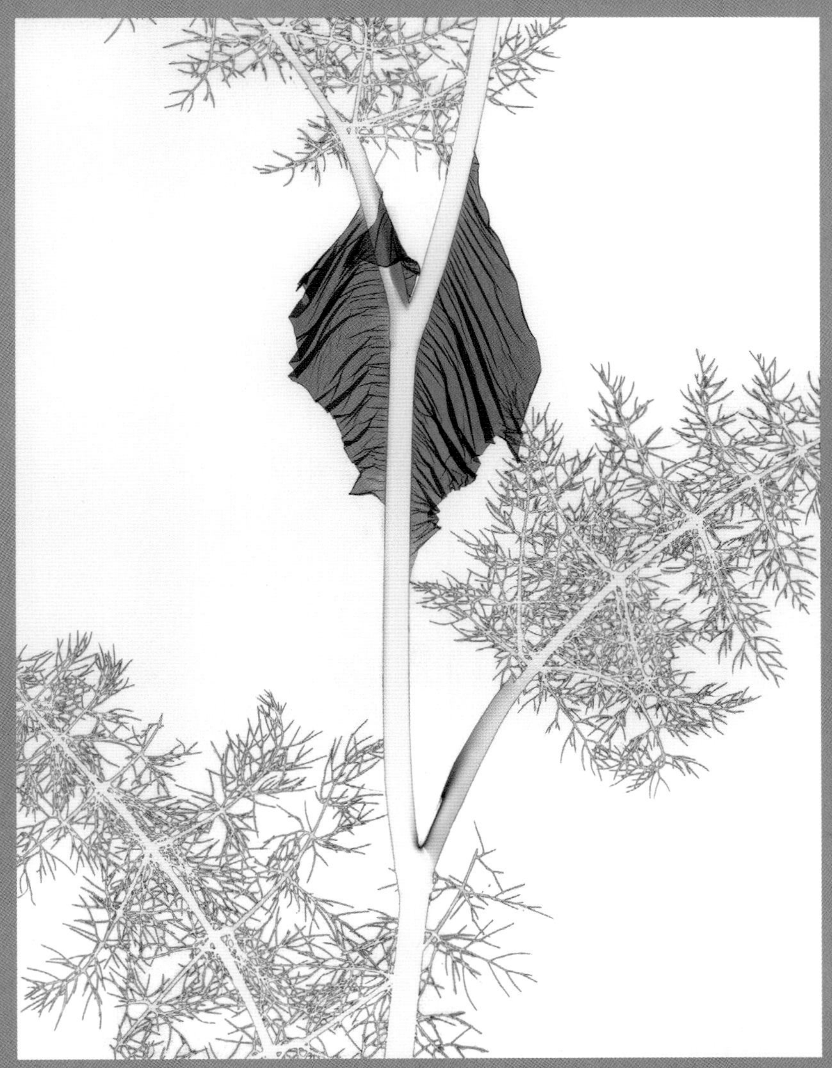

Above:
Le Fenouil Draped, 1991
I believe this was the second image I made in the Sudre
workshop where I saved veils of emulsion. I was using his
subject, but I wanted to add my own signature. He asked
the first veiled image to be signed to him "with love."

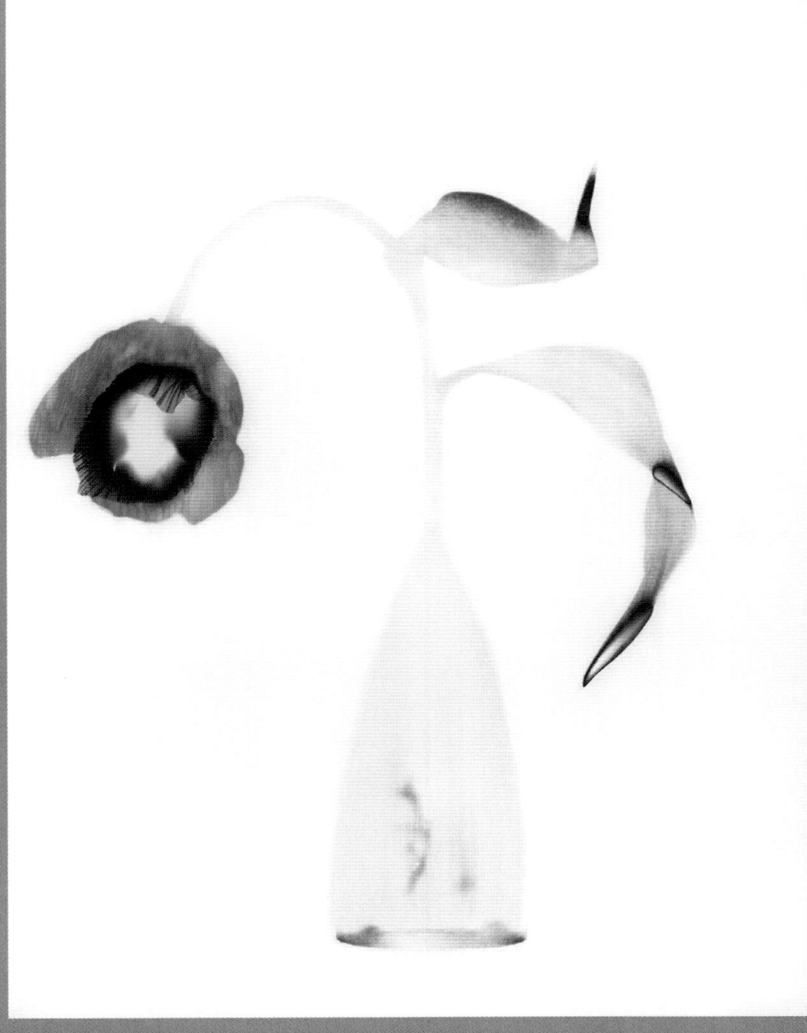

Above:
Tulip #1, 1992
This started as a test print to determine exposures. The
vase was disappearing in the cleaning process, so I chose
to remove emulsion around it, creating a vase form of
my own. Although three other images with a "real" vase
followed, this was my favorite of the day.

Glossary

Aberration An imperfection in a photograph, usually caused by the optics of a lens.

AEL (Automatic Exposure Lock) A feature found on some automatic cameras that enables you to lock the exposure settings so the camera can be moved to recompose the image, without having to re-meter.

Angle of view The area of a scene that a lens takes in, measured in degrees.

Aperture A variable opening in a lens, which determines the amount of light passing through to the film. An aperture is measured in f/stops and is one of the main determining factors of the depth of field in an image.

Aperture priority A camera mode that allows the photographer to choose the aperture (typically to control depth of field), while the camera automatically chooses the shutter speed for correct exposure.

Autofocus (AF) A reliable through-the-lens focusing system allowing accurate focus without the photographer manually turning the lens.

Bracketing The process of taking a sequence of images of the same scene at varying degrees of exposure to ensure that one is "correct."

Bulb mode A manual mode that allows complete control of how long the shutter can remain open.

C41 The standard process for color print (negative) film and some black-and-white films.

Camera shake A cause of blurred images, resulting from the camera moving during an exposure.

Center-weighted metering A metering pattern that determines the exposure for a photograph with a bias toward the center of the scene.

Characteristic curve A graph showing the relationship between exposure and density in a film.

Color temperature The color of a light source, measured in degrees Kelvin (K). Most color film has a daylight white balance of 5500K. Filters may be needed when photographing under different light sources to avoid color casts.

Contrast The tonal range between bright and dark areas in an image.

Depth of Field (DOF) The area in an image in front of and behind the point of focus that appears to be acceptably sharp.

Development General term for the process used to reveal the latent image on film.

Dynamic range The range of light that can be recorded by the camera into one image: from detail in the dark shadows to the brightest highlights.

E6 The standard process for developing color transparency (positive) film.

Emulsion The suspension of light-sensitive halides in gelatin. Can be coated onto a flexible base to create film or onto glass or metal to create plates.

Exposure The amount of light reaching the film, as controlled by aperture, shutter speed, and ISO. Also the act of exposing film to light to make a photograph, as in "making an exposure."

Exposure compensation A control that allows you to manually override automatically set exposure settings, often in ½- or ⅓-stop increments.

Exposure metering The act of measuring the amount of light falling on a scene to determine the required exposure.

f/stop The fractional representation of the size of the aperture. It is calculated on the ratio between the focal length of the lens and the diameter of the aperture.

Fill-in flash Flash combined with daylight in an exposure. Used with naturally backlit or harshly side-lit or top-lit subjects to prevent silhouettes, or to add light to the shadow areas of a well-lit scene.

Filter Colored or coated glass, or plastic, placed in front of the lens to modify the light in some way.

Focal length The distance from the optical center of a lens to the film.

Focal-plane shutter A shutter mechanism in front of the film plane, which typically uses a pair of blinds that open and close to control the amount of light reaching the film.

Latent image The "invisible" image created on film when an exposure is made; this is revealed through development.

Leaf shutter A shutter mechanism which uses an iris arrangement (not dissimilar to the aperture) that opens and closes to expose the film.

Ghosting The recording of a subject that moves during an exposure and is recorded in more than one place. Often happens when using flash with a slow shutter speed, or in pinhole photographs.

Highlights The brightest part of an image. Typically the key consideration when setting the exposure for transparency film.

Hotshoe An accessory shoe that allows synchronization between a camera and a flash.

Incident light reading A light reading based on the light falling onto the subject.

ISO Unit of measurement for the sensitivity of film to light. Other units of measurement have been used in the past, including ASA, DIN, and GOST.

Large format A film and camera format, most closely associated with 5x4in, 5x7in, and 10x8in image formats.

Lens flare An aberration caused when non-image-forming light is reflected and refracted within a lens and reaches the film.

Light leak Camera defect where light gets into the camera other than through the lens. Often a sign that the light seals in a camera need replacing, but can also be celebrated as a "lo-fi" esthetic.

Medium format A film format describing a camera that takes either 120 or 220 format film. Previously included other (obsolete) formats, such as 620.

Mirror lock-up An option on some SLR cameras that allows the reflex mirror to be raised and locked prior to releasing the shutter. This minimizes any vibrations that could cause camera shake.

Multi-area metering A metering pattern that breaks a scene down into a number of areas or zones, analyses each, and then averages out the readings.

Neutral density (ND) filter Reduces the amount of light entering the lens without affecting the color.

Overexposure The recording of too much light in an image leading to bright areas being recorded as pure white and with no recoverable image data.

Polarizing filter Used to filter polarized light, typically to reduce reflections on non-metallic surfaces and intensify a blue sky.

Prime lens A lens with a fixed focal length.

Rangefinder A focusing system—and, by extension, a camera design—that overlays two views of the scene; focus is achieved when the two images align perfectly.

Reciprocity failure The reduction in a film's response to light as exposure times become incredibly short or—more commonly—very long.

Shadows The darkest part of an image. Typically the key area for consideration when setting the exposure for negative film (as in the Zone System).

Shutter priority A camera mode that allows the photographer to choose the shutter speed (typically to control the appearance of movement in the image), while the camera chooses the appropriate aperture for the correct exposure.

SLR (Single Lens Reflex) A camera design that directs the image projected through the lens to the viewfinder using a reflex mirror and prism.

Spot metering A metering pattern that measures the intensity of light reflected by a very small portion of the scene.

Standard lens A lens with a focal length that delivers a similar angle of view to the human eye. Nominally this is the same measurement as the diagonal of the film format.

Stepping rings Rings that allow screw-in filters or filter holders of one diameter to be fitted to a lens with a different diameter. Available as both "step up" and "step down" rings, although use of the latter tends to result in vignetting unless the resulting image is cropped.

Teleconverter A supplementary lens that is fitted between the camera body and lens, increasing its effective focal length.

Telephoto lens A lens with a large focal length and a narrow angle of view.

TLR (Twin Lens Reflex) A camera design that has separate lenses for framing/focusing and making an exposure.

TTL (Through The Lens) metering A metering system built into the camera that measures light passing through the lens at the time of shooting.

Underexposure The result of allowing too little light to reach the film during an exposure. Typically, the highlight areas in an underexposed image will appear muddy and the shadow areas will be dense and lacking in detail.

Viewfinder An optical system used for framing, and sometimes for focusing, the subject.

Vignetting The darkening of the corners of an image. Can either be a by-product of the lens design (optical vignetting) or the result of an obstruction such as a lens hood or filter encroaching on the image projected by the lens (mechanical vignetting).

WLF (Waist Level Finder) Camera design that requires the photographer to look down onto a viewing screen from above, typically by holding the camera at a waist-level position (hence the name).

Wide-angle lens A lens with a short focal length and, consequently, a wide angle of view.

Zone System A system developed to create the optimum black-and-white negative for printing on fixed-grade photographic paper. The system involves steps that are taken at both the exposure and the development stages.

Zoom A lens with a variable focal length.

Useful Web Sites

Film Manufacturers*

ADOX adox.de
AgfaPhoto agfaphoto.com
Argenti facebook.com/argentiphoto
Arista freestylephoto.biz
Astrum (Svema) astrum-ltd.com
Bergger bergger.com
China Lucky Film luckyfilm.com
CineStill cinestill.com
dubblefilm dubblefilm.com
FILM Ferrania filmferrania.it
Film Washi filmwashi.com
Foma Bohemia foma.cz
Film Photography Project filmphotographyproject.com
Fujifilm fujifilm.com
Ilford Photo ilfordphoto.com
Japan Camera Hunter japancamerahunter.com
Kawauso-Shoten (Rera) kawauso.biz/
Kodak Alaris kodakalaris.com
KONO! reanimatedfilm.com
Kosmo Foto kosmofoto.com
Lomography lomography.com
Maco (Rollei) macodirect.de
ORWO filmotec.de
Polaroid polaroid.com
Revolog revolog.net
Silberra silberra.com
Streetcandy oneyearwithfilmonly.com
Tasma tasma.ru
Ultrafine ultrafineonline.com
Wephota wephota.de
Yodica facebook.com/yodicafilms

* note that not all of these companies manufacturer their own films;
some are rebranded versions of other products.

Photography Publications

Ammonite Press www.ammonitepress.com
Black + White Photography magazine www.thegmcgroup.com
Outdoor Photography magazine www.thegmcgroup.com

Index

Acknowledgments

Although it's my name on the cover, a whole heap of people have helped get this book into print, not least Jason and Robin at Ammonite Press who have had to put up with far more excuses and delays than normal, and Tracy and Luke who have had their respective editing and design times moved and reduced accordingly: I probably owe you all a beer or two…

Next up, I need to thank all of the photographers profiled in these pages who allowed me to step into their film-based world and take a look behind the scenes: Francesco and Andrea Padovani, William Jones, Paul Thompson, Wendy Laurel, Matt Pringle, and Elizabeth Opalenik. Your work is truly beautiful and inspirational.

In no particular order I also want to thank Bellamy Hunt at Japan Camera Finder, Adam Scott at dubblefilm, Sandy Phimester, Yasuko Kuroi at Sekonic, Jarrod Whaley at Makers4Good, Mirko Böddecker at FOTOIMPEX, and Ashley Kelemen at CineStill for images and advice. Special thanks go to Leyton Prosser at Fujifilm UK for his technical checks; David Hamrick at VueScan for keeping my CanoScan off the scrap heap; and to Franziska Potsch and Manuel Oberhofer at Metz, and Zernike Au at Zero Image for going above and beyond the call of marketing to shoot product images specifically for this project.

And finally, thanks to Nati and the kids for putting up with the lost weekends and grumpy moods…

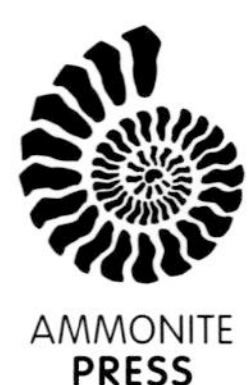

AMMONITE
PRESS

www.ammonitepress.com